THE POLITICS AND POETICS OF CONTEMPORARY ENGLISH TRAGEDY

The Politics and Poetics of Contemporary English Tragedy is a detailed study of the idea of the tragic in the political plays of David Hare, Howard Barker, Edward Bond, Caryl Churchill, Mark Ravenhill, Sarah Kane, and Jez Butterworth. Through an in-depth analysis of over sixty of their works, Sean Carney argues that their dramatic exploration of tragic experience is an integral part of their ongoing politics. This approach allows for a comprehensive rather than selective study of both the politics and poetics of their work.

Carney's attention to the tragic enables him to find a common discourse among the canonical English playwrights of an older generation and representatives of the nineties generation, challenging the idea that there is a sharp generational break between these groups. Finally, Carney demonstrates that tragic experience is often denied by the social discourse of Englishness, and that these playwrights make a crucial critical intervention by dramatizing the tragic.

SEAN CARNEY is an associate professor in the Department of English at McGill University.

The Politics and Poetics of Contemporary English Tragedy

SEAN CARNEY

UNIVERSITY OF TORONTO PRESS
Toronto   Buffalo   London

© University of Toronto Press 2013
Toronto Buffalo London
www.utppublishing.com
Printed in Canada

ISBN 978-1-4426-4573-8 (cloth)
ISBN 978-1-4426-1397-3 (paper)

Library and Archives Canada Cataloguing in Publication

Carney, Sean, 1970–
The politics and poetics of contemporary English tragedy / Sean Carney.

Includes bibliographical references and index.
ISBN 978-1-4426-4573-8 (bound). – ISBN 978-1-4426-1397-3 (pbk.)

1. English drama (Tragedy) – History and criticism.   2. English drama – 20th century
– History and criticism.   3. English drama – 21st century – History and criticism.
4. Politics in literature.   5. Loss (Psychology) in literature.   6. Self in literature.
I. Title.

PR739.P64C37 2013   822'.91409   C2012-905642-1

This book has been published with the help of a grant from the Canadian Federation
for the Humanities and Social Sciences, through the Awards to Scholarly Publications
Program, using funds provided by the Social Sciences and Humanities Research
Council of Canada.

University of Toronto Press acknowledges the financial assistance to its publishing
program of the Canada Council for the Arts and the Ontario Arts Council.

Canada Council   Conseil des Arts
for the Arts   du Canada

University of Toronto Press acknowledges the financial support of the Government
of Canada through the Canada Book Fund for its publishing activities.

Contents

Acknowledgments   vii

Introduction   3

1 David Hare: The Work of Mourning, or, The Agony and the Ecstasy
   of the Bourgeoisie   25

   *The Year of Magical Thinking – Teeth 'n' Smiles – Plenty – The Secret Rapture
   – Skylight – Amy's View – The Judas Kiss – My Zinc Bed – The Permanent
   Way – The Vertical Hour – Gethsemane*

2 Howard Barker: Will and Desire – From the Tragedy of Socialism
   to the Ecstasy of the Unconscious   68

   *Claw – Fair Slaughter – That Good Between Us – The Power of the Dog
   – Victory – The Castle – The Europeans – The Possibilities – Gertrude – The
   Cry – Dead Hands – The Seduction of Almighty God by the Boy Priest Loftus
   in the Abbey of Calcetto, 1539*

3 Edward Bond: Tragedy and Postmodernity, or, The Promethean
   Impulse   123

   *Saved – Lear – Bingo – The Fool – Restoration – The War Plays – Olly's Prison
   – At the Inland Sea – Coffee – The Crime of the Twenty-First Century – Chair*

4 Caryl Churchill: The Dionysian Möbius Strip 175

Seven Jewish Children – Lovesick – Abortive – Owners – Traps – Light Shining in Buckinghamshire – Cloud Nine – Top Girls – Fen – A Mouthful of Birds – Lives of the Great Poisoners – The Skriker – Thyestes – Far Away – A Number

5 New English Tragedians: The Tragedy of the Tragic 231

Mark Ravenhill: *Shopping and Fucking – Faust Is Dead – Handbag – Some Explicit Polaroids – Product – The Cut – pool (no water)*
Sarah Kane: *Blasted – Phaedra's Love – Cleansed – Crave – 4.48 Psychosis*

Conclusion: Late Modernism in *Jerusalem* 285

Notes 301

Works Cited 323

Index 335

Acknowledgments

Research for this book was completed with the support of a Social Sciences and Humanities Research Council of Canada Standard Research Grant, and sabbatical leave from McGill University. Research assistance was provided by Spencer Chimuk, Amanda Clarke, Anna Sigg, and Jeffrey Weingarten.

Richard Ratzlaff at the University of Toronto Press has proved a shepherd to this book in the most profound sense of the word. My thanks to him.

I wish to thank the anonymous readers at the University of Toronto Press. Their meticulous and committed comments on the manuscript were both substantial and inspiring.

Jackie Buxton's contribution to this work is inestimable. I am deeply humbled and grateful for her ongoing support and insight.

This book is dedicated to Barbara Godard – teacher, scholar, mentor.

THE POLITICS AND POETICS OF CONTEMPORARY ENGLISH TRAGEDY

When, for example, the theory and practice of tragedy from Aristotle to the age of Corneille, regard family conflicts as providing the most fruitful subject-matter for tragedy, we glimpse lying behind this view – ignoring its technical merits such as concentration – the feeling that the great changes in society are being revealed here with a sensuous, practical vividness.

Georg Lukács, *History and Class Consciousness* 175–6

Introduction

This book is a study of several contemporary English dramatists, with an emphasis on the idea of the tragic that runs through their work. The idea of the tragic here is in its essence the exploration of the human relationship to loss, be it in literal death, or in acts of mourning, or alternately and crucially in the human confrontation with that which lies outside of the self and which negates the human, 'mortifies' the self, figuratively speaking, by delineating the limits of the self. The playwrights have been chosen for several reasons. First, naturally, they have in common an investment in the representation of the tragic. Sometimes they readily avow this themselves (David Hare, Howard Barker, Edward Bond), sometimes they have been associated with it through recognizable antecedents (Sarah Kane), and sometimes their inclusion is as a result of my own analyses, which must now persuade the reader (Caryl Churchill, Mark Ravenhill, Jez Butterworth). All of these playwrights, and particularly those of the older generation, have been recognized as politically or socially committed at various points in their careers, and my surmise in this book is that the dramatic exploration of tragic experience is an integral part of their ongoing politics. The tragic is also, notably, what marks their break from the Brechtian tradition of political theatre that is still the dominant scholarly category of socially engaged drama. The tragic is not the only way of understanding their work, and will not necessarily encompass their entire oeuvres, but my assertion here, through close reading across many plays, is that the tragic constitutes a dominant 'structure of feeling' in all of their works. The playwrights also have in common their association, particularly at early stages of their careers, with the English Stage Company at the Royal Court Theatre in London, the significance of which I will return to below. Finally, these playwrights, despite such commonalities, are highly diverse and distinctive in their approaches. By examining a broad range of plays stretching from 1965 to 2009, what emerges is not a single structure of feeling but rather several. While my premise is that structures of feeling emerge from individual artists, we will see that even within an individual author's work the structures respond to changing historical conditions.

The phrase 'structure of feeling' comes from Raymond Williams, who is a prominent influence on this book. I highlight his concept to emphasize that this book is neither a work of theatre history nor a theoretical study of the tragic. It finds its object of study in plays themselves, and my analyses are attempts to articulate and emphasize the various tragic structures of feeling discernible in the different playwrights. While the concept of a structure of feeling takes on various shapes throughout Williams's career, the one that is operative here is that articulated in *Drama from Ibsen to Brecht* (1968). The structure of feeling 'in solution,' that is in lived, contemporary experience, is that which singles out the work. It appears to be the work's own unique way of responding to its time, the unconventional aspect of it that may seem incomprehensible, not a sign of technique but rather that which is personal, isolating, alienating, setting the author apart, the *feeling*. The paradoxical connection between the uniqueness of a writer and her larger historical context is often only apparent with the benefit of historical hindsight. That connection is the *structure* of feeling: 'the continuity of experience from a particular work, through its particular form, to its recognition as a general form, and then the relation of this general form to a period' (17). Looking back historically, we can see with the benefit of hindsight how those aspects of the work actually connect to the experiences of the time, how the personal feeling is actually one with a larger structure.

This book, however, is an attempt to historicize the present. For Williams, seeking to identify 'contemporary structures of feeling […] is the most important kind of attention to the art and society of one's own time' (19). Yet it is also very difficult to apprehend such structures directly. All the same, it remains a pressing task for criticism, because it is a means of historicizing the contemporary while also acknowledging the singular quality of art. Thus the present book is understandable as an exploration of a series of possible, emergent structures of feeling within English society from the mid-1960s to the present day. By beginning at a recognizable moment of change in the English theatre (the end of the realist avant-garde in 1965, as Stephen Lacey tentatively determines it [*British Realist Theatre* 6]), I examine what by now are recognizable conventions of plays and then proceed through a series of individual oeuvres with this early work in mind, as a means of making recognizable the structure of feeling emerging from their work in the present. Thus this study takes a long view of the contemporary, with the understanding that the challenge of historicizing the contemporary is an essential undertaking.

The Royal Court in Context

While this is not a work of theatre history, some historical contextualization is important at the outset. The English Stage Company at the Royal Court Theatre in Sloane Square, London, has the dubious distinction of having been a successful and influential venue for new play development virtually from its first season, in 1956, with the performance of John Osborne's *Look Back in Anger*. What was once considered an important moment of historical break, a defining of a period of pre- and post-, has now become a constant target for historical reconsideration: post-war English theatre did not suddenly begin in May 1956 at the Royal Court.[1] But Artistic Director George Devine's plan was to cultivate an Art Theatre outside of the commercial considerations of London's West End, to create a venue where the new, formalist theatre of Europe could be presented and where young English playwrights with similar affinities could be nurtured. However, the first big success of the Royal Court was Osborne's unexpected piece of 'kitchen sink realism.' In a squalid flat, a young, ill-mannered, semi-educated working-class man named Jimmy Porter rails incessantly at his middle-class wife, in whom he invests the full loathing he holds for his entire society, as she silently irons his laundry. This rude and angry play grew slowly into a huge success. As a result, the Royal Court was henceforth compelled to pursue a heterogeneous, catholic (and to audiences, incoherent) mandate, staging the works of Samuel Beckett, Bertolt Brecht, and Eugene Ionesco alongside the new 'social realism' being written by English playwrights like Arnold Wesker.[2] There was never a single Royal Court type of play, but in the years from 1956 to 1965, these two dominant artistic emphases, formalism and social realism, were championed by the Court. This twin emphasis will be important to consider here.

This does not mean that *Look Back in Anger* was itself a piece of social realism, despite the presence of the ironing board on stage. As Raymond Williams points out, *Look Back in Anger* was on the surface a traditional piece of naturalism, yet it was uniquely imbued with 'an intense feeling – a frustrated anger, a prolonged waiting, which must be broken, at any cost, by a demonstration, a shout' (*Drama from Ibsen to Brecht* 318). He insists that the play and its successors, despite the contemporary contexts of their settings, were not 'experiments in social realism' or 'documents of youth and poverty' but rather 'intensely personal cries' (319). For Williams, it is a powerful structure of feeling, and thus a larger social emotion, that is crucially articulated in the work, rather than a transparent social commentary or document of working-class life. Stephen Lacey's insightful *British Realist Theatre* distinguishes Osborne's play from the kitchen sink dramas that followed and posits that while Jimmy Porter's anger has no concrete politics, it led to political plays and politicized consciousness. If Jimmy Porter's anger was trapped, imprisoned, focused futilely upon his wife, Alison, because focused ultimately upon himself and his own lack of agency – and particularly upon his incoherent class status as a working-class man with university education who marries into the middle classes – then this incoherent anger was inevitably a symptom of post-war social change.[3]

What emerged at a broader level in England in the late 1950s was not incoherent anger but the socialism of the New Left, a result of both a perceived failure of traditional class-based leftist politics within the Cold War landscape and a growing disenfranchisement from the ideology of the post-war consensus. Where communism had failed, the members of the New Left of the 1950s were intellectual, young, educated, often middle class, and their social commitment was to causes like the Campaign for Nuclear Disarmament rather than to the class struggle (Lacey 34). The post-war consensus that the New Left opposed was the promise of non-partisan social unity within the growing affluence of English society after the war. 'Consensus' was the broadly lived and accepted myth that in the post-war moment of growing material affluence Britain was becoming a truly unified society, and as Prime Minister Harold Macmillan declared in 1959, 'The class war is over and we have won' (qtd in Lacey 11). Despite such declarations, the vacuous material affluence perpetuated in the ideology of the consensual society only masked, rather than resolved, the social contradictions of English society, and Porter's anger, emerging in 1956, the year of the Suez Canal Crisis and the clear collapse of the British Empire, is an expression of the social incoherence of his society, contradictions demanding resolution. The New Left was the major voice of this frustration.

Tragedy, I suggest, gradually emerges from this situation as a form of political theatre in keeping with the post-communist (and thus post-Brechtian) politics of the New Left. John Orr observes that up to 1956, modern English drama was characterized by 'its stylistic torpor and its neglect of the social content of English life' and also by 'an insular neglect of theatrical innovation and the absence of tragedy' (*Tragic Drama and Modern Society* 241). These twin pairs of failures in fact are identical for Orr because, as he observes it, modern tragedy emerged in Europe in the nineteenth century as a drama of social alienation from bourgeois society (xvii). Since tragedy historically has proven to be a symptom of a culture in a moment of transition, the lack of it is a potential sign of social stagnation. For Orr, Jimmy Porter's social alienation in *Look Back in Anger* has a proto-tragic stance in his anger against a static hegemonic society, but Osborne's play is betrayed by its traditional naturalism, which leaves Jimmy trapped in his bed-sit with Alison, who must suffer his misogyny in the absence of a larger social target (249).[4]

Thus, as Lacey sees it, social realism itself was an inconsistent, contradictory symptom of its social moment, and these contradictions, he argues, eventually led to the emergence of a type of politicized formalism that is characterized by Edward Bond's *Saved* (1965). This is apposite to our concerns, because *Saved* is the earliest play represented in this study (see chapter 3). *Saved* looks like kitchen sink documentary realism, dealing with alienated working-class lives in South London, but it is also a piece of politicized formalism.[5] While it is not necessarily a tragedy as such, its formal experimentation contains the seeds of what will become Bond's formal, tragic dramas, and this connection between tragedy and formalism is the crucial point to note. As Lacey observes, director William Gaskill brought Brechtian sensibilities to the style of the mise-en-scène, notably in the careful emphasis on the 'social significance' of objects (152), and brought deliberate aestheticization to the stylized formalism of the notorious scene where a child is stoned to death in its pram: the stones are mimed; the child, sedated, is uncannily silent throughout; and the scene concludes with the gang of youths buzzing like bees as they leave the stage (153). Like Brechtian realism, this was a selective realism, emphasizing what is material in the social moment (objects) rather than merely inert and in the background (*Saved*, unlike a realist or naturalist drama, had a minimal set). *Saved* is also characteristic of the distance from Brechtian orthodoxy that has always characterized Brecht's anglicization: rather than the notorious Brechtian *Verfremdungseffekt*, *Saved* employs the less clichéd technique of Brechtian *gestus*. *Saved* was deliberately artificial and formal when mere naturalistic mimesis would defuse the social significance of a moment. It was the birth of a new theatrical language of political theatre out of a merging of social realism with the European formalism of Brecht.

Contemporary English Tragedy

It is my thesis that contemporary English tragedy grows out of this hybrid birth, the conjunction of realistic content and formal theatricality that is so carefully balanced in *Saved*. As early as 1960 Caryl Churchill was already diagnosing what was wrong with the English theatre of the 1950s: it was petty and depressed, rather than despairing and tragic ('Not Ordinary, Not Safe' 445). In a polemical piece written shortly after her graduation from Oxford and when she was just beginning to write plays herself,[6] Churchill diagnoses, with a bold, passionate gaze, the ultimate dead end of kitchen sink realism: while the principle of reflecting life with naturalistic form was exciting when *Look Back in Anger* premiered, this style quickly descended into cliché. By 1960, the result was dull plays, reflecting only a dull English society. The essay is fascinating, not only for how it forecasts Churchill's own career as a constant innovator of dramatic form but also for its overall tone: the direction taken by English drama is of crucial import because it both reflects, and potentially will shape, that society itself. It is a reminder to us that within a culture where theatre includes the work of Shakespeare, theatre is, at its best, not simply a distraction from life but an essential participant in social existence. Thus while Churchill praises Pinter's *The Caretaker* for its evocative elements of fear and mystery and for its heightened prose that suggests 'there is more in life than its surface trivialities' (449), the play's naturalistic structure and plotting belie this, valorizing failure and stasis just as does *Waiting for Godot* (444–5). She describes English drama as presenting a despairing choice between banal ordinariness and miserable failure, failure without even the tragic grandeur of a classical fall (444).

Thus Churchill's criticism extends to a failure on the part of the new English plays to grapple with larger classical themes: 'Though progress is a cliché to us, now if ever the intensity of feeling of the late sixteenth century, the awareness of man's increasing power contrasted with his inadequacy, seems to be justified. But we have twisted both sides to mediocrity; we don't think much of man's power, but we don't think his inadequacy matters. We don't even despair; we mope' (447). Churchill does not explicitly call this a tragic theme, but it is one – the perennial theme of the tragic over-reacher as a paradigm of the human – and Churchill specifically makes reference to the absence of tragic heroes in English drama at the beginning of the essay (443–4). While she never qualifies whom she means by 'we,' her frequent use of the word throughout the essay suggests that it is specifically the English themselves to whom she refers, and in the face of the naturalist representation of dull English life she suggests not 'facile optimism' but 'lashing satires or despairing tragedies' (445). 'A play is a poem not a pamphlet,' she asserts, insisting that commitment in art must reach beyond narrow political concerns and be capacious in its scope (447). She finally advocates drama that seeks a tenuous balance between naturalistic investment in contemporary English life on the one hand, and formal concerns such as poetic language and imaginative independence on the other (450). Tragedy, then, is implied as a potential model for a drama that escapes the trap of social realism, managing a view of modern English life that does not descend into the dead end of naturalistic mimesis but instead celebrates aspects of humanity that are invisible to the naturalistic project. And tragedy, by implication, would be a political form more suitable to the post-class, post-propaganda politics of New Left.

Tragedy and Political Theatre

The argument against modern tragedy has always hinged upon the idea that mundane, realistic social content defuses, undoes, or hobbles the formal, distanced artifice of tragedy, but Churchill's polemic instead offers tragedy as a means of balancing a New Left commitment to social content with an equally New Left political commitment to poetic language and formal experimentation, precisely as a means of avoiding the politically stagnant despair of social realism. The present study is devoted to political playwrights who explicitly or intuitively recognized and responded to that challenge. To suggest as I do here that tragic experience has become a key concern of socially committed dramatists in Britain since the late 1960s is to suggest that political theatre has adapted its parameters to a changing sense of what constitutes 'the political' in relation to dramatic art. All of the authors considered in this book are identifiably leftist political playwrights (or have been considered as such at points in their careers) with social agendas for their dramas. All of them have at some stage been associated closely with the English Stage Company at the Royal Court Theatre. All of them write tragedy rather than pursuing the recognizable clichés of what constitutes 'political theatre.' It has become a commonplace to argue that the election of Margaret Thatcher in 1979 signalled the end of the moment of traditionally progressive, overtly political theatre in England (see Patterson), and it is true that the tone of political playwriting in the country during the 1980s changed, but without being extinguished. But my surmise here is that it was not only since Margaret Thatcher's election that political theatre acknowledged its failure to foment social change, collectivity, or activism, or to create a politicized audience, perhaps with the understanding that this was never a feasible or potential task for artistic representation emanating from a left-leaning middle-class theatrical establishment in the first place.[7] In fact, Thatcher's election seems only to have confirmed what a generation of politicized socialist playwrights had been reluctantly diagnosing since the early to mid-1970s: the promise of revolutionary change proclaimed by the 1960s had foundered after May 1968 and dissipated. Playwrights such as David Hare, who had begun their careers as radical agitprop situationists, appeared to modify their views of what they, as committed dramatists, could do with their art, but without losing their sense of commitment.

Here again, some larger historical context informs the analysis. Were I to be asked to pinpoint specifically the moment of this open acknowledgment of failure, I would offer 1973–4, the years of the global economic crisis that led to the recession of the 1970s, and the years that Fredric Jameson suggests are when both the 1960s and also progressive historical change in a traditional Marxist sense came to an end. In 'Periodizing the 60s,' Jameson discusses 'the 60s as a moment in which the enlargement of capitalism on a global scale simultaneously produced an immense freeing or unbinding of social energies' (208). Traditional class-based Marxist socialism was pronounced defunct by these new revolutionary projects and dismantled in favour of new forms of progressive politics (resulting, in England, with the emergence of the New Left, as we have seen with Lacey). Jameson's point is that this new progressive potential of the 1960s was a result of, and inseparable from, late capitalism's globalization of advanced industrialization.

To translate this into Lacey's terms, the very discourse of the so-called affluent, consensual society and its ideology of a post-class England led not to a renewal of orthodox class consciousness on the part of the Left but the emergence of a New Left, the condition of which was the affluent, materialist society itself, thus engendering a leftism attempting to cut across traditional class lines. The great year of possibility for this new collectivity was 1968, and its greatest moment of nascence May 1968 in Paris, when university students and workers united across class lines in an enormous general strike. This strike seemed like a moment of utopian possibility for social overturning, and it failed. Jameson, as a traditional Marxist, points out that this political energy was merely a possibility engendered by, and dependent upon, the effects of late capitalism itself, and was duly undone by the inherent instability of capitalism. Universal reified industrialization heralded the arrival of postmodernity on a global scale and was the triumph of late capitalism, which led, as capitalism periodically does, to an economic crisis in 1973–4, within which the new progressive energies and new social formations were left scattered, depoliticized, and fragmented. The key English play that articulates this structure of feeling is Trevor Griffiths's remarkable *The Party* (performed at the National Theatre, significantly, in 1973), a drama that describes the English attitude towards May 1968 as one of nostalgia, envy, and mourning for a lost revolutionary moment denied to Britain in the 1970s. It is a remarkably elegiac play by a committed socialist playwright who was himself involved in the New Left, looking back at the 1960s as a moment of failed possibility.[8]

What I suggest has emerged from this post-1960s repositioning is a feeling that the central role of the political playwright is the representation and interrogation of human suffering from a dialectical perspective. Another word for this is tragedy. In distancing (but rarely divorcing) themselves from the most oppressive and stifling cliché of political theatre, namely the looming, smothering shadow of Bertolt Brecht's theory and Epic style, these writers nevertheless focused their energies on the problem that Brecht returns to again and again: the role and function of suffering in human life.[9] Brecht's famous warning to the audiences of *Mother Courage and Her Children*, that suffering in itself is a poor teacher, encapsulates the Epic theatre's core concern in the form of a dictum. Yet that Brecht had to shout this declaration again and again at audiences who were determined to heroize Mother Courage indicates not only the persistence of this piece of ideology in the minds of his public, but also the failure of Brecht's plays themselves to take so strident and unambiguous a stance. Brecht's concern was that this key dramatic ideologeme – the idea that suffering in itself is humanizing, a tenet of neoclassical theories of the tragic – had become, within modernity, a bourgeois justification of the status quo. This collective assumption is what Raymond Williams quite rightly describes as 'the tragic ideology' (*Modern Tragedy* 63) and is the reason for a long-standing suspicion of tragedy on the part of leftists. Brecht's rejection of tragedy is ultimately a rejection of tragic ideology rather than tragedy as such. The tragic ideologeme is a means of eliminating the dialectical contradictions of the tragic and of transforming it into a cautionary tale.[10]

Yet Williams (and later, Terry Eagleton in his book *Sweet Violence*) are both committed to exposing the dialectical action at the heart of the tragic in order to reveal the importance of tragedy for leftist politics.[11] Williams explores this because tragedy, emerging at moments of historical contradiction and change, thus serves as a sign of historical openness and possibility, and Eagleton engages with the tragic because the dialectical aspects of tragedy have the potential to illuminate the contradictions of late capitalism within the contemporary moment. Crucially for our concerns in this book, in both of their studies the dialectical aspect of their materialism insists on the consideration of metaphysical absolutes, of the idea of the Absolute itself, even if this runs contrary to conventional materialist thought. Without the concept of the metaphysical as such, material reality becomes static, inert, and unchanging, but with the concept of the metaphysical engaged, dialectics becomes possible as the potential overcoming of opposition and the finding of an identity between opposites. As such, tragedy, with its inevitable considerations of metaphysical issues, is uniquely suited as an aesthetic form for a particularly *dialectical* materialism.

The Idea of the Tragic

The definition of the tragic that I engage with here, in which the human relationship to loss is the central feature, may raise a query for some readers, since the tragic is often understood as a narrative of fatality, predetermination, or necessity, in which the outcome of a turn of events is understood retroactively to be inevitable. Such vulgar determinism is not necessarily a part of my definition of the tragic, although the experience of necessity certainly is, as long as we understand the experience of necessity itself as a facet of loss, namely alienation from human agency. As Williams demonstrates in *Modern Tragedy*, the Greek experience of the tragic is not a cancellation of human agency by inhuman divine fate, but the collision of the two within a social mindset that did not suffer from a rigid binary opposition between human freedom and inhuman destiny: Oedipus is both free and predetermined, and this contradictory experience defined the tragic for the Greek mind.[12] In the condition of postmodernity, we have come full circle and are re-experiencing this coincidence of agency and necessity. Thus the tragic today is concerned with the intersection of humanity's will with situations of the loss of human agency in (apparently) unavoidable, inhuman situations. Yet there is no disastrous event anywhere on earth today that does not warrant speculation upon whether or not it was avoidable, because humanity as a whole effectively has the means to take control of its own destiny. Today the mind asks of catastrophic, tragic events whether or not they were necessary, rather than flatly stating that they were tragic because they were unavoidable.

While this book is not a work of critical theory, it is informed by theoretical ideas about the tragic. The following is primarily a study of the dramatic representation of tragic experience rather than a study of tragic plot in the classical Aristotelian sense. In this I am in accord with William Storm, who separates the tragic as such from both tragic vision and dramatic tragedies. Storm develops a theory of a transhistorical tragic derived from the idea of Dionysus and the Dionysiac ritual of the *sparagmos*, the rending of a sacrificial victim into pieces. For Storm, this tragic rending is a metaphor for the permanent dispersal of selfhood in tragedy. While tragic figures strive for a coherent selfhood, tragic actions deny this striving, as an expression of 'a fundamental condition of mortality' (*After Dionysus* 29). The tragic, then, is neither an aesthetic vision nor a philosophical one but rather the fundamental condition of being a mortal human being: 'It is eternal to precisely the extent that mortal beings live and continue to be aware, not only of their own mortality but of the divisive forces that inevitably separate being from all that is held as valuable' (32–3). As George Hunka writes, 'Tragedy, both as genre and as consciousness, presupposes a metaphysics' (9). As an absolute, the tragic as a subject forces a presentiment of metaphysical conditions, of the *meta* as such as that which lies beyond the bounds of the human. This has been a source of ire on the part of leftists with regards to tragedy and tragic experience, but as Hugh Grady points out, '[M]aterialism [...] needs to acknowledge the existence of and limits to human nature [...]. [A] basic datum of human nature is mortality, and tragedy is centrally about some of the consequences of our mortality, or it is about nothing' (132–3). Yet all particular tragic visions, philosophies, and aesthetic tragedies will view this human relationship to the metaphysical from within an historical perspective, and this accounts for a diversity of aesthetic forms of tragedy.

The Dionysiac impulse as it appears in drama is properly dialectical: 'Dionysus is, of necessity, contradictory: he is both the maker and the dismantler of the human individual as portrayed through dramatic character' (Storm, *After Dionysus* 26). A tragic vision will necessarily be a dialectical collision and attempted identity between the human and that which is outside the human, but for Storm, the dialectic of the tragic proper refuses the idea of a final dialectical synthesis, and insists upon discord in the self (43). Meanwhile, more politicized critics like Williams and Eagleton will insist that a tragic action always has within it a dialectical promise of the resolution of contradictions, the possibility that we might find in tragedy an identity between coherence and incoherence, wholeness and fragmentation. Thus while John Orr will agree with Raymond Williams that '[t]he essential tragic experience is that of irreparable human loss' and that loss always points to 'the predicament of human alienation, of which tragedy is the supreme literary expression' (*Tragic Drama* xii), Williams himself refuses a single, transhistorical absolute sense of even the seemingly unavoidable fact of death: 'To read back life from the fact of death is a cultural and sometimes a personal choice. But that it is a choice, and a variable choice, is very easily forgotten' (*Modern Tragedy* 56). Even absolutes like death are always mediated historically. To read mortality as the absolute negation of life is only a cultural code, one so deeply engrained in Western society that it goes by the guise of the universal, and this entrenchment forgets that mortality can, potentially, be interpreted in a dialectical identity with life, as part of an ongoing historical process.

Such considerations are necessary because I have no intention here of slavishly applying theories of the tragic in a formulaic manner, but rather wish to allow the plays under consideration to articulate their own attitudes towards tragic experience. The great failure of theories of the tragic is when they find that actual dramas fall short of the established theoretical parameters and are then found not to be tragedies. This is particularly true of considerations of contemporary dramas, which are inevitably and necessarily held up for comparison against past forms of tragedy. The most notorious example of this critical tendency is George Steiner, who provides a definition of tragedy in its 'absolute mode,' a kind of negative ideal that no existing play might actually fulfil but that can nevertheless be conceived of as an ur-form.[13] For Steiner, tragedy in its absolute mode presents a highly specific world view: '"It is best not to be born, next best to die young." [...] The proposition implies that men and women's presence on this earth is fundamentally absurd or unwelcome, that our lives are not a gift or a natural unfolding, but a self-punishing anomaly. We are unwelcome guests' ('Tragedy, Pure and Simple' 536). For Steiner, this vision of absolute tragedy is a kind of black hole, a 'pure tragic axiom' that is rarely realized as a 'performative act' (537). Earlier, in *The Death of Tragedy*, Steiner uses the word *Unheimlichkeit* to encompass this world view: that the human is fundamentally, radically alienated and homeless in life.

Steiner holds to a consistent scepticism about the possible re-emergence of tragedy within the condition of postmodernity: '[I]t is difficult to imagine a renascence of high tragic theatre in a positivist climate of consciousness, in a mass-market society, more and more of whose thinking members regard the question of the existence of God, let alone of demonic agents intervening in mundane affairs, as archaic nonsense' ('Tragedy, Pure and Simple' 543). Steiner's notorious thesis, reiterated many times over the years, is that tragedy demands a metaphysical view of the universe, and that accordingly, secular tragedy is not possible. For Steiner, tragedy is at its heart an image of humanity radically estranged within the world, an 'ontological fall from grace,' as he put it recently ('"Tragedy," Reconsidered' 32). Yet Steiner's investigation into the possibility of contemporary tragedy, far-reaching as it is, is always biased towards the attempt to locate what he considers 'authentic "tragedy"' (32). He locates Euripides's *The Bacchae* at the core of this 'absolute' tragedy, as a play in which there is a complete abandonment of hope. Such tragic drama is, for Steiner, inherently and necessarily metaphysical and theological in its contours. However, while Steiner privileges *The Bacchae* as being at the absolute, authentic core of the tragic, his argument does not always remain in the realm of antiquity and abstraction, and he is willing to allow that the last potential practitioner of tragedy is Samuel Beckett.[14] When Steiner elevates Büchner's *Woyzeck* and Yeats's *Purgatory* to the precious status of absolute tragedy, it is as secular plays that, in his estimation, come close to the absolute negativity he assigns to pure tragedy. He only looks to the modern with an eye to recovering something authentic from antiquity. In short, he is a high modernist lost in postmodernity.

Steiner's thesis is, I believe, finally flawed by his unreformed modernism, by his relentless insistence upon metaphysical absolutes, such as the idea of an authentic tragedy, when even in his own definition, tragedy is an image of the human not as authentic at all but as an ontological fraud. This contradiction is productive: Steiner assumes as a constant given that tragedy has a metaphysical essence and that the perfect Platonic tragedy exists somewhere, when the very definition of tragedy that he gives is of a universe bereft of hope, thus drained of essence. Steiner's assumed premise dictates in its logic that tragedy invokes a theological universe, one where humanity exists in a fallen state, and there must be a perfect, metaphysical reality from which we have fallen. As a metaphysician, his logical approach itself is classically tragic, asserting that all actually existing tragedies exist in a post-lapsarian state of artistic imperfection and failure. He describes contemporary plays as far from the tragic because they have fallen from grace. However, this lack of authenticity within actual works of art is, ironically, what allows them to fulfil his definition of tragedy. For our purposes, we should appreciate that the most crucial aspects of Steiner's thesis are its inconsistencies.

As a means of responding to this interpretative dilemma, Sarah Annes Brown suggests that 'if we are asking the question of a text "is this a tragedy?" then my view is that the answer is probably "yes"' ('Introduction: Tragedy in Transition' 2). The typical qualities by which a contemporary tragedy will be identified are either through a recognizably Aristotelian plot, or by a deliberate intertextual evocation of Greek or Shakespearean precedents. As Williams is at pains to argue throughout *Modern Tragedy*, this constant reference to the past with regards to the present always risks a further tragic alienation of our own historical moment, an assertion that if tragedies of today are not like tragedies of the past, then they are not 'truly' tragic, and this stands as a symptom of the post-tragic and less meaningful age in which we live. Thus in order to explore the possibility of the tragic as equally valid in the contemporary context as in the classical, Edith Hall turns not to Aristotle but to the German philosophical tradition for a 'working definition of tragedy [as] the expression of an enquiry into suffering, an aesthetically articulated question mark written in pain' ('Trojan Suffering, Tragic Gods' 20). Building from a similar premise, tragedy in the present study is about suffering and loss, frequently but not always manifested as literal death, and just as frequently figured as the experience of the internal death of the self that comes from various forms of alienation: social, personal, or psychic.

Importantly, the artistic representation of tragic experience is tragic not through the mere representation of suffering but through the dialectical interpretation of the tragic, and the hopefulness inherent in moments of the dialectical identity of opposites. As Peter Szondi puts it with reference to Schelling's theory of the tragic, what matters most in the dialectic of the tragic is 'the identity of freedom and necessity' that resolves itself in 'indifference in conflict.' Yet this 'indifference of freedom and necessity is possible only at the price of the conqueror simultaneously being the conquered, and vice versa. The site of the conflict is not an intermediate zone that remains external to the struggling subject, rather, it has been transferred into freedom itself, which, now at odds with itself, becomes its own adversary' (*An Essay on the Tragic* 10). This is seen in the Greek tragic hero, who is punished by the gods for a fate he was not able to avoid, and in enduring this senseless punishment asserts his freedom through the loss of his freedom (7). Thus the tragic is the peculiar and unique human experience in which loss and gain become, however fleetingly, indistinguishable from one another. Fleetingly, because this singular occurrence will be glimpsed as a part of the ongoing human work of mediating and managing loss or suffering, and as such it is an impermanent phenomenon. The tragic is a moment of dialectical identity between necessity and freedom that might be experienced by consciousness as the phenomenon of the impossible, or the intimation of the unconscious, of Derridean *différance*, of the Hegelian concrete, or of Lacanian truth or the real. At the heart of the tragic is the apprehension of the human as both sacred and profane, free and determined, metaphysical and material, soul and body, high and low, and thus as incoherence in response to the rigid oppositions of binary thought. The idea of the tragic and of tragic experience is, in the argument of this book, an affirmation of the value of loss within the rationalized positivism of a conservative society and an assertion of dialectical negativity within postmodernity. Within an ideological situation where hardship and misfortune are rewritten as personal weakness and destiny, the tragic explores both the fact that suffering is unavoidable and that the struggle to end suffering is a part of a humanizing process.

As we shall see here, contemporary English political dramatists, while by no means endorsing the idea that suffering as such is itself humanizing, are deeply concerned with the fact that humans make themselves – 'humanize' themselves if you will – out of their struggles to end their suffering and the suffering of others. We make ourselves out of loss and out of our losses, and this is a dialectical contradiction. The younger generation of playwrights considered here write plays questioning whether this humanizing process is still possible in postmodern capitalist society. In all cases we find an insistence that the tragic aspects of human existence be avowed and dramatized, as if these aspects have been repressed and disavowed within the contemporary cultural and political imagination. The task of representation is to represent, to copy, to imitate, and the plays studied here represent the performance of the tragic dimension of human life as a political intervention into the public discourse concerning the human. To claim that humans are defined as human by their failures and by their losses, by the negativity of their existences, is to engage in a radical social critique in the face of a conservative political establishment. I suggest that in the political environment of the 1980s, human failure was reconfigured as the failure to be human, and human misfortune was dismissed as human weakness: one's accidents became one's destiny. The dramas I analyse are avowals of aspects of humanity that have been repressed or disavowed, 'buried,' so to speak, within public discourse; in a sense they are public acts of mourning, with the understanding that public mourning is a political act.

Tragedy and Englishness

Again and again we shall see that tragedy confounds ideology. Here the particular ideology on display is Englishness, a uniquely English sense of national identity. Antony Easthope, in *Englishness and National Culture* (1999), presents an articulate and flexible thesis about national identity, arguing that Englishness as a sense of national identity arose in the latter half of the seventeenth century. Easthope's focus is on Englishness as it manifests itself in poetic language, and in defining Englishness he takes his critical lead from the moment in the 1960s when

> the New Left picked up Marx's account of the English philosophic tradition as empiricist, building it on to a more contemporary, Althusserian foundation. On this basis they advanced a historical narrative which, known now as the Nairn-Anderson theses, would explain the backwardness of English economic, political and cultural development and consequent failure of working-class revolution as all due to *empiricism*. (62)

Easthope modifies their critique on the grounds that national identity cannot be reducible to a form of ideology in a narrowly Marxist sense of a false belief system, imposed from above by dominant class interests. Instead, Easthope explores empiricism as a *discourse*, the truth or falsehood of which is irrelevant: 'Not to be confused with the "factual" or the "empirical," empiricism affirms that reality can be experienced more or less directly by the unprejudiced observer and that knowledge derives more or less directly from that experience' (63). Empiricist discourse is common sense and Lockean, taking itself as transparent and immediately communicative of objective, external reality. Naturally, it is not, because all language is rhetorical, yet it is invalid to say that empiricist discourse is an ideological 'lie.' First, since empiricist discourse is based upon rigidly entrenched binary oppositions of real and apparent (90), to attempt to criticize it as a 'false' view of reality is to participate in an empiricist discourse. Second, as a discourse it creates a valid sense of national identity that cannot be reduced to ideological false consciousness, since in Easthope's opinion Englishness crosses class lines.

The ultimate goal of any analysis of nationalism cannot be to escape it altogether, but rather to rethink it, and in so doing, change it. Easthope is interested in estranging national identity so that we might see what it is and how we might reconfigure it differently. Englishness is obsessed with the transparency of representation and the idea of a simple homology of subject and object. Yet what any national identity, including Englishness, constitutes itself out of but refuses to acknowledge is its disavowal of Otherness. Here, the tragic has an opportunity to intervene into selfhood and estrange Englishness through the avowal of that which is outside the self. Easthope analogizes national identity formation to the Freudian-Lacanian theory of the ego, a selfhood that is structured around a central lack, or primordially lost object. Yet ego identity constitutes itself precisely as a mirage of fullness that occludes its own fundamentally incomplete status: 'In its reflected image the subject aspires to an ideal of unity and permanence which it feels will make good its lack (*manque à être*), and identifies itself there' (Easthope 15). Here is where the tragic, in the sense defined by William Storm, can intervene through the Dionysiac *sparagmos*, the rending of the self that affirms its fundamental incompleteness and lack of unity. However, while Easthope knows that national selfhood needs a repressed unconscious, his focus on the discourse of Englishness becomes hermeneutic and tautological. He only considers examples of Englishness in discourse. So while he does consider the idea of paradigmatically English tragedy, using the literary example of Orwell's *1984*, it is as the tragedy of Englishness, a tragedy eminently suited to Englishness, rather than dialectical tragedy proper, which might challenge this English sense of self. Specifically, Easthope reads Winston Smith as a common-sense, empiricist thinker whose English individuality is tragically destroyed by Big Brother's totalitarian doublethink (Orwell's satirical representation of dialectical logic).

We can, however, usefully reverse the terms of his reading of *1984* for the purposes of this study: dialectical tragedy proper serves as an intervention into the empiricist discourse of Englishness precisely through the refusal of empiricist transparency and through the tragic insistence upon an identity of opposites. This dialectical identity is potentially an avowal of Otherness, an acknowledgment of the opposite that is identical with identity. Four well-known mythological figures make appearances throughout this study, modelling four different attitudes towards the tragic from within the perspective of Englishness: Oedipus, Antigone, Prometheus, and Dionysus. The tragic stages a confrontation between selfhood and Otherness, that which refuses selfhood, and in the plays in this study the selfhood on display is frequently seen to be an eminently English one, confronted by that which refutes the English sense of self. This confronted self can be understood to be an Oedipal Englishness: the tragic English figure confronted by an Otherness that demands the subjection of the self. Alternately, on other occasions it is the protagonists of the plays themselves who stand in the position of the Other to English consciousness, and in these cases the protagonists take on a more Antigone-like stance: tragic refuseniks who will not be contained by Englishness. A third, Promethean tragic figure stands against Englishness as a triumphalist assertion of the affirmative will to live. Finally, there are glimpses of what I will call the Dionysian tragic, which hints at a joyful union between self and Otherness. This book can be understood – at times implicitly and at times explicitly – as a study in what Easthope calls 'historicized subjectivity,' a sense of Englishness with a relationship to the Other in all of its guises, inner and outer.

The Freudian psychoanalytic theory of Jacques Lacan will be drawn upon in this study, largely due to Lacan's evocative reading of Sophocles's *Antigone*. While the importance of the Oedipus narrative for Freudian thought is well known and overdetermined, Lacan offers *Antigone* as an alternative paradigm of the tragic because it emphasizes the role of acknowledging desire and the unconscious rather than asserting Oedipal repression and subjection. For Lacan, the ego is an aspect of human selfhood residing properly in the register of consciousness he calls *imaginary*, an essentially narcissistic register from which the *symbolic* dimensions of human language liberate the human, because it is symbolization that engenders a further human relationship to the unconscious and to the Other, of which the unconscious is the discourse. The beautiful image of Antigone stands for the capacity in tragic experience to be purged of the imaginary register of consciousness (*Seminar, Book VII* 247–8). Antigone, whose intransigent insistence upon performing forbidden funeral rites ends with her 'buried alive in a tomb' (248), stands in the position of the unconscious and the Other. The play can be understood as a tragic avowal of the Other (be it mortality, the id, or desire) as the essential outside of the subject. Antigone is, as Lacan puts it, 'beyond a given limit,' *meta* (264–5). Thus, this study considers figures in contemporary plays who take on the position of the unconscious, like Antigone does, and who represent the symbolic death of the subject for English consciousness, engendering an avowal of and relation to the Other.

The presence of the Promethean and the Dionysian is the most unexpected and forceful political intervention into the contemporary representation of the tragic, and it is for this reason that the philosophy of Friedrich Nietzsche is occasionally drawn upon in the following analyses. As James I. Porter explains, Nietzsche's theory of tragedy is inconsistent and transitory, even within the pages of *The Birth of Tragedy*, but the crucial and unique importance of Nietzsche's thought is his insistence that the affirmative, joyful energy of Dionysus underlies all tragic experience. This can seem surprising and irrational, since tragedy emphasizes negativity, loss, and mourning. Indeed, in *The Birth of Tragedy* Nietzsche gives a highly contradictory account of the Dionysian, metaphysical One-ness that underlies the illusions of material reality, yet which paradoxically cannot be accessed except through the aesthetic veil of art. The core tragic knowledge that it is better never to have been born, the prize elevated by Steiner to the position of the Absolute, cannot 'be immediately apprehended: it must pass through an aestheticizing filter' (Porter 74). Thus as Porter concludes, it is impossible to decide whether tragedy, for Nietzsche, is an illusion that gives us a glimpse of metaphysical reality, or an illusory image of a glimpse of metaphysical reality (76–7). Dionysus may be, in Nietzsche's thought, not so much what underlies the veil of everyday life as the experience of everyday life as a veil that both promises and denies the presence of something metaphysical beyond it. 'There is something sublime and comical about mankind's persistent inability to live in the absence of metaphysical illusions,' Porter writes

(85). Tragedy is a form of celebration of the illusion of existence itself, of life as sheer appearance. Dionysus is, among other things, the god of masks and the theatre, and the well-known influence of Nietzsche on modernism also finds its way into the contemporary playwrights considered here, particularly in their affirmation of the here and now in all of its painful facets.

The Promethean assertion of the human is one dramatic mask of that Dionysian joy. The tragic dramas on display throughout this book are frequently united in their condemnation of a social sphere that stifles and hobbles human potential; the dramatic response is often a valorization or a tragic-heroic encomium to protagonists who assert their *right to live*, an ambiguous phrase that contains a multitude of human positions within it. As we shall see, the many theatrical representations of what it means to live are varied in their differing details but the commonalities are startling. The angry and often violent assertion of both a right to be and a right to one's desire, no matter what the antisocial consequences of such an unflinching position, are at the heart of the tragic playwright's project today. As a result, the idea of the tragic on display here will gradually mutate from nihilistic renunciation to joyful affirmation, from Oedipus to Antigone, and from Antigone to Prometheus and Dionysus.

Most of the plays and all playwrights here have been written about before. What I hope to do is examine a familiar series of objects from perspectives that are slightly askew, and in so doing reveal new facets for our appreciation. The tragic as an absolute object will not be discernible in and of itself in this book. As a traumatic ripple of loss it is much like a wave form: we will see this energy as it passes through different objects and substances, and we will be able to deduce things about tragic energy from the various forms of resistance it encounters as it passes through these different conductors. Each play or author will thus be one lens upon the tragic, but none will be final or definitive. Rather, the totality of views onto the otherwise intangible, seemingly metaphysical object is our concern. No matter how antagonistic the approaches on display here may be towards one another, they are all complementary in their articulation of tragic experience.

Such a caveat on my part responds to contemporary critical arguments about tragedy and the tragic. As Simon Goldhill argues lucidly in a recent article, contemporary attempts to define the essence of the tragic tend to draw their inspiration from Romantic Idealism and posit a relationship between the tragic and the sublime (as one might reasonably argue that the present study does). This search for an unambiguous, transhistorical definition of the tragic risks two things: the dehistoricization of tragedies at the expense of their particular social and political contexts; and the flight into abstraction and the eliding of actual dramatic tragedies that do not necessarily fit the parameters chosen by the critic or philosopher. This latter risk entails a further hazard, Goldhill surmises: actual Greek tragedies are often, he demonstrates, concerned with the dangers of abstracting and generalizing about the particularities of human suffering and political turmoil. 'Greek tragedy seeks the general,' but 'the plays themselves repeatedly question the value of the exemplary or explore the blurring between the general and the specific' ('Generalizing about Tragedy' 59). They warn us about generalizing an idea of 'the tragic' itself, a rhetorical gesture that risks the separation of concept from experience, with potentially tragic results. A dialectic between the general and the particular is needed, and the Greek tragedies offer the model of a 'productive and dialectical tension' between the general idea of the tragic and particular tragedies themselves (62). The ideal goal is a criticism that at once historicizes and politicizes the object of study while also attending to the general aspects of aesthetic experience. Thus I attend to both the politics and the poetics of contemporary English tragedy throughout this book.

The Structure of the Book

I begin with the work of David Hare rather than with Edward Bond, because Hare's realism and his concerted attention to his own contemporary social context give us a clear dramatic picture of the fabric of Englishness and demonstrate most articulately what is at stake in the insistence upon tragic experience within English society in the post-war environment. Thus 'David Hare: The Work of Mourning, or, The Agony and Ecstasy of the Bourgeoisie' sets the stage, so to speak, by providing three things that are essential to my overall argument. First, it establishes for us a useful picture of Englishness and English ideology against which to position the discussion of tragedy and the tragic throughout the book. Second, it discusses, critically, the ideological stakes in realism of dramatic form and realism of character, something that subsequent chapters on more formalist playwrights will problematize. Finally, through an exegesis of ten plays by Hare (and one recent instance of his directing work), it examines the use of tragic, Antigone-like protagonists as oppositional figures who stubbornly resist the substance of English life, contrarian figures who affirm an ideal of life in the face of a woefully negative and renunciatory English society. This chapter also considers the possibility for reading Hare's tragic figures dialectically, and in so doing finding the kernel of resistance to Englishness in his work.

The second chapter, 'Howard Barker: Will and Desire – From the Tragedy of Socialism to the Ecstasy of the Unconscious,' serves as a marked comparison and contrast to the first: Howard Barker's form of tragic theatre that he terms the 'Theatre of Catastrophe' is in every way the exact opposite of Hare's tragedy. Hare abandoned Royal Court socialism because he felt it was not speaking directly to its audience, an audience that was, finally, middle class rather than revolutionary. Barker abandoned Royal Court socialism because it was, in his opinion, pandering to its audience and preaching to the converted, namely comfortable middle-class leftists who were assured rather than challenged by doctrinal socialist content. Hare and Barker come at the same problem from fundamentally different ends of the spectrum. Hare presents oppositional, tragic characters as a means of affronting middle-class ideology, while his plays ultimately condescend to this social group. Barker, a contrarian in dramatic form, rejects the idea of communicating with his audience altogether, and thus presents not only characters but also plays that in their formal experimentation take a tragic stance in relationship to their society. Barker's plays fulfil the promise that Hare's plays make but can never satisfy owing to Hare's investment in realism of form, which ultimately reflects his audience back at itself. My analysis of Barker's Theatre of Catastrophe begins with his political theatre of the 1970s and its emphasis upon the contradictions, failures, and ultimate tragedy of socialism itself, and then moves into a study of catastrophic theatre proper from the 1980s to the present. Through a study of eleven plays, I examine how Barker's characters, attempting to unite their wills and their desires, offer an image of tragic protagonists triumphing over the negativity and repression of contemporary existence. In my analysis I enlist Nietzschean and Lacanian theories as a means of describing Barker's aesthetic. The goal of his theatre is the creation of a form of anxiety in his audience, an apprehension of a certain philosophical cruelty, as a passage to the appreciation of ecstatic, tragic beauty. Yet while Barker's aesthetic resembles the claims to the sublime in Romantic literature or high modernism's aspirations to the Absolute (thus the seeming similarities to Artaud's theories of cruelty in Barker's work), for Barker ecstatic experience is an opening into the unconscious, or what Lacan calls the language of the Other. In form, Barker's plays offer a contemporary expressionism that celebrates contradictions and incoherence as a means of staging a violent intrusion of the id into the ideology of Englishness.

The third chapter, 'Edward Bond: Tragedy and Postmodernity, or, The Promethean Impulse,' addresses the concept of the tragic and the work of tragedy as it appears in theoretical essays and eleven plays by Edward Bond. With Bond, we find a fully developed theory and practice of overtly politicized, dialectical materialist, socialist tragedy. Here, tragedy exposes the dialectical contradictions within society. These incoherent fissures are the foundations of suffering, but the fact that they exist is also a sign of hope, since it is by consciously resolving the contradictions that social change can take place. Bond's vision of the tragic is relentlessly critical of situations of dehumanization and also pragmatically optimistic in its assertion of small, humanizing gestures that serve to negate the inhumanity of contemporary existence. Bond's theoretical essays also broaden the horizon of interpretation within which the contemporary tragic operates to include not only the ideological fabric of Englishness but also the conditions of late capitalism, otherwise known as postmodernity. Bond unites this critique of the condition of postmodernity with attention to the tragic aspects of human existence, all within the rubric of a Marxist analysis. Through a detailed exegesis of Bond's theoretical writings, combined with close readings of plays written throughout his entire career, I suggest that the tragic in Bond is located in the small, sometimes futile gestures with which his characters materialize, often failingly, their humanity in the face of postmodern dehumanization. These are manifestations of a celebratory Promethean tragic, acts of *hubris* located within tiny objects and gestures and also within crimes, which Bond offers as humanizing instances of tragic heroism.

The fourth chapter, 'Caryl Churchill: The Dionysian Möbius Strip,' addresses a playwright who might be considered an unexpected participant in this discourse of the tragic. With the exception of *Fen*, Churchill does not write formal tragedies. However, my argument here is that Churchill's career so far demonstrates a continuing engagement with human subjectivity from a tragic perspective. From early in her career to her most recent work, Churchill grapples with the problem of negativity as foundational for the human subject. Effectively, she begins in her early work with a traditional Freudian concept of the subject as constituted around primordial lack, and thus suffering from a tragic, alienated subjectivity. In particular, her characters grapple with the alienation of their desire. They struggle with the unconscious. Churchill's gradual consideration of the possibility for what I call 'post-Freudian' Dionysian subjectivity means that her plays explore the transformation of the subjective tragedy of alienation into the tragedy of difference. This post-Freudianism resembles, to some degree, the post-structuralist revisioning of selfhood: away from a self defined around loss, negativity, and social *ressentiment* and towards a Dionysian definition of self that affirms difference. In Churchill's plays there is a movement away from the alienation of the unconscious and towards the forging of a relationship with the unconscious as the Dionysian Other. Far from being a utopian project, this affirmation of difference remains firmly rooted within tragic parameters for the self, but the tragedy of difference offers an affirmative attitude towards the aspects of existence that a traditional concept of subjectivity sees as facets of alienation. Churchill's tragic is a socialist-feminist intervention into questions of social and individual alienation as a means of articulating the vitality of tragic experience. For example, in Churchill's dramas, mourning and loss are affirmed as enabling aspects of the self rather than repressed or disavowed by consciousness. The social diagnosis that emerges from this analysis is that it is specifically tragic experience, and particularly an affirming relationship to the unconscious and to the Other, that has been rendered pathological within a conservative political environment.

In the final chapter, 'New English Tragedians: The Tragedy of the Tragic,' I take this analysis a step further and examine two key exemplars of the 1990s generation of playwrights and their attitudes towards tragic experience. By reconsidering their 'shock' theatre within the paradigm of the tragic, I argue that Mark Ravenhill and Sarah Kane are best understood as contemporary tragedians whose political plays are social commentaries on the effect of the postmodern condition upon tragic experience. What is a tragedy for them is that postmodernity makes the tragic – specifically the humanizing mediation of loss – impossible. The tragedy of the tragic is that postmodernity dictates that the tragic is dead. This is something different from the 'death of tragedy' that George Steiner famously diagnosed. In response to this threat, these new tragedians analyse the cost of this repression of the tragic both for individual subjectivity and for society, while also fashioning tragic dramas as interventions into the postmodern condition. Loss, grief, melancholy, mourning, trauma, and pain are not the opportunity for mere 'shock effects,' as the 'In-Yer-Face' theatre was deemed to be in the 1990s. Rather, these playwrights articulate vital, humanizing confrontations with suffering and necessity while at the same time demonstrating an awareness of the political risks bound up within such a seemingly reactionary project. As the inheritors of Royal Court socialism themselves, they know their Brecht and the associated warnings against tragedy, but they also know that tragedy offers access to aspects of human experience to which the postmodern remains blind. Ultimately, the work of Ravenhill and Kane demonstrates that formalism and the tragic are associated responses to the alienating conditions of postmodernity itself, and the tragic serves as a dialectical mediation between form and content, as a corrective to postmodern reification. The tragic is the reintroduction of the political and the social into a privatized contemporary setting.

My conclusion explores the implications of the seemingly metaphysical concerns regarding the Absolute that have – incontrovertibly – crept into the work of socially committed playwrights. In Hare it is spiritual experience and the soul, in Barker the ecstasy of desire and the unconscious, in Bond the Promethean 'radical innocent,' in Churchill the Dionysian Other, and in Ravenhill and Kane it is 'evil' and 'love.' Taking my cue from Fredric Jameson's surmise that 'we cannot not periodize' (*A Singular Modernity* 29), I suggest that this trend in English theatre might best be characterized as 'late late modernism,' precisely for the ways in which it combines politicized formalism with tragic claims to the Absolute. Accordingly, given the parameters of this study, Jez Butterworth's recent Royal Court success *Jerusalem* (2009) offers a particularly apposite endnote. *Jerusalem* encourages us to reframe the critical debate around the so-called In-Yer-Face playwrights with an eye to Englishness, the Absolute, and the tragic, and suggests the vital possibilities for tragic experience within the contemporary English theatre.

David Hare:
The Work of Mourning, or, The Agony
and the Ecstasy of the Bourgeoisie

'Do we just suffer? Is that what you want? Fight and suffer to no purpose?
Yes? Is everything loss?'

Hare, Racing Demon 88

Joan Didion's *The Year of Magical Thinking*

Watching director David Hare's production of Joan Didion's *The Year of Magical Thinking* at the Royal National Theatre in May 2008 was a uniquely decentring experience. Arriving in London after its successful Broadway premiere a year before, the UK production enjoyed sold-out audiences and an extended run. Yet one suspects that the play's appeal to the American audience and its attraction to an English audience were based on different objects: in the first instance, Joan Didion's devastating memoir about the sudden death of her husband, a book immensely popular in America (Hare calls it 'the one indispensable handbook to bereavement' in the United States [Introduction, *The Year of Magical Thinking* viii]) being adapted to the Broadway stage; and in the second instance, Vanessa Redgrave appearing in a one-woman show directed by David Hare at the National Theatre. Certainly the discomfited, slightly confused grumbling that rippled through the English audience in the play's first moments confirms this: here was not Vanessa Redgrave at all but a gaunt, unglamorous American woman with a peculiar Yank accent talking with great familiarity about various New York hospitals as if the audience were assumed to understand these distant cultural references.

The momentary alienation of the middle-aged, middle-class English audience in the face of Redgrave's portraying a character completely unlike her public persona was palpable. Not only has 'Joan Didion' lived a uniquely Californian existence, iconoclastic and improvised, an un-English life of adventure, travel, and unending jet-setting; not only is she arrogant, aloof, cool, and indifferent to what the audience thinks of her; she also announces at the opening of the play that she has come here to teach the audience a lesson: *You think what happened to me won't happen to you. You are wrong.* What happens to Didion is that her husband dies suddenly in July 2003 of a heart attack while their grown daughter is in the hospital with dangerous complications from pneumonia. In August 2005 her daughter, who never fully recovers from these complications, dies of acute pancreatitis and septic shock. In between those two events, Didion cares for her ailing daughter and writes a book about her own disjointed mental state: while knowing rationally that her husband is dead, Didion nevertheless finds herself engaging in what she calls 'magical thinking,' which she likens to so-called primitive thought (Didion, *The Year* 23). For instance, she must keep her husband's shoes, because if she performs the right actions, pretending to go along with funeral arrangements and the like, she can make him return. She wants an autopsy performed, because if they can locate the exact cause of death, perhaps they can fix it. If she does the right thing, then she can make him come back.

David Hare takes no credit for a script constructed from what is obviously Didion's personal experience; his role in the development of the play was to help Didion to shape the material into properly dramatic form. My interest here is not in the script but rather in the style of performance that Hare coaxed out of Vanessa Redgrave, combined with the presentation of a resolutely American tale of tragic grief to a resolutely English audience. This combination of form and content tells us something about Hare's own work. It is the style of performance, so directly in evidence in a simple monologue play, that makes *The Year of Magical Thinking*'s protagonist a representative member of Hare's dramatic pantheon. Didion is a creature of style who mistakes this style for substance and finds that it cannot sustain her through her ordeal. She radiates brittle, distant aloofness: reserved, isolated, a little cold, and perhaps even unfriendly to her audience, she brings them a warning about human mortality that is laced with sarcasm, wry self-deprecation, and an ironic detachment towards herself. It is a cautionary tale about the futile attempt to control the uncontrollable and, as Hare himself puts it, a *Lehrstück* about the fate of being human (Introduction, *The Year of Magical Thinking* xvii).[1] Despite the direct address of the monologue, there is an invisible wall between stage and audience, a thin veneer of untouchability radiating from 'Didion,' most noticeable when it is subtly stressed or tested, as in two rare moments when she extends her wrist, almost haughtily but with composed grace, to show us a bracelet that we eventually learn was a gift to her daughter. This gesture seems not generous or inclusive but faintly superior and condescending. Worst of all is the sense that Didion knows all this and doesn't care: she is utterly, dangerously self-possessed. Didion is indifferent to what the audience thinks of her behaviour. Her description of her 'magical thinking' is alienating and frustrating to the audience not because of its irrationality, but because she in her arrogance finds this thinking strange. Her lack of self-insight is perturbing.

I begin this discussion of the tragic with reference to this recent example of Hare's directing work in order to highlight a central point: in Hare's oeuvre, the tragic encounter with mortality, the human experience of loss, grief, and mourning, does not ennoble or strengthen consciousness. Instead, the tragic reveals the seeming fraudulence of consciousness as such, by exposing the virtual pose of the self. Hare, in working with Didion and in casting Redgrave, worked from the understanding that the right voice needed to be created for the narrative and the right stylist found to express that voice (ix, xv). Thus what matters here is just as much how Didion presents herself as what she says. And she presents a brittle figure of *hubris* attempting to control the uncontrollable, finding herself confronted by a profound lack of understanding or of self-insight when subjected to the machinations of her own psyche, and estranged from her self by the experience of loss. Such a distanced, self-possessed, and self-conscious poise as demonstrated by Didion at the beginning of the play courts accusations of fraudulence and inauthenticity, of disingenuously theatricalizing one's self. By the end of the play this figure is humbled but not necessarily any more sincere. Rather, she is now troubled by a dread of a lack of integrity: she fears that she has survived because her love for her husband and daughter was not substantial, and that the two of them have been joined together in a loving bond that excludes her. The haunting conclusion thus offers the intimation that Didion now harbours doubts about her own authenticity and sincerity as a human being: the experience of loss has revealed to her that her own attempt to control reality is a false mask concealing an inner emptiness. This tragic ambiguity guides us towards the matters that are of concern to Hare the tragedian.

Rather than commencing this study with Edward Bond, the playwright who represents the senior generation in relation to other writers here considered, I address Hare first because Hare is the English playwright whose tragedies are most deliberately immersed in the theatrical inheritance of dramatic realism, particularly when compared to the other dramatists in this book, all of whom venture more daringly into realms of formal and stylistic experimentation. Hare's dramatic realism is valuable here as a starting point because it serves to define the theatrical legacy against which the more formalist playwrights under consideration rail. Howard Barker serves as the most directly parallel counter-example of this, which is why he is addressed in the next chapter, as a contrast to Hare. Hare's realism also serves as a crucial vehicle for content: realism allows him to engage with historical events and social circumstances in a manner that paints a substantial picture of English life and Englishness and makes clear the ideological stakes at hand for this study. Finally and importantly, the dramatic tradition of realism is inseparable from the representation of middle-class values through this conservative stylistic inheritance, and it is the ideology of the middle class that this first chapter will sketch out through a study of Hare's plays. While Hare's focus on the middle class is often wielded as a tool of dismissal against him, it is nevertheless what defines his particular explorations of the tragic.[2] Moreover, while there is middle-class realism in Hare's plays, I will argue that his tragic characters are delineated as formal, 'unrealistic' creations precisely as a rejection of the parameters of this dominant style.

In his early days as co-creator and active member of the Portable Theatre, Hare's work was confrontational and agitational, yet like other playwrights shaped in this touring crucible of theatrical experimentation, Hare found himself eventually working in the established London venues and speaking to the mainstream, middle-class audiences that dominate British theatres.[3] Perhaps more than any other English political playwright, Hare has grown increasingly conscious of this audience and has sought to reflect the thoughts, lives, and experiences of this group back from the stage, refracted through the lens of the social critic. Fascinated by English life, Hare is nevertheless deeply critical of English thought and behaviour, and he presents tragic figures, usually women, as powerful affronts to entrenched English values. Maggie, the protagonist of *Teeth 'n' Smiles* (1975), represents the first of Hare's Antigone figures: uncompromisingly stubborn tragic characters who find themselves at a remove from the conventions of the society in which they live. Susan Traherne in *Plenty*, Hare's Oscar Wilde in *The Judas Kiss*, and the actress Esme Allen in *Amy's View* are further extrapolations on this figure. They are dedicated to ideals of social change, love, or art that both elevate and debase them in their dramatic plots, isolating them, strengthening them, defeating and martyring them. Finally, in their unflinching and theatrical stances, they risk accusations of inauthenticity or insincerity.[4]

The results are problematic dramas to interpret, much as Sophocles's *Antigone* has withstood a multitude of conflicting readings. On the one hand, Hare's writing radiates clarity, lucidity, and the powerful impulse to communicate clearly with an audience. The pleasures of his work arise from the craft and technique evident in his dramas, combined with the compassion and conscience he displays in his choice of subject matter. A less cynical Ibsen for the modern age, Hare creates conflicts between characters that represent differing social perspectives and clashing philosophies. On the other hand, and also like Ibsen, Hare's seemingly clear-eyed conflicts, when they are performed, become less than obvious in terms of their meanings. When interpretive ambiguity enters into the realm of these middle-class tragedies, the plays become truly, productively tragic in their lack of clarity. It is my contention here that Hare explores tragic protagonists who demonstrate a kind of theatricality derived from their privileged class positions, a theatricality that reveals the fraudulence of English society itself. These characters all, to some greater or lesser degree, reject their class backgrounds, yet this ability to renounce their own class is conditional on the privileges of that very class, and thus their tragic stances resemble a pose or posturing, like the fragile tragic stance assumed by 'Joan Didion.' As we shall see, this dialectical contradiction between the individual pose and a society bereft of values realizes precisely Raymond Williams's definition of 'liberal tragedy.'

Teeth 'n' Smiles

As a tragic figure, Maggie of *Teeth 'n' Smiles* is a composite of Antigone and Oedipus: she is at once self-willed and self-destructive, radiating a blinding glamour onstage embodied in the energy of Helen Mirren's performance of the character at the Royal Court Theatre in 1975. At the same time she is a scapegoat, victimized by her own supporting band when the intensity of her drunken tour schedule provokes them to give her up in a drug bust. She actively assumes this victimization in a classical tragic turn, preferring to go to prison rather than remain free in England. This particular gesture on her part is, retroactively, of special importance to Hare himself, because it is Maggie's consummately un-English action: 'a girl chooses to go to prison because it will give her an experience of suffering which is bound in her eyes to be more worthwhile than the life she could lead outside: not one English critic could bring himself to mention this central event in the play, its plausibility, its implications' (Introduction, *The Early Plays* 9). We are immediately in the central formal problem of Hare's work: barring the early satires (for example *Slag*, *The Great Exhibition*, *Knuckle*) or his collaborations with Howard Brenton (*Brassneck*, *Pravda*), Hare's dramatic rhetoric is firmly couched in the rhetoric of realism. Maggie is offered to us as a figure with recognizable parallels in everyday experience – '[H]ow many people here have close friends who have taken control of their own lives, only to destroy them?' Hare asks (9) – but she is also too much of a member of a dramatic continuum of wilful stage women (Hedda Gabler by way of Janis Joplin) to be mistaken for an imitation of life. Mundane settings, events, and characters populate Hare's oeuvre, yet in immediate contradiction to this are the self-consciously formal dramatic conceits he employs again and again: the tragic gestures, events, and characters he unleashes into his realistic dramas are jarringly at odds with 'reality,' if reality is understood as the social consensus. This conflict is key to Hare's representation of the human, torn between the mundanity of 'realistic' behaviour and the self-conscious performativity of the tragic, dramatic gesture. There is an unavoidable theatricality in Maggie, a vacillation between authenticity and pose: 'Tragedy's easy. I pick it up, I sling it off. Like an overcoat,' she claims (*Teeth 'n' Smiles* 193).

This tension is a key challenge in the interpretation of Hare's plays: the clash between his realism and his formal exploration of tragic characters. It is typically realism that wins out in critical evaluations of Hare, with the result that his tragic characters are examined according to the twin criteria of realism: psychology on the one hand, and morality on the other. Consider, for example, Carol Homden's reading of Maggie as a Nietzschean tragic heroine: 'She is [...] Dionysiac Man feeling the pain of understanding that nothing she can do can change things' (14–15). For Homden, 'Maggie's suffering is heroic: she denies the power of the establishment to decide her fate by her own act of choice' (18). Such readings of Hare's characters are problematic, because however extreme the behaviour of the characters, they are nevertheless held up as models of human behaviour, to be ideally emulated. They are implicitly read realistically, out of the desire to find political models for action in their deeds. John S. Su's exploration of *Plenty* and *The Secret Rapture* argues from a similar premise: '[T]o what extent can a nostalgic vision of a Britain that perhaps never was provide a moral structuring principle allowing the possibility of right action in the present; more pointedly, can a moral response prove an adequate solution to what Hare has cast as political problems?' (23). Such a search for ethical models in Hare's protagonists is inevitably defeated from the beginning, because it holds his tragic characters up against a positive paradigm of political theatre from which his plays are deliberately distanced.

Hare insists that despite his turn away from situationist confrontational work with the Portable Theatre, he has always remained a committed political playwright with a socialist agenda. It is his definition of what constitutes political theatre that has made him an elusive subject for critical analysis: 'We are living through a great, groaning, yawling festival of change – but because this is England it is not always seen on the streets. In my view it is seen in the extraordinary intensity of people's personal despair, and it is to that despair that as a historical writer I choose to address myself time and time again' (Introduction, *The Early Plays* 8). Hare asks us to transcode individual conflict – personal despair – into social allegory, but despair does not, and is not intended to, provide an individual's code of conduct. What, then, are the causes and qualities of Maggie's despair? How is her despair political? On an immediate level, we must consider the formative situation of her youth: Maggie's despair is the product of

growing up affluent and well educated in the rural town of Stevenage, specifically. She insists that she sings from real, authentic pain (*Teeth 'n' Smiles* 195),
but the members of her band have heard this line so many times that they scoff
at her claim to authenticity (198).

In her self-willed posturing she is a hard character to like, which is precisely
Hare's point. In fact, the reasons behind Maggie's unrelenting alcoholic debauch-
ery become more vague as the play proceeds (200–1), and her disgruntled entourage, arguing about the roots of her self-destructive behaviour, are all too
cognizant of the dramatic antecedents that inform her performance: 'I knew a
Viennese teacher who said that desperate people who try to kill themselves but
only succeed in shooting their eyes out, never, ever attempt suicide again. It's the
sense of challenge you see. Once you've lost your eyes, it gives you something to
live for' (202). In these parodic, indirect references to Freudian theories of
Oedipalization, the suggestion here from Maggie's manager Saraffian that Maggie
is going through a maturation and socialization phase, and is dramatically like
Oedipus, raises the contemporary problem that will emerge again and again in
the exploration of tragic experience by contemporary playwrights: the problem
of whether or not the experience of tragic submission is or can be authentic, since
for the contemporary human, individual agency dominates the register of consciousness, and the concept of human actions being determined by inhuman
conditions is largely dismissed. Laura, the long-suffering tour manager/roadie,
replies, 'It's just possible anywhere, any time to decide to be a tragic figure. It's just
an absolute determination to go down. The reasons are arbitrary, it may almost
be pride, just not wanting to be like everyone else. I think you can die to avoid
cliché. And you can let people die to avoid cliché' (202). Hare portrays a resolutely secular, mundane universe, and while, as we shall see, he is fascinated by
questions of faith, spirituality, and belief, there are no gods or miracles on his
stage. As a result, the agency of his characters seems absolute, their responsibility
for their deeds their own: in this same scene, the decision is made to sack Maggie
because of her behaviour. The tragic paradox redoubles and folds back onto itself:
observing that she is behaving in a theatrical, inauthentic fashion specifically designed to avoid a clichéd life, her entourage make of her a scapegoat, thus placing
her in a tragic narrative by thieving from her agency over her fate. They not only
fire her, but when a drug bust goes down and the band's drugs are found in her
luggage, unbeknownst to her, she is allowed to take the blame. In the second half
of the play, questions of agency and the paradoxes surrounding this aspect of the
human emerge as a central facet of Hare's portrayal of Maggie.

The question of alcoholism, for example, leads to a familiar argument about
the problem of human agency within a tragic paradigm. Saraffian suggests that
people drink to excess as a means of absolving themselves of responsibility for

their actions: 'They want to be addicted so's to have something to blame. It's not me speaking. It's the drink. The drugs. It's not me can't manage. They want to be invaded, so there's an excuse. So there's a bit intact' (225). As we shall see, Hare's consistency of themes can be observed in the fact that this question is at the heart of his recent play *My Zinc Bed* (2000). Yet equally as consistent in Hare's work is a refusal to answer or to settle these questions. Rather, the plays will gesture allusively to a reason why the problem of human agency is or should be unanswerable. The breakup of the band and the firing of Maggie is rationalized by Saraffian: '[T]hey break up because they don't feel any need. I don't mean fame, that's boring, or money, that's a cliché, of course it goes without saying that money will separate you from the things you want to sing about, we all know that. I mean – need. Maggie. Where's the need?' (227). Saraffian's deployment of this eminently philosophical term becomes cryptic in its supposed self-explanatory meaning. The word 'need' immediately takes on a metaphysical weight for being apparently self-evident. His criticism of the absence of need in the lives of rock musicians is immediately recognizable as a critical commentary on their artistic activities as not being *work*: it is not whether they are successful either financially or in terms of popularity that separates them from the experience of necessity, but by living lives of hedonistic pleasure *as artists*.

Furthermore, there is another possible meaning to this diagnosis: art takes place in the superstructure rather than in the productive economic base, where real work, the articulation of necessity, occurs. With this interpretation in mind, the play is self-reflexively commenting on its own inability to speak to the question of necessity, since from a rationalistic point of view art itself is unnecessary. This seems to be how Maggie interprets Saraffian's critique in her reply, as she retorts that the absence of need from their lives has nothing to do with singing or being an artist: 'In Russia the peasants could not speak of the past without crying. What have we ever known?' (227). While Maggie understands Saraffian's comment to be directed at the immateriality of art, she broadens the critique to include all of English society. It is a familiar fetishization of the suffering endured by other, less economically developed cultures as providing more authentic human experiences and a greater sense of history, thus a more meaningful existence, than life in the West can. She tells an anecdote of her childhood, a rosy idyllic life of privilege and care, and then mocks this narrative by dousing herself with liquor. It is moments later that she is informed that the drugs are in her bag. She takes a long pause and accepts this fate: 'O.K. Try prison for a while, why not?' (228). The implication of this moment is that Maggie's self-destructiveness arises from her feeling that life in England is meaningless because its people have no experiences through which a submission to necessity might be endured, and thus tragic experience is not available to them.

Saraffian's reply to this surmise comes near the end of the play in the form of a long narrative describing the bombing of the Café de Paris in 1941, the looting of the corpses of the rich, and the refusal of a cab driver to let the wounded wealthy get blood in his cab. Saraffian, present at this event and in spirit on the side of the looters, suggests there is necessity in England and that the class war has continued since the Second World War. His pleasure in telling the narrative seems to suggest that life in England is not as meaningless as Maggie takes it to be, and particularly that those who truly suffered in the war, the members of the working class, have experiences of necessity that a member of Maggie's privileged class does not. Yet Maggie accuses him of living in the past, in a comforting fiction of the class war. The play itself seems torn, in the end, between their contrasting perspectives on the possible location of necessity in English life at the end of the 1960s. The possible existence of such a ground, upon which a meaningful and significant tragic gesture might be erected, remains an unresolved question within the play's dialectic, but there is a possibility of tragic authenticity to be found not at the level of content but of form.

Formally, *Teeth 'n' Smiles* is a highly self-conscious play, enacting the 'the play is in the air' theory that Hare would go on to espouse in a controversial 1978 talk at King's College, Cambridge: 'A play is a performance. So if a play is to be a weapon in the class struggle, then that weapon is not going to be the things you are saying; it is the interaction of what you are saying and what the audience is thinking. The play is in the air' (Introduction, *The Early Plays* 6).[5] Hare's Cambridge lecture was also a performance, but one terminally mismatched with its audience, and its message resulted in heckling.[6] With this talk, Hare was infamously branded a political apostate for his refusal of the idea of political didacticism in the theatre and his acceptance that the audience to whom he speaks is middle class. I would suggest that he is ultimately arguing that the political efficaciousness of a play is found in its unique *form* as theatre, and this form is of a singular event that happens in communication with an audience. This uniqueness bears a content of its own. The politics of *Teeth 'n' Smiles* emerge in the context of the dramatic action, which is also when the play becomes its most formal and self-reflexive. The action takes place over one evening, at a Jesus College Ball at Cambridge University in 1969, and the audience of the play is in the position of the privileged college students who find themselves being reluctantly entertained by a raucous and ill-mannered rock-blues outfit. Tragic authenticity arrives in the form of this performance. The uniqueness of *theatrical* form demands our attention: theatre is itself, and it is an imitation. The human onstage is both real and virtual.

Helen Mirren is the raw, authentic human here, embodying Maggie. Onstage, Maggie ruins the band's numbers with stumbling, out-of-control performances that baffle her band mates, who argue about the causes behind her drama (211) and how she can claim to have real pain in her life that fuels her despair: 'Somethin' ta do with bein' unloved, but she don' wanta be loved, she wants to be flattened by a Sherman tank' (212). The songs are riddled with rock R n' B cliché, yet the emotions of the performer are sincere. When does the cliché of the self-destructive has-been rock star transcend its contours and become something else? In the unique moment of live performance, in the particular, unrepeatable event. Theatre provides a response to the problem of the life bereft of authenticity: a utopian space where the authentic and the inauthentic will overlap and blur their borders. In the focusing of Maggie's pain into song, a pain that, we must note, is a grief over her lack of need – a sense of loss *for* the experience of loss – she makes, through the work of her art, a gain out of this loss. It is fitting, then, that the last scene of the play is 'Maggie's Song,' which is at once a lament for the sinking of the Titanic/England and a mournful celebration of the song itself: 'The ship is sinking/ But the music remains the same' (248). The audacity of Hare's conceit is that a realistic play about a rock performance should risk tragic themes, and the tragic here emerges as the final end of the post-war promise with the close of the 1960s.[7]

Plenty

Hare's location of the Second World War as a touchstone for English experience is well known: 'Really it's to do with the Second World War – I only see this with age, with perspective – that I was born having just missed the most important event in my life, which happened just before I was born. And I can now see that my parents' behaviour, which I didn't understand at that time, was related to that event I had missed' (Interview with Harriet Devine, *Looking Back* 160). Hare's description is a piece of tragic paradox: to have a distanced yet possessive relationship with an event that took place before he existed, and thus was not an event in his life at all. He expands upon this sentiment in a lecture from 1996: 'The most important fact of my life happened before I was born. In the Second World War millions of people died in defence of a belief, and the sense of squalor and disappointment of the post-war period seems to me inexorably to have stemmed from the feeling that the sacrifice they made has somehow been squandered' ('When Shall We Live?' 72). Hare's most explicit dramatization of this experience of alienation is found in *Plenty* (1978), one of his most well-known plays, and which was revived in 1999 with Cate Blanchett in the principle role. Like *Antigone*, it is a play about the cost of holding to one's ideals beyond all reason, but *Plenty* also emerges as a response to *Teeth 'n' Smiles*. The moment of the Second World War is presented again as a past experience in relation to which the present pales by comparison, but in *Plenty* those past moments are presented directly for the audience rather than recounted through dialogue.

Famously confusing to the critical establishment, *Plenty* is at once Hare's most merciless critique of post-war Englishness and his most elusive play.[8] Hare's précis of the play and the difficulty it poses to English audiences is an apt summary: 'I intend to show the struggle of a heroine against a deceitful and emotionally stultified class, yet some section of the English audience miss this, for they see what Susan is up against as life itself' (Introduction, *The History Plays* 15). This is, however, not the fault of the audience in the least; the play itself frankly encourages this idea by portraying no alternative to the way of life that Susan Traherne so bridles against and is so much a part of, other than the aimless and transitory Bohemianism of her friend Alice. The alienation Susan feels from the society around her in the years from 1947 to 1962 is the result of her experiences as a seventeen-year-old in Special Operations in France from 1943 to 1944. During the war she found herself in constant danger for her life, living for a cause that she believed in unquestioningly and having experiences of such vitality that after the war she is left at a permanent remove from her present circumstances, constantly revisiting in her mind a past moment against which the present pales in comparison: 'I think of the war more than I tell you. [...] The most unlikely people. People I met only for an hour or two. Astonishing kindnesses. Bravery. The fact you could meet someone for an hour or two and see the very best of them and then move on' (*Plenty* 158). It is not simply that England after the war isn't as exciting for her, it is that England after the war is an ontological fraud. Englishness itself is, in the post-war decline of Empire, nothing more than a hypocritical pose. Leaving her work in a shipping office (the remnant of Empire), Susan drifts into the new economy of affluence and 'plenty,' eventually finding herself working in advertising, manufacturing point-less deceit to sell cheap footwear, which compares poorly to the 'glittering lies' that she engaged in during the war (166).

Nothing is more vacuous, shallow, or vapid than the stupidity of advertising in consumer capitalism, except perhaps for the one other form of employment substantially represented in the play: the diplomatic corps, a career pursued by Susan's husband, Raymond Brock. Diplomacy is a major form of activity in the play, serving not only as a sign of the remnants of England's overseas presence after Empire but also as a metaphor for the decrepit nature of Englishness itself in the 1950s and 60s. Diplomacy is a profession in which 'nobody may speak their mind,' and 'in its practice the English lead the world. [...] As our influence wanes, as our empire collapses, there is little to believe in. Behaviour is all' (193). Having nothing left to believe in after the war (except for the ideology of 'plenty,' in other words an undirected, decadent promise of affluence and comfort), the English are left with nothing to believe in at all, and are as a result left meaningless themselves. They are hypocrites, crass materialists, sexually repressed and emotionally stifled, casually racist, and carefully, deliberately classist, narrow-minded, self-important reactionary conservatives.

Throughout the play Susan is torn between trying to fit into the English world she is inevitably a part of, through marriage and work, and indulging fitfully in periodic losses of control, which are interpreted as loss of sanity by others. Yet at the same time it seems self-evident to me that in scene 7 it is England's deceitful hypocrisy itself during the Suez Canal debacle that is driving Susan beyond reason. However, this must be taken literally, not figuratively: her loss of control is at once something she indulges (she acknowledges that she likes losing control in the penultimate scene of the play) and something provoked. The only authentic human response to being English, *Plenty* suggests, is to go mad. Thus Susan's agency over herself is ultimately unknowable in the play. Her husband, eventually, accuses her of never facing life (199) and summarizes the all-too-sensible English attitude towards her apparent wilfulness:

> Your life is selfish, self-interested gain. That's the most charitable interpretation to hand. You claim to be protecting some personal ideal, always at a cost of almost infinite pain to everyone around you. You are selfish, brutish, unkind. [...] I won't surrender till you're well again. And that to me would mean your admitting one thing: that in the life you have led you have utterly failed, failed in the very, very heart of your life. Admit it. Then perhaps you might really move on. (200)

Brock attempts to help her by promising to have her institutionalized. She retaliates by drugging him, giving their home to her friend Alice to use as a women's shelter, and leaving him permanently. The play attempts to present a true dialectic, but it is all too easy to identify with Brock's perspective, much harder to find the flaws in his attitude. Susan is disliked, not just by audiences but also infamously by the woman who created the role: Kate Nelligan.[9]

In order to see from Susan's perspective, we may need to evoke Oscar Wilde's definition of selfishness in 'The Soul of Man under Socialism' (an idea which is far from irrelevant, as we shall see it return in *The Judas Kiss*).[10] Selfishness, for Wilde, is exactly what Brock displays in his words: the insistence that another should live and behave according to the same rules as oneself. For Wilde, selflessness was found in a life lived privately and individually, without regards for the concerns of others. Selflessness is minding your own business, while selfishness is minding others' business. From such a perspective, Susan lives without ego, or seeks to do so, by being utterly and only concerned with her own affairs. The ego (and here I am evoking a Lacanian definition) is aggressively narcissistic and seeks to remake the outside world into a mirror for itself.[11] When Susan divests herself of her material possessions (198) she is stripping away the trappings of ego, culminating in the gifting of the house to Alice. Susan flees her life and is shortly found by a man she met during the war, Lazar, to whom she explains, 'I've stripped away everything, everything I've known. There's only one kind of dignity, that's in living alone. The clothes you stand up in, the world you can see' (204). Having divested herself of material, worldly goods, Susan retreats into a cannabis haze that culminates in the final dramatic image of the play: a hotel doorway opens onto the rolling green hills of France and a scene in 1944, after the end of combat. We end the play within Susan's memory of a happy moment in the past, an almost pastoral idyll.

Susan Traherne is in no way a socialist heroine, nor should she be taken as an attempt at creating one. The closest she comes to espousing any progressive sentiments is her response to the Suez Crisis in 1956, which she first mocks for England's bungled, emasculated show of aggression when compared to the war effort, then somewhat deliriously offers as a moment of possibility: 'Isn't this thrilling? Don't you think? Everything is up for grabs. At last. We will see some changes. Thank the lord' (179). There may also be gleaned some small progressive impulse in her comment that being a bastard won't always be a stigma in England: 'England can't be like this forever' (163). In fact, in Susan Traherne's romantic idealization of the past, *Plenty* offers a recognizably middle-class reaction to an unsatisfying present. Nostalgia for a more meaningful past, a lost plenitude, reinforces the ideology of an unalienated existence that predates or in some way lies dormant within the self. This is the paradigm of tragic ideology: a sense of living in a fallen, meaningless world. Of course this is the rational way of interpreting the experience of alienation: if you feel alienated, you must feel alienated *from* something, and if you feel distanced from something, you must have a relationship to the thing from which you are distanced, and that thing stands as the imagined solution to the problem of one's alienation.

At the end of the play, Susan, mentally having retreated to the end of the war, speaks with a Frenchman about a characteristic of her nation: 'The English ... have no feelings, yes? Are stiff' (207), he says. She replies that it is true that the English *hide* their feelings from the world, but it may be that things will change now that the war has matured the British. Susan's tragedy may be that she is at once a thorough Englishwoman, repressed and alienated from her emotions, and at the same time distanced from her national sense of self. Her conflict and her struggle is to reconcile her tragic self with her English self, her feeling self with her social identity, but the impossibility of this risks madness and produces only her isolation within her nation. Finlay Donesky singles out *Plenty* as Hare's definitive state-of-the-nation play because of how carefully the drama balances the 'interplay between personal despair and national decline' (63). For Donesky, what allows the play to maintain this tension is its formal status as a *tragedy*, balanced admirably between 'the personal and social' reality, which 'define each other in an active process without either sphere being relegated to a passive reflective role' (86). *Plenty* thus satisfies the criteria for modern tragedy defined by Raymond Williams, as Donesky sees it: 'a tragedy about a society in decline because of seemingly intractable social and political causes' (86). What is missing from *Plenty*, Donesky argues, is a possibility of resolution or restoration, of any progressive sense of social transformation.[12]

This, I would agree, is necessary to Williams's vision of ideal tragedy, but we must take the analysis of *Plenty* a step further and consider how it is the unique problems of interpreting the play that are the site of its properly tragic contradictions. In liberal tragedy, Williams argues, we find not a simple conflict between a tragic hero and a hypocritical, false society, but a dialectical contradiction: 'the hero defines an opposing world, full of lies and compromises and dead positions, only to find, as he struggles against it, that as a man he belongs to this world, and has its destructive inheritance in himself' (*Modern Tragedy* 98). *Plenty* explores this contradiction in Susan herself. When Brock first encounters her, he remarks, 'Don't you think you wear your suffering a little heavily?' (147). The falseness she loathes in post-war English life reproduces itself in her English pose of standoffish individuality. Moreover, her inevitable immersion in her own culture, despite this culture's destructive effects on her mental health, is indicated when she and Brock return from Iran: 'I knew if I came over I would never return,' she says cryptically (187). Finally, the most moving contradiction of Susan's character is found in the plot: her increasing isolation, alienation, and loneliness over the course of the drama appears to be the effect of her search for meaningful connection with others, connections she fetishizes nostalgically as authentic emotional experiences she had during the war. She seems to lose contact with others through the very action of seeking meaningful human contact. Her cannabis dream in the play's conclusion is a theatrical image of her contradictions: the scene is false, a delusion in form, but it is also a hopeful aspiration for a meaningful, connected, and emotional English society in content. The delusion is all that is afforded her by a false society, but it remains a vehicle for her desire, her aspirations for something more than her emotionless, vacuous society, and this desire, this aspiration, remains a place of integrity. 'The desire fails, or is broken, but is never denied,' Williams writes of Ibsen's characters (*Modern Tragedy* 99). The result, in liberal tragedy of the late nineteenth century, is 'tragic deadlock' (98).

Yet *Plenty*, despite its remarkable revival of dramatic tensions portrayed by Ibsen's characters, is not an Ibsen play. Susan's dramatic forebear, as has been observed many times by critics and commentators, is clearly Ibsen's Hedda Gabler. Susan's affection for her handgun, her impatience with her surroundings, and her refusal to compromise her ideals, combined with her periodical fits of uncontrollable extreme behaviour, all evoke the shadow of General Gabler's daughter. Yet this comparison also reveals the importance of a crucial formal difference in Hare's play. In Ibsen we find, as Williams puts it, 'tragic deadlock.' Hare offers a way out of the tragic deadlock of liberalism through formal innovation. Ibsen's maintenance of the unities of time, place, and action, combined with the single, realistic setting to which Hedda is confined throughout the play, make tangible the confining and deterministic naturalism that underpins Ibsen's vision of the human: there is no way out for Hedda, no way to reconcile her desire with her society. In contrast, Susan Traherne's environment is merely sketched in, always shifting throughout the play, and never really at the forefront of the dramatic focus. Susan's relationship to her environment is, accordingly, not entirely that of liberal tragedy.

Thus if the play resists in any way the tragic deadlock of its narrative, this takes place at the level of form. *Plenty* unfolds over a period of more than nearly two decades and is composed of twelve scenes. Unlike the dramatic unity of *Teeth 'n' Smiles*, *Plenty*'s epic narrative form resists the reduction of the play to Aristotelian plot elements through the provocative use of short, aphoristic scenes throughout the play, each separated from one another by substantial gulfs of time. This snapshot form, in which we glimpse disparate moments in Susan's life over twenty years, seems evocative and telling in reference to the play's most powerful emotion: nostalgia for the past. What is characteristic about Susan's wartime experiences and her memories of them is that by necessity of circumstance, they take this aphoristic form themselves, of brief but deeply emotional and honest encounters:

> For instance, there was a man in France. His code name was Lazar. I'd been there a year I suppose and one night I had to see him on his way. He just dropped out of the sky. An agent. He was lost. I was trying to be blasé, trying to be tough, all the usual stuff – irony, hardness, cleverness, wit – and then suddenly I began to cry. On to the shoulder of a man I'd never met before. But not a day goes by without my wondering where he is. (158)

Susan has described the second scene of the play, which in typically theatrical form shows the audience a moment of dramatic intensity in the narrative of a character. For Susan, the war gave her such moments of life shaped with the intensity of art, and most importantly, heavy with the *emotional* weight, the 'plenty' that she finds absent in English life. *Plenty* itself, the play that we see, is not, however, predominantly concerned with the war but with life after the war, and it is impossible not to see that the play is determined to provide, for an audience in 1978, an artistic shaping of post-war experience that actually renders it meaningful and offers the emotional connections that Susan herself finds absent. The play is far less nostalgic than Susan herself is, and far from being as alienated as she is, the play utilizes the epic form to present intense, vivid snapshots of human life filled with emotional plenitude. For an audience in 1978, as for Hare himself, the war is emotional and psychic prehistory, not an experience of the past but the presentiment of an absence of an experience of the past. It is a sense of loss that cannot be filled but can only be inhabited through art.

The Secret Rapture

Unlike *Plenty*'s lament for a lost moment in the past, Hare's work in the 1980s seems to become increasingly conscious that ideals are not actual locations or events in time and space (such as the war) but rather aporias in human consciousness, leaving traces within the self while never allowing themselves actually to be represented. While Maggie in *Teeth 'n' Smiles* and Susan in *Plenty* are ultimately figures of tragic negativity, Hare attempts to define the contours of an affirmative tragic in the face of Margaret Thatcher's ideological domination of the 1980s.[13] Here, some critical assessment of this shift is appropriate: Hare moves from gestures of angry resentment towards an exploration of ideal, selfless love. Why the change in this decade? The ideological fabric of Englishness moves from a visibly class-divided society, as was evident in the 1970s, to a triumphant repression of class through the dominance of conservative ideology under Thatcherism. With the arrival of the 1980s, Thatcherism and its legacy in fact shift into the full disavowal of the possibility of loss as gain. Love, for Hare, is the paradigmatic instance of loss as gain, of the affirmative tragedy of love, and he asserts it as a political intervention into the ideology of Englishness.

The titles of plays such as *The Secret Rapture* and *Skylight* describe the shape of an open, tragic consciousness, formed through the intimate privacy of spiritual or metaphysical experience. The tragic figures in these plays become exemplars of human consciousness as fraught and open to loss and emptiness through the activity of mourning. *The Secret Rapture* (1988) begins and ends with an activity that lies at the heart of the puzzle of the human being: funeral rites. Isobel Glass and her sister Marion French are forced into proximity with one another by the death of their father. 'Funerals shouldn't have politics dragged into them' (10), comments Marion, a Junior Minister in the Department of the Environment. *The Secret Rapture*, however, is determined to demonstrate that there is nothing more political than funerals. It is in the activity of mourning that we see an essential political aspect of the human. It is the human experience of loss that makes us social creatures, and the ability to mourn, to be open to loss, is represented as stifled in the most emotionally repressed aspect of conservative Englishness: the Tory of the 1980s. By the end of the play, the neurotic Tory Marion will be forced to mourn for her sister Isobel, and the experience of loss will open her emotionally and render her sympathetic in her grief.

At the beginning of the play the sisters are tested in their personal beliefs by the need to provide support to their alcoholic stepmother Katherine, who becomes a burden upon them, a piece of family baggage to be handled and managed. Katherine is 'chronically dependent' (32), a crass, rude, outspoken woman; self-destructive, self-pitying, and exploitative of the goodwill of others. Yet in her late husband's eyes she was a free spirit, resolutely un-English in her bad behaviour. Isobel idealizes her late father and believes that his love for this thoroughly unlovable woman redeemed life for him: 'The great thing is to love. If you're loved back then it's a bonus. [...] He saw himself as a failure [...]. The only thing that distinguished his life – as he felt – was this late passion for a much younger woman' (5). Isobel is challenged to live up to her father's example when Katherine is foisted upon her as an employee in Isobel's small commercial art business. In her attempts to be kind, generous, and good in the face of individuals in her own family who are more than willing to exploit her idealism, Isobel is much like Shen Te in Brecht's *The Good Person of Setzuan*, but without recourse to an alter ego who will allow her to survive. The imposition of Katherine onto Isobel's small firm is the first step in a series of intrusions that see the business incorporate, expand, and become liquidated by its board of directors because it is not profitable and competitive enough. Isobel's resistance to the grasping materialism of the 1980s in England is overwhelmed by her sister Marion's insistence that Katherine must be supported by Isobel's firm (42). To refuse would be selfish, Marion claims. Again as in Brecht's play, the innocent commerce of a small business is corrupted when it is subjected to full capitalist expansion, which warps the goodness inherent in individual acts of human exchange.

The title tells us that *The Secret Rapture* is about the *jouissance* of the Christian martyr, a moment of utter privacy and transport when a person who has made a vow to the divine is granted contact with God. The image contains all of the exclusivity and detachment that may be associated with an outsider's view of a bride of Christ who has been given a glimpse or intimation of a totality inaccessible to the uninitiated. Isobel's stoic goodness, her claims to an ideal certainly may be interpreted as selfishness from the utilitarian perspective of the altruistic Tory ego, which seeks to dictate the greatest good for the greatest number in the image of its own interests. Marion's arrogance and accusations of selfishness are a paradigmatic rendering of that Lacanian definition of the ego as an aggressive altruist, which seems to have found no more ideal representative than the 1980s Tory minister. Yet Hare has also stated that this play was a deliberate attempt to write a tragedy with a female heroine, at a time when neither tragedies nor female heroines were fashionable.[14] The unreasonable, unswerving arrow of a tragic figure like Isobel is powerful and frustrating because she refuses the hypocritical mask of goodness. Yet at the same time, she is defined quite simply as someone who does not want to expand her business simply for the sake of making money, and who would rather sit in the park of an afternoon than attend a board meeting in which her business is to be asset-stripped. She is neither self-destructive nor a masochistic martyr in love with suffering.

That Marion is revealed over the course of the play to be easily frustrated and angered by Isobel's self-possession and lack of interest in the ideology of the 1980s – and emotionally repressed in her own life – indicates the neurosis that lurks at the heart of the aggressive, confident ego: 'I can't interpret what people feel,' she laments at the play's conclusion, and speaks of being confused and frightened as a child by human behaviour, and reduced to 'watching and always pretending' (82). This insight into her own failure to be human comes only after Isobel's death, and represents the chief redemptive achievement that this loss provides. Previously, Marion had espoused a ruthlessly inhuman efficiency model for the emotions: 'If it breaks, just mend it. I was talking to some people at the Ministry of Health. The modern theory is that a lot of so-called unhappiness is actually a product of diet. It's all avoidable' (63). When Isobel is intransigent and refuses to be bullied any longer, Marion's retort summarizes her attitude towards the irrational, emotional side of relationships: 'God, how I hate all this human stuff' (70).

Isobel, for her part, is quite mercilessly doomed by the plot of the play: she falls out of love with Irwin, her fiancé, when he is caught up in the expansion of the business, and he, unable to maintain a value to his existence without her self-possessed grace, kills her for her unflinching emotional honesty. She is destroyed by the collision between the circumstances of England in the 1980s and her self-possession, which is bound to seem a perverse and stubborn weakness in Thatcherite times. She is almost intolerably human and all the more admirable for it, and one way to understand the message of the play is that it suggests that the price of Thatcher's ideology is the suppression of humanity. Yet there is an indeterminacy about this message, what might be thought of as a lack of clarity or as ambiguity, since the point is conveyed negatively through a tragic action that is largely interested in a harsh critique of the behaviour and mentality of the privileged members of English society at the time. The play is not suggesting that Marion and her ilk should be like Isobel, preferring to sit in the park on a sunny day rather than drive themselves mercilessly in their work. Here I mark a point of disagreement with other interpreters of the play, who argue for Isobel as a role model or a tragic heroine whose goodness is a fatal flaw.[15] Antigone, Lacan suggests, is not a vision of the human in general but of unconscious desire, and in her unswerving movement towards death she is a mark of loss that humbles the ego and opens it towards its being-for-death.[16] Her fascination and splendour are found in this terrifying drive towards something that lies beyond the illusions of common good that the ego lives within. The final words of the play belong to Marion, who says, 'Isobel. We're just beginning. Isobel, where are you? (*She waits a moment.*) Isobel, why don't you come home?' (83). Evocative of Marion's new-found awareness, these questions convey a phenomenological transformation within her. Now speaking from the position of the family home that she had never cared for and wished to sell off, Marion gives voice to the sense of absent presence created by the loss of a loved one, the sense that the person is there even though she has died.[17] Moreover, the absence is an absence from the familiar, specifically the familial setting, location of ground and origin. It is a matter of Being, that ephemeral metaphysical sensation that describes the human experience of the soul or of one's floating consciousness, separate from yet connected to the material body. Isobel's legacy to her sister is a gift of loss, of distance or difference, of absence from the home, and Marion is humanized by this spectral trace of her sister.

Skylight

The titular image of *Skylight* (1995) evokes a similar openness to death's beyond, an openness necessary to the ongoing social, political work of being human, but understanding the relevance of this image to the plot of the play demands some interpretive excavation and a connection of *Skylight*'s Kyra Hollis to the experience of loss and mourning. The effect of loss upon consciousness and the lingering spectral presence of the lost loved one are hauntingly evoked as concerns in the play's opening moments: 'Once they're dead, I find they keep changing. You think you've got hold of them. [...] But then they change again in your memory. [...] Now I'd like to find out just who she was' (5). Here, teenager Edward Sergeant is speaking of his late mother Alice, who has been dead for a year. He is speaking to Kyra, a woman who three years earlier abruptly ended a secret love affair with Edward's father, Tom, when Alice learned of this adultery. The play's protagonist, Kyra, is a further exploration on Hare's part of characters that are fascinating in their nearly impossible self-possession.

Skylight demonstrates that it is not accidental that audiences have sometimes claimed to find Hare's female characters unbelievable. This is evidently because they are designed to skirt the edge of what is considered humanly possible by the middle class: Kyra, by choice, lives in a cold ground-floor flat in North London and suffers a long daily commute to work teaching troubled and un-derprivileged teenagers in East Ham, yet she seems perfectly at ease with this situation. She has no desire to return to her previous life of privilege. Speaking with Tom, who appears on her doorstep shortly after the visit by his son Edward, Kyra explains the comfort she felt in their secret affair and why she felt it neces-sary to leave literally the moment that Alice found out about them: 'I always felt profoundly at peace. (*She waits a moment, wanting to be precise.*) I don't know why, it still seems true to me: if you have a love, which for any reason you can't talk about, your heart is with someone you can't admit – not to a single soul except for the person involved – then for me, well, I have to say, that's love at its purest' (38). It is this sentiment, combined with her unflinching and passionate dedication towards her teaching work, that presents Kyra as a political chal-lenge to the middle-class audience of the play.[18]

Tom Sergeant is a highly successful restaurateur of working-class upbringing who built an empire during the financial boom period of the mid-1980s and became extremely wealthy when he took his business public. Now in the mid-1990s he reports to a board of directors and a management guru (21) and spends all his time with lawyers and bankers rather than working as a proper businessman, as he sees it (25). As the audience's comfortable, wealthy middle-class spokesperson, Tom tests Kyra's motivations in the second half of the drama. He argues forcibly and reasonably that there must be some kind of re-pressed pathology behind Kyra's behaviour and her choices in life. As a daugh-ter of privilege and with abilities that would easily allow her to find work commensurate with her class background, she must have some subtextual neu-rosis that drove her away from a relationship with a man who, he claims, wanted to marry her, and into a life that cannot possibly provide her with happiness or fulfilment (75–7). In other words, it is inconceivable that she might be living *honestly* and in good faith with herself. If this is so, then by implication her unflinching belief in a pure relationship of trust where love is only given must be a rationalization of her fear of commitment.

Kyra's response to Tom's attempt to psychoanalyse her and her purportedly 'tragic' (76) waste of her gifts is one of the most forceful monologues in Hare's oeuvre. Kyra lists off all the expected clichés that dismiss, from a conservative perspective, social work's apparent pathology: those who dedicate themselves to helping others must be failures in their own lives, deeply miserable and unful-filled emotionally. She then speaks from the heart: 'I'm tired of these sophistries.

I'm tired of these right-wing fuckers. They wouldn't lift a finger themselves. They work contentedly in offices and banks. Yet now they sit pontificating in parliament, in papers, impugning our motives, questioning our judgements' (78). With a moral force that is indisputable from within the play's frame of reference, she skewers the *ressentiment* of the members of the middle class.[19] Guilty about their lack of suffering and misfortune, the privileged are also resentful of that guilt and repress it so that it emerges as condescension towards those who act instead of unconsciously loathing their own affluence. Kyra is not doing what she does because she is repressed or emotionally stunted. Her motives and beliefs arise from an inner space of intense privacy and immovable conviction that is also the source of her abandonment of Tom. She left, she finally states, because Tom deliberately allowed Alice to find Kyra's love letters, and this betrayal of trust destroyed the perfection of their relationship (92–3).

Her unyielding ideal encompasses both her belief in a perfect love and her teaching work. Kyra is a teacher because here, to be a teacher is to be dedicated to an ideal of the human. She explains to Edward in the final scene of the play what drives her to continue her difficult, dangerous, and largely frustrating work: 'I mean, to be a teacher, the only thing you really have going for you … there's only one thing that makes the whole thing make sense, and that is finding one really good pupil […]. You set yourself some personal target, a private target, only you know it – no one else – that's where you find satisfaction' (99). To be dedicated to the pupil with a spark, a challenge to be faced, and achieve this is an utterly private, goalless activity. Goalless, because it is not oriented towards an instrumental logic of education: 'I wouldn't say the kids are all great. But at least they're not on the ladder. So perhaps that means … they do things for their own sake. […] You don't need a CV to get a UB40' (10). Kyra teaches outside of the utilitarian means-and-ends instrumentality of the world around her. She doesn't teach because she wants to train poor students to get jobs. She teaches them because they have a potential, because they are human. From an instrumental perspective they are not worth teaching, because they have no serious chance to ever make anything of themselves. It is a waste of her time and talent, says Tom. She could be teaching at a university. Her unyielding self-sufficiency as a human is reflected in her private targets as a teacher. This is the most important and challenging idea in the play. It is the unyielding part of Kyra that creates the unbridgeable gulf between her and Tom, and she cannot explain it in any other terms. Her ideal is utopian in the sense that it imagines within each and every person something that is human for its own sake, something cut off from the world and self-sufficient and the most important part of a person, something that has no use to the outside world but is worth nurturing as the human. It is utopian work because it is not alienated, and it is doing something for its own sake: the human work of being human. It is the work of acknowledging the Being of the other and as such is the inverse side of mourning: avowing the unique humanity of those beyond one's own consciousness.[20]

The political connection between Kyra's private ideals and the larger concerns of the play are found when Tom's dramatic action is articulated fully. The titular image of the skylight refers to the view from Alice's sickbed as she was dying of cancer, a window that Tom had built for her and through which she watched birds (18). Yet the skylight is also something that, while providing Alice with peace as she died over the course of a year, isolated her from Tom, because it offered a space where she could attain something she described as 'spiritual' (44). Tom is antagonized by the privacy of an intimation of metaphysical experience, which he contrasts disparagingly to the comfortable clarity and organized rules of religion: 'It's one of those words I've never quite understood. I mean, I've always hated the way people use it. [...] Spiritual, meaning: "it's mine and shove off." People use it to prove they're sensitive. They want it to dignify quite ordinary things' (44–5). Having spent a 'great deal of money' (46) renovating the room, Tom is frustrated to be shut out of Alice's isolated brush with transcendence. 'Skylight' is the troubling opening onto something outside the hermetic closedness of middle-class consciousness. This opening provides a peace that is unsettling to a figure like Tom, a man for whom wealth constitutes the full material achievement of life. The implications, however, of the logic of this play are that since such exits or openings like the skylight or the secret rapture are also windows into the experience (or non-experience) of death, the position of death is also associated with the self-possessed goodness of an Isobel, or in this case, a Kyra. Such figures of insufferable goodness occupy, for the illusions of the centred ego, the negativity of death itself, much as Antigone is understood as a figure between life and death. Yet this is of course complicated by Hare's realism and his creation of fully rounded characters like Kyra and Isobel, who nevertheless occupy an unsettlingly abnormal location in the register of consciousness for others. What places them in this disturbing position is their unwavering insistence on the importance of loving others, regardless of whether or not this love is returned.

Elusively, the play is offering us as its action the productive emotional work of mourning, with the implication that Tom has, unknowingly, come here to allow loss to enter his life. Tom arrives on Kyra's doorstep while still in the process of grieving for his late wife, and his attempt to recover the terminated relationship with Kyra is inextricably bound up with his mourning process. Here a coincidence of the antecedent action must be understood as a meaningful turn of events, at least for Tom's psychic life – it was not long after Kyra left that Alice first showed the signs of illness: 'We were in such total confusion, at that time things were already so tough, so that news of the illness … to be honest, at first, when it was first diagnosed, it seemed like kind of a joke. How much misfortune? and so on. Where are the gods?' (44). This coincidence of events suggests that Tom's inability to resolve his relationship with Kyra is entwined with his unresolved grief for Alice. Moreover, the terms within which Tom understands his situation are a trial of classically tragic proportions, although he is caught within the dilemma of the modern, secular mind when faced with the incomprehensibility of suffering, death, and loss. He admits to his shame that he bears the guilt of having fled Alice when she was close to death: 'All right, I'm not proud. We both knew what was happening. I kept thinking, it's not like a test. What's happening is chance. […] But I couldn't fight it. I felt … […] This is some sort of trial of my character' (52). From Tom's perspective, he has suffered, been tried, and now wants to be redeemed and absolved of guilt by having Kyra back. From Kyra's perspective, Tom is living in the hermetically sealed world of wealth and middle-class values with no perspective on reality, specifically no perspective on how everyone except himself lives (70–1). The gulf between them is insurmountable.

Tom leaves at the end of the play, having failed to reclaim Kyra, but this failure may be understood as a success, a classical humbling of him for his *hubris*. She insists that it is too late for them to recover their relationship and instead forces him to confront his shameful behaviour, his guilt, and his attempts to exorcize this guilt through antagonism towards his son. Tom will not be redeemed by Kyra's love and he will have to live with his past actions. The implied result is that a sense of mortality, fatality, and responsibility, a sense of the tragic, are forced into his consciousness despite his resistance. The play is elusive and open-ended, but there is a sense that Tom has, unconsciously, achieved what he sought while failing to achieve what he consciously sought. He has been forced into a presentiment of the limits of his own agency. His confrontation with Kyra is a confrontation with his own repressed unconscious, and the result of this confrontation cannot be a success, it can only ever be an acknowledgment of the loss of self that is the unconscious as such: it is an openness to mourning. Avowing this loss means avowing his loss of Kyra, or Kyra as loss. It also means coming to terms with the inherent guilt that is an inevitable and necessary part of being middle class, which is why Bill Nighy, who played Tom (after Michael Gambon first performed the part), asserts that the play is concerned with 'one of the central facts of our lives: what do you do about the poor, about being more wealthy and powerful than the people around you? How do you live in the world when it's so unbalanced? Yet it is shown in the form of a love story […]. But it's a love story which exactly mirrors the larger struggle outside' (qtd in Boon, *About Hare* 179). *Skylight* avows the unconscious of the middle class: women, social workers (and gay people, as we shall see with *The Judas Kiss*), avatars of what the centred, narcissistic ego disavows and negates as *not* being an aspect of itself.[21] They embody the repressed content of the lives of people like Tom and Marion.

Amy's View

While Hare portrays Kyra as a figure of unflinching integrity, a woman of middle-class upbringing whose abandonment of her class is an act of unimpeachable heroism, he continues in the 1990s to explore the contours of stubborn women whose stances are deliberately theatrical and thus seemingly poses. A dialectic is thus established between tragic protagonists like Isobel and Kyra, whose stances are affirmative in their opposition to society, and characters like Maggie and Susan, who take a renunciant stance towards the world and simultaneously risk being seen as frauds. This latter stance is a metatheatrical commentary on the place of theatre in society and theatre's potentially tragic renunciation of the world. *Amy's View* (1997), for instance, is a deliberate attempt on Hare's part to evoke a traditional dramatic, theatrical legacy in England. As the play's director, Richard Eyre, puts it, '[Y]ou set up the world of a country-house play with a vague echo of Noel Coward [*sic*] about it, and you put at the heart of it a character who literally embodies that world of light comedies. [...] It's an attempt to speak to the much-derided middle-class audience, and to do it by playing with a particular form and then subverting it from within' (qtd in Boon, *About Hare* 226). The character that embodies this dramatic and ideological tradition is Esme Allen, a role created by Judi Dench. In its broadest strokes, the play represents a conflict between tradition and change, between values and commerce, between England and capitalism, and between theatre and the media. Esme, a successful West End actress in 1979, stands for all of the former, and in each case these older icons are eroded or pushed aside by changes in England during the 1980s.

Dominic Tyghe, boyfriend of Esme's daughter Amy, represents the changes in England that threaten what Esme stands for: from a meek young intellectual film critic interested in becoming a filmmaker, Dominic eventually becomes a highly successful television producer responsible for an arts program that is highly antagonistic towards the arts. He is a textbook representation of philistinism, of someone more interested in tearing down the valorization of art by others than in appreciating it oneself, mocking anyone who claims to like a cultural product as a liar or snob. Eventually Dominic will go on to become the filmmaker he aspired to be: his first film features a notable shot of a man's head exploding graphically (*Amy's View* 124). Esme is never able to appreciate what

Amy sees in him, and Amy's refusal to part from Dominic even after he has betrayed her becomes an insurmountable barrier between the women. There is very little to admire about Dominic, particularly in the play's original production, where, as portrayed by Eoin McCarthy, he largely sounded like a narrow-minded idiot, a man too unintelligent to understand intelligent ideas, who then decides that he is more interested in power and success and the destruction of those responsible for said ideas. The audience is forced to take on good faith the positive qualities Amy sees in him. Moreover, his ideological opponent, Judi Dench's Esme, offers an impossible challenge, particularly when the subject turns to the question of 'whether the theatre is dead' (51). The deck is stacked against him.

Yet Esme herself begins very much like a flighty and difficult Bohemian woman from a Noël Coward play like *Hay Fever*, completely out of touch with reality and stubborn in her blinkered prejudices. It is the fact that Esme was played by Dench, and more recently by Felicity Kendal, that renders her an admirably stoic heroine. There is, however, a moment in the play where the action risks suggesting that the choice between Esme and Dominic is no choice at all, because they each represent at this point one mask of empty, false values as embodied in Thatcher's England. In scene 2, we are in 1985, and while Dominic's crass television program is enjoying popular success, Esme has just returned from opening the proceedings at the local village fête, where the Berkshire residents pretend they are living in an Olde English village that enshrines traditional English heritage. The '[t]hatched cottages' are a 'sort of fantasy theme park,' a fake, Esme insists, which is why they have invited an actress to appear there (45). Changes in England have left them with a choice between two empty and hypocritical value systems, both of which are essentially compatible with Thatcher's ideology: the heritage industry and the capitalist culture industry. Esme speculates soberly that people perform these vacuous echoes of tradition because 'they no longer know who they are' (47). Neither provides the English with an actual identity.

That Esme is not apart from the opportunism of the 1980s but deeply implicated in it emerges in act 3. It is 1993 and not only is she bankrupt, she is permanently destitute, indebted in perpetuity due to her participation in a Lloyd's of London insurance syndicate that saw her provide unlimited liability to the insured in return for lucrative cash up front. Ruined financially, she is forced to work in television to make ends meet. Her foolish participation in the scheme can be attributed to her willingness to believe in a fiction of the English class system, namely that privilege and wealth are deserved and unassailable. She was seduced by all that Lloyd's represented as a venerable English institution: 'All right, I can see it's England as sheer bloody theatre. But there are times when theatre's pretty hard to resist' (99). Her willingness to be seduced by this class snobbery is undamaged by her financial ruin: she refuses to join an action group of judges and Tory Members of Parliament suing Lloyd's. If they won't hold to principles, she still will. She took the money unquestioningly and now she insists on accepting responsibility for her decision. Esme's unwavering adherence to her principles drives Amy away from her and the women are not reconciled before Amy dies suddenly, struck dead while walking down the street.[22]

Esme loses her family, home, and security, and is left with less than nothing, if to be permanently indebted financially can be understood in such a way. Having all of the trappings of her comfortable existence stripped away from her, she is on the one hand stubbornly isolationist, but on the other she has gained something from her loss: she is, it seems, a better actor than she ever was, and she speaks from a position of painfully achieved wisdom that demands a level of admiration for her humility and her strength. She has learned from her loss, but what it seems she has gained is the value of loss itself. She confronts Dominic about the gratuitously violent content of his first film: '[I]s it that you just don't dare to deal with real experience … with the things that go on in real life? Like grief … and betrayal … and love and unhappiness … and loss … the loss of people we love' (120). Like any valuable lesson, she has learned it at some expense to herself: the loss of Amy. Esme concludes the play in 1995 absolutely isolated and alone, but having returned to the theatre in a small West End production by a young playwright, a show that has achieved unexpected success: 'I have my life here in this theatre. My life is when the curtain goes up. My work is my life. I understand nothing else' (123). Esme felt whole when with her late husband Bernard, himself an artist (125). All life afterwards is alienation: her final words, the final words of the play, are 'So we're alone' (127). Yet this harsh statement is rendered ambivalent by the powerful image that follows: she and her fellow actor turn away from the audience towards a rising curtain in the upstage area, and step forward into a blinding light. It is potentially understood as an image of transcendence through the theatre, through the dedication to an isolated and endangered art form that has no foundations and turns its back on the outside world's concerns and timeliness. It is an image of the theatre itself as unapologetically heroic in its refusal to be a part of the world. It is, then, the transcendent inner truth, the indestructible ideal kernel at the heart of Esme that she retains through the stripping away of the material trappings of her middle-class Bohemian life: art remains truth for her and for the world of the play. It is the middle-class value that she retains when all else from her seemingly solid class background is proven to be transitory and unstable. Her co-actor Tom tells her that everyone says that as an actor, Esme now has 'something extra,' and he himself observes that onstage, 'You never play anything outwards.

I've noticed you keep it all in. So you draw in the audience. So it's up to them. And somehow they make the effort … […] they have to go and get it themselves' (113). Through loss, she has gained loss, which manifests itself as *interiority*, as the presentiment of subjectivity to others. She has, with time and experience, gone 'deeper […] down to the core' (114). She has gained a depth of self that isolates and alienates her, even onstage, where she does not reach out to the audience members but withdraws from them.

The Judas Kiss

The theatre is the art of human beings pretending to be human beings, and so Hare's portrayal of himself in the dramatic monologue *Via Dolorosa* (1998) should be seen not as aberrant but as integral to his dramatic work overall; it is also indicative of his representation of a theatre of consciousness – in the case of *Via Dolorosa*, the playwright's liberal-socialist middle-class consciousness, struggling to understand the thoughts of those living in Israel and in the Palestinian territories. Hare's insistence on the middle-class self as a form of theatre, a constant repetition and re-enactment of one's humanity, is indelibly tied to his interest in the tragic. The result of this interweaving raises an essential tragic problem, particularly in the condition of postmodernity. As we have seen with a character like Maggie in *Teeth 'n' Smiles*, the tragic performer risks a fraudulent veneer in her theatricality. The final image of Esme Allen onstage is moving, integral, and tragic while simultaneously appearing selfish, petulant, and stubbornly wilful. The problem of middle-class authenticity cannot be solved but must rather be appreciated for its problematic representation of the human being as a theatrical posturing. However, Hare's casting of stars like Liam Neeson and Judi Dench as his tragic protagonists problematizes this problematization, since an authenticity is re-entrenched in these figures by virtue of the public personas that perform them. *The Judas Kiss* (1998), Hare's dramatization of the betrayal of Oscar Wilde by his lover, Lord Alfred Douglas, is from one perspective an unapologetic portrayal of Wilde as a tragic figure. Yet the fact that this is a status that the character Wilde cultivates and is all too cognizant of within the play troubles the representation, since a tragic figure is understood as one whose agency is undermined by circumstances. At the same time, a tragic figure is also one who is understood to take responsibility for a fate that is forced upon him, merging agency with an inevitable situation. The result is necessarily an interpretive ambiguity.

As an illustration of this, Wilde wilfully portrays himself as a man who is crucified by his love for Bosie: 'I am cast in a role. My story has already been written. How I choose to play it is a mere matter of taste. The performance of the actor will not determine the action. [...] I am trapped in the narrative. The narrative now has a life of its own. It travels inexorably towards my disgrace. Toward my final explusion. And it bears me along on its crest ... [...] Yes, in fact, for me, borne along by this story, there is even an odd kind of freedom. I may wear whatever mask I choose' (37). Bosie mocks these ideas as romantic posturing, mere poses disguising weakness (40–1). Yet through the action of the play Wilde demonstrates that his dedication to a personal ideal is material to him and that his dramatic posturing is sincere: he is trapped in a narrative of exile, it emerges, not so much because of the imminent arrest, trial, and incarceration, but because he is to be tried for his love for Bosie. It is this love, finally, that isolates him from others and sends him into an exile that is both inner and outer at the same time.

Wilde is exiled from England, significantly, and as an Irishman the persecution he suffers is bound up in his refusal to behave in a manner acceptable to the English: 'I wish I shared your faith in the English. Nation to them is just as important as class. They have united at last in hatred of the foreigner. Yes, because I am Irish' (28). It is tempting to speculate that the antagonism towards Wilde is based just as much in his dedication to his private beliefs as in his nationality. To be English, here as elsewhere in Hare, is to be a hypocrite. Robert Ross, Wilde's friend, serves as the most benevolent example of this English hypocrisy in the play. His attempts to help Wilde are based in good faith, but all fall short of respecting the tragic arrow at the heart of Wilde's character. Wilde explains: 'What is the fatal human passion? What is the source of all sin on this earth? This propensity in all human beings to indulge in the improper rapture, the gratuitous pleasure of giving others advice. [...] Is there not some small part of us which is purely our own? Which is our soul? Which is our innermost being? And which we alone should control?' (50). This inner purity or truth will seem false and theatrical to the public eye, because in its unreasonable intransigence it appears to be a pose, a piece of theatre, not least because the most effective way of articulating it is through dramatic, specifically tragic, imagery. It is an affront to Englishness.

Wilde's insistence that perfection and truth are found in loving others, regardless of whether or not the love is returned, is tested in the dramatic action of the play: in the first half he sits in his hotel room and decides not to flee England, even knowing he is about to be arrested. In the second half we see Wilde after his prison term, a broken man, yet still in love with Bosie and having followed him to Naples. Bosie interprets their fates according to a familiar dramatic formula, a moral, cautionary tale: 'Do you think that human beings just live? The lot they are handed, the ordeals they undergo ... do you think these depend purely on the workings of chance? [...] [H]ave you never thought that perhaps we live like this because this is what we deserve?' (100–1). Bosie espouses a tragic ideology, just the kind of rigid moral narrative that dictates that people are judged for their actions and punished by their circumstances, as a means of justifying his betrayal of Wilde's love and his disavowal of his own homosexuality. Wilde's response to such fatuous moralizing is to refuse the very terms upon which it is based: 'So the world seeks its revenge. [...] No longer is punishment enough. The moral *of* my punishment must be stuffed down my throat. I must choke on it' (89). Wilde's wife Constance threatens to divorce him, barring him access to his children, unless he leaves Bosie. From Wilde's perspective, this censure is a moral judgment upon his love, upon the one ideal he holds to when he has nothing else left. It is inhumanity masquerading as humanity (91). Moreover, he is obstinate and stubborn and refuses to defend himself publicly because to do so would be to acknowledge the existence of the court of public opinion (110). He will not defend his homosexuality: 'Even to ask, even to plead my case is to admit their right to judge me' (110). Such a refusal to allow himself to be publicly judged is in keeping with his earlier self-fashioning as a tragic protagonist in a piece of self-willed theatre, but it is also an articulation of his soul.

In his ambivalence, Wilde is an allegory of the human as theatrical representation. The force of this self-fashioning is that it refuses the empirical logic of Aristotelian oppositions such as false and true. Hare is fascinated by the reversibility of these terms, particularly in the realm of human emotions and passions. In *The Blue Room* (1998), his adaptation of Arthur Schnitzler's *Reigen* (1900), Hare extracts and amplifies the original play's central conceit: love is always a love of an ideal person, felt to be lost by the self and sought out in actual human relationships. As a result of this ideal truth that drives human passion, realized love is always a form of betrayal, a falsehood that is still true love. In other words, in the realm of human emotions, there is no such thing as fidelity. Schnitzler's theme is an affront to the values of the bourgeoisie, the class that is the subject of the play, and an exposure of the underlying hypocrisy of these values. This is where the force and persuasiveness of Liam Neeson's performance as Oscar Wilde is necessary to the realization onstage of Hare's concerns: the imparting of an unquestionable sincerity and integrity to the character of Wilde that cements the drama and the posturing within a bedrock of honesty. Otherwise, Wilde's final self-fashioning as Christ would risk a hollow and fatuous falseness, particularly when he deigns to suggest an improvement to the narrative: 'It seemed to me the greatest story I ever read. But it has one flaw. Christ is betrayed by Judas, who is almost a stranger. Judas is a man he doesn't know well. It would be artistically truer if he were betrayed by John. Because John is the man he loves most' (117). In the end Wilde stands as a tragic protagonist as the German Romantics or the existentialists would have described one: he submits to an unjust and inhuman fate, to exile and loneliness, and in his silence and refusal to defend himself from this callous and indifferent judgment, he condemns his invisible yet omnipresent judges, judging his judgment.

In *The Judas Kiss*, and also in *Amy's View*, the formal rules of realism are followed with an intimidating level of respect. *The Judas Kiss* contains two locations, the hotel room in London and the villa in Naples. The action of the first act in particular exploits a unity of time, place, and action to convey a palpable sense of circumstances closing fatally in upon Wilde. Throughout the act he is warned again and again by Robert Ross that he must leave immediately or he will be arrested. Wilde's repeated delays in the face of this foreboding doom finally give way to a decision to do nothing: to merely sit and eat his meal. It is precisely this behaviour on the part of the tragic protagonist that flies in the face of the play's oppressive realism: if Wilde's behaviour is unrealistic from the perspective of respectable English society, then the stylistic commitments of the play come to embody that ideological tradition of Englishness itself. Wilde is an unrealistic tragic protagonist imprisoned in a world of dramatic realism.

My Zinc Bed

This exploration of inner subjectivity with an emphasis on the psychic conflicts between agency and the loss of agency has become increasingly Hare's focus in his recent work. Traditionally in the theatre, such concerns, particularly when couched within the stylistic tradition of realism, signify ideologically middle-class anxieties. Thus the deliberate decision in *Amy's View* to speak overtly to the rhetoric of this theatre tradition and yet still hope to force it to question itself, allowing a core belief or value to emerge at odds with all others that dominate this particular privileged background. Yet there is nothing that emerges from such a narrative that is particularly subversive or challenging in the end, other than Esme's resolute refusal to capitulate at the end of the play. It is the use of a tragic narrative arc to finally affirm the value of suffering and submission for the building of a genuine, profoundly middle-class character, which is then the basic element in the creation of theatre. In particular, the interest in the creation of complex, ambivalent characters through the machinery of a realistic drama, with two or three main characters, may be understood as a dramatic legacy from a moment when the bourgeoisie dictated the content of stage action.

The representation of human beings as complex, fraught individuals with divided subjectivities is just the form of representation of selfhood that Brecht interrogated as a fetishization by the bourgeoisie of its own self-fashioning. Yet Hare has a rereading of such character representation within a postmodern situation:

Contemporary consumer culture makes us feel that people don't run very deep. The whole endeavour of advertising, newspapers, television, cinema, is to make it seem that people are no longer very profound and mysterious. [...] The theatre seems to be the place where you go back to be reminded how deep and dark human beings run. [...] I wanted to do the same in *My Zinc Bed*. It's about addiction. It asks if we are doomed to act out patterns from which we can't escape and if we are simply running around like rats, along a course which our addictions commit us to. Or is there such a thing as a free act of will any more in a consumerist, capitalist society? Is there such a thing as an authentic action any more? (qtd in Boon, *About Hare* 163–4)

Hare offers the experience of alcoholic addiction as an analogy for the loss of individuality within consumer capitalism. Thus for Hare the flattening of human character and the elimination of individuality is both a symptom and product of the reification of capitalism itself. By analogy, we can argue that Brecht's modernist representation of character and his attack on qualities such as depth of character and individuality ('the continuity of the ego is a myth'; *Brecht on Theatre* 15) in fact borrowed its stylistic tools from capitalism itself, from the factory and the production line. The bourgeois response to the loss of truth, authenticity, free will, or agency is almost universally negative, since these are sites where basic humanity is located by the self: in the location of will. Alternately, the logic of a Brechtian artistic strategy is that the problem itself is inhabited and processed into its own solution: through the emptying of aura or authenticity from art through the reification of mass production, a new subjectivity might be sought, one free of nostalgia for a lost truth. In dramatic terms, tragic alienation might be inhabited and liberated from a sense of loss, and be transformed into a freedom of its own.

My Zinc Bed (2000) does, as Hare avows, explore the questions he describes in interview, but it also stands out for a stylistic strategy that is a sharp departure within his oeuvre, and demands attention with reference to the content of this form. It is an unusual break from realism, and in this also seems inspired by his experiences as an actor in *Via Dolorosa*, where he simply sat upon a stage and spoke to an audience, and found remarkable the audience's willingness to believe that the persona Hare represented onstage actually allowed them to get to know the real David Hare. In content, *My Zinc Bed* is concerned to communicate the idea of human beings as unsolvable problems, contradictory knots of logic that cannot be untangled or known. While the play seeks to *tell* us this, in form and style it also seeks to *show* us this. It seeks to be what it is about.

The narrative is told in retrospect by the central character, Paul Peplow, a recovering alcoholic and struggling poet, who conducts a newspaper interview with the wealthy and reclusive entrepreneur Victor Quinn. Victor is a former communist who has retained from his previous life as a party member the Marxist's demystified interpretation of social antagonism between the rich and the poor, and a mocking, deprecating attitude towards the *hubris* of capitalism. These socialist lessons in *realpolitik* have also made him a successful business-man, a software guru who seems to specialize in the kind of rushed, defective computer applications that characterized the rapid expansion of the 1990s. Victor is a contradictory figure, a man cynical about the present but who re-mains idealistic at his core: 'Of course, there was one time something called good. [...] Socialism was the present the British gave themselves for winning the war. Or so it now seems. [...] Maybe we don't feel we deserve presents any more' (57). His willingness to be interviewed by Paul, it emerges, has to do with Paul himself. On the one hand, he admires Paul's poetry, and on the other, he is fascinated by Paul's participation in Alcoholics Anonymous, but only because he feels it is a mistake. Victor espouses a critical attitude towards AA, which for all its callousness echoes the common accusations that are made against the American-born abstinence association: AA is a kind of modern cult that re-places one kind of addiction with another, and maintains its strength as a cult by espousing the unfounded idea that alcoholism is a disease without a cure and that complete abstinence and permanent participation in AA is the only means of combating and managing the addiction.

As a recovering alcoholic, Paul is in complete retreat from life: he stays at home alone listening to music when not at AA meetings, shuns human con-tact, and seems to fear most of all any passionate relationships. Here the central idea of the play emerges: addiction is a metaphor for any repetitious human activity, be it drinking or loving another person, that begins as vital, emotional, and liberating, yet becomes lifeless and dehumanized through repetition. Such a conceit logically suggests that there is some alternative to addiction, some freedom from repetition. Victor in particular insists that a person can be 'cured' of addiction through force of will alone: 'Life being – as we know – all too easily – a series of patterns, a series of addictions. I'd rather break free of the addictions, thank you' (70). However, the play does not suggest that Victor actually has the solution to the problem of being human. Gradually, Victor emerges as a much less secure and confident person than he makes himself out to be. His wife, Elsa Quinn, is, like Paul, also a former alcoholic, one that Victor claims to have cured of her addiction both to alcohol and to AA when he picked her up off the floor of a bar and took her home with him. Elsa and Paul fall in love with each other seemingly the moment they meet. Paul insists that he can only love Elsa with alcohol, perhaps because in some way they are the same thing to him: 'Alcohol is bound up in love' (64). At the same time, addiction is the result of the temptation to lose oneself in passion, love, and desire. Their hour of lovemaking is, Paul observes in retrospect, the happiest hour of his life (96). When, at the end of the first act, he decides to accept a drink, he is consciously letting desire and life flood through his veins (73–4), but this romantic moment of temptation degenerates into a drunken binge. Anything that tempts one out of the safety of isolation into the risk of vitality and instability can also become enslavement.

Thus the play argues that while we can conceive of a free and unfettered existence outside of addiction or repetition, and that we are drawn to this escape from automatism towards Dionysian excess and the abandonment of control, this outside cannot actually be lived. Victor seems to summarize what is learned over the course of the play: 'If we do not enjoy what is attractive we do not feel we are living. Submit to its attraction and we soon lose our way. If God had not intended us to drink, he would not have invented the sidecar' (119). Desire, it seems, is at the heart of the plot, figured as a drive that humans struggle against but are drawn to follow through the lure of beauty. Beyond beauty, however, desire continues and risks the coherence of the subject that follows behind. The alternative to this risk to the self is the numbing tedium of routine. Victor and Elsa demonstrate that for all of their confident rhetoric, they are trapped in a pattern of routine as stifling as Paul's AA meetings. The affair leads to a confrontation between the married couple in which Elsa forces Victor to accept that she cannot be cured (117–18). The result is an acceptance on the parts of all three that there is no cure for being human, and that various attempts to control one's own existence, to be centred in one's agency and master of the self, are both a retreat from vitality and an avoidance of what it means to 'live.'

Thus there is a tragic view of the human at the heart of the play, of human beings as terminally self-divided and flawed, alienated from their own desires, doomed to continuing failure, yet this avowal of the tragic is also the play's progressive core, since this incomplete, flawed nature of the self means that humans are always doomed to be perpetually in process, constantly making themselves anew: 'Contradiction. At the very heart of life. Wouldn't you say? [...] Contradiction at the heart of everything. Life and death. We're here. Then we're not. It's a dynamic conception of the world. No still, no pause' (50). Victor appears to have inherited this philosophy from his Marxist-communist past, and, as he claims, he still believes in history (15). This is not, however, simply a description of a philosophy of history; it is a description of the human psyche, but one from which humanity on the whole veers away. 'People are frightened of conflict,' Paul comments (51). It is the importance of the destabilizing, insecure force of mortality that deserves our attention here: death negates life, and the force of the determinate negative is such that it ensures the ambivalent hopefulness of change. 'Victor says we shall know nothing until we are laid out on our zinc beds' (70), Elsa remarks, and Victor affirms that he feels that since life is just a series of patterns he places his hopes in some actual, authentic *meaning* to life being provided after death. Yet for all his romanticization of change and flux, Victor clings to his own anchor: the hope for fidelity and constancy in his own life (60). The fact that Victor meets his end while driving drunk asserts that death trumps all attempts to live as a centred, 'cured' human being.

This is not just an exploration of seemingly eternal metaphysical questions about the nature of the human psyche and the self's relationship to its desires. The play is a social diagnosis of the massive widespread disavowal of the unconscious in a contemporary Western context: 'It's the world that's changed, not me. [...] The word "ideological" is never now mentioned. [...] Now we solve problems. Everything is a problem, and we solve it. We say, what is the problem? We define it. Nothing is decided in advance, because nothing is believed in advance. It's as simple as that. That's how we proceed. That's how we get things done. The containable life. [...] You could say the whole world's in AA' (19–20). What is missing from the modern world, Victor argues, is ground or foundation, be it a sense of belief, faith, ideological origin, or tradition; some bedrock, material or metaphysical, upon which the human stands. As a result, there is no more political or ideological conflict, there is only the management of problems.

The Internet and e-commerce serve as a central image of such contemporary unanchored existence, and when Victor's business is devalued by speculators in the second act of the play it is merely representative of the fact that the modern virtual economy is just as groundless as is the modern subject, founded upon speculation, confidence, and the ephemeral promise of future profits: 'An economy used to *make* things. Now? A world in which ten people do something and the other ninety speculate' (97). However, the play is careful to avoid the fantasy of nostalgia for a lost plenitude in the past, of a past time when faith, be it political or spiritual, was within human grasp: 'But that's the very thing I'm saying,' Paul explains in reference to his poetry. 'I'm saying we can't go back' (53). Victor's response to this could be taken as a description of Hare's playwriting work: 'I know. But you sound as if you want to. There's a longing. [...] Poets always want to go back. Childhood. Lost love. How would poets get by without them?' (53). Paul replies: 'We might wish – what? – to be happy peasants again. But we can't' (53). Change, Paul's poetry says, is experienced by selfhood as regrettable loss, provoking an impossible nostalgia. Art sounds mournful when in fact it is articulating the meaning of mourning instead.

Here, *My Zinc Bed* offers something new in Hare's oeuvre and speaks directly to his ongoing concerns. The solution to the problem of nostalgia for a lost ground of faith or ideology is not to solve the problem but to grasp the problem itself as its own solution. The ground that humans have lost contact with is loss itself, manifested as the unconscious, which is a peculiar kind of ground: it is the bedrock of trauma, the unrepresentable aporia within the self. Alcoholics Anonymous stands for a particular approach to the self that centres, ultimately, upon ego management and disregards the idea of any possible relationship on the part of the self with the unconscious. Victor, for his part, seems to espouse in the first part of the play the idea that the id can be conquered with a voluntaristic act of will, but the action of the play foils such *hubris*: the unconscious will neither be denied nor befriended by the conscious self. As this vital experience of loss can only arise from love for others, Hare's vision of human desire is to be found in the intersubjective relationships between people. It is for this reason that Hare's notion of the tragic is dramatized through the desire of people for other people, particularly people outside of the nuclear family. Hare's unconscious is not interior, although it will seem as such to the ego. The id is social here, but this is specifically a repressed social desire. Paul comments, 'Jung says that when we love another person what we are really doing is trying to compensate for a lack in ourselves. But Jung also says that the search to complete yourself with another person can never succeed' (48). There is nothing at the heart of the self that has been lost. The lack in the self that drives love is a traumatic ground: a loss that is foundational.

What Hare seems to want to conjure with this play is not a confident, stable, grounded sense of the human but rather the human as a flawed creature with a deep mystery at its centre: the humans represented in the play, for all their intimate complexities, remain contradictory and unknowable. The style of *My Zinc Bed* is a notable departure from Hare's typical realism: onstage there is very little in the way of naturalistic mise-en-scène, and setting is instead created through the use of *light*, against which the human figures stand as the only constant objects. This style reflects the content of the play: its interest in the groundlessness of modern life, in the trick of confidence that the Internet presents, or in an overall sense of artificiality and emptiness upon which humans float. The image can be read in two ways: with the sense that something vital has been lost, or with an understanding that this is what humans are, and that the postmodern condition is in fact a chance to see this clearly and without nostalgia.

This returns us to a logical problem that we saw established with 'Joan Didion,' with Maggie in *Teeth 'n' Smiles*, and that has been reiterated in various guises through Hare's tragic protagonists like Oscar Wilde and Esme Allen: they are *actors*, self-fashioning performers who perform the human as a virtual reality, frauds whose only truth seems to be found in their resolute commitment to the performance. Yet this is a mask of self that floats over a foundation of loss and trauma, a ground that is no ground at all, but simply *absence*. The epigraph to *My Zinc Bed* comes from Virginia Woolf: 'There is no Shakespeare; there is no Beethoven; certainly and emphatically there is no God; we are the words; we are the music; we are the thing itself' (*My Zinc Bed* 1). In reference to *My Zinc Bed*, these words come to signify the human as an aesthetic object, as a self-created creation, defined through the negation of metaphysical presence, be it canonical authors or monotheistic deities. The idea of the human as an unanchored fiction is evoked joyously and affirmatively, but presented within the body of the play itself tragically. This difference of tone is notable because it delineates two diverging attitudes towards the philosophical apprehension of the human as an ungrounded being, alone in the cosmos. To assert that the human is an unsolvable problem that must nevertheless be confronted as such is to insist that human beings are in their essence theoretical: they are a question rather than an answer. Terry Eagleton writes,

> Tragedy reminds us of how hard it is, in confronting non-being, not to undo ourselves in the process. How can one look upon that horror and live? At the same time, it reminds us that a way of life which lacks the courage to make this traumatic encounter finally lacks the strength to survive. Only through encountering this failure can it flourish. The non-being at the heart of us is what disturbs our dreams and flaws our projects. But it is also the price we pay for the chance of a brighter future. It is the way we keep faith with the open-ended nature of humanity, and is thus a source of hope. (*After Theory* 221)

We can describe this non-being negatively as alienation, or we can affirm it hopefully as *différance*.

The Permanent Way

Thus we find ourselves at the heart of Hare's tragic paradox. He often seems to long for a nostalgic past and has been criticized for a reactionary investment in the post-war consensus (see Donesky *passim*). His protagonists hold to private ideals that do not offer positive models for constructive social engagement. In fact, what Hare valorizes is far more problematic and challenging than this: communities united in the present by the experience of meaningful tragic loss and personal isolation. The only significant social connection that will emerge in his work is connection founded on the private isolation of suffering and grief. This is not nostalgia. Instead it is a description of an historical consciousness, one enabled by the experience of negativity. *The Permanent Way, or La Voie Anglaise* (2003) is about mourning, the work of grieving. It is Hare's most articulate exploration of the problem of the tragic within a modern, secular England. It asks whose agency is responsible for a terrible train crash, a tragic accident, which nevertheless must be traced back to someone responsible. *The Permanent Way* is also, significantly, a return to the methods and the director with whom Hare worked on *Fanshen* in 1975, which thus suggests that *Fanshen* is far from the early anomaly in Hare's career that critics have often taken it to be. With *The Permanent Way*, Hare returned to group research with a troupe of actors who would also subsequently perform the show, under the directorial supervision of Max Stafford-Clark and the Out of Joint theatre company (Stafford-Clark's follow-up to Joint Stock). And like *Fanshen*, *The Permanent Way* is about a community shocked into action and into taking responsibility for a situation of suffering that is imposed upon it. Most of all, *The Permanent Way* is about how human beings struggle with the tragic ideology that they have internalized when they are confronted with a situation of terrible loss. Williams calls 'the received ideology of tragedy [...] the old tragic lesson, that man cannot change his condition, but can only drown his world in blood in the vain attempt; or the contemporary reflex, that the taking of rational control over our social destiny is defeated or at best deeply stained by our inevitable irrationality' (*Modern Tragedy* 74). Those affected by the disasters depicted in *The Permanent Way* must struggle with trauma and loss and attempt to contain these alienating wounds within their humanity.

The Permanent Way employs a troupe of actors to represent a series of interview subjects to the audience. 'It's very English, David' (50), remarks one speaker, addressing the audience but speaking to the playwright. Her words remind us of the 'verbatim' form of this play, transporting us momentarily out of the theatre and into the interview that underlies it. The speaker is a bereaved mother (the second of two in the play), speaking about the callous behaviour of the head of Railtrack at a public enquiry into the causes behind a catastrophic train crash. What is 'very English' is the head's disregard for the feelings, even the existences, of the families who lost loved ones. At the same time, the bereaved mother's phrasing is a hint that Hare seeks to diagnose something about the English character through his study of differing human reactions to a series of train collisions and derailments that occurred after the railways were privatized in England in the early 1990s. The speakers are individuals, each distinct and largely but not entirely anonymous. The characters speak in the first person to us throughout the drama, occasionally letting proper names slip into their narratives. They engage in storytelling, Epic theatre, as a means of creating a particular *Verfremdungseffekt*. This strategy both distances us from the narrated action in order to allow us to reflect, and heightens the humanity of the characters, their depth of experience and emotions, placing in the foreground not the events recounted but the emotional and rational responses to these events. The play functions as a paradigmatic instance of Brecht's 'The Street Scene': after the fact, the spectators to an accident recount from their perspectives the witnessed event with an eye to answering pointed questions: Did this need to happen? Why did this happen? Could this have been avoided?

The immediate social moral that emerges from the interwoven interviews over the course of the entire play is that privatization and unrestrained capitalism lead to an emphasis on profit over safety, a lack of centralized accountability, and competition rather than cooperation. Hare's familiar diagnosis of the collective psychic ills that plague the English is reiterated here: England is a society that no longer holds to any firm beliefs and thus has no faith upon which to stand. The symptoms of this are found in chronic blaming of individuals and attempts to assign individual guilt both to oneself and to others, rather than the shouldering of constructive collective responsibility. Yet while this social commentary is at the heart of the play's criticism of the tragic waste resulting from the regrettable and irrational political decision to carve the British railway into 113 pieces and sell them to different companies, the play uses this polemical exposé as a framework upon which to paint a canvas of the human psyche at odds with the events.

Perhaps the most striking instance of this is the contrast and conflict that emerges between a Survivors' Group and the bereaved families of the dead. The Survivors' Group forms out of the second train collision, the 'Ladbroke Grove' disaster, and is represented by two characters, a Young Man in Denim who works in business, and a Founder of the Group, an independent financial advisor who was so badly burned in the crash that she now wears a plastic mask. These two young professionals represent a constructive attitude towards the train crash that seems in part informed by their own class backgrounds. The Survivors' Group describe themselves as democratic in their decision-making, such as in the determination to exclude the bereaved from the Group due to their conflicting aims and the fact that the bereaved are in mourning and the survivors, largely, are not: 'I realised they weren't on the same wavelength. When they were talking, they wanted to talk about people they had lost, which was understandable, but they almost wanted to dump their emotional baggage on you' (44). The play is careful to portray these differing attitudes respectfully and with a sense of balance. The Survivors' Group is not villainized as callous. Certainly their desire to be constructive rather than to seek revenge seems admirable: '[T]his has happened to us, we don't want it happening to anyone else, so let's see if we can stop it' (46). Yet there is also the slight hint that their cooperative and positive attitude is as much the result of an affinity with corporatism as it is a genuine desire to prevent further disasters: 'We were huge and we were very similar. We'd either run our own businesses, we were high up within our companies, we were directors of companies, same sort of background' (46). They court publicity and press attention as a means of furthering their cause and hold televised prayers with the head of Railtrack at Paddington station on the first anniversary of the disaster (47). 'My attitude is: we can do something here, so let's do it. Let's keep our drive and enthusiasm to keep going. The Paddington Survivors' Group is a very strong brand and image' (54).

The Survivors' affirmative, constructive attitude, standing in contradiction to the emotions of the bereaved, finally emerges as potentially suspect. What seems like a desire to get along and work together rather than nurture counter-productive antagonism may in fact be an aversion to a true accounting. Without such accounting, there can be no real guarantee that no further disasters will not occur, and the subsequent Hatfield and Potter's Bar derailings in 2000 and 2002 ratify this endemic problem: '[N]o apology. No prosecution. No admission of liability. No proper compensation. No inquiry. The fourth crash – and in the response, the worst of the lot' (64). A further comment from this Scottish Literary Editor – 'To be honest, I don't think the English are good at the communal. [...] It's as if we don't want fully to commit to the notion of living together. [...] The truth is that nowadays governments want to shed responsibility' (68) – seems to summarize the play's diagnosis. In Hare's estimation, Englishness today is characterized by a failure to get along, to agree, to live together, but what distinguishes this sentiment is the assumption that the people of a nation are expected to live in harmony with one another and have failed. Such a view sees an underlying social consensus as both the lost ideal and the solution to current malaise. Divisions are made sharp and painful over the course of the dramatic action: between those who want to escape the past and those experiencing a protracted mourning; between people in general, who can sympathize, empathize, and understand the pain of loss, and persons in positions of political and economic power, who are corrupt, self-serving, and unable or unwilling to understand the emotions of others. Meanwhile, the bereaved come to take on a tragic isolation, but one that results in a paradoxical sense of belonging, what one of the bereaved calls 'hysterical friendship,' the last words of the play (70). Playing upon the idea of 'hysterical pregnancy,' this idea of a friendship that is somehow imaginary or fantasized has an ambiguous resonance, since a friendship is a state of mind rather than a biological fact. In their losses, the bereaved have found connections with others who have similarly suffered. This has offered them a kind of community, one that emerges through an avowal of the Being of others: '[Y]ou don't stop loving him. You don't stop because he dies. You still want to do things for him. You need to find out why' (70). The dead still live on in the psyches and in the work of the bereaved, offering them an experience of loss that opens them to a renewal of community with others similarly touched. 'Hysterical friendship' describes the tragic paradox at the heart of Hare's dramatic vision: his vision of social consensus is grounded in isolation and private loss.

The Vertical Hour

The productive result is an unresolvable, properly dialectical contradiction between the private and the political within the psyches of Hare's protagonists. In his recent play, *The Vertical Hour* (2006, New York; 2008, London), the tragic heroine returns, not as a possible simulacra of dubious authenticity and not as a comfortable myth resolving the anxieties of the bourgeoisie, but as a tormented figure whose politicization within the contemporary world is contingent upon this self-torment. To be politically engaged today, as a Westerner, means to be tragically self-divided. *The Vertical Hour* is an attempt on Hare's part to explore the intersection of psychic life and political life, the public and the private, while suggesting that these necessarily overlapping spheres do not negate one another, but productively mark or leave a trace upon each other that makes them both unavoidable, and mutually antagonistic. Nadia Blye is an American Professor of International Relations at Yale University, a former war correspondent whose experiences in Sarajevo and Iraq have left her permanently marked by a self-righteous anger and a passion for danger that she describes as an addiction (44). She has attempted to flee this aspect of herself by taking up an academic position and by engaging in a safe relationship with Philip Lucas, an Englishman who has gone American, embracing the optimism and confidence that he associates with the American ethos. 'I don't feel self-doubt when I'm in America' (40), he tells his father Oliver, a General Practitioner who has retreated to the self-imposed isolation of a medical practice in the countryside on the Welsh border.

It is by meeting Oliver Lucas that Nadia is forced to confront her repressed social conscience. The fascinating ambivalence of this irrepressible aspect of herself, her unconscious, so to speak, is that her political convictions are her *private* self that Nadia is in flight from. Part and parcel of this repression was an attempt to argue herself out of her anger and righteousness: 'walking around feeling *that* all the time doesn't make anyone happy – unless of course they're a psychopath, or – I don't know – one of your poets,' she tells Oliver, referring to his preference for poetry over patriotism (46). Living as an American, Nadia focuses on work as an academic to the exclusion of all else: her relationship with Philip is, ironically, in fact an attempt to avoid having a private life, and she is violently defensive in the face of the idea that human psychology has any relevance in the modern world, when social reality is so much more pressing in its demands. In the war-torn zones where she found her righteousness and her ideals, neurosis and repression seemed like the irrelevant luxuries of Westerners. Yet she finds that in order to function she has to repress her righteousness. Oliver sees through Nadia's defences from the moment his son Philip brings her to the English countryside. Oliver has ruined his own life and marriage by his dedication to 1960s ideals of free love, which eventually mutated into endless philandering and a car crash that killed two people. The lesson he learned was that one cannot spend one's life in flight. He abandoned his former life and went into retreat: 'I see life for what it is: fragile. Every moment for what it is: potentially disastrous. And, at all times, I try to take care' (97). Oliver's intervention into Nadia's pathology is to affirm the validity of the emotions she has repressed. He points out, simply, that her anger is right, politically: 'You were right to be angry. Why should you be ashamed? Those people *did* die. And nobody *did* care. Why to apologise?' (47). It is wrong that the West ignores what happens in other parts of the world; it is wrong that there is such a vast disparity between the few who are wealthy and the many who live in poverty on this planet (21). And it is right to feel angry that these things are not changed, and to want to actively, practically effect change.

Yet Nadia, as a Westerner, feels this to be a pathology on her part, a self-destructive obsession with danger and adventure, a confusion of inner morbidity with larger social conscience. The night she spends speaking with Oliver serves as a kind of brief psychoanalytic passage for Nadia. She must accept, by the end of the dramatic action, that her pathology is her inner truth, and that this 'private' life that she has fled from is in fact her political life. Her personal emotions are her social conscience. So Nadia herself chooses to leave America and return to Iraq: her choice is to accept the part of herself that she can repress but never eradicate, her political commitment. Hare suggests, with this recent work, that the privileged Western psyche within the twenty-first century remains, due to the actions and inactions of Western nations, self-divided, and that the only real agency available to the Westerner is found in avowing this tragic alienation and laying claim to an authentic, 'heroic' sense of self rather than remaining mired in the complacency of Western self-absorption.

Gethsemane

This tragic agency was most in evidence in the performance of *Gethsemane* I saw in February 2009 at the National Theatre, which features as its heroine a social dropout: a former teacher, Lori Drysdale, who has quit her job and now works as a busker on the District Line tube. *Gethsemane* completes a trilogy of state-of-the-nation plays, but unlike *The Permanent Way* and *Stuff Happens*, which draw upon fact, *Gethsemane* is fiction. Hare presents a dystopian look at present-day England in which craven, avaricious fundraising, suppressing scandal, and controlling immigration are the most pressing matters for the government, while the Prime Minister meanwhile practises his rock drumming in his office, preparing, presumably, for his post-political career as a pop musician, assisted by his top fundraiser, boy-band impresario Otto Fallon. Amidst what seems like a political environment in the midst of its death throes, Lori Drysdale emerges as a figure of integrity who is somehow essential to maintaining the cohesiveness of society itself, simply by virtue of her refusal to be a part of this corrupt world. Nicola Walker's performance of Lori embodied the essence of Hare's heroines: she conveyed, from her opening moments onstage at the play's beginning, a calm and serene sense of selfhood, untroubled by events around her. Without arrogance or assumption, she demonstrated the supreme self-possession that is the egoless ideal Hare aspires to articulate in his plays. Lori has withdrawn from her society in a decision that she terms her 'Gethsemane': '[T]eaching had become nonsense, filling in forms, ticking boxes, manipulating statistics, achieving targets – proving you were doing the job, rather than doing it – [...] I had what I call my Gethsemane. [...] My moment of doubt. I wondered what on earth I was doing. I locked myself in the staff-room lavatory. And I gave up' (121). Lori is a disenchanted version of Kyra from *Skylight* who has been beaten by the system and, in her own eyes, has walked away.

Yet Lori, perhaps unbeknownst to herself, is possessed of a grace that belies her own sense of failure. She is drawn back into the world of the play when a former student of hers, Suzette Guest, daughter of the Home Secretary in charge of immigration, is involved in a sex scandal. Lori is asked by Suzette's mother to handle the girl and be her confidante. When the scandal is revealed in the press and the government's foundations begin to shake, Lori takes Suzette to Sicily. It is here, in the play's final scene, that Lori describes her Gethsemane moment, and Suzette, in turn, wryly points out that Lori has misunderstood the meaning of the word: 'Jesus went through with it. Gethsemane's when you have a night of doubt but you go through with it. You go on' (122). Lori's interpretation of her own moment of failure is turned inside out at this moment. We are left to consider whether she has in fact experienced a Gethsemane, holding to her own personal ideals rather than capitulating to the failing system. More fundamentally, Lori's self-narration through Christ's moment in the Garden of Gethsemane has not been an attempt to fashion herself a martyr but as a failure. Lori is no martyr, but neither is she a failure in the eyes of this play. She is the embodiment of ideals that remind the other characters in the play of their own lack thereof. Most importantly, in her theatrical performance as the only happy person in this world, Lori's integrity is demonstrably intact, and she displays a beatitude that is Hare's vision of the purity of soul without which his society could not, finally, function.

This undecidability with regards to Lori's Gethsemane moment serves as a fitting conclusion to a study of Hare's tragic protagonists: it is common for a critic to interpret a figure like Isobel in *The Secret Rapture* as either a Christian martyr or a rejection of Christian sacrifice.[23] With Lori in *Gethsemane*, Hare appears to be engaging in a metatheatrical critique of this tragic trope that runs through his own work. Has Lori failed or has she succeeded? Was her gesture an act or will or an act of renunciation? This question, and the manner in which it strains at the ideology of Englishness, is the value of tragic experience, and it arises from intersubjective relationships and an awareness of the unresolvable contradictions of the self. These hopeful tragic contradictions are various in Hare's work: a rock singer who finds integrity in the fraudulence of the stage; a quintessential Englishwoman who nevertheless rails against her class, only to finally retreat into a dream of the past. Tragic ironies define his characters: a woman whose grace and self-possession leads to her ironic destruction within the selfish avarice of the 1980s; an Irish homosexual whose unflinching dedication to an ideal of love is at once a theatrical pose and a willed submission to a unjust tragic fate; a successful restaurateur whose failure to find redemption with his former lover opens him to the process of grieving for his late wife; and a middle-class actress who finds artistic honesty in stubborn self-abjection. Within these reversals Hare locates the human: in an alcoholic who finds in his lapses of will the vitality and integrity that arise from a failure to control his addiction; in the collective isolation of private bereavement that creates a sense of mournful community; in a journalist whose public political commitment is also the repressed private emotional core of her self; and in a woman whose abandonment of her teaching career is both a sign of her failure and of her success. This ambiguous vacillation is Hare's artistic intervention into the ideology of middle-class Englishness. Its effect in his work is to distend and estrange this ideological fabric without ever, ultimately, snapping it.

Howard Barker:
Will and Desire – From the Tragedy
of Socialism to the Ecstasy
of the Unconscious

'The liquidation of tragedy confirms the abolition of the individual.'
Horkheimer and Adorno, Dialectic of Enlightenment 124

Howard Barker was born in 1946 into a working-class family and started creating theatre in 1970. He is of the same generation as Hare, who was born in 1947 and started working in the theatre in 1968. While they are of the same generation of playwrights and developed in the same politicized, left-wing milieu, the many similarities between them are offset by a pronounced difference. Both wrote 'Royal Court' style political theatre in the 1970s and espoused socialism, both became apostates to such hard-left politics, and both became self-professed tragedians, but at this point their aesthetics diverged sharply. While Hare's apostasy from a far-left socialism is embodied by his (in)famous 'The Play is in the Air' talk, a defence wherein he insisted that the play was an intersubjective phenomenon consisting of the communication between audience and stage, Barker's apostasy follows from an opposing view of art: while a work of art inevitability communicates, it does not exist to do so. That is not its function, and in fact art as such cannot be reduced to the role of functionality at all. Thus while Hare's riposte to the unwavering theatrical Left of the 1970s was to claim that it wasn't communicating with its audience, Barker insisted that 'social realism' of the Royal Court variety was pandering to the yearnings and expectations of its audience. As a result, Hare's work became more mimetic, moving into domestic, middle-class spaces and small rooms, maintaining unities as a means of heightening recognizability and social content, while Barker eventually abandoned interiors, then later left behind social content and class consciousness, forging an expressionistic formalism designed to challenge and sometimes shock an audience rather than engage it with the familiar and the recognizable.

There are, nevertheless, remarkable parallels to be found in these two play-wrights who have taken widely diverging paths in the theatre. Hare is a cele-brated member of the theatrical establishment, while Barker is a proverbial black sheep whose challenging scripts are appreciated by actors but have led to his outsider status.[1] Yet Barker's critical lambasting of his own culture often sounds like a less well-mannered, angrier version of the voice we have encountered in Hare. For instance, it is the English, Barker is at pains to remind us, who in-vented the modern concentration camp.[2] The dehumanizing totalitarianism that lies at the heart of concepts of historical progress and social consensus is key to grasping Barker's development of a form of contemporary tragedy for which he has coined the phrase 'Theatre of Catastrophe.'[3] Barker's tragic must be delin-eated along two parallel tracks: first, it is a philosophical world view centred upon an unmitigated confrontation with alienation and 'pain,' a term that Barker will eventually employ as a trope for necessity; and second, Barker's tragic is a political intervention into ideology with the weapon of the aesthetic, a form of social critique and a map for individual psychic liberation. In this chapter, I con-sider the metamorphosis of the tragic throughout Barker's work. In his early plays of the 1970s, we see a political playwright whose unique focus is upon the tragic contradictions of the historical process and the contradictions of social-ism itself. This emphasis gradually moves into an increasingly expressionistic landscape, where the tragic provides an opening to acts of individual will and desire, attempts to produce ecstatic experience on the stage through the drama-tizing of contradictions that allow momentary glimpses of the unconscious.

A key point to keep in mind throughout this analysis is Barker's assertion that '[c]atastrophe in my theatre is willed, as opposed to simply endured' (*Arguments* 193). The revision of traditional tragedy here is found in how Barker's characters attempt, often throughout their dramatic arcs, to merge their wills with tragic, catastrophic situations of necessity, frequently but not always the catastrophic situ-ation of war. This results in strange new forms of human subjectivity in Barker's plays. In the romantic vision of the tragic Oedipal figure, the merging of freedom and necessity happens at a key moment of dialectical identity, when the unjust fate determined by the gods, from which Oedipus has initially fled, is finally and wil-fully assumed. Alternately, in Barker's plays, the shouldering of this Promethean burden is an activity that visibly defines his protagonists from the outset and deter-mines their oppositional status in relation to their societies. The artistic image that emerges from this tragic vision is celebratory, 'ecstatic,' in Barker's terms, as the individual struggle to will catastrophe creates an image of painful beauty, recog-nizable to audiences as 'the appalling strain of being human' (*Arguments* 204–5).

Barker's plays appear to be the assertion of metaphysical values in the face of postmodern and secular society, and might fruitfully be considered as a modernist resurgence of the sacred through the vehicle of the aesthetic, and specifically the tragic. Yet this seeming appearance of high modernism must be passed through in our analysis, with certain premises about Barker's attitude towards spiritual posturing in mind. He writes: 'Tragedy is *hope-less*. Death is *hope-less*. Neither is bereft of hope, rather they have *dispensed* with hope. They exist in a vortex, not of *hopelessness* ("the situation is hopeless" always contains the plea for a miracle) but a vortex without categories of optimism or pessimism' (*Death, the One and the Art of Theatre* 32). There is a kind of negative ideal imagined here, a non-space where concepts fundamental to human thought cannot be located, either as presence or as absence. Consider Barker's deliberately contradictory attitude towards the idea of prayer. To suggest that prayer is an expression of anger over present conditions and a desire for an alternate state of affairs 'would be to reduce prayer to a practical statement of aims and desires. It is without anger, it is uttered without hope, to a wall of silence ... the cosmological oblivion to which it is addressed does not, however, detract from its passionate need, its value as *expression*' (Rabey and Gritzner, 'Howard Barker in Conversation' 34). Barker refuses the idea of prayer as a promise or as a demand but asserts its purely formal value, bereft of content. This is a unique but recognizable response to the conditions of postmodernity: the necessity for spiritual gestures without the possibility of metaphysical fulfilment of said gestures. Barker's tragedies, as we shall see, take place in a godless environment but nevertheless promise ecstatic experience. His tragic manifests itself through the ecstatic abandonment that comes from intimations of the unconscious, which is now the locus of what was once the experience of the divine. His plays are themselves responses to the purported impossibility of the tragic within postmodernity, through attempts to articulate the unrepresentable: the unconscious.

Yet Barker's rhetoric in his many polemical essays, couched in an impassioned valorization of individual will, has also subjected him to scholarly chastisement, both for his seemingly naive investment in the 'bourgeois individualism of the nineteenth century' and his apparent attempts to curtail and control interpretation of his own plays through his critical writings (Barnett 463, 464). David Barnett claims that Barker's Nietzschean individualism fails to take into account Marxist and Lacanian analyses of the concept of the individual, which leaves him anachronistically somewhere 'between Romanticism and Modernism' (463). Others are less troubled by Barker's terms of reference. While Barker's aesthetic has been illuminated by critical attention to the concept of the sublime, or through comparison to the Romantic elevation of the tragic individual, my approach situates the Theatre of Catastrophe in relation to the rubric of (late) modernist thought.[4] Whereas critics have suggested that Barker wishes to resuscitate the experience of the sublime or the Romantic divinity of the heroic

Übermensch, I want to offer an historically grounded assessment of the Theatre of Catastrophe.[5] Within Barker's frame of reference, I argue, it is the unconscious itself that has been domesticated into the merely recognizable or entirely denied by postmodernity. The importance of the unconscious (and its notable absence as a term of discussion from Barnett's aforementioned essay) is that it is equally a Romantic, Modernist, and postmodernist concept; it is both quaintly nine-teenth century and of use to post-structuralist critics. And it is a term that Barker himself draws upon in his polemics. It is the unconscious – and desire – that counterbalance Barker's emphasis upon individual will. As for Barker's polemi-cal essays, they are, in my estimation, less attempts to control the meaning of his plays in advance than they are attempts to describe the hoped-for theatrical *ef-fect* he envisions. In these essays, he is less an authorial, controlling presence than he is a spectator to his own work.

While Barker's playwriting distances itself from the concept of the political, critics have insisted that it is this very distance, within a contemporary context, that is its own political act. David Ian Rabey's work is fundamental to our un-derstanding of this playwright's politics and aesthetics, and for understanding how Barker's work is, as Rabey sees it, an attempt to clear a space for a true de-mocracy. Rabey writes, 'Whereas Christianity promotes an ethic in the present and promises a good life in the hereafter, and Marxism promotes the value of struggling and suffering today in order to achieve future perfection in material terms, existentialism insists that we are creatures of infinite possibility with an obligation to self to live in the present, as a priority to creating community' (*Howard Barker: Politics and Desire* 243). Rabey's approach is exemplary for its insistence that Barker's emphasis upon the will and desire of individuals is a precursor to the emergence of democracy. More recently, Rabey has assessed Barker's oeuvre as a project to 'reclaim language from a sense of social crisis expressed as fatalistic determination (the presumption that there is only one possible way that things can turn out). [...] [H]e has countered the implicitly authoritarian presumption and proposition of supposedly "natural" diminu-tions or "inevitable" restrictions of the options whereby one might think, feel, speak, act, love and exist' (*English Drama since 1940* 182). It is this latter senti-ment that most accords with our concerns here: the determinism of tragic ide-ology, as it manifests itself ubiquitously within contemporary Western thought, is set upon by the violence of tragic experience in Barker's plays.

Claw

Like Brecht, Barker is a fascinating theorist of the aesthetic and a theatre po-lemicist. He is also a remarkable re-reader of his own early work, but as Brecht re-interpreted early plays like *Baal* or *Man Equals Man* through the lens of his developing Marxism, Barker re-visions his early political plays through the theory of catastrophe that developed in his work after the 1970s.[6] Barker's reflections in 1988 on the early play *Claw* (1975) demonstrate a lucid sense of the heterogeneity of the dramatic text: 'I regarded this play at the time as a didactic play of politics demonstrating false consciousness, the futility of individualism and the myth of social mobility' (*Arguments* 55). Yet in the light of his later aesthetic theory, Barker finds within it a stylistic, formal politics that trumps the directness of didactic content. The play's protagonist, Noel Biledew (named after Noël Coward), is a war baby born from adultery while his mother's husband is in a POW camp during the Second World War. The elder Biledew, upon his return to England, becomes a disciple of Marx and espouses class consciousness as the only salvation available for them, while Noel learns from Marx that the social corruption and decay that are endemic in Barker's England are both a problem and their own solution. *Claw* may be read as a satire of the Marxist dialectic of history: 'It seems to me the point of old weirdbeard's diagnosis was to hasten the corruption, not run after it with a dustpan and broom. Which confers on me the status of a hero, so sit down and shut your gob' (155). As a self-styled political agitator, Noel/Claw's name signifies his status as a human weapon against the upper classes, seeking to corrupt and ravage them from within. He engages in 'an Odyssey' (the subtitle of the play) of self-creation, renaming himself and deciding, after a brief dalliance with the Young Communists, to become a pimp (he refuses to glorify the profession with any other word) as a means of escaping his class background. This adventure takes him into the homes of upper-class Chelsea politicians, and in particular the residence of Tory Home Secretary Clapcott, whose work appears to consist largely of denying men parole. Noel eventually attempts to blackmail Clapcott as a means of entrenching his place in this privileged social sphere, only to find himself imprisoned in a mental institution, where he is summarily drowned in a bathtub by a former hangman's assistant and a former IRA bomber who now work for the government by disposing of embarrassing individuals.

The play is clearly the product of a highly politicized culture and sensibility, reserving its most scathing satire for Clapcott's Conservative hypocrisy: 'In the Tory Party, as in life, discretion is the difference between success and abject failure. If you have integrity, but no discretion, then you are nothing. If you have brilliance, but not discretion, then you are nothing. But if you have nothing else, but you have discretion ... then you are like unto a God' (202). No less biting is the final speech of the play, in which Clapcott describes, in Parliament, Noel's death as an unfortunate accident. *Claw* is a rough, lurching, angry, and energetic play, ferocious in its satire and cruelty and merciless towards the angry young man at the heart of the plot, particularly when he is abandoned and forgotten, crying out for the elder Biledew, the only father he has ever known. In his odyssey Noel goes from alienated undesirable with coke-bottle glasses to leather-clad rocker pimp to hapless scapegoat.

Noel is granted a particularly moving final speech, in which, inspired by a vision of his father imploring him to appeal to the common humanity and class background of his jailors, Noel fashions a rough and poetic articulacy out of the narration of his own journey through life. It is an awakening class conscious-ness and appeal to solidarity: 'Because our little squabbles and our playground fights and little murders in the entrances of flats are hardly crimes compared to that crime they are working on us, all of us driven mad by their brutality and no coppers to protect us against their claws! [...] And we have nothing except each other. Our common nothingness. And our caring for each other. And our re-fusal to do each other down' (229). Naturally this speech has no effect upon two killers, who identify thoroughly with their masters. In his retroactive reading of the speech, however, it is not the political message that matters to Barker but the long silence following the speech, combined with the subsequent drowning of Noel:

> This silence is, I suggest, the supremely beautiful moment of a play which is a jour-ney through the stagnant pool of unlived life, soiled feeling and the moral destruc-tion of both poverty and privilege. [...] He is drowned, without resistance, on the stage. Thus the optimistic possibility is exploded – if optimism it is – and didacti-cism is scattered in a surge of terror. [...] In effect, the play subverts itself, the conclusion, in its failure to project the message [...]. The frustration of the message sets up an anxiety, while the beauty of the scene locks it in the imagination. (*Arguments* 56–7)

As we shall see, this is, in a nutshell, a description of the desired effects of the Theatre of Catastrophe. It is achieved only in performance. This may only be Barker's personal interpretation of the effect of this moment onstage, but we should note that it is the description of an audience member, as distanced as any other spectator from the avowed authorial intentions of the play. The scene is also punctuated with long, ten-second silences, indicated at several points, which are the play's response to the everyday atrocities in which these men have been active. A number of long monologues from the two professional murder-ers describe their acts of mundane, dehumanizing violence and their perfect compatibility with not only political institutions but also the trivial details of daily English life. For instance, the Irish terrorist describes how he completed his bomb attack with the decision to buy a record, the tune of which he couldn't shake from his head all day. This is a manipulation of dramatic substance to canny effect: both the demand for some articulate response to the horrors described and the pitiable plea to live from Noel are refused by the play. Silence is offered instead. Here is the potential for inducing audience anxiety that Barker will eventually see as a key effect of his theatre.

There is also discernable in *Claw* an awareness of the stifling straitjacket of the tragic ideology and the inevitable politics that arise from apprehending this world view: when Noel cries out to his stepfather for help, he is granted a vision of the elder Biledew, who describes his own awakening class consciousness as an inspiration to the young man. The truth that gradually emerged for Biledew is a rejection of a certain tragic vision in favour of an orthodox dialectical materialism: 'I had suffered the kicks and cuts of what I had assumed was Fate, and followed the circumstances that what I thought was Fate imposed on me. […] And it dawned on me. […] I saw it as a whole, I knew the way the world ran wasn't some divine miracle but was a machine, which came to pieces and was comprehensible.' From this revelation he apprehends that there are no gods, and that humans are the source of all actions and events: '[W]hat is, is not what has to be, but what we have allowed to be. And the consequence that flows from that is that we can change it' (225–6). The speech describes a paradigmatic transition from the false consciousness of tragic ideology into a dialectical apprehension of social change. The understanding that human suffering and pain are not inevitable but avoidable is a central keystone to materialism, but, as we shall see, Barker's own philosophy is that pain *is* necessity, which is something different than to state that it is necessary. In response to Biledew's realization, the play retorts with the destruction of Noel: a tragic death, but not an inevitable one.

Fair Slaughter

There is a conjunction between tragedy and materialism established in Biledew's speech, one explored in evocative terms in *Fair Slaughter* (1977). At the beginning of *Fair Slaughter* the protagonist, Bert Gocher, has just become England's oldest living murderer, braining another old man with a bedpan in a rest home. Over the course of the play Gocher emerges as an idealistic socialist struggling to reclaim or return to this ideal, represented for him by the totemistic severed hand of a man who claimed to be Trotsky's engine driver. Gocher claimed and bottled the hand while in Russia in 1920, where he also found international socialism, and in a series of flashback scenes we see Young Bert Gocher return to England from Russia with the hand of 'Tovarish,' and subsequently undergo a series of humiliating escapades in England working in the Music Hall with the hand as both his prop and a taunting reminder of his compromised ideals. In the present tense of the play, Old Gocher eventually persuades his warder Leary to help him return the hand to the body of its rightful owner, and they go on a parodic quest through the English rail system, which Leary, in an obvious echo of Edgar and Gloucester in *King Lear*, tries to convince Gocher is Europe.

The two narrative threads, one moving literally from past to present, the other moving figuratively back through time and space, embody and enact the inner fissures of the socialist divided by his creed. Old Gocher is on a journey to reconnect with the humanitarian ideals that embody the best of socialist aspirations, while Young Gocher moves further and further into the realm of pragmatic, immediate survival. The stakes in the dramatic struggles that divide the two Gochers (they travel along the same paths but in opposite directions, doomed, of course, never to meet) are articulated by arch-capitalist Staveley, whom Gocher encounters at various points throughout his life:

> I am personally of the opinion that pain is the dividing line between East and West. The attitude to it, I mean. [...] the abolition of pain simply does not seem a worthwhile object to them. I would go so far as to say that without it they would feel deprived. Whereas to us, that is the starting point of our national will, the common object of our efforts. [...] There is so much pain in them. [...] We are so alone. We are born alone, and we die alone. And there is nevery [*sic*] any contact. Isn't there enough agony for you? (68–9)

'Pain' as a concept finds kinship with isolation, alienation, and the agony of being a human being, and this is a form of metaphysical suffering that England seeks to eliminate.

Meanwhile, Soviet socialism is portrayed by Staveley as a politicized culture that is really just an offshoot of the Russian mindset, where dehumanization is accepted rather than fought, but the dramatic irony of the elder Gocher's quest to return the severed comrade's hand to its body is that England serves as the theatrical substitute for Russia, indicating that the differences between the two locales are more apparent than real. Staveley *implicitly* refers to the Leninistic tendencies that tolerate mass famine and gulags as a means to the presumed end of a socialist utopia, whereas Staveley's own ideal of civilization and progress is *presumably* the English elimination of needless suffering through humanizing and rationalizing society with consensus-building to the benefit of the greater good. As Barker himself puts it when he discusses the importance of pain for his tragic theatre: 'The political and social project of the twentieth century has been the elimination of pain, the elimination of conflict, the prolongation of life. The corollary of this is the promotion of happiness' (*Arguments* 215). However, I am going to offer another interpretation of Staveley's critique, one based on Barker's later theorization of the Theatre of Catastrophe as a theatre in which pain is understood as necessity (*Arguments* 186). Staveley remarks that he would prefer any degree of triviality to pain (*Fair Slaughter* 87), hinting that a numbing superficiality of existence is endemic to English life and the prime national means of avoiding pain.

Thus Young Gocher is eventually employed by Stavely in the 1930s as a music hall entertainer, and his performances insulate and numb the English to their own pain: 'Every voice lifted in song was one less calling for the revolution. Every hand clap was a clap for putting up with it,' reflects Old Gocher in retrospect (79). Tellingly, these memories of his revolutionary compromises now cause him 'PAIN' and 'MISERY' (80). What Staveley describes in reference to the Russian national character may be similar to Barker's own eloquent definition of what it means to be 'European':

> To be European is to hold to opposites and live, if not rejoice, in the contradictions. Read Céline, and read Thomas Mann. [...] What is more, migrate from one to the other, for it's impossible to extend one's treasured *tolerance* to all of these. [...] It is perpetual oscillation, and all talk of harmony is false, a self-deception. Further, whether or not Europeans invented beauty, they have argued beauty to an extreme, it dominates every street in an old city, and we sense the agony of these streets, that also is our way ... if you cannot relate pain to beauty, I think you are not a European in your soul. (Rabey and Gritzner, 'Howard Barker in Conversation' 37)

If we can apply such a philosophy of existence to what is avowedly a play written at a much earlier moment in Barker's career, *Fair Slaughter* in its aesthetic *form* is European, a play in which Gocher the socialist is represented as contradictions that cannot be harmoniously reconciled, which remain resolutely open at the play's conclusion. Thus in its form it offers an experience of pain, and this offer is counter to the English consciousness as described by Staveley.

Socialism is also represented as a contradiction here, an open question. As Barker explains in self-reflection: 'I always knew socialism was tragedy. I had represented it as tragedy early on, in *Fair Slaughter*. I had repeatedly studied its failure. But in the breaking of the politics of the time, I needed to know what meaning socialism had for me. [...] I found it possible to begin the play without socialism but to find socialism within the play. So the audience had to share my not knowing, when it was accustomed to being taught' (*Arguments* 21). I think we can find a conjunction between the idea of socialism as tragedy and Barker's project to begin from a state of unknowing in his exploration of the nature of socialism. It is, in a sense, the discovery of the solution within the problem: socialism *is* tragic, in that its essence is not a simple set of prescriptions or solutions to problems, but rather a process of fully confronting and articulating social problems, exacerbating and clarifying contradictions, to the point where the process of change is seen as organic and intrinsic to the situation that one might seek to transform. The title of the play refers to one of the central sticking points for socialism, the role of violence and specifically killing in the service of a socialist project: if socialism seeks to create a more human society where alienation is decreased and dehumanization minimized, this is contradicted by the use of dehumanizing means to achieve such an end. As a result, such socialist revolutionary activity is a kind of ongoing project of failure.[7] Gocher cries for 'fair slaughter' after a life of disillusionment and betrayal in England, after suspending his revolutionary sentiments in favour of the war effort during the Second World War (89), and after ending up in a bedsit, sole guardian to his daughter.

Barker crafts a dramatic narrative that moves with the force of inevitability towards the staging of the tragic problem of socialism: 'You cannot serve the people if you cannot pull the trigger,' Leary proclaims at the end of the play, having been converted to Leninist *realpolitik* by his apprenticeship to Old Gocher (104). Having stumbled upon Staveley, now an enfeebled resident of a mental institution, during the ultimately unsuccessful quest to return the hand of Tovarish to his body, Leary gives Staveley a quick trial for being a capitalist and wants to execute him. The play ends with the unresolved, tragic problem of socialism: a non-choice between the dehumanization of 'fair slaughter' and the madness of grasping, thieving capitalism. Ideals, meanwhile, are rendered in grotesque parody: Gocher dies to the accompaniment of a black gospel song while having a vision of Tovarish in heaven; Leary, still convinced that Staveley is not mad and deserves punishment, flees with the bottled hand; and Staveley, in his doddering madness, clutches a crumbling, cheap reproduction of a Picasso, gloating in his success at looting this work of art from the old world.

That Good Between Us

While Barker's theatre seems to take as its chief antagonist the oppressive disavowal of 'negative' human experience that characterizes the English attitude towards suffering, when Barker's aesthetic breaks out fully into the Theatre of Catastrophe he entirely abandons the representation of 'social content' in any traditional sense, which is to say he ceases to represent Englishness in any mimetic manner. Thus we are left to scrutinize the plays that predate the Theatre of Catastrophe in order to understand that to which catastrophe is a reaction. Chris Megson calls these Barker's 'State of England' plays and suggests that they span a ten-year period, from *Claw* in 1975 to *Downchild* in 1985 (Megson 125). For instance, *That Good Between Us* (1977) portrays a decaying England in which a

Labour government slides into the suspension of civil liberties and other quasi-fascistic measures, such as the mass arrest of intellectuals and murder of dissidents, as a means of quashing unrest. The play is sketchy in its social background, leaving the concrete social problems that exacerbate the unease largely unexplained. To draw a blunt political point from the action, one need look no further than to the fact that it is *only* when the arrests of the largely ineffective, self-questioning, and unorganized dissident group begin that these dissidents become militant, organized, and murderous. The government's brutal measures provoke the conspirators to don balaclavas and perform the execution of politicians. These chief dissidents in the drama are in fact disenchanted servants of the Empire: a group of soldiers planning a vague revolutionary coup, who are sickened by their work as strike breakers and brutalizing communist protesters. Yet in an embodiment of the ongoing contradictions of revolutionary activity, they continue to perform the violence they abhor as a means of maintaining their cover. *That Good Between Us* is a dystopian social satire in which the ideology of English decency and 'goodness' has congealed into stiff-lipped English totalitarianism: '[T]he creature who ran Auschwitz was a perfect family man,' remarks the Home Secretary's daughter Rhoda (22). Here, the specific representation of historical circumstances is less important than the expression of a general fury at the state of the country. When the police break up a gang rape, the victim's emotional response encompasses the play's social commentary: 'I had a ticket to Australia … I could have got out to Australia …! […] This bloody country! I HATE THIS PLACE!' (28). Her vitriol at being assaulted is directed at her society as a whole, taking the rape as a sign of the overall social decay plaguing Britain. It indicates a pre-existing, entrenched disenchantment with the social fabric of England that immediately contextualizes the individual crime as a symptom of a larger one.

The play dramatizes two unusual forms of radical individuality as violent interventions into the impoverishment of social ideals and the bankruptcy of the post-war English dream: two men who work as spies for the government, rooting out conspiracies. The first is Michael Godber, one of Barker's amoral, protean figures who seems untroubled by human qualities such as conscience or values, and thus is in the position to act on unanticipated, immediate impulses such as the sudden urge to seduce or be seduced, a spontaneity that seems to have an aphrodisiacal effect on those around him (43–5). Godber also introduces a thematic concern that will eventually grow into a crucial philosophical world view in Barker's work: the absence of faith. When confronted about his beliefs, Godber explains that he believes '[i]n cutting ice. (*Pause.*) In all this falling down of everything. In this howling wind that all the good old souls are struggling in, staggering from wall to wall, lurching to the great Calcutta of the future. In all this chewing and spewing and spitting out of people. I believe in cutting ice. [...] Down here. In the alleys and the pubs. In the new rage of street politics. I am going to be a star, Billy. And you can be my roadie if you like' (29). Ironically, this is a refusal to hold credence with fidelity or trust, perhaps a rejection of 'that good between us' to which the title refers.

This rhetoric of stardom as an interior emptiness of self, a performance borne from an apprehension of vacuity at the heart of existence, comes to a climax when Godber finally betrays his fellow spy, Billy McPhee: 'When you're a star, nobody asks you to apologize for your act. No Bay City Roller ever got upset when he hit old women with his Mustang. Keith Moon didn't weep when he reversed over his chauffeur. It's all blood to the erection, Billy. It's all tinsel to the act' (57). Having watched Billy be willingly taken away to his own execution, Godber reaches a terminus in his own life. In this final betrayal of the man with whom he swapped blood in an oath of friendship (20), Godber appears to escape from humanity altogether by embracing a creed of infidelity as the foundation of existence. He seems to become one of Barker's 'social suicides,' individuals so bereft of connection to society or to other individuals that they are reduced (or alternately elevated) to a living death, represented here by Godber symbolically assenting to his own death through a sudden machination of the plot. This action of conquest, victory, or self-overcoming (potentially in a Nietzschean sense) is a characteristic of the Theatre of Catastrophe proper, but as with a Nietzschean *Übermensch*, the actual contours of this being's selfhood are so far from what are generally recognized as human as to be nearly incoherent to consciousness. Godber seems to present precisely such a challenge and constitutes one of Barker's early attempts to describe a tragic subjectivity.

For all the importance of Godber's enigmatic selfhood in the play, it is Billy McPhee, the second example of radical individuality, who both serves as his antithesis and exercises a fascination and a charisma that Godber cannot match. It is perhaps an irony that while other *characters* find Godber mesmerizing, McPhee's gormless, indestructible affability has the greater potential to captivate, if not seduce, the audience. As David Ian Rabey points out, there is something of Hašek's Schweik or Brecht's Galy Gay in Billy McPhee (*Howard Barker: Politics and Desire* 54). Rabey highlights McPhee's wide-eyed trust and naive innocence, his concern to be no trouble to others. We should add that the play begins and ends with him. In the opening scene, we see an attempt to murder him by forcing him into the sea, and in the play's final scene he steps from the sea onto the beach, having survived his ordeal and swum to shore. Throughout the play, this unlikely spy and clumsy infiltrator of the military conspiracy manages to succeed despite his own incompetence. The scene in which he is quizzed by the revolutionary leader Cadbury about his problems with the government is particularly affecting. Utterly without resources with which to fashion a reply,

McPhee squirms and attempts to circle around the question until finally hitting upon a one-word reply: 'Immigration!' (38). His charm is in no small part located in his Scottish wit and non-stop monologues of sarcastic invective. He is also clearly designed to be one of Barker's abject and unsympathetic characters: he describes to Godber his youthful participation in the aforementioned gang rape, which is acted out in flashback for the audience.

Having been established as a part of this decrepit social dystopia, McPhee is distinguished by an indestructible optimism, which is all the more notable for having no discernible support from the events McPhee suffers. 'I will no believe that life is nothin' but a pan of piss,' he tells Godber (29). While Godber the hollow man seems to will his own extinction, McPhee survives, seemingly unstoppable, swimming five miles in the sea to a lighthouse on the Devon coast and giving an ecstatic cry 'I! I! I!' in celebration of his achievement (59).[8] The lighthouse that guides McPhee is a beacon of hope in an otherwise hopeless play, and there is a sense of McPhee as a figure of tragic affirmation, alienated from his society not because he says 'no' to the world but because he cries 'yes' without qualification. The play suggests that the reward for McPhee's uncrushable humanity is his continued existence, but *That Good Between Us* is also profoundly suspicious of the concept of goodness as a mask for a socially acceptable form of inhumanity. We should connect Rhoda's contempt for her politician mother's English goodness to the narrative Rhoda later recounts of her participation in a theatre group, which dragged an audience member up onstage during the performance and literally mugged him, assaulting him and taking his wallet: 'And when the show was over, they all clapped, including him, and we all waited for him to ask for his money back. But he didn't. He left the pigskin wallet with the money in. And I thought that was very, very decadent. I thought that was VILE, STINKING DECENCY on his part. I said we had to go on from there and actually maim someone. Do someone an injury. Really FUCK THEM UP a bit!' (49). It is tempting to read this as a self-diagnosis on Barker's part, a reflection on the intractable goodness of well-heeled English theatre audiences, which his gradually emerging aesthetic sets itself to disrupt with generous lashings of pain and desire in an assault on the hollow English masks of goodness and decency. We should not grant priority to Billy McPhee's optimistic effort of will: both he *and* Michael Godber succeed in their journeys, and both, in the extremity of their tragic subjectivities, constitute attempts to maim the ideology of decency that holds Englishness together.

The Power of the Dog

The conflict between, and conjunction of, History and pain is explored in much of Barker's work.[9] In fact, Barker's theoretical conclusion that pain is necessity

(*Arguments* 116) is essentially a counter-philosophy of history. If the concept of necessity is understood to refer traditionally to the determining circumstances to which human beings must submit in order to survive, necessity entails a dehumanization that is experienced when human beings are yoked by the necessary, a sense of the inevitable that conflicts with agency and freedom. The Marxist project, told in broad terms, is the reduction of the realm of necessity and the expansion of the realm of freedom for human beings as a whole, with the understanding that necessity cannot be eliminated altogether: there must always been some quantity of work upon which human beings build their lives. History in the abstract, from such a socialist perspective, is this work of eliminating necessity and maximizing freedom. This History is progress and its enemy is suffering. Yet if in Barker's cosmography God likes pain, and pain is necessity, then we are faced with a vicious inversion of this emancipatory history.[10] From the perspective of the Enlightenment, the progress of history was a manifestation of the divine in the work of human reason. In Barker's historiographic vision, then, it is not progress that is 'history,' but the negative. *The Power of the Dog: Moments in History and Anti-History* presents Barker's most thoroughly envisioned philosophy of history in just such terms. In a sense this play serves as a social critique of all that he would cease to address explicitly with the Theatre of Catastrophe. Written in 1981 and staged in 1984 by Joint Stock, *The Power of the Dog* is a stark parody, a kind of negative X-ray image, of the materialist conception of history.

History in the play is represented by Joseph Stalin, caught in a profound melancholy during the infamous post-war meeting in Yalta with Winston Churchill to carve up Europe between their nations. For Barker, this crude historical demonstration of political power was so grotesque that satire was the only possible response (*Arguments* 33). The result is an opening scene in which a Scottish clown named Archie McGroot finds himself in the Kremlin, summoned by Stalin to entertain Churchill. McGroot assays an increasingly desperate and unsuccessful series of jokes and one-liners, becoming a jester-like Fool figure as counterpoint to the political monarchy present (there are perhaps echoes of *King Lear* in the moment when the politicians start carving up Europe on the back of an envelope). The meeting ends with a drunken decline of energy and focus, an encroaching entropy that signals the decay that lies at the root of the whole play, but not before the question of history is raised by Churchill, who asks for Stalin's definition of it, expecting 'something of the dialectical mumbo jumbo of the communist mind' (*Power of the Dog* 4). Stalin's reply, 'The incredulous overwhelmed by the incredible,' is baffling to the translators, who try to substitute words like 'unbelievable' and 'unlikely.' McGroot offers his own demystification of the nature of history: 'History! A will tell ye wha' history is, it's a woman bein' raped by ten soldiers in a village in Manchuria' (4). Left behind, McGroot becomes inexplicably ensconced at Stalin's side and spends the rest of the play fashioning an appalled and undercutting commentary on the dehumanizing terror of official history's machinations.

Stalin is concerned that in becoming the great man of history, he has eliminated spontaneity: 'Accident, which is the essence of experience, has been eliminated from my life' (5). He hallucinates that a waiter is rubbing him out of the film of history, and, succumbing to an existential crisis, he orders a photographer be brought to him from Poland, seemingly in order to capture an authentic image of him rather than the sycophantic portraits that are the official picture. Anti-History is figured in a Hungarian fashion model and photographer named Ilona Ferenczy, who along with her photographer companion, Victor, travels the post-war wasteland of Poland documenting the entropic decay of History: 'the most comprehensive collection of documentary suffering in the history of photography' (16). Yet Ilona poses in all of these photos, using the grotesque images of death, pain, and barbaric suffering as 'a mere stage for her own beauty' (*Arguments* 180).[11] The two plot threads of the play represent History and Anti-History, and the final scene is titled 'History Encounters Its Antithesis.' As the antithesis of History, Ilona represents one of those curiously Brechtian figures who survive in the modern landscape of twentieth-century atrocities by emptying themselves of everything recognizably human. Ilona has abandoned emotional investment and espouses a philosophy of will that is crucial to Barker's aesthetic of catastrophe. In her first scene, Ilona poses before the spectacle of a hanged woman, putting on her 'human condition face' (10), takes the corpse's stockings, and states the beliefs that allow her to survive in this desolate situation: 'I believe that every murder is an acquiescence, and every victim possessed the means of her escape. I believe in your eyes and in your mouth you own the means of your salvation, whether you want to be loved, or whether you want to be saved. At the door of the restaurant, or the gate of the camp ...' (10). Only then does she recognize this to be, improbably, her sister Hannela's body and go on a quest to find out what happened to her.

Ilona's view of human involvement in one's own fate is not, I think, meant to be reduced to some callow libertarian ethic of voluntarism, such as the banal and all-too-familiar belief that victims ask for what happens to them. It is this aspect of Barker's plays that demands that we cease reading them as acts of mimesis or lessons for life. His abandonment of the typical codes of realism (entrenched in domesticity) must be understood to also mean a refusal of the typical codes of audience response, and particularly the means by which audiences relate to characters. It is fair to say that *The Power of the Dog* contains no characters, if by 'character' we mean consistent, coherent, psychologically recognizable imitations that seek to fabricate a recognizable semblance of 'the human.' Much as August Strindberg insisted that he had not created characters in *Miss Julie* but something new, Barker fashions new aesthetic beings that may have no accountability to anything but their own fictionality. It is, after all, one of the tenets of tragic figures that their destinies are inherent to their beings, and that their agency is inseparable from the fates to which they succumb. This is the aspect of Barker's catastrophic characters that is self-willed. Stalin remarks, 'There are only two classes of person able to be unreservedly themselves, to follow the absolute dictation of their personality. The supremely powerful and the utterly insane. It is the power of Marxism-Leninism that prevents me sliding from one to the other.' Stalin speculates that this grants him a special aura, possibly perceptible to a phenomenologist: 'I believe the man who has emptied the cupboard of his personality creates around himself a powerful magnetic field' (19). A scene later, Ilona explains to Lieutenant Sorge that she has survived the fascist occupation by virtue of her aura (21). She is like a postcard that she received from her sister from this place, Czernovitz: 'What is it about a postcard that it passes through wars with no more than a dog-ear when every ditch is full of people whose faces have been crushed? I felt such affection for this postcard that could slip through wars and politics' (21). It is, ironically, by objectifying herself that Ilona manages to escape dehumanization by the war, creating a protective aura or magnetic field.

Lieutenant Sorge belongs to a Russian motorized division whose members are film students exploring the problem of the aesthetic representation of history, through the creation of a revolutionary 'celluloid-free film entitled WAR' (12). As a celluloid-free film, the soldiers are essentially performing a piece of Epic theatre, dramatizing their experiences during the war by acting out their scenes in person and punctuating them with directorial cries of 'Cut!' and 'Sound effect!' These filmic interventions are, of course, perfect instances of the Brechtian *Verfremdungseffekt*, interruptions of the dramatic representation through techniques borrowed from modern technology (we should note that Barker's script contains seemingly Brechtian titles for each scene, such as 'The Soldiers Fictionalize Their History' and 'A Great Man Hallucinates'). From this perspective, we can consider *The Power of the Dog* to be Barker's most direct grappling with the shadow of Brecht that loomed over British political theatre in the 1970s, and a kind of radicalizing of Brechtian aesthetics. The play may be a kind of dialectical inhabiting of Brechtian theory and practice and a working through of the theory of the Epic theatre as a means of transforming (or purifying) it, and the plot may be understood to be a kind of X-ray of *Mother Courage and Her Children*'s desolate, decaying, entropic landscape.

While Brecht's theories espoused the presentation of open, unsolved contradictions, the dividing of the audience into individuals and the encouragement of audience members to draw their own conclusions, Brecht's plays are sometimes less ambiguous than they are didactic, evincing the confidence of an orthodox socialism that has drawn its conclusions long before opening the debate. Brecht's contradictions frequently contain their implicit solutions in barely concealed guises. Barker, who is not afraid to use the word contradiction in reference to the ambiguity in his own plays,[12] may be understood to 'out-Brecht' Brecht, presenting a properly dialectical theatre or what Theodor W. Adorno calls a 'negative dialectic' (and we should note Barker's affinity for quoting Adorno in essays and epigraphs[13]). Consider how Barker situates his aesthetic in relation to both traditional tragedy and to the Epic theatre: 'Traditional tragedy was a restatement of public morality over the corpse of the transgressing protagonist – thus Brecht saw catharsis as essentially passive. But in a theatre of Catastrophe there is no restoration of certitudes, and in a sense more compelling and less manipulated than in the Epic theatre, it is the audience which is freed into authority' (*Arguments* 54). In *The Power of the Dog* a series of pseudo-Brechtian theories of representation are bandied about, consciously evoking familiar concerns. Sorge explains to film student Georgina Matrimova that she must escape the technique of satire if she is to create something properly *new*: 'It is easy to satirize the bourgeois film but difficult to cut free from its principles. For example, the principle of courage – [...] I think it is the principle of individual courage that you do not like. [...] So we must represent artistically a new form of courage, mustn't we? [...] And this courage will not consist of sacrifice but will celebrate survival. [...] It will be the opposite of bourgeois courage. [...] Not heroics, but endurance. Not bravery, but cunning' (14). From such a perspective, Ilona is a radicalized version of Mother Courage, in which the tenacity of sheer survival replaces values altogether rather than suggesting, as Brecht's play ultimately does, that the loss of values is a casualty of war that should ideally be lamented. Instead, we have in Ilona and in Stalin something closer to the representation of the human in the early version of *Man Equals Man*, in which Galy Gay's emptiness of personality is a valueless but vital form of strength and his means of survival in any circumstances.[14]

The new subjectivity emerging in this war-torn space has a cosmology that is both new and very old: a soldier espouses the pseudo-Nietzschean theory that 'God is neither good, nor bad. He is stupid. [...] We say of Him, as we say of an insane murderer, He is responsible for the crime of which He is accused, but not guilty of it' (34). Such a metaphysical discourse is the result of the suffering of the war itself: while from a rational perspective widespread pain should lead to an increase in reason, in Barker's counter-Enlightenment vision of history, 'all pain leads to metaphysics' (35). In the parsing of responsibility from guilt, the soldier's philosophical world view echoes, in a recognizable but distorted manner, Nietzsche's description of the Attic Greek tragic view of life: according to Nietzsche, the Greeks endorsed a vision of their own agency and culpability in their fates, but without a sense of bad conscience or guilt for their deeds. Since the cruelty of the gods and the agency of the Greek were identical within their pre-Socratic, pre-Aristotelian world view, their mindset saw men as responsible for their own fates but not guilty, since their fates were at the whims of the gods. It is the gods who are guilty of that for which men are responsible.[15] Unburdened by the logical laws of non-contradiction, they were as Ilona sees humanity: agents in their own destinies, no matter what those destinies might be.

This sense of responsibility without guilt is key to Barker's tragic vision of the individual. The encounter between Lieutenant Sorge and Ilona results in a surge of desire for her on his part and a yearning for her to reciprocate, but when Ilona offers the same submissive, emotionless acquiescence that has allowed her to survive the war, Sorge baulks, asking instead for something on her part that is of telling importance in Barker's representation of human desire and will: 'When I set eyes on you … […] I felt … she is unspoiled by History … (*Pause*) I want you to **want** to be my mistress … […] Not to acquiesce, but to will, and therefore – to suffer … […] For wanting …' (boldface in original, 39). What he demands of her is a merging of her will and her submission to her desire, thus to make her suffering into her own willed agency. He wants a tragic consciousness from her. It is the *wanting* that is key here, the willed owning of one's own suffering. Yet Ilona refuses to resist, refuses to, as she puts it, 'have substance' (39). Substance, a sense of truth or authenticity, fidelity to selfhood, is a liability in this post-war desolation. What remains ambiguous up to the penultimate scene of the play is whether Ilona is being true to her self in refusing the idea that she has any truth. Sorge is infuriated by her insistence that this is who she is and believes that she is hiding something of herself, while she holds to her own empty untruth.

Sorge's arrest for having a personal relationship with Hannela and Ilona, which conflicted with his service to the Party, and Ilona's subsequent refusal to demonstrate or feel emotion for him when he is detained have two effects upon the film student Georgina Matrimova, who has come to admire Ilona's unusual selfhood. In her detachment Ilona becomes saint-like (39, 40). But Matrimova has also decided to make Ilona the subject of her WHOLEFILM project (37). WHOLEFILM begins as another pseudo-Brechtian theorem for the innovation of aesthetic forms as a means of containing a politicized, materialist sense of reality within the work of art. By employing three film screens simultaneously, WHOLEFILM would refuse the bourgeois autonomy of the single authorial point of view and offer instead a triad of perspectives in dialectical relationship with one another: first the individual bourgeois perspective on events, then events in the wider context of historical causality, and finally the synthesis of these two in screen three, which 'offers the alternative prospect available given the conditions described in one and two, and for the first time places responsibility on the audience, which escapes its passive role' (29). Ilona is to be the content of this new realism and thus be 'everything! What was, what is, what should have been!' (37), but the arrest of Sorge throws a new factor into WHOLEFILM for Matrimova, who finds the idea that he has done wrong impossible, yet actual. If the impossible can be, 'It calls for a fourth screen! A Fourth Screen which says – notwithstanding all that has been registered on screens one to three – there is always the possibility that –' (40). Barker's historiography implies the inclusion of the impossible, not just the necessary and the possible, as a part of history.

It seems to be this impossible possibility, the fourth film screen, that the final scene of *The Power of the Dog* stages. Ilona is chosen as the photographer to capture Stalin's selfhood. She attempts to be cold, fearless, and stony in her demeanour, but her continuous dropping of photographic plates belies this pose, and when Stalin informs her she is under sentence of death for some incriminating photographs of her that Lieutenant Sorge secretly had on file, Ilona cracks entirely, begging that Sorge's life be spared and then asking if she herself is going to die. When Stalin dismisses the very idea, she unexpectedly falls into his arms and he consoles her. It seems that when confronted by the terrifying, empty personality of Stalin, the powerful aura of history embodied, Ilona is finally bested and falls back into a previously stifled humanity. It is possible that here she succumbs to that tragic being, that suffering of want, that Sorge so needed to draw from her for the sake of his desire. The achievement of this merging of will with suffering demands a confrontation with a terrifyingly, inhuman godlike being who holds her fate in his hands and who sets her entire narrative in play with his order for a photographer in the play's opening scene. If film screen one is naive subjectivity, screen two historical causality, screen three the possibility for change that is the opening into the future, then screen four, the screen of the impossible yet actual, is Barker's tragic screen, where catastrophic historical circumstances become the ground for individuals to merge their wills with historical fatality.

Victory

The repeated motif of the end of a moment of war – a social and political upheaval that leaves the social consensus in disarray, the human landscape in chaos, and the individual psyche wounded and open to transformation – becomes a crucial component of the Theatre of Catastrophe. Equally essential in this disarray is that in the aftermath of the conflict, the dramatic action of the catastrophic plot is initiated by the resonant tragic trope of the disinternment and violation of human remains. In the aftermath of the Second World War, the remains of Hannela Ferenczy in *The Power of the Dog* are the object of dramatic concern and the locus of dramatic anxiety, as they are laid to rest over the course of the action. It is this action of *deferral* that demands our attention, the prolongation or the delaying of funeral rites for the human being, the result being the metaphorical attenuation of mourning into an interminable condition, a process that becomes an allegory for the tragic human subject. Human subjectivity is articulated as a relationship to mortal loss. That the chief grieving subject is a woman is also material. The spectre of *Antigone* arises once more, the perfection of its plot being the distillation of this catastrophic situation into an elementary form: in the aftermath of war, the remains of Polynices are denied funeral rites, and Antigone's intractable insistence upon laying her brother to rest leads to her own living death.

In *Victory: Choices in Reaction* (1983) we see Barker perfect this particular catastrophic template: in the aftermath of the English Civil War and the tumultuous restoration of the monarchy, the decayed corpse of revolutionary polemicist Richard Bradshaw is exhumed from its hidden grave and the body parts put on display for the King to throw skittles at. The dead man's widow, Susan Bradshaw, goes on an odyssey to London to reclaim the pieces of her late husband and return them home. Yet there is, I think, a crucial difference in Barker's tragic protagonists, which differentiates them from the Sophoclean paradigm and which perhaps needs to be connected to Barker's refusal of *catharsis*. If Antigone is a 'no' to the world, then Susan Bradshaw is a 'yes.' Or rather, if Antigone's refusenik stance brands her as undead in the eyes of her society, and to some degree in the eyes of Sophocles's play, the ambivalence of *Antigone* and what constitutes its tragic stature is that there is a hopeful resistance in her negativity: she renders perceptible the instability of her society and the productive incoherence of kinship relations, as Luce Irigaray and Judith Butler have argued.[16] If Antigone's action is in Butler's terms a 'promiscuous obedience,' a performative submission that is also a refusal, then Susan Bradshaw reverses this into a kind of affirmative negativity, an attempt to fashion authenticity out of *ressentiment*. Susan's pain in *Victory* is the suffering that comes from saying 'yes' to everything in life. Far from being engaged in acts of self-destruction, Susan has turned the tragic gesture inside out. It is for this reason that Barker will argue, as I have mentioned, that '[c]atastrophe in my theatre is willed, as opposed to simply endured' (*Arguments* 193). Thus it is crucial that his protagonists will themselves through their ordeals from the outset (unlike Oedipus, whose act of conscious will is his late act of self-blinding, a submission to his fate and a carving of a 'no' into his flesh), and that characters like Ilona Ferenczy and Susan Bradshaw survive their narratives (in contrast to Antigone). These factors of will and survival grant to some of Barker's plays qualities that might be understood as optimism or hopefulness, and so this action of survival must be carefully parsed and excavated to distinguish it from the naive and simplistic assertion of hope. Key at all times is the fact that Barker describes the Theatre of Catastrophe as a form derived from tragedy and thus it is a certain new type of tragedy, without key identifiable markers of the traditional form.

We see this exemplified in *Victory*, the first play to officially inaugurate the Theatre of Catastrophe. Susan Bradshaw makes the decision to set out on foot for London to gather the dismembered remains of her husband and bring them home. There is something pure and elegant about this dramatic action, in its clarity and simplicity evocative of the spiritual backbone of the human subject. Her eighteen-year-old son tries to persuade her that it is not the mortal remains of a human being that we love: '[W]hen you love – it is not the flesh, is it, that one loves? Am I being indelicate?'(16). Bradshaw's rebuke to him is to slam home the contradictions inherent in the experience of love and the loss of this love: 'I LOVED HIS HEAD. […] YOUR DAD'S HEAD' (17). Rather than argue with him, Susan asserts the materiality of her emotion. Reminding her son that it was his father's head is a means of forcing him to acknowledge the inarguable validity of her investment and that it transcends reasons. The laying of human remains to rest is an avowal of the being of the human, and the violation of these remains opens that psychic wound once more.

In Bradshaw's case, this catastrophe undermines all of the values inherent in humanism: 'I accuses no one. I am done with accusing. I am done with shame, and conscience, duty, guilt, and power, all of it! All of your words, chuck out! […] [W]e must crawl now, go down on all fours, be a dog or rabbit, no more standing up now, standing is over, standing up's for men with sin and dignity. No, got to be a dog now, and keep our teeth. I am crawling and barking, stalking, fawning, stealing breakfast, running when I see a stick, taken when I'm taken, pupping under hedges, being a proper four-legged bitch' (31). There is little psychological motivation provided for this sudden turn in her life and we should not seek plausibility. If we wish to read subtextually we might imagine that she is driven beyond the bounds of her life by the destabilizing experience of her husband's unfinished death. A forced confrontation with the psychic equivalent of an open grave unmoors the boundaries of her self. She becomes a kind of self-willed criminal, like one of Jean Genet's thieves, abandoning the central human value of faith and insisting on its opposite: her creed henceforth becomes a fidelity to betrayal, and thus to infidelity itself. She steals from peasants who idealize her as the wife of a revolutionary hero, and when her servant

Scrope berates her for this attack on their faith and friendship, which he claims threatens the sanity of those she betrays, she retorts, 'Do you think I found it easy? It wasn't easy. But that's my triumph. Any fool can rob his enemy. Where's the victory in that?' (43). Bradshaw forces herself outside of the realm of human relations where the principles of friendship and faith are paramount. It is not just that she abandons them in self-interested acts of survival but that she wilfully attacks the very idea of fidelity itself. She offers them instead 'an education [...]. Ask a rat about his faith!' (43). Thus the title of the play comes to refer to private acts of betrayal, anti-human deeds in which agents affirm their wills against the values that shape their societies and that give conceptual meaning to existence.

Susan's new creed of betrayal is an anti-philosophy, akin to a Nietzschean, Artaudian, or Derridean destruction of concepts (concepts being 'your words,' as she puts it to her son). Underlying the genealogical destruction of values such as truth and fidelity is the exposure of the 'cruelty' that is at the heart of human existence. Cruelty means that loss is the primary bedrock of existence, but when Nietzsche and Artaud each call it cruelty, they are liberating the idea of loss from its burden of negativity.[17] They are insisting that cruelty is an affirmation of life in every aspect, a saying 'yes' to life that is an attempt to live without conscience, *ressentiment*, repression, or bad faith, all of which are reflexes of the psyche that allow the human to say 'no' to some trauma that wounds the self. If at the origin of the human is not fidelity but cruelty, then there is no wholeness that lies outside of the realm of the human: there is no Eden at the origin and there is no redemption in the afterlife. There is only the liberating falseness of existence itself. The idea that life is a theatre but that there is no metaphysically authentic presence offstage is the contradiction of Artaud's Theatre of Cruelty: a theatre that refers to nothing but itself.

Susan espouses such a view of the world when she insinuates herself into the employ of the Duchess of Devonshire, mistress of Charles II. She manages to seduce Devonshire into accepting her by asking about the Duchess's pain. Devonshire describes the wickedness and cruelty of a God who would make a woman highly prone both to getting pregnant and to miscarrying, which has happened to her seven times. Devonshire's experiences of pain render her a kindred spirit to Bradshaw: 'What's your advice? I believe in asking strangers for advice, you cannot trust your friends. I believe in essence all your friends wish you dead' (58). Susan's advice is simple agreement, a 'yes' in reply that encapsulates the entire education she has to offer Devonshire. Faced with the cruelty of the world, Bradshaw's response is to say 'yes' to all of it: 'Yes means no resistance. Yes means going with the current. Yes means lying down when it rains and standing up when it's sunny. Yes urge. Yes womb. Yes power. [...] No is pain and yes is pleasure, no is man and yes is nature. Yes is old age and no is early death. Yes is laughter, no is torture. I hate no' (58–9). In the very same scene, Bradshaw's affirmative embrace of life is put to the test as she is discovered by a violently libidinous Cavalier named Ball. His libido is inflamed by her puritan modesty, and he insists she submit to him sexually. Confronted with an unavoidable, catastrophic situation, she refuses to become a victim, and instead she performs the paradigmatic tragic gesture in Barker's cosmos. She submits to the rape as a conscious act of will and agency, and after he leaves, '*by a great effort of will she resumes exactly the posture she occupied before his arrival*' (63). She compares Ball's sexual aggression to the sterile neglect with which her husband treated her, leaving her untouched for seven years as a result of his mental servitude to his idealistic political beliefs. In contrast, Ball has 'opened' her to her desire (63). It is a discomfiting tragic action. Acts of will are not idealized in the play: Bradshaw does not perform her faithless deeds with the ease of her convictions in some voluntaristic piece of libertarian propaganda. Her 'victories' are entwined with her own self-willed dehumanization, her debasing herself into a state of inhumanity, like an animal.

A curious scene in *Victory* where Susan Bradshaw encounters John Milton, now in hiding and sheltered, ironically, by the court poet Clegg, finds an unusual conjunction between Bradshaw's acts of victory and the larger historical narrative of counter-revolution in which the characters find themselves, suggesting that the privacy of her willed crimes is not without some connection to the failed political moment. Reminded of how she had once been in a state of awed fear of Milton, one connected obliquely to the submissive silence that she performed for her husband, Susan receives a sudden inspiration and slaps Milton in the face. She is exhilarated by the liberation from her past self that she has achieved. 'I have broken myself into pieces to do this,' she explains (68). Milton finds some connection between the slap and a question posed to him earlier, the problem of why their political struggle failed. Milton's explanation is that man is both shit and God. The God in man is his willingness to sacrifice anything, even himself, in the name of change, while the shit in man is his willingness to seize all the power he can grasp should he be allowed. These two aspects of the human, the sacred and the profane, are in contradiction with one another, and the shit in man was allowed to have its way following the war. 'When the war is won, wage war on the victors. Every civil war must be the parent of another. [...] Next time, should we start there must be no finish, or we shall slap one another's faces in the gardens of our enemies' (69). The slap is interpreted by Milton as an expression of heartbreak on Bradshaw's part at the stifling and failure of their revolutionary change. If this is so, then her victories are a compensation for the failure of the social change sought in the civil war, an irruption by other means of the antagonism towards tyrannous authority and power that was the spirit of the revolution.

Yet such a politicization of Bradshaw's criminal quest must be considered alongside one of Barker's own interpretations of her journey as derived from two different performances. Her revolt against social conventions is most of all a 'revolt against Utopia' (*Arguments* 117). In Julie Covington's 1983 performance, Barker saw a Bradshaw whose keen intelligence and sharp wit were inherent to her character, stifled by the oppressive idealist rationalism of her husband ('the intolerable presence of the harmonious achieved by force and reason, abolition, exhortation and the ban' [*Arguments* 117]) and unleashed or liberated in her journey to gather his remains. Her acts of will were the vengeance of a repressed youth, an unfolding of some authentic self that lay beneath her puritan veneer. In Tricia Kelly's 1991 performance, her acts of will were more ambivalent and perhaps closer to the true intentions of the Theatre of Catastrophe. She was a collaborator first and foremost in her husband's politics, and her journey was one where her sense of duty was 'beaten out of her.' Thus her voyage was 'disassembling a life and a household [...]. She had been a collaborator, so that her freedom was wrung only from strenuous will' (117). The difference in the two performances is between two expressionistic theories of the human, one in which society represses the authenticity of the human being, and another where this social repression, while functional, does not shackle or cage a true human at all. Freedom arises from the fragmented pieces of self that are left when the chains are broken. Both evinced what Barker calls a 'will-to-life' through the 'internal excavation of illicit feeling,' and both performances demonstrated that 'the reassembling of the man was the pretext for his abolition, the breaking with a past whose lingering inspirations generated nothing in them but a ferocious pity smothered with contempt' (117–18). Thus Bradshaw's deeds are, from Barker's perspective, anti-utopian, because in their irrationality they insist on the presence of the unrecognizable, the incorrect, or morally wrong, that which a bland and rational utopian idealism banishes from its borders. Milton's rationalization of one of these deeds, the slap to his face, into his historiographic narrative, is not necessarily utopian, since it posits the need for endless change, but it does attempt to contain her antisocial deed within a harmoniously reconciled plot.

This ambivalence on the part of the play towards Dick Bradshaw's politics, which contain both a stifling and repressed rationalism and the potential for something more emancipatory and transformative, remains an important contradiction up to the end of the play. It is not possible, really, to determine what the play's attitude towards the late Bradshaw's polemical 'Harmonia Britannia' and its socialistic aspirations are, and this is perhaps a part of the productive, unsettling anxiety *Victory* has to offer its audience. Susan Bradshaw returns to her home with the pieces of her late husband, a new child in her arms and the Cavalier Ball as her new spouse. Bradshaw has been transformed and seems happy and comfortable with her new selfhood and family, yet when she asks her daughter Cropper to look at the remains of the dead man, Cropper denies that these bones are her father. As her brother did at the beginning of the play, Cropper separates the body from the human being, and in explanation describes how she has secretly learned Latin so she could read the 'Harmonia Britannia,' translate it into English, and print it. It seems that for the daughter, the man is his ideals and political beliefs. Bradshaw has no direct response to this but the play implies that her attempt to lay him to rest has failed because his politics live on in her daughter, which while perhaps noxious to Bradshaw is to Cropper like a 'birth' (85). Cropper's situation asserts the persistence of hope and the stubborn survival of idealism; her learning to read Latin is a direct affront to her mother, who stopped her husband from educating Cropper as a means of keeping the girl 'bovine, religious and clean' so that she would survive (19). Thus while from Cropper's perspective her self-education is a liberation, perhaps even a victory, from Bradshaw's perspective it is a resurgence of the rationalistic idealism that so imprisoned her in her marriage. While Cropper is in the process of abandoning the flesh in favour of the mind, Bradshaw's journey has been in the opposite direction, trying to perform funeral rites for the rational mind as a means of releasing a bodily self.

The Castle

The shift from history to allegory is the representative formal move in Barker's work in the 1980s. We see this happening in *Victory*, where the historical situation takes second place in comparison to the hermetic, expressionistic continuum he constructs on the stage. With *The Castle* (1985) the creation of allegorical theatre comes to full fruition. *The Castle* was popularly read and remains readable as a transparent and unsubtle allegory for the arms race in the 1980s. Set during the Dark Ages in England, the locale immediately suggests a Brechtian analogy between a contemporary failure of reason and an historical moment of intellectual darkness. The knight Stucley returns from the crusades after seven years to find that in the absence of husbands, his estate has fallen fallow as the women, both noble and peasant, have attempted to create a pre-Christian commune resembling a utopian variation on Celtic matriarchy. The church has been abandoned and elderly men enlisted as studs, resulting in rampant human fertility even as the land has been allowed to go to seed.

The dramatic action of the allegory is not so much an action of apotheosis but of counter-revelation, not an illumination but the assertion of darkness, understood not as the Gothic darkness of ignorance within feudal history but the obscurity in the self that is the crevice of difference and desire. Stucley has brought with him a captive Arab architect named Krak, an individual of cold and calculating intelligence and inscrutable silence, who surveys the land and instantly envisions the titular edifice that he will design and Stucley will have built. While Stucley appears to see the building of the castle as a part of his plan to restore enlightened order to the feminist chaos of his estates, the resulting effect is the reverse: late in the play, once the absurdly large and overly complex castle is completed, a series of sudden and deafening crashes herald the arrival of new, rival fortresses just over the horizon, seeming to suddenly sprout from the land or perhaps fall from the sky, replete with modern defences and battlements that make Krak's castle utterly useless. The castle has spawned its own enemies as an organic result of its inner architecture. The dialectic of Enlightenment results in a proliferation of dehumanizing technology. In response, pregnant women begin to throw themselves from the towering walls of Krak's now-vulnerable masterpiece as acts not just of individual but also social suicide, the ultimate act of terrorism found in the most privately violent of deeds. The absurdity of the enterprise becomes apparent to labourers and servants, who kill Stucley in an attempt to end the project and then attempt to give the keys to the castle to the widow Skinner, chief spiritual leader of the women and Stucley's principal rival for his own wife's love. Skinner, hungry for power, is tempted by the chance to indulge her vengeful spite and envy, but realizing she will be too cruel as a result of the torture to which she, as a witch, as been subjected, she throws away the keys. Krak's sudden presence and his suggestion that '[d]emolition needs a drawing, too ...' offers an ambiguous ending: the sound of jet fighters overhead is counterpointed by Skinner's strained attempt to recall a time when there was no government. Skinner, physically and emotionally tortured, may or may not have been transformed by her experience of suffering.

The most immediate and superficial allegorization of the play is to read it as an open and accessible parable about the nightmarish escalation of nuclear weaponry during the 1980s, and there is certainly nothing in the play that precludes such a reading.[18] While the chief narrative of the castle describes the self-perpetuating effects of military deterrence, the conclusion asks the open question of how and if this cycle can be broken. Krak suggests ambiguously that this disarmament too needs an architecture, while Skinner yearns for a prelapsarian utopia such as the women temporarily enjoyed in the absence of their husbands. Yet as with any kind of allegory, there are less and less literal, more and more capacious horizons of interpretation within which the particular story can be located. Barker himself understands the castle to be 'the outcome of spiritual despair,' which shifts attention away from dramatic arc of the castle itself and towards the situation to which it is a reaction (*Arguments* 21). Barker's suggestion hints that beyond the immediate political allegory (which is admittedly a fairly literal and mimetic reading with strong 'social realist' overtones) there is an expressionistic reading that is perhaps broader and less mired in reflective concerns.[19]

Somewhere between a Celtic commune and a troupe of bacchae, the women have attempted to create a perfect world. The failed utopia was an attempt to live without divisions of any kind, material or mental: '[W]e threw the fences down and made a bad word of fence, we called fence blasphemy, the only word we deemed so' (28). Moreover, this attempt to free humans from all hierarchies and impediments to their freedom was also a release from the repression of religious and sexual alienation. It is not the castle and Stucley alone that can be considered the chief enemy of this women's utopia, but desire, which divides the characters from themselves and stifles attempts to create a harmonious society. Stucley's wife Ann is immediately seized with desire for Krak when she first lays eyes on him, and Skinner feels betrayed by Ann's inability to resist the force of heterosexual desire. At the same time, when Krak is initiated into the mysteries of desire through Ann's seduction of him it shatters his veneer of reason and sends him on a mental quest to understand this self-dividing force at work within him. He seems changed by desire at the end of the play, and this may fuel his new project to demolish the castle, for which he needs Skinner's help: desire, subversive of institutions, may also drive hope.

Desire and the force of seduction are essential to Barker's metaphysical vision because these inner fissures in the self are the tragic self-division that cannot be cured by social utopias. In The Castle, an attempted utopia without differences or division instead opens wide the fissure of betrayal and cruelty that desire creates. Cruelty is, above all, the cruelty in the self, which is evidenced by the loss of coherent self-possession that occurs when desire thieves agency from the conscious self and when seduction undermines the coherence of one's will. Skinner, for example, fights a lonely, losing battle against heterosexuality. In The Castle, the central fissure that asserts itself like the return of the repressed is the fundamental difference between men and women. It is 'the difference in women' (32) that drove Skinner's husband away from home and to the crusades, from which he refused to return, while for Skinner herself, women's difference presented an opportunity to make themselves anew in acts of self-overcoming: 'LISTEN, we all bring to the world, inside our skulls, inside our bellies, Christ knows what lumber from our makers BUT. You do not lie down to the burden, you toss it off. The whine "I am made like that" will not wash, will it?' (35). She encourages the women not to revert to their previous submissive sexual attitudes towards men and instead to hold to the new bonds of love they have created. Explicitly coded as a lesbian, this status is Skinner's key to both her self-possession (her will) and her self-division (her desire), as she cannot accept Ann's return to the social contract and her abandonment of their vows of love. The irreparable divide in the self, the foundation of the self that is not a foundation but the absence of such, is what lies beneath political utopias and modern states. Politics, for Barker, is the disavowal of this division.

Skinner seduces and murders the master builder as a means of holding back the construction of the castle, and for her punishment is, perversely, bound to his corpse and released. The crime she committed, significantly, is considered not just an isolated act of violence but also a violation of the 'universal trust, that universally upheld convention lying at the heart of all sexual relations marital and explicit' (56). Binding her to a corpse is a potent visual allegorization of the inner mortification of the self that she has suffered for her own spurned desire. The human literally burdened with mortality and negativity, loss, and decay, is a blunt form of poetic justice heaped upon a woman whose desire thieved from her the will to live. In a play dominated, like all of Barker's plays, by strong poetic language, this key theatrical image of a woman wandering with a rotting corpse strapped to her belly is a more immediate theatrical metaphor than the castle itself, which was, in its original production, suggested by words rather than represented, 'shouted into place' as Barker puts it (*Arguments* 21). Barker includes a telling stage direction describing Skinner's burden, describing the effect as '*a grotesque parody of pregnancy*' (*The Castle* 63), and Skinner herself describes it in such terms. Pregnant with rot and death, she may serve as an image of the human itself as a tragic, mortified ruin. Wandering as a pariah, she becomes an object of new religious worship, a kind of Oedipal outcast or *pharmakos*.

Stucley finds his own way of articulating this agonistic metaphysic of humanity tortured by desire through the 'Gospel of the Christ Erect' (42). It is a narrative of a Christ whose central crucifixion was his inner division by his own virility and desire. The passionate suffering of heterosexual desire becomes the profane and tragic transcendence within the human, an inner Golgotha of suffering and mortification that simultaneously drags the human down to profane existence and promises to elevate the human beyond the bounded walls of the self. Any allegory or parable is potentially such an apocalypse, a narrative of redemption and the map to utopia, like the parables in Christ's gospels that are offered as directions to the kingdom of heaven. Yet *The Castle* is a self-conscious allegory, since it is about the failure of social transcendence and the ruining of social projects by desire. It is an allegory describing the failure of the key allegorical action, namely transcendence. It is thus an allegory of cruelty, suggesting that there is no perfection to be sought outside of the here and now. Yet *The Castle* is not so much an obscure play as it is a play about obscurity. It is, relatively speaking, one of Barker's most humanistic plays, lacking one of the unsympathetically criminal individuals that we find elsewhere. Here, his tragic protagonists, crucified by desire and lost love, are all-too-recognizably human in their sufferings and their contortions, and the elevation of their pain into a source of beauty is an accessible, recognizable, tempting alternative to the inhuman machinations of the castle itself.

The Europeans

The Europeans: Struggles to Love (written 1987, performed 1991) feels in many ways like a sequel to or recasting of the earlier *Victory*, with certain key alterations of that dramatic pattern, the effect of which is nevertheless to create something resolutely new in dramatic art. The title of the play guides us towards two key innovations: first, this is not a play about an individual; and second, this drama about struggles to love is also a break from what we might recognizably call tragic. So while Susan Bradshaw's journey is arguably the spine of *Victory*, in *The Europeans* no single character's alienated state can be understood to hold a privileged position of importance. Instead, *The Europeans* shows us a group of characters, all of whom encounter a catastrophic situation and lose their moorings in life. They respond to this unanchoring of self in differing ways, some through the aesthetic, some through a kind of hyperbolic performativity of self, and some through an embracing of their pain and loss as a resistance to a conciliatory and victorious social environment.

While Barker describes the Theatre of Catastrophe as a modern permutation of tragedy, there is little about a play like *The Europeans* that seems recognizable in terms of traditional tragic plots or patterns. Instead, the concern here appears to be with a representation of a human world as philosophically tragic without recourse to a paradigmatically Sophoclean or Aristotelian plot. In fact the story itself seems to be an attempt to dramatize an idea, specifically that the Theatre of Catastrophe is tragedy without *catharsis* or reconciliation. Thus reconciliation gradually becomes a principal concern over the course of the play, something against which two of the characters struggle while also struggling to love. Reconciliation here means the recontainment of individual loss and suffering within grand narratives of History, and the Theatre of Catastrophe is what characters attempt to create out of their alienation and pain as a means of escaping History.

The Europeans wants to present such a rebirth of the self in catastrophe as a possibility, but it also wishes to question whether or not it is actually feasible to escape History. Thus the play may in fact be an exploration of whether or not the Theatre of Catastrophe, understood as an expressionistic rebirth of the self, is in fact an impossibility that is nevertheless conceivable. If the play is in fact an exercise in the impossible, this is encapsulated by a key character's description of the new art he envisages arising out of the rubble of post-war Europe: 'What I need. And what there will be. I need an art which will recall pain. The art that will be will be all flourishes and celebration. I need an art that will plummet through the floor of consciousness and free the unborn self. The art that will be will be extravagant and dazzling. I need an art that will shatter the mirror in which we pose. The art that will be will be all mirrors. I want to make a new man and new woman but only from the pieces of the old. The new man and new woman will insist on their utter novelty' (135–6). This is the conflict that Barker's art itself confronts: an art of pain in a time when society seeks to celebrate.

The events are set in Austria in 1683, at the historical moment when the Turkish siege of Vienna was repulsed by European armies and the Hapsburg Empire restored to power in Europe. Barker has created an authentic modern politicized expressionism, enacting the mutual contamination between social circumstances in disarray and individual selfhood in crisis. The spine of the plot is a birth, both literal and symbolic, that arises from the trauma of the war, and at stake in the birth are the differing factions that vie to contain that birth within either tragic or conciliatory narratives. As with the expressionism that arose in Europe at the end of the nineteenth century and around the First World War, the concept of birth contains an important ambivalence, since a birth can be conceived of as something new, a creation *ex nihilo*, or as a repetition, a re-birth, a liberation of a repressed, more authentic aspect of the self that society has prohibited. But what General Starhemberg calls the 'unborn self' is not a quasi-fascistic vision of the new man but rather a new person constructed out of the fragments shattered by the moment of catastrophe. The unborn self is the patchwork self.

Starhemberg's importance in the play arises from his status as both hero of the siege, 'the man who saved Vienna' (101), and an alienated dissident who cannot share in the triumphalist spirit of the times. Starhemberg's post-war melancholy manifests itself in a loss of faith in his fellow men, an inability to love men (140), away from which he cannot reason himself. The siege of Vienna brought about a crisis in fidelity for Starhemberg because of the widespread betrayals of European values that he was witness to: 'I received a delegation who proposed the burning of all effigies of Christ, and as for the Imperial standard, I saw it stuffed inside a drain-pipe. [...] I forced freedom on them, and when they applaud me, their claps are drowning out the shame which roars inside their ears' (105). He has seen his fellow men abandon the underpinnings of their sense of selfhood, and now he refuses to help them recover a sense of identity, preferring instead to attempt to manufacture a new self out of the pieces of the old. Moreover, having seen how betrayal and infidelity ruled during the siege, Starhemberg's crisis of faith may in fact be an escape from the illusion of values: a self created out of fragments is not a true self at all but the fashioning of self out of betrayal.

His loss of faith leads him into comical confrontations, first with outcast beggars and finally with an officer with whom he seeks to create a rapport and find brotherly love. Their bemused and confused responses to his alienated and hyperbolically overdramatic sense of his own detachment from humanity indicate to us that the tragic condition in the play does not extend to the lower classes, who stand aside from the action and serve as ironic spectators to the suffering of figures like Starhemberg. Yet while the play is willing to mock Starhemberg's self-obsessed state, it also portrays his struggle to love as of the utmost importance. While Starhemberg is too isolated by his faithlessness to be the hero that the Emperor and Empress want him to be, it is in fact this very same state of torment and self-absorption that elevates him to saint-like status in their eyes and makes him the object of the Empress's desire: 'I think you are a cold and wonderfully imagined man, I mean, you are your own invention, isn't that so? [...] No real man is worth the effort, but one who invents, and re-invents himself! He can keep us heated! [...] Starhemberg, we must invent the European now, from broken bits. Glue head to womb and so on. And fasten hair to cracked, mad craniums. And stop being ashamed. Now, go, you excellent actor, do go ...' (106–7). As is so often the case with such alienated figures, they occupy a state of performativity where their lack of an authentic self resembles falseness or a pose. They are *actors*, but with the key distinction that they have no offstage lives to which they might retreat. It is for this reason that betrayal, infidelity, and falseness become their only truths, since truth itself does not exist in their catastrophic situations.

Starhemberg's quest to love brings him into two new relationships over the course of the play. The first is with Katrin, a young, literate peasant woman who was raped by Turkish soldiers and now carries a child as a result of this violation. It is the eventual birth of this child that becomes the symbolic birth in the play. Katrin is in many ways Starhemberg's spiritual kin. We first encounter her in a convent, attempting to recount the rape, the cutting of her throat and the removal of her breasts, and finding herself in a violent struggle with words. Words for her have become mere euphemisms, barriers to the event rather than the means of communicating it. In her struggle she demonstrates the force of her trauma and pain as she attempts, unsuccessfully, to throttle this experience into the stifling shape of language. Yet Katrin does not wish to escape her pain and recover her life. The word 'home,' for example, evokes revulsion from her when it is used by her sister: 'I can't go home because – and do listen, this will be difficult for you, perhaps beyond your grasp – home is the instrument of reconciliation, the means through which all crime is rinsed in streams of sympathy and outrage doused, and blame is swallowed in upholstery, home is the suffocator of all temper, the place where the preposterous becomes the tolerable and hell itself is stacked on shelves, I wish to hold on to my agony, it's all I have' (99). The paradox of her state is that her only possession is a lack of self-possession; her only object is loss itself. Accordingly, Katrin embarks on her own performative journey to theatricalize her suffering, volunteering her disfigurement, as she puts it, to the Institute of Science (107). The gathered physicians welcome this offering to science as the deed of a 'courageous and patriotic woman,' but Katrin's insistence that thousands of full-colour illustrations of her mutilated body be printed and circulated throughout the city indicates that she has less altruistic intentions in mind. Her appearance here is part of a larger campaign: 'The birth is for the seventeenth. I want it public in the square, and banks of seats. No awnings, even if it rains, and let actresses be midwives if nurses have their scruples' (110). The birth will be a public performance, an open and ostentatious display of her agony. Both Starhemberg and Katrin are actors whose performance is their catastrophic and fragmented selves: the shattered mirror of the ego, cracked by loss and trauma.

Katrin's experience effectively overturns the world for her, reversing all values and granting her a tragic knowledge of the infidelity at the heart of existence. The result is a seemingly illogical, irrational view of cause and effect: 'It is not a matter of you wanting a child. It is the child wanting. I know. I never wanted a child. But the child wanted. [...] The unborn, the unconceived, force the act upon the parents' (125). In this reversal the idea of causality and origins behind deeds is disrupted. It is a Nietzschean genealogy, a sense that if cruelty and betrayal are the motive force behind deeds, then what drives events is overcoming rather than progress. This is 'knowledge' according to Katrin, which is necessary if one wishes to make oneself again. The overturning of given values evokes a kind of Brechtian logic, without the moralizing of the Marxist dialectic: 'I dread the criminality of motherhood. It is a criminal relation' (126). She describes the image of a gas chamber, one of the play's many deliberately anachronistic references, to suggest the betrayals that a mother would indulge in order to save her own child: 'Imagine the mother of the infant trampling the occupants, her heels, her spikes, go into eyes and cheeks as she climbs the dying mound for the last cubic inch of oxygen, the infant stretched aloft, SPARE MINE!' (126). As Brecht did in *The Caucasian Chalk Circle* and *Mother Courage and Her Children*, Barker takes the human relationship that is most revered as natural, honest, and 'good' and overturns it, revealing it to be not natural but social. If motherhood is not natural, then for the human there is no nature. If motherhood is a criminal relation, then all relationships are criminal: they are not bonds of fidelity but infidelity.

While Starhemberg and Katrin are similarly alienated, outsider figures in the play, the difference between them is that Starhemberg seems to actively seek a remedy to his disenchanted state, while Katrin revels perversely in hers. Thus when Starhemberg asks her to help him for fear that they will die alone, Katrin rebukes him for dreading such isolation (130). Yet Starhemberg does not want to bring Katrin back into a society or a community; instead he seeks to aid her in her goal of theatricalizing her pain as an isolated state. When Katrin's new-born daughter is claimed by the Emperor as a sign of historical conciliation and the child is christened 'Concilia,' Starhemberg hatches a plan to thwart those who have tried to steal Katrin's 'horror' and make it into 'reconciliation and HISTORY' (141). At the end of the play, Starhemberg gives the child to a Turkish Commander while stationed in a fortress in Wallachia. Starhemberg appears to conclude that the loss of the child by the Europeans will essentially frustrate historical closure: 'Oh, the great chaos of this continent. [...] How do we escape from History? We reproduce its mayhem in our lives' (153–4). His deed of betrayal perpetuates History as mayhem and chaos rather than prog-ress. The word 'History,' notably capitalized by Barker as a means of echoing the grand narrative of progress, is thus a reversible concept, containing two sides: patriotic, civilization-building endeavours such as the Hapsburg Empire, and the dehumanizing violence and trauma of war, emblematized by the rape of Katrin and the resulting child. History is both reconciliation and pain, oppo-sites that nevertheless transform into one another as a part of the historical process itself.

While Starhemberg and Katrin are engaged in a struggle to love, acts of phys-ical self-maiming are described as the opposite of their heroic, psychic cruel-ties. Physical self-castration 'has to do with the fear of love. I think in the very moment of the cruelest torture, the perpetrator suffocates the possibility of freedom in himself' (153). Freedom and love become coterminous here, and are only possible through an act of overcoming that sublates negativity: Katrin is appalled by Starhemberg's granting of her child to the Turks, but her final moments in the play are acts of pure, triumphant will, as she endorses jubilantly his statement that since the child is a Turk, this is merely a restitution of Turkish property (155). The play ends with an agonized but joyful embrace and kiss between the lovers. What matters is the separation of physical acts of cruelty, which are in fact self-negating deeds, from the inner psychic struggle that turns characters like Starhemberg and Katrin into *Übermensch* figures, and thus Antichrists for others similarly afflicted by catastrophe: 'Christ also suffered the intensest hate, or He could never have found charity. [...] [Y]ou follow him who triumphs over himself, who boils within and in whose eyes all struggle rages' (140).[20] These words are spoken by the third catastrophic figure in the play, the Catholic priest Orphuls, who will make Starhemberg into a kind of private messiah for himself. It is Starhemberg who is cruel according to the Emperor Leopold, worse than any Arab butcher (105). It is Katrin who is cruel according to her sister Susannah, 'more cruel than any clot of raping mercenaries' (99). Cruelty is a refusal of fidelity, of bonds, of faith and friendship and family. Cruelty becomes a creed, and as such is exemplified by Orphuls. Orphuls experiences not so much a crisis in his Christian faith as an overturning of it in profoundly Nietszchean terms: he admits to the admiring Starhemberg that he no longer thinks of Christ when he serves Mass, rather he thinks he *is* Christ (112).[21]

The catastrophe of the siege has forced Orphuls into an understanding that to live is to engage in acts of overcoming, breaking from repetitive existence and creating oneself anew. But this raises the problem of what can be truly new and unique within human consciousness. Orphuls appears to have come to an understanding that negation and self-denial are the only condemnable acts; indeed, they are criminal non-acts. When Orphuls learns that Starhemberg's mother has died, Orphuls murders his own mother. His crime is a kind of self-canonization, a 'second birth' for which Starhemberg was the midwife (144). Before being arrested and executed, Orphuls delivers a sermon summarizing the knowledge he has learned from his crime. 'Is there evil except not to do?' he asks (145). He describes the unlived life, the ascetic existence lived in humility and gratefulness to God, as an affront to God. A life of repetitions, in which humans 'sleep even in their waking hours,' is the worst of all sins, and the only Gospel to be studied is the unwritten Gospel of Judas, who was, like Orphuls, 'cruel for knowledge' and not a betrayer of Christ but key to the resurrection (146).

The repetitive subversion of Christian imagery in the play is both contradictory and meaningful: any attempt to envisage what it would mean to create a new human being at the psychic level will be forced to confront the fact that the only vocabulary upon which one can draw contains the language and concepts that carry the baggage of the old human. And so while the fragments of the old are necessary to conceive of the new, those fragments will risk the possibility that the new human seems like a repetition of the old. The Nietzschean idea of an Antichrist, for example, describes a figure who will, Dionysus-like, reverse the Christian reversal of values, affirming life rather than negating existence. Yet the very imagery of an Antichrist remains burdened with Christian negativity, down to the very idea of a negation of Christ. However, as Ian McDiarmid has pointed out in interview with David Ian Rabey, Barker's tragic is a unique attempt to present a Nietzschean world view in which there is no 'no' but only 'yes' to everything in existence.[22] This is ultimately to affirm joyously the cruelty

that is the affirmative fissure at the heart of the world, and thus it is entirely appropriate that *The Europeans*, this strange and unique piece of expressionistic
theatre, should be framed by an unusual and highly theatricalized form of
laughter. The play begins, ends, and is periodically punctuated by the interjections of Emperor Leopold, who not only laughs at the shocks, horrors, and
surprises of this catastrophic war but performatively states that laughter in
words: 'I LAUGH,' he exclaims again and again, explaining to his courtiers that
if they feel embarrassment or nausea at his japing and fool-like behaviour, this
is only a symptom of a deeper underlying unease: 'The Emperor only acts the
insecurity of all order' (102). Internalizing within himself both monarch and
court jester, Leopold embodies that Dionysian attitude towards the tragic that
affirms, with a kind of theatricalized laughter, everything in existence. If in its
energy and force this laughter and his flamboyant behaviour seem like a false
mask, perhaps we should assert that while it may be a mask, it is not false, since
there is no truth to be hidden or revealed by it.

The Possibilities

In his theoretical assertions Barker insists that his art takes as a key antagonist
clarity, transparency, recognizability, and coherence: '[T]he spectacle of the
tragic penetrates beyond pity and achieves its effects in that place of irrationality which is also home to desire' (*Arguments* 173). In linking his own modern
theatrical innovations to tragic art, he also makes an explicit appeal to a pre-
Socratic aesthetic in which the dramatization of the inhuman and the irrational
is at once a form of affirmation: tragedy is 'the most devastating to social orders
and consequently, the most de-civilizing, the darkest and yet simultaneously
the most life-affirming, for precisely by standing so close to the rim of the abyss
it delivers expression to the inexpressible, and stages emotions the so-called
open society finds it almost impossible to contemplate' (172). Turning to classical narratives for examples of the inscrutable darkness and obscurity to which
he aspires, he describes 'the sadomasochistic undertones' of the narrative of
Christ as one instance (174). Suffering, pain, and cruelty, the unavoidable yet
disturbing qualities of art from antiquity, make such narratives both 'forbidden
and enticing' (174). Barker's turn to allegory and parable is congruous with
such classical forms, rejecting contemporary trends in realistic narrative and
setting and amplifying the carefully crafted formalism in his work. Yet the challenge of a truly obscure and disturbing parable is one that will legitimately frustrate the receiver, who will ultimately be unable to recognize him- or herself in
it while simultaneously feeling as if there is still something there that should be
recognized. If the Theatre of Catastrophe truly 'drags the unconscious into the

public place' (*Arguments* 19), then the result can only be a fleeting experience of something that is wholly alien to consciousness yet inarguably true: a thing of darkness that the self must bow down before, like Dionysus's appearance at the end of *The Bacchae*.

The Possibilities (1988) comes close to this intimation of the unconscious. The play consists of ten short parables 'on the theme of making terrible but necessary mistakes, the very idea of the Necessary Mistake being wholly inappropriate to the Theatre of Saying or a Theatre of Solutions' (*Arguments* 122). The very idea of a necessary mistake is an elegant description of the force of the unconscious made manifest to the self, but what distinguishes the ten scenes of *The Possibilities* is that the necessity of individual mistakes is imported into highly politicized social situations, creating a series of moments in History and Anti-History in which Anti-History, the insistence on the necessary mistake, is presented as an essential part of History itself, as if they are two sides of a Möbius strip (the necessary and the accidental), or facets of an unending, ambivalent process. Certainly the situations in *The Possibilities* are immediately recognizable as common dialectical moral quandaries, in which individuals are torn between two imperative necessities that are nevertheless incompatible and mutually contradictory. We have seen this in Brecht's major plays such as *Mother Courage*, where the woman is torn between the need to feed her children by profiting from the war and the need to protect her children from involvement in the war: both are essential to the survival of the children, but the needs conflict with one another and it is impossible to serve both. It is a real contradiction and as a result her children are doomed. But the contradictions of history are also apparent in Brecht's early *Lehrstücke*, the sometimes controversial and often misunderstood 'Learning Plays' for Marxist activists. Short, parable-like in form, and didactic in their directness and tenor, these plays, as Andreas Huyssen has argued persuasively, were ideally designed not to impart passive moral lessons to an unquestioning audience but as opportunities for engaged critical thinkers to explore problems without solutions, such as the conflict in *The Measures Taken*, between immediate, short-term political solutions and long-term political projects (in other words, the untenable yet unavoidable separation of means and ends, and the temptation to use ends to justify means). The failure of these plays is to be found in Brecht's willingness to compromise and bow to Leninist *realpolitik*, asserting that the goals of long-term historical projects take precedence over humanity's short-term needs.

The Possibilities may be a series of *Lehrstücke* for the Theatre of Catastrophe.[23] 'The Weaver's Ecstasy at the Discovery of New Colour' begins the play, and its Brechtian overtones are apparent. A family of Turkish weavers attempt to continue their rug work during a bombing campaign by a Christian nation: they are painfully aware that their survival after the war is dependent on their ability to continue their work during the war, but the constant bombing hampers their concentration. The son objects to the continuation of work on the rugs, insisting that armed resistance to the Christians is their only means of survival. In effect, both positions are right, but the contradictions of survival during the politicized situation of war are irreconcilable. '[W]ithout the rifle there's no rug! I don't know why, but the rug and rifle are the same' (162). They are both necessary to their survival, but cannot both be maintained.

While the scene evokes familiar dialectical concepts, exemplified in an ethical conflict where a correct solution is impossible, it is Barker's concern to insist that this tragic deadlock can only be broken by a mistake, through the intrusion of the accidental and the contingent. The scene's accident occurs when the daughter slips in a flood of human blood that has flowed across the stage, thereby staining the wool with a new shade of red that the weaver becomes convinced will be highly desired by customers. He sends his son to the hospital to bring home the blood of casualties, and meanwhile Christian soldiers arrive, murder the weaver, take the rug, and abduct the daughter. With Brecht's plays, solutions to impasses, however imperfect, are the domain of the rational, centred mind, and these actions and decisions are vital participants in the motor of history. Barker's re-visioning of the problem removes agency for history from the enlightened mind and places it in the hands of the unconscious, and locates the intimation of change in accidents. History is no longer the progressive assertion of transparency and totalitarian sameness but rather the tripping up of transparency by the intrusion of the non-identical.

While the scenes are self-contained and there is no continuing narrative, the succession of moments presents a series of themes that echo and evoke one another. In the second scene a woman makes the mistake of opening the door to three terrorists who abduct her husband. Her error here is a result of her goodness and humanity, which she could not resist: 'I had not killed the instinct of a neighbour,' she explains, but as a result of good intentions, her husband will die and be unable to help his village through his selfless work (167). He struggles to forgive her before he is taken away to his death: 'To survive, we must learn everything we had forgotten, and unlearn everything we were taught, and being inhuman, overcome inhumanity' (168). These eminently dramatic situations, in which the stakes for the characters are never less than life and death, demonstrate the struggle between humanity and inhumanity that is the agonistic movement of humanity in creating its own history. The husband's forgiveness of his wife means that when she tries to smother her own child a few moments after he is taken away, she grapples with her own loss of humanity and finally overcomes this loss, ceasing her attempted infanticide and insisting that she will 'open the door,' thus asserting that she hasn't lost the sense of goodness and neighbourliness that were the cause of her mistake in the first place. Mistakes are 'necessary' because, it seems, they force these characters to confront their own inhumanity and struggle with it. In the struggle itself they manifest their humanity.

A scene such as the above, which can be interpreted as optimistic and humanistic in its overtones, is followed by a reminder that human history is a history of failures and retrogressions rather than successes: in a post-revolutionary society with Eastern European overtones, a woman who was a participant in the revolution argues about the past with her daughter, who is a successful and prosperous prostitute catering to corrupt communist politicians in the present. While the daughter believes in nothing, the mother still believes in the ideals of the revolution despite the failure of events to live up to those ideals from the very moment of revolutionary inception: she describes seeing a police station's records being burned, and then seeing revolutionaries secretly saving the records themselves. The daughter is tired of her mother's insistence that History advances not in a straight line but in zigzags, because this eminently dialectical rule of thumb can be, and has been, used to justify any number of grievous political crimes as 'errors' to be admitted and corrected (170–1). The scene concludes with an open-ended argument about which group lacks humanity: whether it is the older generation who participated in 'the slaughter of the unnecessary [...], the terrible scorching of all dissonance,' yet who did it in the name of ideals like humanity, love, and desire; or the younger generation who harbour neither hopes, ideals, nor illusions (172). The force of error as a fuel for historical transformation is drawn in the contradiction between the two women: errors are both regrettable and to be avoided, and absolutely necessary.

The scenes are dense, aphoristic, and ambiguous in a manner that truly frustrates rational, clear-eyed attempts at analysis. Often a scene of relatively simple composition will be marred by a moment of irrational and unexpected behaviour. For example, in 'The Philosophical Lieutenant and Three Village Women,' an officer planning to demolish a village is offered three bribes from three women: the first offers him an opportunity to extend pity, the second a chance to develop his own superior sense of humanity, and the third a chance to dominate a woman through sex. He rejects all three temptations and so the women of the village declare they will murder him and the other soldiers. When he exposes the flaw in their plan it makes no difference to them. The fact that more soldiers will come and kill the women anyway will not stop them: 'We are the village and the village is us,' they explain, and the correctness of the Lieutenant's observations makes no difference to them (209). He is a man of logic confronted by women for whom there is no logical solution to their problem, merely the need for an action, however full of error it may be from a rational perspective. They are dialectical beings who see themselves as inevitably a part of the historical zigzag to which they are subject, and thus they are, potentially, at one with their own irrational mistakes.

Accordingly, the final scene of *The Possibilities* presents a dream-like situation in which rational logic is suspended and we can no longer take the action to be situated in social realism. It is as if each scene of the play has gradually moved further away from the realm of logical explanation and into the unexplainable realm of the unconscious. Finally we find ourselves in a world turned inside out, where it is the irrational and the inhuman that dominate and are ubiquitous rather than the isolated aberration. Two women await the return of one woman's husband from war after a seven-year absence, and with his arrival they are uncertain of his identity. Their failure to recognize him is the scene's most surreal aspect, as it is not explainable in the terms of logical opposition, which would dictate that he either is, or isn't, this woman's husband. He seems at once to be her husband and not her husband. He arrives with a bag of heads, which he tips out on the floor, and tells stories of rape and murder. Filled with desire for him as a result of these blood-soaked narratives, his wife sends him to bathe and then takes him to bed, where, it seems, she murders him after having sex with him. Only after this can they confirm with certainty, with a kind of joyful abandon, that it was indeed him. The scene, entitled 'Not Him,' is one of Barker's most evocative and elusive pieces of writing, pressing itself upon consciousness without offering any easy moral or logical lesson, or even a comfortable paraphrase. While it is certainly not nonsense, it is a powerfully expressionistic scene in the most legitimate sense that the term can be used. The woman's great fear is that it will not be her husband, and she cannot recognize him, it seems, until she has loved and murdered him, as if knowing him and recognizing him is something that can only take place in the (importantly offstage) space of ecstatic abandonment. Her friend suggests that she has waited patiently for so long that she finds herself refusing the possibility that it is him because her committed love has become a kind of ideal trap: the slightest difference in the real man will mean she cannot recognize him.

What makes the short scene itself compelling is the fact that even at the end of the action his identity is not certain to the audience. The wife's final line, 'It was him. Did he think I was fooled?' (216), leaves us in a state of indecision and confusion even as her own uncertainty is fully resolved: at no point has the man ever gestured to any other identity than husband to this woman. Far from being nonsensical or illogical, 'Not Him' creates a persuasive dramatic space poised between clarity and obscurity, knowing and not-knowing. It at once offers and withholds meaning. Barker's gloss on *The Possibilities*, that it is a series of necessary mistakes dramatized, is useful here, since there isn't an obvious error or mistake in 'Not Him,' in contrast to the previous nine episodes. I am tempted to suggest that the dramatic force of 'Not Him' is found in its employment of a key element of dramatic plot, namely *anagnorisis* or recognition, defined by Aristotle to be elementary to the construction of tragedy. Barker takes the classical moment of recognition and estranges it: in the Sophoclean paradigm that Aristotle singles out and elevates to canonical status, the moment of recognition is a moment of clarity in which the tragic protagonist's *hamartia* – his serious mistake, error, or 'missing of the mark' – is brought to light. Barker manages a strange distortion of this Sophoclean rationalism, or at least of Sophocles's subjection to Aristotle's logical laws of non-contradiction. Barker blurs together the act of recognition and the mistake, turning those opposites into one and the same: a woman's recognition of her husband and her mistaking of him for someone else (or someone else for him) become the same dramatic action. The result is a violent ecstasy of desire, a criminal betrayal of the lover that is at the same time a kind of erotic worship of her own desire for him.

The concept of ecstasy and its importance for Barker's tragic is the final endpoint to which any analysis of his work must proceed. Barker comments on the potential irritation experienced by the audience of *The Possibilities*: 'I persistently refuse the answer an audience anticipates from the predicated situation. There is an element of frustration in it, but what prevents the witnesses of the plays from becoming vociferous in their unwilling subjection to the wholly unpredictable nature of the pieces is the peculiar, simultaneous ecstasy of recognizing the appalling strain of being human' (*Arguments* 204–5). The agony of being human is rendered taut and visible within these small dramatic crucibles, wherein the dehumanizing force of subjection compels these figures to struggle against their own inhumanity. Barker suggests that there is an ecstasy to be experienced in the recognition of this elemental psychic work of the self. In his attack on rationalism and the transparency of the reified society, Barker consistently asserts the power of desire to shatter the coherence of the bounded, conscious self and the ability of theatre to effectively create a situation where sublimity, with all its mingled experience of pain and beauty, can be offered to an audience, specifically through the vehicle of the actor's agonized performance of suffering, alienation, and servitude.

Increasingly, the experience of the ecstatic has become Barker's primary concern, while the term has nonetheless been a point of reference in his work from very early on.[24] Ecstasy describes a transport and abandonment of the self that is at once erotic and spiritual, pleasurable and painful, blurring the line between the limits of corporeal experience and the sublimities available to the soul or the being of the human. The ecstatic is a position outside of selfhood where boundaries and oppositions collapse along with coherence (and so with this in mind perhaps we should think of the dramatic experience offered by 'Not Him' as potentially a kind of anxiety that is a window into aesthetic beauty beyond the bounds of comfort, clarity, and logical ease.) Ecstasy is the tragic experience of beauty that arises from loss. The ecstatic is ultimately that paradoxical non-space of failure where loss becomes gain, but in exploring the potential for such tragic experience in the contemporary theatre, Barker is again forced to operate within a Judeo-Christian vocabulary and frame of experience, when in fact the goal of his aesthetic runs counter to such religious orthodoxy. While suffering is at the forefront of Barker's vision of the human, he is at pains to insist that suffering, endured and significant, is nevertheless never redeemed in a Christian sense, as God is absent from Barker's cosmos (see Barker's preface to *The Ecstatic Bible*). His tragic is not one in which the human is dignified or ennobled by the endurance of pain and suffering: tragedy for Barker 'is the *unbearable* – literally, what *cannot be borne*, what cannot be carried and spills, which falls to the ground and is seized up again, like a woman struggling with the too-many burdens of the refugee ... this failure [of the actor] to transport the load is the ecstasy of Catastrophic theatre' (*Arguments* 144–5). Yet importantly, this failure to overcome dehumanizing circumstances and events is precisely where humanity can be glimpsed.

Gertrude – The Cry

Hamlet Prince of Denmark is a tragedy with such a long and overdetermined history of interpretation that it would be folly to assert a single, primary meaning to this ambiguous, open and nevertheless obscure text. However, playwrights who write counterplays to *Hamlet* seem to do so with a sense that *Hamlet* is singular because it represents the crisis of inner subjectivity in the modern subject. As a result, it is a text seemingly out of joint with its time, inspiring critics like Walter Benjamin to find a post-Romantic failure of self-reflexive consciousness in the titular figure. Hamlet's melancholy, narcissistic, downward gaze provokes an ambiguous, obscure enlightenment: 'a distant light, shining back from the depths of self-absorption' (*The Origin of German Tragic Drama* 157). But at the same time, Benjamin's friend Brecht infamously interpreted *Hamlet* as the tragedy of the early modern Enlightenment mind asked to act within a feudal circumstance, and finding his university-trained rationality useless to him within a blood-soaked mode of production (*Brecht on Theatre* 201–2). In any case, *Hamlet* is the tragedy of thinking in the modern sense, and of the problems that plague the inner contours of the thinking, self-conscious mind. Interestingly, Barker's parodic iteration of the play, *Gertrude – The Cry* (2002), seems to align itself with

Brecht's somewhat demystificatory reading of the play, at least with reference to Hamlet himself. Near the end of *Gertrude*, it is announced that Hamlet had commissioned architects to rebuild Elsinore in glass: 'All acts of love he wanted under public scrutiny/Lying/Darkness/Secrecy/Hamlet abhorred' (165). Representative of the rational mind that seeks to chase all darkness and shadows from the world, Hamlet is ultimately the villain of Barker's piece, an antagonist representative of that totalitarian movement of Enlightenment described by Horkheimer and Adorno in *Dialectic of Enlightenment*. As a result, there can be no more important tragedy for Barker to attack and mutate into an instance of the Theatre of Catastrophe, since *Hamlet* is, at least here, the ultimate example of the drama of reason.

Barker's betrayal of *Hamlet* is in many regards largely faithful to the dramatic arc of the source text, indicating that there is already a catastrophic tragedy within the play waiting to be excavated. As many other playwrights have also done, Barker takes the characters that receive the least stage time and the thinnest characterizations in Shakespeare and places them centre-stage. Whereas with Tom Stoppard it was Rosencrantz and Guildenstern, Barker writes the story of Gertrude and Claudius. What Barker seems most of all to interrogate or overturn in *Gertrude* is Hamlet's infamous inaction in Shakespeare's play. It is one of Barker's criticisms of the reception of classical drama that whatever the inaction of Shakespeare's and Chekhov's characters meant for audiences in their original contexts, to modern audiences these beings who do nothing have become emblems of the 'the assigning of spiritual wealth to impotence' through the 'bypassing of moral will and the aestheticization of stasis which accords with a social climate itself embarrassed by personal autonomy, willing itself into conformity and charmed by the spectacle of the unshakeable power of the domestic' (*Arguments* 168–9). Barker's protagonists are those who act, for good or ill, exercising will while also serving as vehicles for unleashed desire. 'When I came here I said/Funny/THE SHEER SAYING OF THESE PEOPLE/THE SHEER DOING OF THEM,' remarks Hamlet's girlfriend Ragusa, moments after she has finally committed a 'sheer doing' of her own by drowning Hamlet's newborn half-sister (173). With such a valorization of will in mind, Hamlet's only heroic deed in the play comes at the very moment of his death, when, having been poisoned by drink, he sinks to the ground and '*by his final exertion, stands the glass on its foot, an action of perfect will*' (159). Otherwise Hamlet is portrayed as a repressed and prurient prude, tortured by the prospect of his mother's eroticism and by his general loathing of women.

The play itself opens with an act of will: the murder of King Hamlet. The betrayal of the King is charged with erotic energy, and the pouring of poison in his ear convulses the Queen into an ecstatic state, which compels the lovers to have sex over his dying body. She emits a cry, the object of the play's subtitle, which will go on to manifest itself as an inhuman and disembodied force of desire, beyond the Queen's agency. Watching the act of erotic criminality, her servant Cascan remarks, 'All ecstasy makes ecstasy go running to a further place that is its penalty we know this how well we know this still we would not abolish ecstasy would we we would not say this ever-receding quality in ecstasy makes it unpalatable on the contrary we run behind it limping staggering I saw it there I saw it there' (84). Allowing form to become content in the shape of his sentences, Barker has in his recent works eliminated punctuation and allowed the rhythm of the dialogue alone to determine the patterns and shapes of sentences, giving a breathless, unstoppable force to the speeches of his characters. It is as if Barker's characters pursue in their spoken language the force of desire that stays just out of reach of their lips and with which their words strive endlessly to catch up.[25] The cry is Gertrude's ecstasy, the manifestation of the pain and pleasure that come from the commingling of the murder of her loved husband and the passion of her lover's embrace.

This ecstasy is not an intimation of the divine or contact with an otherworldly holiness; it is the pleasure of a betrayal that enacts a deicide: 'IT KILLS GOD [...] And that is our ambition surely to mutiny is mundane a mischief which contains a perverse flattery no killing killing God is our [*sic*]' (97). The cry becomes an obsession for Claudius, something he longs desperately to hear again, but it is a force beyond Gertrude's agency. The cry cannot be repeated at will because it is not an act of will: the cry is, in effect, a singularity, a manifestation of both grief and erotic longing in a single aural exclamation that is, potentially, unrepeatable, and thus outside the purview of representation and theatricality. In its unique autonomy, the cry occupies a position like that of the divine: 'IT IS THE CRY OF ALL AND EVERY MOVING THING AND ALL THAT DOES NOT MOVE BONE BLOOD AND MINERAL,' Claudius raves (107). In its privileged metaphysical position, the cry is like unto a god, but as a deicide the cry is the betrayal or destruction of the monotheistic, of the faithful and of fidelity. The implication of the cry is that Gertrude is and is not at one with her desire, and that while she loves Claudius, the cry is a drive of cruelty that manifests itself only through acts of betrayal. Gertrude seduces and betrays Hamlet's friend Albert, Duke of Mecklenburg, egged on by her mother-in-law to wilfully act the role of prostitute. Gertrude begins to speak of herself in the third person, as if she has become, performatively, alienated or estranged from her sense of self. Yet 'MY CRY IS NEVER FALSE,' Gertude explains (96). The cry is an impersonal force of integrity that manifests only through acts of betrayal: it lies at the interstices of truth and falsehood.

The autonomy of the cry allows it the freedom to manifest itself through any kind of physical agony in which the human is willed to submit to the experience of mortality. This reaches beyond the *petit mort* of erotic *jouissance* and into the realm of other types of dispossessing corporeal transport. The cry comes again when Gertrude gives birth to her daughter, and Claudius, obsessed with every sound she makes, speculates that 'birth might be an ecstasy' or that she may be experiencing the agony of mortality in this act (146). Whatever wounds the self, breaks open the bounds of ego, is ecstasy: 'We prefer the wounds of women to the women,' Gertrude's servant Cascan remarks, 'it's incontrovertible that whilst men scale the fences of desire it's only for the wounds they give' (135–6). Moreover, as the only servant in the play, he has another, privileged perspective unavailable to the royalty. When Isola attempts to bribe him he throws the offer back in her face, explaining that his devotion to the Queen is itself an ecstasy (127). His willing submission is a subjection of self that, in its alienating servitude, offers him an ecstatic pleasure beyond the bounds of the self.

Gertrude's ecstatic cry comes again when Hamlet impulsively drinks the poison offered to him by Claudius, and Claudius finally realizes that the cry is not a part of Gertrude at all: 'Always I thought the cry was in you / But it's not / It's outside / It waits / It walks / Some long hound pacing the perimeter' (168). The expansive movement of the cry is into a fully expressionistic manifestation, as Cascan eloquently describes ecstasy: 'A haunting mirage on the rim of life' (84). The murder of the newborn daughter by Hamlet's girlfriend brings Claudius to the edge of death, and with his demise the cry comes once more, not from Gertrude, who is seized by the cry, but from the land. Ecstasy here is reminiscent of the Lacanian concept of 'extimacy,' a neologism coined to describe the idea that desire, the most intimate aspect of the subject, is nonetheless exterior to the subject.[26] Desire, and moreover the unconscious itself, is *outside* rather than, as in a classical Freudian model of the id, a subterranean, submerged, or repressed aspect of consciousness.[27] Ecstasy is not a matter of the body or the disruptive power of natural instinct, but the 'extimate' and uncontainable product of the activity of consciousness itself. It is 'THE AGONY OF BRAIN' (160). The final words of Albert, Duke of Mecklenburg, are 'BURN AND SCATTER THESE' (175), referring to the corpses that have populated the stage by the play's end: symbolically, this *sparagmos* refers to the scattering of consciousness in the face of the force of ecstasy, the shattering power of the cry to rend the coherent self to pieces. The savagery and merciless conclusion of the play (Gertrude mourns the dead Claudius and a moment later composes herself for her new lover) must finally be understood as a dramatic manifestation of the cry itself, which is avaricious, cruel, and merciless in its drive to destroy, again and again. It uses humans as its vehicles and instruments, much as the wind passes through a harp, and the pleasure of this possession is inseparable from the objectification that comes from one's loss of agency. Ultimately, it is the play itself that must be understood as the cry, since its linguistic and dramatic force and effectiveness will only be made manifest through the bodies, voices, and emotions of the actors, and in particular the actor portraying Gertrude, a role that requires convulsions of agony onstage of such magnitude that a similar ecstatic abandonment might be triggered in the audience.

Dead Hands

Gertrude – The Cry is an avowed rewriting of a classical tragedy that inverts the terms of *Hamlet*, valorizing not consciousness but the outside of consciousness (Ragusa remarks that Gertrude and Claudius live 'outside' and that 'YOU MAY NOT LIVE OUTSIDE AS YOU TWO DO' [173]). While it is not a declared revision of a canonical tragedy, the dramatic action and thematic concerns of *Dead Hands* (2004) announce it to be Barker's ravaging of the Oedipus myth in catastrophic terms. *Dead Hands* returns to the tragic theme of mourning rites: the protagonist of the play, a university lecturer named Eff, returns to his family home for his father's funeral to find that he experiences not grief at this loss but rather a general and pervasive sense of estrangement. Eff experiences a thorough defamiliarization of his surroundings, an uncanniness in which distance and difference, rather than proximity, recognition, and familiarity, characterize his relationship with his environment and his own thoughts. Throughout the play he comments on how situations and words such as 'father' have taken on a strange tenor: the word has become 'funny' to him in the sense of being unfamiliar (10–11). No less strange to him is his absence of grief, which is replaced by an overwhelming and unexpected surge of desire for his father's mistress. Described in the stage directions as 'a widowed mistress,' Sopron, the late father's lover, is a little less than a stepmother but more than a lover. Eff's desire for her presses against an unspoken social taboo which, while it is not strictly speaking the ban on incest, is a virtual simulacrum of it. Sopron's strange hands, which seem both infantile and decrepit to him, are the fetishized objects of Eff's obsession (7). The fixation on her mortified hands, old but infantile, seems to be a metonymic manifestation of the larger context of the drama: a funeral rite.

Eff's unusual but not unrecognizable response to a confrontation with human mortality, namely his sexual arousal, takes place within a compressed dramatic environment that deliberately eschews realism in favour of the logic of dream: over the course of the play Eff is tempted three times by Sopron, who repeatedly sheds her coat and, weeping, drapes her naked body over her lover's coffin. Eff repeats a long and highly stylized phrase again and again, 'I wanted her whole cunt in my mouth the flesh the fluid and the hair stiff hair I imagined and if she pissed so much the better' (8). Eventually these words become a kind of mechanized mantra that seems to summon the act into existence. Indeed, the possibility exists that the action of the drama is entirely a dream or fantasy of Eff's mind. The play begins with him engaged in a monologue with his father's corpse, in which he both blames and thanks his father for the psychic legacy of *thought* that he has inherited from the older man: '[T]his incorrigible speculation it comes from you of all the many gifts bestowed on me by you this mode of argument is the most precious if argument itself is precious [...] I'm alone / In the world and in my imagination / Utterly / Utterly / I blame you / Utterly / Blame and thank you simultaneously' (9–10). By articulating the inexplicable fantasy of Sopron entering the room naked but for her shoes, Eff seems to summon this fetishistic piece of sexual titillation into existence. Tellingly, it is Hamlet in *Gertrude – The Cry* who provides us with an articulate estrangement of the image of women in high heels:

> [I]t is as if you held your body in contempt as if you found your shape unsatisfactory shoes are a consequence of nature certainly of cold and winter but should shoes not enhance the action of our limbs should they not encourage us to act in sympathy with the body's functioning not trick us into grotesque parody [...] By this perverse and extreme elevation of the heel your posture is so tilted by the shift of gravity a stranger unacquainted with our habits would howl (155)

Mentally tortured by his mother's sexually performative behaviour, Hamlet describes from the perspective of the distanced, alienated consciousness the deliberately unnatural, irrational, and theatrical display of a woman in high heels. It is a parody of the human body, an exaggeration of stature and movement. Through the visual image of Sopron, naked but for her heels, the presumed natural ground of the human body is dislodged from such an ideological position of material givenness and repositioned within the realm of consciousness and representation: the body on display is not just the 'natural' body, it is the body as theatre. Moreover, it renders palpable the idea that the voyeuristic desire of the onlooker that is aroused at such a fetishistic display is the evocation not of a biological imperative but rather of desire found in the realm of representation and theatre. Sexuality in Barker's plays is always carefully detached from the concerns of biology or reproduction, and desire is portrayed not as natural instinct but, as in *Dead Hands*, the product of consciousness confronted by mortality and loss. Desire is death-bound. Tellingly, Eff's desire for Sopron is embodied in a visceral image of oral sex rather than genital copulation: in taking her cunt in his mouth and having her piss in it, he will find a perverse pleasure closer to the invocatory drive – the locus of speech – than to any mundane biological imperative.

The central concern of the play is established in Eff's conversation with his father and particularly in Eff's remark that he is tragically alienated and isolated within his own mind because of the torture of his own thoughts, and that he has his late father to both thank and blame for this estrangement. He is in this sense a paradigmatic tragic protagonist, resembling Hamlet. Eff speculates that everything that takes place in the dramatic action is happening by design of his father, as a legacy or a curse in which the son repeats or acts out a narrative constructed by the paternal authority, and thus his agency, while never foreclosed upon absolutely, is always troubled and in doubt. Sopron too, he fears, may be acting out a script composed by her former lover, and her exposure of herself to him is a provocative spectacle because it is balanced 'between spontaneity and utter calculation' (41). This anxiety in the face of repetition and determination, when overlaid with the surreal and dream-like logic that suggests we may be within a mental landscape of Eff's fears and desire, creates the general intimation that the play is ultimately about subjectivity itself, and the psychic mortification of the self through the experience of grief, suffering, loss, and desire, all of which inflict upon the ego wounds that are the equivalent of decay and dying.

Moreover, the injection of these themes into a tragedy wherein the protagonist fears that his actions are predetermined by a narrative dictated by his dead father ties the theme of the mortification of the self to the loss of agency through desire and the unconscious: God, Lacan reminds us, is the unconscious, and Eff is all too aware that 'father' is a funny word like 'God,' 'God who was a father' (11).[28] Tempted by Sopron, who offers herself to him, Eff resists out of a sense that it is a planned conspiracy or trap, and to participate will dehumanize or objectify him, reduce him 'to the status of an instrument played by a man nearly if not literally in the grave' (14). He is agonized by his dilemma, because while he feels the threat of his demotion to an object, he is also acutely aware of his own agency in his desires, yet he cannot grasp the motivation behind his own betrayal, a betrayal or infidelity that he senses is, crucially, merely a repetition of his father's deeds: '[D]id I ache to emulate my father or surpass him copy him or rob him of his place' (42). It is impossible for him to separate betrayal from loyalty or fidelity.

The solution to this classically tragic paradox is found in Barker's peculiar and theatrical view of human will, which extends even to one's own death. The possibility occurs to Eff that this manipulation by the father may also extend to his younger brother Istvan, who arrives shortly and, grief-stricken, confesses that to his own shame, he fled the father on his deathbed and refused to comfort him in his ordeal. Eff immediately comes to the conclusion that Istvan's betrayal in his father's hour of need was merely another one of the father's machinations; he was paradoxically 'the instrument of some other' (20). 'I fled him to deliver him [...] My cruelty was kindness [...] My selfishness was generosity,' Istvan concedes (23–4). Eff concludes that this logic of reversibility is a kind of natural phenomenon, but then he realizes abruptly that his brother has been having an affair with Sopron; the betrayal of the father by Istvan, he imagines, was thus twofold, and imagining Istvan and Sopron together while his father died provokes a new estrangement of the word 'father': 'I think it must mean sacrifice' (31). In the ambivalent confusion of betrayal and fidelity, of crime and repetition experienced by Eff, he finds himself merging these opposed terms within the phenomenon of ecstatic sacrifice. If 'father' means sacrifice, then it is 'a willing one an ecstasy if sacrifice can be yes to be murdered by the son is ecstasy you murdered him but I might have done' (44). It is an ecstasy because it is an event that takes place in a psychic zone beyond the facile oppositions of free will and determination: it is a willed submission, a discovery of agency in the renunciation or loss of agency. A sacrifice means here a willed abandonment of self, and the powerful psychic result of this deed seems to be the elevation of the dead father into the authoritative position that is the privileged place of the absent patriarch: 'The appalling servitude endured by my father will inevitably be reproduced in me no matter how vehemently I proclaim my determination to avoid it' (45). His father thus takes on the force of a haunt or a ghost. When Sopron appears naked and grieving for a third time, Eff finally submits to this narrative and they depart to act out his fantasized erotic scene.

With his final recognition of his own agency in the uncanny homecoming, Eff's will and the legacy of his father merge and are one. The result is that Eff takes his father's place fully, submitting to his love for Sopron and to her love for him. The inheritance is an inheritance of betrayal: 'one is simultaneously privileged and punished so to speak [...] what a cruel gift I thank you what a cruel gift' (70). Alone onstage, Eff's final realization is that he had every opportunity to avoid this fate. *Dead Hands* is accordingly a tragedy of the utmost cruelty: the determining force of an absent god cannot be separated from the vehicle it finds in human agency. In a cruel universe such as this, the betrayal of the father and faithfulness to the father are rendered identical: tragic knowledge is located precisely in that apprehension of the cruel theatricality of such an existence, where repetition and originality blur into one another. It seems that the experience of loss cannot happen in good faith because there is no good faith, only, in the end, false consciousness marred by repetition and *ressentiment*. For Eff, the fear that his deeds are not his own is a torture. Most importantly, it is the experience of loss, here found in the loss of the father, that is troubled by the threat of inauthenticity. In characters for whom existence has become theatrical, even the spontaneity of grief becomes a performance. Yet what this finally reveals is that there is no authentic self, and that such an autonomous ego is itself the illusion. The mortified self is the self that has submitted to loss and thus feels inauthentic because it is marked by a lack of self-possession. This lack of self-possession is the only truth available to consciousness: the intimation of an absent truth, the agency of the unconscious, which is always beyond the boundaries of ego and in the realm of desire.

The power of the father's ecstatic sacrifice sends the son on both a literal and a psychic journey of homecoming, one where all that is familiar has been rendered strange, including the self, because the very concept of familiarity has been permanently imbued with uncanniness when betrayal and fidelity become a single operative force of disruption and change. Without familiarity, there is no ground or transparent self-presence available to consciousness. Ultimately, the power of such an ecstasy must be to offer to the audience a defamiliarization of self that is an intimation of the unconscious, and that will mortify consciousness, transforming it into a form of theatre. Yet ecstasy is not just a matter of personal loss but emerges from a long Christian tradition of religious ecstasy, in which spiritual devotion allows moments of metaphysical transport and intimations of divine bliss. It is an inevitable endpoint in such an expressionistic movement from outer social reality to inner psychic conflicts that the tenor of Barker's dramatic explorations should ultimately echo directly with spiritual issues.

The Seduction of Almighty God by the Boy Priest Loftus in the Abbey of Calcetto, 1539

Like Hare, Barker diagnoses a general social malaise in English society arising from the secularizing process of rational reification in Western society. Loss of faith and lack of religious belief are the result of the demystifying march of reason in post-Enlightenment thought, but as Hare has suggested in his work, a cognitive void seems to be left behind when traditional religion is abandoned. The ability to understand the importance, inevitability, and potential value of loss is itself lost. This is of primary concern for the tragedian, not because the decline in orthodox Christianity in England is to be lamented for its own sake, but because both religion and theatre are arguably concerned with the same philosophical topic: the mediation of loss by the human subject. Historically a necessity, such a psychic activity now becomes repressed or disavowed as irrational or irrelevant within a strictly secular consciousness, banished, for example, as a superstitious investment in a bogus afterlife. Arguably less superstitiously, we can translate this into a refusal or dismissal of the unconscious and the attempt to centre the self within an ego whose agency is unquestionable and inarguable. Yet the result of such an ideological disavowal of loss and failure of will is Thatcherism, which constructs an image of the human as whole and individuated without dependency upon other subjects for coherence, and without acknowledging failures and flaws as essential and determining aspects of the self. The tragedians under consideration here offer theatre itself as the response to religious decline, not with the sense that theatre will replace religion and serve its function, but with the determination that theatre will displace religion with something new and progressive that nevertheless will seem superficially to echo religious belief and faith. The difference between the two is simple yet essential: religion's narrative demands a faithful adoption of and belief in metaphysical truths, while theatre's narrative demands a faith in a willed and conscious lie, which is to say, a faith in faithlessness, deception, and infidelity, the paradoxical substances of theatre itself.

Thus Barker's recent play about Christianity, faith, and prayer should be first and foremost considered as theatre rather than as some kind of modern religious rite. *The Seduction of Almighty God by the Boy Priest Loftus in the Abbey of Calcetto, 1539* (2006) is an anachronistic parable, set ostensibly at the beginning of the Reformation and hinting at some possible analogies with the rise of Lutheranism, while the presence of bicycles and umbrellas in the opening scene japes the idea of historical verisimilitude. Certainly the immediate action of the play, in which the devout and ascetic seventeen-year-old, Loftus, forces his presence upon the decadent and self-indulgent members of the Abbey, shaming their indulgence in physical pleasures and chastising their lapsed faith, both gestures loosely towards Luther's attack on religious hypocrisy while also portraying, allegorically, the contemporary decline in religious faith. The half-dozen remaining priests at Calcetto have been selling off the sandstone of the Abbey as construction materials and have taken to fucking the local women while eschewing devotion, suffering, self-deprivation, and regular prayer.

Loftus, with all the integrity of a young Christ, prays fervently and discovers that his prayers have unexpected results: consoling the dying Abbott Ragman, Loftus becomes physically enraged, attacking with vicious slaps the hypocritical philanderer Penge, who most represents the abandonment of the Abbey's values. Penge dies inexplicably, while Abbott Ragman is suddenly overwhelmed with health and liveliness. Realizing that there is a brutal form of poetic justice in this reversal, Loftus is seized with a satisfaction that he knows to be '[i]ncompatible with the teaching of Christ' (18). It shortly becomes apparent to the members of the Abbey that Loftus is indeed privileged by God and a conduit for some kind of divine agency. While they mock his frequent ecstatic fits and profess to find his asceticism tiresome, they cannot deny his power and influence on them. Yet while Loftus seems to be some kind of messianic figure, the ensuing events complicate the idea that he is a manifest saviour. The arrival of a series of Crown Commissioners sent to the Abbey to inspect the government's property and then liquidate its assets propels the drama into a semi-absurd farce as these officials spontaneously drop dead, one after another. Loftus is horrified that he might be wishing people to death (35), but cannot deny that he might be elected to bear God's hate (32).

At issue, however, are the murky motivations behind these divine actions. At first they seem directed against the enemies of the Abbey, thus affirming that a somewhat unchristian sense of vengeance or retribution might be behind the deaths, but the fact that the Abbott, who is fully restored to his faith by Loftus, suddenly dies and then two intruders who rape Loftus go away un-scathed indicates that God may have wished this agony upon the Boy Priest (52). Thus Loftus cannot determine God's motivations: he wonders if God has simply become fatigued and in his decline subordinated his powers to this devoted young follower. This metaphysical quandary is actually a problem of secularization and the increasing human agency and responsibility for the world: 'The fatigue of God far from relieving us of our responsibilities places us under a yet greater obligation,' he remarks (58). For Loftus, this seems to mean that he must attempt to overcome human feelings and frailty, including hatred. By the conclusion of the play, he appears to achieve this: he overcomes his ha-tred of the enemies of the Abbey and in so doing achieves divinity. The fatigue of God is interpretable as the metaphorical Death of God, which seems to be ratified by the purchase of the Abbey and plans to dismantle it and furnish manor homes with the raw materials (61). Loftus, calm, can only conclude that his tolerance of this betrayal indicates that in his indifference, Loftus has him-self become God (63). He is free of antipathy now, contemplating the problem of hatred from a detached distance, and resurrects one of the dead bureaucrats as a demonstration to himself of his divinity.

Loftus is no Nietzchean Antichrist: in his self-denial and ascetic devotion he is as far from one of Barker's criminals of the will as one might seek to find. He is a bar to enjoyment, but in his negativity he may be a necessary, though inhu-man, aspect of the self. The suffering offered by Loftus is a doorway into further obscurity, not the clarity of truth. Loftus also generates around him a devoted cult of women, the officials' wives who find themselves first drawn to the site of their husbands' inexplicable deaths and then erotically drawn to Loftus himself. They form a bacchic triad of worshippers shaped by the confluence of loss and desire: each is compelled to offer her body to Loftus and is rebuked as he over-comes his own desire in an act of will (55). The women, who both ache for him sexually and worship him religiously, become a kind of group consciousness, acting as one, speaking like a chorus from Attic tragedy, and becoming enraged like a pack of furies when Loftus resurrects the third Crown Commissioner. As an expression of this anger they move as one and, wordlessly, castrate him, an act of violence that is both symbolic and enigmatic in its overtones, because it is impossible to determine if this is a further act of worship or an antagonistic attempt to escape him. Their desertion of him is a further ambiguous devotion. While they perform this in anger, the castration both literalizes and symbolizes his transformation into the self-abnegation that he performs as prayer. In betraying him, they fulfil him.

One might be entitled to wonder if this represents some kind of reversal of perspective on Barker's part, since it can be taken as a highly Christ-like turn.[29] The final image of the play, of Loftus alone, arms extended as in a crucifixion, castrated, and his bloody loins enclosed in a towel, is a powerful image of beauty and suffering entwined. Anthony Cooter, the priest who purchases the Abbey, curses Loftus for his repressive asceticism while acknowledging its potential necessity: 'I have a feeling / A terrible feeling / That people like you must exist / If only to / Oh / If only to remind us how beautiful life is / YOU HATE LIFE' (46). If his description of Loftus is to be taken as valid, then Loftus the boy god is a manifestation of Necessity and offers something essential and valuable to humanity in his own self-denying inhumanity. Shallow materialism and self-indulgence, unrestrained and untempered by self-scrutiny or conscience, results in an eventual abandonment of a more aesthetic kind of experience: that of beauty. The life-denying self-sacrifice of Loftus is necessary not as an object of admiration and reverence but as a demonstration of one who has renounced life, and who thus reminds onlookers of the beauty of life.

Is the image of Loftus in a position of crucifixion an offering of ecstatic sacrifice to the theatre audience? It is an obscure image and an image of obscurity, perhaps a rendition of the crucifixion as Barker sees it: not as a revelation but a bloody and violent cruelty without redemption. Even Loftus's ecstatic contacts with divinity are subject to a doubleness and to a performativity that suggests that all of existence is a deception and that there is no truth to be revealed lurking behind it. Midway through the play, after suffering one of his painful ecstatic fits, Loftus returns to himself and remarks that, despite appearances, this was not his sickness manifesting itself: '[t]hat was an exquisite reproduction of my sickness [...] I have discovered falseness in myself' (42). It was a false ecstasy, as may be his final crucifixion. For all its concern with Christianity, faith, and the manifestation of God's presence in the human world, *The Seduction of Almighty God* remains a play of darkness rather than light, of betrayal and falsehood rather than truth and apotheosis. The seduction of God by Loftus referred to in the title of the play seems to refer only vaguely to the action of the drama, and demands exegesis. If Loftus seduces God unwittingly, through his abstinence and devotion, then paradoxically he corrupts God through this seduction, for what is a seduction but a dividing of someone from within, a separation of will from desire, the introduction of difference and cruelty into the perfect self-presence of the divine? Seduced by perfection, God becomes imperfect, and as imperfect, less than God. Thus there is no God in the play. The signs of God's attention in the play, the seemingly divine acts, in fact open room for doubt, confusion, and scepticism about God himself. Loftus's ecstasy, his intimation of divine truth, accordingly becomes troubled by a lack of authenticity.

Barker has fashioned a pure tragedy, in which the final image of pain and suffering is ultimately obscure in its significance. The imperative to find meaning here falls on each individual. For my part, I will choose to think of it within the context of theatre itself. The second Crown Commissioner, having arrived at the Abbey and assessed its vastness, looks around and remarks on the space itself: 'Are you never lonely here? […] It's huge […] Huge and Embarrassing' (51). To the bureaucrat for whom reality is understood through the dehumanizing factors of value and economy, the idea of a great, empty space without any obvious utilitarian function is irrational to the point of embarrassment. It is impossible to sit in the audience of a theatre and not realize that this is, of course, a description by the reified, rational mind of the theatre space itself, an open emptiness the value of which cannot be calculated in fiscal terms and which cannot be justified. While Loftus at one point in the play concludes that as long as he is in the Abbey, it cannot be dismantled (52), he finds by the play's end that he is wrong. It is the theatre itself that is under attack here, and Barker's own theatre, which has always struggled to find support, sympathy, and spaces for performance, is allegorized in the Abbey's struggle to survive. Finally, Loftus's ecstatic sacrifice is overdetermined by just such a theatricalization: an experience of sublime pain and suffering rendered in the theatre, an uncompromisingly tragic gesture that dwells outside the mindset of the bookkeeper. What the theatre has to offer is an experience that destroys the balance-sheet mentality where losses and gains reside in different columns and never find coincidence within a single event. The castration of Loftus, performed by his frenzied bacchae, is such a single event: as much a bloody act of Dionysian exultation performed upon a righteous young Pentheus as it is a vision of Christ's passion.

This vacillation between meanings within an image of sacrifice brings us to the same place we arrived at with the analysis of Hare's *Gethsemane* and Lori's act of renunciation, interpreted through Christ's test. It is also here that the contrast between Hare and Barker is most apparent. In Hare, the ambiguity of sense is comforting, a blessing. In Barker it is a terrible, pressing imperative: equally a curse. Hare's protagonists are, finally, saints, both standing aside from his society yet embodying a social promise inherent in their goodness and values, an ultimate sign of their sociality. Barker's characters are an expressionistic X-ray of

Hare's realism: criminal-saints. Hare sees the role of the playwright as communication with his audience. Barker describes his hope that his theatre will engender *anxiety* in its audience.[30] As Barker sees it, the audience's potential anxiety in fact arises from the refusal of realism, a realism that is the benchmark of Hare's drama. Barker writes: 'This tension is the effect of *failing to recognize* an action, a character or a type, an uneasy rocking of all popular cultural modes. [...] [E]lements of the unconscious are stimulated which are denied in humanist drama' (*Arguments* 111). However, the inducement of anxiety in the audience is not an end in itself but a passage to an aesthetic experience unique to the tragic, both 'the ecstasy of moral uncertainty' (113) and what Barker calls the 'State of Loss.' This concept encompasses 'a state of lost morality, an ethical vacuum, a denial, a rebuke to order, a melancholy and a pain. It is a revelation of the essential terror of the world, and an abyss. [...] The Theatre of Catastrophe is not the comfort of a cruel world, but the cruelty of the world made manifest and found to be – *beautiful*' (116). Through the vehicle of anxiety, the Theatre of Catastrophe offers a passage through pain and cruelty into an experience of the beautiful.

A Lacanian intervention articulates how the experience of anxiety may lead to an experience of the beautiful. Dylan Evans explains that for Freud, anxiety is a response to trauma, such as a loss of or separation from the primary caregiver, while for Lacan it is something related but more ambivalent, namely the failure of symbolic castration itself, which provokes anxiety: 'All desire arises from lack, and anxiety arises when this lack is itself lacking; anxiety is the lack of a lack. Anxiety is not the absence of the breast, but its enveloping presence; it is the possibility of its absence which is, in fact, that which saves us from anxiety' (Evans 12). Anxiety is the response to an unresolved relationship on the part of the subject to its own unconscious desire: anxiety is the disavowal of unconscious desire. For Barker's plays to provoke anxiety means that they must unsettle the narcissism of the ego, an ego that seeks to close itself off from the experience of the unconscious and the traumatic wound of loss. This is Barker's social diagnosis of English ideology: it denies desire, that which unsettles the self. Anxiety, the unsettling of certainty, is a psychic chafing of this denial.

Meanwhile, for Lacan the beautiful is not an apprehension of 'ideal beauty' but a sign of 'both a presence and a pure absence,' an apprehension 'at the very point of the transition between life and death' (*The Seminar of Jacques Lacan Book VII* 297). Lacan uses the example of Dutch still life painting to evoke the idea of the experience of the beautiful as art that 'both reveals and hides that within it which constitutes a threat, denouement, unfolding, or decomposition' (298). This has a particular relationship to tragedy, at least as exemplified for Lacan by *Antigone*. He posits that the 'image' of Antigone exerts a fascination that is an unbearable splendour. The function of this beautiful image is to purge us and purify us of the order of the imaginary, the register of the ego, by attracting our desire (247–8). The effect of this beauty on desire is not to satisfy it, however, 'for one cannot say that it is completely extinguished by the apprehension of beauty. It continues on its way, but now more than elsewhere, it has a sense of being taken in, and this is manifested by the splendor and magnificence of the zone that draws it on' (249). Desire is led on into the zone that Lacan calls man's 'second death, the signifier of his desire, his visible desire' (298). This is the function of the beautiful: 'to reveal to us the site of man's relationship to his own death, and to reveal it to us only in a blinding flash' (295). This is not literal, biological death, but the subject's relationship to death, the mortification of the self that is the truth of the subject's desire.

In my analysis I have charted a path through a series of plays representative of Barker's investment in the tragic and in my readings I have tried to emphasize the striking contradictions of these plays, while resisting the scholarly temptation to resolve or dismiss those contradictions. To do so would be to avoid the anxiety of uncertainty and to embrace the imaginary confidence of the ego. Instead, I have observed the modernist silence of *Claw* in the face of the false optimism of English life, the open, tragic contradictions of socialism in *Fair Slaughter*, the tension between nihilist and optimistic models of betrayal in *That Good Between Us*, and the tragic collision between historical necessity and individual will in *The Power of the Dog*. In the Theatre of Catastrophe proper we find Susan Bradshaw's inhuman and unrecognizable gestures of tragic affirmation in *Victory*, and moreover the conflict between Bradshaw's wilful acts of anti-history and her daughter's perpetuation of the 'Harmonia Britannia.' *The Castle* demonstrates how desire emerges in moments of catastrophe as a counter-utopian force that wrecks social projects. We see the fraudulent integrity of the heroes of *The Europeans*, for whom betrayal is integrity and the cosmos is *Unheimlichkeit*, and the 'necessary accident' in *The Possibilities*, the intrusion of the unconscious into the contradictory fabric of History itself. Tragic experience is found in the 'extimacy' of Gertrude's cry, an image of ecstatic desire that is at once within and without her, and thus the ecstasy of the loss of agency, the impossible, tragic identity between fidelity and betrayal, authenticity and fraudulence. *Dead Hands* reveals the tragic as an opening to the mortification of the self, while the castrated Christ is at once an image of both a true and false messiah, an eminently reversible image of sacrifice without redemption, yet one that still embodies such a promise. It is by embracing these contradictions rather than resolving them or retreating from them that we glimpse, however fleetingly, the possibility of the beautiful in Barker's theatre.

Edward Bond:
Tragedy and Postmodernity,
or, The Promethean Impulse

One of Edward Bond's earliest pieces of juvenilia is an unproduced play for radio entitled simply 'The Tragedy.'[1] Throughout his career, Bond has never ceased to explore the importance of tragedy and tragic experience from the perspective of a highly politicized, socialist playwright. Bond, born in 1934 to a working-class family in North London, is slightly older than Hare and Barker, and would typically have been addressed first in this book's analysis, particularly considering how Bond's playwriting work at the Royal Court Theatre in the 1960s both helped clear a space for the other writers here considered and also served, to some degree, as a point of contestation for their early careers.[2] I address Bond third in order to highlight an ongoing argument about the tragic in this book, a logical progression rather than a chronological one. The tragic serves as a pebble dropped in a pond, rippling outwards across broader and broader horizons of interpretation.[3] With Hare, we saw the tragic within a framework of realism, functioning as an exposure and distending of the middle-class ideology of Englishness; with Barker, the tragic moved beyond an estrangement of ideology into an attack upon it with the psychic weapon of the unconscious, that which realism excludes from its borders. Barker also opened the question of the place of the tragic within History. Bond places the tragic within a still broader social horizon, beyond ideology and Englishness, mapping the tragic onto issues of class consciousness, capitalism, and postmodernity. In other words, with Bond, we arrive at a vision of the tragic within a traditionally political horizon of interpretation.[4]

Here, I will analyse Bond's early explorations of tragedy in *Saved, Lear, Bingo*, and *The Fool*, plays written during his time at the Royal Court Theatre; then consider *Restoration*, another Royal Court production staged shortly after Thatcher's election and which terminated his relationship with the Royal Court; *The War Plays* trilogy, which ended his relationship with the Royal Shakespeare

Company; and then consider his more recent plays, which have been performed by Theatre-in-Education groups, community theatre groups, and companies outside the United Kingdom. Once heroized as a paradigm of the socialist playwright in the 1970s, Bond became increasingly a discomfort to a more conservative theatre establishment in the 1980s due to his dedication to socialism, until he finally turned his back on professional English theatre.[5] Long self-exiled from the mainstream British venues, Bond has over the years found alternate venues for his work with the children's touring company Big Brum and with the Théâtre Nationale de la Colline in Paris,[6] though recently the commercial London stages have seen new productions of his 1970s work, such as the recent production of *The Sea* in 2008 and a cycle of six plays from throughout Bond's career, produced at the Cock Tavern Theatre in October through November 2010. Most notably, in February 2012, Patrick Stewart played Shakespeare in *Bingo* at the Young Vic. Yet Bond remains irascible, tenacious, unbending in his commitments and intimidating in his socialist idealism. He is mercilessly political and harshly critical of other theatre artists, garnering a controversial reputation, some of which is consciously self-generated, that precedes him.

He is also, like Barker, a remarkable polemicist, re-reader, and theoretician of his own work. This tendency to theorize his own work can readily be understood as an attempt on Bond's part to pre-empt or control the interpretation and reception of his plays. In this regard, I am of the same opinion as Michael Mangan, who points out that Bond's essays

> are not repositories of simple truths about 'what the plays really mean,' and anyone looking for this in them will almost certainly go away disappointed and probably more confused than before. Bond's polemical essays should be considered – the same way as his directing of his own plays should be considered – not as attempts to tie down the meanings of his play, but as further explorations in themselves of the questions and issues which the plays raise. (3)

The complexity, ambiguity, and intensity of his commentaries may either alienate or captivate readers, but rarely does what he says simplify our understanding of his plays. Bond's extensive theorizing not only about his own plays but also about the nature of the human itself is essential to his politics, because this theorizing is an assertion that the human is not self-evident. In contrast, consider that David Hare's paradigm of the human is precisely and specifically untheoretical: it is ultimately a view of the human as straightforward and transparent, a given and easily recognizable quantity. Hare's insistence on a theory of the unconscious merely supports what is in the final instance a middle-class paradigm of humanity as 'realistic' and suitably represented within the techniques of realism. Hare's view of the unconscious and of the tragic are familiar and verifiable by commonplace middle-class experience (Freudian slips, desire, blind spots in our knowledge), and this is confirmed by his view of a play as a straightforward moment of communication between stage and audience in which the receiver is a crucial component in the message. Theory is ultimately unnecessary in Hare's playwriting, because his characters are finally recognizable to his audience, even when they behave in irrational ways. Thus what is most crucial about Bond (and also Barker and his extensive theorizing of the human) is that the human is precisely not recognizable within the paradigms of realism and does not behave in a 'realistic' manner. While the topics Bond explores in his essays may often seem tangential to the dramas, I find the ideas salient and acutely relevant to understanding how the tragic functions within his work, particularly because his polemics, like Barker's, differentiate his plays from the traditions of realism and naturalism that dominate the stage, and within which Bond's work might be mistakenly included.

Saved

Consider, for instance, an early example of Bond's polemical commentary. When Bond describes his seminal 1965 play *Saved* as 'irresponsibly optimistic,' in the original published Author's Note to the play (Appendix, *Plays: One* 309), he seems to offer to the spectator a key to deciphering the political message of the play. Yet as Luc Gilleman appropriately points out, the image of a broken chair being mended at the play's conclusion, while apparently intended to 'press this point home,' is overshadowed by the notorious scene of a baby being stoned in its pram at the end of the first half ("'Juss Round an' Round'" 69, 72). Michael Mangan, in contrast, argues that if *Saved* does not quite succeed it is because the play lacks analysis of what it shows, not 'because the low-key "optimism" of the play's final moments is insufficient to balance the trauma of the play's earlier violence. The smallness of the gesture of mending the chair does not diminish its theatrical power: indeed, the fact that it is such a small and concentrated gesture is part of its intensity' (17). Mangan's study of Bond is important for its emphasis that even in an early play like *Saved*, which inhabits the trappings of kitchen sink realism, Bond's theatre is highly formalist, symbolic, and anti-psychological. This is an uneasy place to inhabit for a political playwright who represents working-class characters. Despite Bond's socialism and the class consciousness of his dramatic content, the relationship of his plays to social reality does not function mimetically or transparently, but highly formally.

The concept of the tragic, particularly but not only as Bond theorizes it himself, opens his plays to such formal political interpretation. At the conclusion of

his insightful study, Mangan observes that there are images like 'the faint optimism of the mended chair' running throughout Bond's oeuvre, images that
'open out the meanings of the plays and their arguments' (96) and gestures that
'make a connection between the biggest philosophical and humanitarian questions and the material details of everyday life' (94). Bond's understanding of the
tragic provides a very specific way of opening out such meaning. In a recent
essay called 'Modern Drama' (in the collection *The Hidden Plot*), Bond describes the importance of small objects in his plays. An important, extended
quotation from this essay serves to unify various strands of his thought and is
particularly illustrative of his dramaturgy:

> The experiences the world offers – and impedes – in the child's mind are freedom
> and happiness, which later in adults have the rational form of justice. Freedom and
> happiness are necessarily associated with the tragic, with offering and impeding.
> This freedom-tragic is not abstract. It is the experience created by situations and
> objects. For the child the objects are small and concrete: existential utensils. [...]
> Although the objects are trivial the response to them is absolute. Justice is total
> whether it concerns the trivial or the great. Usually in life and drama justice is as-
> sociated with an 'object-moment,' an object made critically consequential or re-
> vealing by a situation. The object-moment is the site of the freedom-tragic and its
> paradoxes, the site of the pleasure of freedom and the suffering of the tragic (frus-
> tration, mortality, the loss of freedom or its prospect). ('Modern Drama' 15)

Strikingly, and unusually, Bond is suggesting that in their investments in small
objects and in conflicts with each other over small objects, what is at stake for
his characters is their very humanity – their active self-humanizations, their
strivings for freedom – which is an expression of the need for justice. Bond is
encouraging a dialectical vision here, a mediation between the particular and
the general, the very small and the very big, within intersubjective relationships. The tragic for him is thus a site of both necessity and freedom, loss and
gain, inhumanity and humanity, failure and success. What Bond at an earlier
stage in his thinking called 'irresponsibly optimistic' has been given as a less
ambiguous but more deliberately contradictory formulation: the freedom-
tragic – not optimism, but the struggle to be human.

Saved's protagonist, Len, is an intractably giving and considerate young man
who finds himself in a relationship with a young woman named Pam and living
in a small flat with her parents and her newborn child, who may or may not be
Len's progeny. As Pam rejects Len and seeks attention from his friend Fred, Len
shows no signs of jealousy or anger, instead demonstrating reasonable open-
mindedness and compassion, in particular towards Pam's child and the need to

care for the infant. While Len's instances of goodness throughout the play are numerous and evident to the point of being maddening to Pam, he is not an impossibly utopian character: he secretly watches the infant being stoned rather than intervening, and his presence in the flat introduces strife to the household and creates conflicts. As a lodger who is welcome because he is employed and pays rent, but who is not officially a member of the family, Len's outsider status in the home is the abrasive grit that drives the play's action, and it is a situation that Bond himself interprets in explicitly Oedipal terms: Len arrives in the home as a part of his sexual maturing, snogging with Pam on the couch as her father, Harry, pokes his head in the room, interrupting them. Later in the play Len finds himself in a subtly eroticized situation with Pam's mother, Mary, which eventually leads to a violent confrontation with Harry. This recognizable dramatic pattern is broken by the fact that Len defuses the conflict, and the problems are resolved through communication and understanding. It is thus an 'Oedipus comedy' (Appendix, *Plays: One* 311) without the cathartic moment of *pathos* or purging violence that Aristotle dictates as necessary to a tragic plot.

While the stoning of the child, the subject of great controversy and debate when *Saved* first appeared, is notorious for its graphic imagery, it is not the play's most original or groundbreaking invention. This distinction belongs to the final scene of the play, an almost wholly wordless pantomime in which Pam, Mary, and Harry silently go about mundane, isolated activities such as reading the *Radio Times*, tidying the living room, and filling in football coupons. Meanwhile Len goes about noisily mending a chair that lost a leg in an earlier argument in which Harry confronted Mary about her supposed infidelity. Symbolically, the mending of the chair is the play's most pragmatically utopian gesture, represent-ing Len's indomitable determination to repair any damage suffered by the house-hold. It absorbs his attention completely, as in the absence of a hammer he is forced to slam the chair down loudly upon the floor in an attempt to drive the loose leg into place. Yet even the mundane act of mending a chair is rendered strange, intense, and significant by both the near absence of words from the scene, itself a forceful break from realism, and the bizarre convolutions Len twists himself into as he struggles with the chair. He turns the chair upside down and right side up, sits upon it facing the audience, and finally crouches next to it on the floor, facing away from the audience, one arm wrapped around the back of the chair, one hand touching the floor, and his head resting upon the seat of the chair. It is the combination of silence and Len's physical contortions that make this a site of the freedom-tragic, a locus where we are invited to grasp the magnitude of the stakes lurking within the mundane.

This is a uniquely theatrical vocabulary of gestures and actions, in which meaning and content are liberated from the vehicle of language and instead conveyed through the movement of the human body and its interaction with its environment. A chair is one of the most elemental and seemingly organic pieces of human technology, shaped by human reason to receive the human form in a manner that seems entirely purposeful, natural, organic, and intentional, following the contours of human joints and offering to the human body a place of rest in its self-made environment that is harmonious and liberating. Len, struggling thoughtfully and patiently to mend the chair, creates an image of the human seeking that simple, mundane place of rest in the universe, a momentary home. He seems to find it not through the traditional position of rest on the chair but through an estranging image: sitting on the floor next to it, head at rest on the seat as if in slumber. In being positioned facing upstage from the audience, Len is perhaps depersonalized but also rendered vulnerable and available to the eyes of onlookers. There is something mortal and inherently human about the back of a head presented to our conscious attention. Finally, the chair onstage, ostended in this way, evokes a theatrical awareness of the consequences of sitting onstage. As Bert O. States remarks in *Great Reckonings in Little Rooms*, the historical moment when characters begin to sit onstage marks the transition from the mythological world of high tragedy to the merging of the human with her material and social environment. When tragic characters sit, they become more human and descend into their environments, becoming less god-like, increasingly mortal, and closer to the comic. Surrounded by indifferent, private isolation on the part of Mary, Pam, and Harry, Len's mending of the chair represents *Saved*'s irresponsible optimism. Bond locates the greatest humanizing gestures, the most transcendent of deeds performed by characters as a means of escaping their alienation, in the most mundane and everyday of activities. It is tragic because in this final scene Len is, in Bond's words, living with people 'at their worst and most hopeless' (309), and still he maintains a stubbornly realistic hope, drawing affirmation *from* the negativity of his situation, not in spite of it, finding humanity within an everyday domestic object.

Lear

This focus on the smallest of gestures perhaps accounts for the well-known change made to the published script of *Lear* (1971), in which Lear's final action, the attempt to personally dismantle with a dull shovel the immense wall that has been his life-long political project, leads to his being shot by an onlooker. Between the first published script and the version anthologized in Bond's collected plays, Lear's death was rewritten: originally, he keeps working for a few moments after being shot, while in the revised play Lear drops dead immediately. It is clear that for Bond these physical details of movement, action, and gesture are deeply meaningful, perhaps more so than the readily understandable imagery and ideas available within dramatic dialogue. Bond comprehends that the dramatic performance of death is laden with geological strata of meanings, concepts long sedimented from abuse, misuse, and cliché, none more easy or obvious than the idea of the attenuated, noble death, the struggle to continue the final task even while life seeps from the wound, the glorification of suffering and pain as elevating and ennobling of the tragic hero. While it would seem that Bond, in his refashioning, refining, and purifying of Shakespeare's play, still wishes to see Lear as transformed by his suffering and endowed with knowledge and wisdom by the play's end, the playwright is also at pains to purge the drama of false hope. Whereas Len continues to mend the chair at the end of *Saved*, Lear is felled instantly with a single gunshot, although he significantly leaves the shovel stuck upright in the earth. Unafraid to speak of the importance of hope, Bond is nevertheless deeply suspicious of the salving, sedative qualities of such optimism in the theatre. 'The ideal only has a practical significance when it's embodied in the mundane,' he writes ('Introduction: The Rational Theatre' xiv). The shovel, stiff and upright in the earth, is perhaps the glimmer of hope in *Lear*, a humanization of the tool rather than an ennobling of the man. If *Saved* is a working-class tragedy with a stoically optimistic ending, then *Lear* offers the possibility of a pure tragedy, a materialist tragedy without the distortions of ruling-class bias.

This inversion may also help us to understand the conscious artifice with which Bond infuses the plot, language, and characterizations in *Lear*. Gone are the intimate, human details of lived life as he demonstrates it through the language, attitudes, and behaviour of his working-class characters. Instead, *Lear* presents a strangely theatrical realm, a kind of alternate reality in which historical situation is suspended and anachronism proliferates, in which subtext and indirection of speech are effaced in favour of a harshly presentational style. Characters announce themselves with cool directness, speak simply and clearly, and any inner dissembling is explained openly and obviously to the audience in broad, artificially theatrical asides. We will not, then, be offered a series of psychologically tormented aristocratic characters with complex interiorities here. There will be nothing traditionally 'human' about Lear or his scheming daughters Bodice and Fontanelle with which a sympathetic theatre audience might yearn to identify. Paradigmatic of the bourgeois valorization of conscience and the tragic torments of consciousness, such a representation of the self as a deep and bottomless well of introspection is wilfully abandoned by Bond as useless to a socialist project.

Lear demonstrates that for the class-conscious socialist in the early 1970s, tragic paradigms were both the problem and the solution, and traditional tragedy was a form to be inhabited and worked through dialectically rather than rejected altogether. While *Lear* may be misunderstood as a paradigmatic instance of 'bardicide' (as may *Bingo*), this estimation does not accord with the socialist praise Bond heaps on Shakespeare, whom Bond describes as a playwright of profound passion and conscience, one whose intellect and acumen allowed him to level a trenchant gaze upon the historical contradictions of his own society and describe, in various forms throughout his career, those problems, while nevertheless remaining enclosed within his own class bias. This bias prevented Shakespeare from envisioning solutions to the problems that he described. Shakespeare asked the question of what justice is and what a just society might be, but could not answer these questions because the only justice that existed in his world was the justice of the ruling class. 'And although he could not answer his questions he learned to bear them with stoical dignity: this is at least an assurance that he was facing the right problems – otherwise his dramatic resolutions would have been sentimental and trite,' Bond surmises ('Introduction: The Rational Theatre' ix–x). While he could not solve the problems because no solutions existed in his time, Shakespeare, in bearing the questions honestly and directly, thus suffered nobly and tragically by refusing to lie (xi).

Accordingly, the political contradiction that Bond sees as crucial for his revision of *Lear* is a dialectical materialist problem, one understandable only with the hindsight available to the socialist looking back on the failure of socialism in the twentieth century: 'It is so easy to subordinate justice to power, but when this happens power takes on the dynamics and dialectics of aggression, and then nothing is really changed. Marx did not know about this problem and Lenin discovered it when it was too late' (Author's Preface, *Lear* 11). Bond demonstrates this problem through a dramatic action in which a tyrant is overthrown by his scheming and power-hungry daughters, tyrants who are themselves subsequently defeated by a civil insurrection, the leaders of which engage in violent and dehumanizing rebellion as a means to their end. It is these rebels, for example, who have Lear blinded as a means of rendering him politically ineffective without taking the drastic action of having him executed. Once in power, the rebels construct a government that is repressive and totalitarian, abusing this means in the name of a worthy end and continuing the construction of Lear's wall, believing it is necessary to protect them from their enemies while they build a good government. Lear himself eventually learns that the wall itself is the problem and that nothing will change until it is pulled down. The wall is ultimately both an inner and outer prison for society and the self: 'I left my prison, pulled it down, broke the key, and still I'm a prisoner. I hit my head against a wall all the time. There's a wall everywhere. I'm buried alive in a wall,' he explains near the end of the play (*Lear* 94). Having escaped his own inner wall by the play's end, Lear attacks the wall surrounding his society.

Lear has the broad contours and archetypal imagery of a modern political parable, hinged upon the central image of the huge wall, that most modern of human phenomena and paradigmatic of a key political use of power and force: employed to divide, enclose, contain, exclude, and otherwise aggressively delineate the borders that separate human beings from each other and maintain privilege and resources for some and not for others. The wall is a political tool for possession and the maintenance of property. It is the instrument of alienation within capitalism, serving at once to imprison those within and those without, and in that sense the wall is an image of the tragedy of capitalism. And most challengingly, while the play eschews psychology or realism, there is a relationship mapped between Lear's selfhood and the play's larger dramatic action, a connection suggested by the idea that the wall is both an inner and outer alienation. Thus, while he borrows his dramatic structure from Shakespeare, Bond's rejection of realistic representation of character complicates the connection between the play's central tragic character and the larger political themes.

Jenny S. Spencer's detailed and articulate reading of *Lear* through the lens of theories of tragedy suggests that this is Bond's most recognizable and traditional inhabitation of tragic form. Bond's play, like Shakespeare's, is about 'the causes and consequences of intense human suffering' as explored through a protagonist who gains 'some insight' in the play (79). Her analysis is most illuminating when she suggests that Bond was intervening into two popular interpretations of *King Lear* that were dominant in 1971, both of which explored the topic that is central to the concerns of the present study: the meaning of suffering in human life. The publication of Jan Kott's *Shakespeare Our Contemporary* in French in 1962 had purportedly influenced Peter Brook's Beckettian absurdist production of the play at the Royal Shakespeare Company the same year (Spencer 80). At stake is the incoherence of the original play in the face of crucial tragic questions, specifically whether *King Lear* presents a Christian redemptive reading of the meaning of suffering through a providential vision of human history (based on A.C. Bradley's reading of the play), or an absurd 'anatomy of a cruel and indifferent universe [and] inexplicable suffering at the hands of some inexorable "mechanism" beyond human control' (80). Spencer offers to us the insight that the meaning of suffering is crucial to consider for the socialist playwright, and that Bond's *Lear*, unsurprisingly, presents a tragedy whose action is not 'tragically inevitable' (81). Thus Bond rejects both Bradley and Kott/Brook. Moreover, Bond's Lear becomes a 'militant hero' and his final gesture in the play is the result of a long and arduous process of gradual, partial enlightenment and the learning of compassion. While Lear's attempt to dismantle the wall is not a constructive 'moral action' indicative of class consciousness (88), the gesture of defiance nevertheless breaks from tragic inevitability and hands responsibility for social change over to the audience (92).

Spencer's essential study of Bond is laudable for its desire to search for models of moral, ethical, and political behaviour in Bond's work. Yet the implication of such analysis is that the questions asked of the play remain those asked of social realism, an approach that sits uneasily next to an understanding of the drama as a tragedy.[7] What makes the mining of the play for models of political action problematic is not just the tragic action of the drama but the representation of Lear as a character, which Spencer notes is a key break from the Shakespearean precedent: 'Bond's dialogue constantly points outward toward social relationship and away from the murky depth of psychological interiority; even Lear's most reflective moments starkly present rather than psychologically create an inward-looking subjectivity' (89). While Lear does look inward, he does not do it realistically but theatrically. In short, there is no realistic subtext, and finally, no traditional interiority on display here. Yet this innovation affects everything in the play, because Lear remains a drama about a tragic protagonist and his humanizing turn towards insight.

Thus my argument is that the political content of the play is found not in the actions and behaviour of the characters but in the representational mode that Bond forges as a critical intervention into the ideology of the human as a paradigm of bourgeois consciousness. His politicized formalism shows a vision of the tragic human that breaks from its Shakespearean precedent. When Lear is betrayed at the beginning of the play he flees to the woods and is given shelter by an unwitting young swineherd and his wife, Cordelia. In the mental crisis that results from his betrayal, Lear begins to see himself as an abandoned dog turned out by his daughters. It is the first sign of the descent into madness that eventually seizes him. From the swineherd Lear begins to learn compassion and the peace that comes from a quiet and simple life conducted at a remove from society. This idyll is shortlived: the first act closes with the arrival of his daughters' soldiers, who kill the swineherd, rape Cordelia, and seize Lear. Lear is tried and here displays the tragic protagonist's apparent flight from coherence that is in actual fact an entry into a deeper lucidity. He refuses to recognize his daughters and when shown a mirror denies that the face within is that of the King: 'This is a little cage of bars with an animal in it' (49). The animal he sees in the mirror is imprisoned behind bars and must be released. This image of the tortured and caged animal plagues Lear throughout the play.

In Lear's imagery we find an ambivalence in Bond's work, a contradiction perhaps, that his own socialist project struggles with, for although Bond in his recent writings is at pains to insist that human alienation is not an alienation from our human nature, but rather the social condition of being human itself, there seems to be an irresistible impulse in a play like *Lear* and in its prefatory material to fashion human beings as, essentially, a kind of animal and as underpinned by biological imperatives and millions of years of evolution. He writes, for example, '[W]hy do we behave worse to one another than other animals? We live in ways for which we are not designed and so our daily existence interferes with our natural functioning, and this activates our natural response to threat: aggression' (Author's Preface, *Lear* 4). The unjust, class-based society is at heart an unnatural way to live, and for this reason it distorts and enchains human lives: '[T]he child soon learns that it is born into a strange world and not the world it evolved for: we are no longer born free' (6–7). This is of course a tragic problem and a tragic paradigm of the human, but Bond's logic bears all the marks of the Enlightenment thinker's mythological valorization of the state of nature as a Rousseau-esque paradise.[8] There is no sign here even of the modernist, Brechtian twist on such alienation within capitalism. While Bond claims that he rejects the notion of original sin as just a rationalization of violence into an inevitable part of human nature ('On Violence' 10), there are strong images in *Lear* evoking the idea that natural pre-lapsarian human innocence and goodness have been corrupted by humanity.

The most profound break from the realistic representation of character in *Lear* is the appearance of a ghost who serves as a kind of alter ego to the deposed King, and this ghost also serves as a theatrical counterweight to Lear's naturalistic language. In his cell, Lear is visited by apocalyptic visions of the disasters that will occur if the caged animal is not released, and it is here that he is visited by the ghost of the swineherd. The ghost pleads to stay with Lear and becomes his companion, an expressionistic manifestation of some aspect of Lear's damaged mind healing itself through the estrangement of aspects of his psyche: 'I had a terrible pain in my head and he stopped it and now I must help him,' Lear remarks of the ghost (65); 'He saved my mind when I went mad' (68). Conscious that he is responsible for the fate of the swineherd's ghost, Lear now owes him help, care, and kindness. Yet the ghost is also an aspect of himself that Lear must gradually lose as he gains insight: imprisoned by the rebels, Lear observes the corpse of his executed daughter Fontanelle and, to the ghost's dismay, begins a mental process of transformation. Lear realizes that he, ultimately, created and destroyed her, and that she was beautiful, though he never knew it (72–4). 'I must open my eyes and see!' he cries, moments before he is surgically and hygienically blinded as a means of making him politically ineffective (74, 77). Lear's *anagnorisis* here is crucial to his humanization, but it also entails the slow loss of the ghost, whom he sees as a kind of surrogate son.

While Lear himself seems trapped within the rhetoric of natural man, struggling with the estrangement of aspects of his selfhood that are perceived as animalistic, Bond provides a small hint that there might be another vision of the human available in the play, which is located in this strange, surreal, and highly Shakespearean conceit of the ghost of the swineherd. Lear makes mistakes throughout the play that leave others dead and lives ruined, but Bond assigns a special status to the death of the young swineherd, who is murdered by soldiers looking for Lear: 'I think [Lear] had to destroy the innocent boy. Some things were lost to us long ago as a species, but we all seem to have to live through part of the act of losing them. We have to do this without guilt or rancour or callousness – or socialized morality' (Author's Preface, *Lear* 12). Becoming the being he is by play's end means that Lear must actively repeat at the psychic level the experience of loss or separation that Bond imagines is the legacy of alienation endowed by our biological heritage. Yet there is a difference between the two: as a conscious being, to actively experience loss is to affirm the necessity of this experience for the humanization of the self. It is to make of loss an act of agency, and Bond hints that this may be the importance of the ghost to Lear in the play. It is not a question of bad conscience or *ressentiment*, Bond explains.

There is, then, a loss of innocence or loss of self that humanizes one's subjectivity rather than tormenting one with class-based guilt and morality. Lear's experiences with the ghost are an expressionistic process of loss. The ghost tries earnestly to tempt Lear into a happy and long life of peace and quiet, forgetting about 'crowds, wars, arguments' (96), but Lear's growing political awareness and his frustration with the repressive bureaucratic military regime that has sprung from the rebellion seem to wither and desiccate the ghost. Over the course of the play the ghost appears to age and decay, until by the end of the play the former swineherd is attacked by pigs. Having come full circle, he is able to die, and Lear encourages him to do so. The gesture seems to be one of avowing and owning the experience of loss. In this highly original and unexpected piece of theatricality, we are offered an expressionistic insight into the experience of selfhood on the part of a tragic protagonist, an insight that avoids the pitfalls of bourgeois interiority while nevertheless demonstrating how a man learns the political necessity of pity for others without the sentimental valorization of his tortured selfhood as an end in itself. A ghost is not an animal in a cage, a ghost is rather a sign of *différance* and Derridean spectrality. While Lear may comprehend himself as an imprisoned natural creature that must be released so he can be whole and free, *Lear* itself shows him to be a being who must own the division and loss embodied in the ghost for whom he has come to feel compassion and pity, emotions that are no more fully avowed than when he releases the ghost into the death from which it has come. It is a theatrical image of mourning as a self-humanizing act.

Bingo

For Bond, the strength of Shakespeare's art is found in his ability to ask questions about his society rather than provide clear and didactic answers. Within such a paradigm of the aesthetic, the function of art as a reflection of its ideological, cultural, and economic surroundings must be seen as a revelation of real contradictions, a contradiction in the realm of the social being a problem without an existing solution. A real contradiction is specifically some conflict that creates a rift or a gap in society, such as the divide between classes, something that cannot be corrected without radical social transformation at the most fundamental level. In other words, art's function is to make clear the problems of society and to resist the representation of easy resolutions, since no such solutions exist. Shakespeare, in Bond's opinion, bore the questions stoically: '[I]f you understand so much about suffering and violence, the partiality of authority, and the final innocence of all defenceless things *and yet* live in a time when you can do nothing about it – then you feel the suffering you describe, and your writing mimics that suffering. When you write on that level you must tell the truth' (Introduction, *Bingo* 4). To suffer a question, to be conscious of a contradiction for which there exists no solution in one's time and place is to grapple with a mental alienation against which one cannot triumph. In Bond's paradigm, Shakespeare the artist becomes a tragic figure himself, when viewed through the lens of his art.

Thus the play *Bingo* (1973) is a poetic distillation of Bond's theory of the social function of the artist. Bond portrays an aged Shakespeare as a man so tormented by his own clear vision and his sympathy for the suffering of the poor and underprivileged that when he looks back retrospectively on his own economic success and privilege, he realizes that he has wasted his life. He is destroyed by the compassion that marks his plays with their profound humanity. 'If children go in rags we make the wind' (63), Shakespeare explains before taking his own life, voicing a sentiment that seems to echo King Lear's most profoundly lucid moments of empathy. *Bingo*'s action concerns Shakespeare's historical participation in the Welcombe enclosure, a financial scheme in which wealthy landowner William Combe and his associates sought to enclose, with hedges and ditches, common land from which Shakespeare drew rents. The eviction of the peasants who were to be displaced from the land would cost Shakespeare lost rent, and so in return for a signed document saying he would not oppose the enclosure, Shakespeare received from the enclosers a guarantee against potential financial loss. Bond finds in Shakespeare's action a troubling contradiction: that a man who articulated in his plays the kind of compassion for the destitute that one finds in *King Lear* could, when his own financial security was threatened, side with the wealthy rather than the poor. The problem that torments Shakespeare in the play is elementary: how does one remain human within a capitalist society, since capitalism makes the dehumanizing reification of human relationships essential to society's functioning?

Bingo is notably balanced in its assessment of this modernization: as Combe observes, this kind of transformation means that in the short term some will suffer, while in the long run the town as a whole stands to benefit. The play does not demonstrate the effects of the enclosure on the town (which, as Bond points out, was resisted and not completed until 1775 [Introduction, *Bingo* 6]), and it seems more salient to attend to the disenfranchised figure in the play that is the direct beneficiary of Combe's modern treatment of the poor. In the opening scene of the play a young transient woman arrives in Shakespeare's garden, seeking charity. The vagrant is apprehended by Combe and whipped for leaving her own parish, a treatment she has received before and which she claims has given her serious physical and mental damage. When we encounter her again half a year later, she has survived the winter through the charity of Shakespeare's old gardener. She is tormented by shaking as a result of the further whipping she received, and it appears that the mental damage she has suffered has unbalanced her and now provokes her to set fires around the town. Once more Shakespeare tries to offer her charity, but his daughter Judith betrays the girl to Combe and when the transient woman is caught again, she is hanged and gibbeted as an arsonist.

Sitting near the corpse, Shakespeare appears to reach a point of simultaneous incomprehension and comprehension, as he is no longer able to reconcile the sheer quantity of human suffering he has witnessed in his lifetime, of which this dead woman serves as a visual metonym for the audience, with the fact that some few are privileged to benefit and profit from the suffering of many: 'What does it cost to stay alive?' he wonders, searching his thoughts for the 'right question,' one that will articulate the mental anguish that torments him (40, 41). He explains, 'I'm stupefied by the suffering I've seen. The shapes huddled in misery that twitch away when you step over them. [...] What it costs to starve people' (40). A long monologue in which he describes the gory violence of bear baiting in London allegorizes the dehumanizing treatment of the disenfranchised poor by the rich and powerful that Shakespeare has witnessed and to which he has been a party. His security, comfort, and humanity have been achieved through the dehumanization and brutalization of others, even if he himself never raised a hand against them. This fact is the contradiction that he struggles to voice, but it is also a riddle that he cannot solve and that, in his humanism, he cannot attribute responsibility for to a divine power: 'There's no higher wisdom of silence. No face brooding over the water. [...] No hand leading the waves to the shore as if it's saving a dog from the sea' (40). Perhaps his most trenchant and disquieting realization is that '[e]very writer writes in other men's blood. The trivial, and the real. There's nothing else to write in' (57). Within this formulation, art is made of suffering itself and thus is inherently tragic in its form: shaped from the substance of loss.

If the writer always writes in other men's blood then the onus to tell the truth and eschew all illusions is paramount, and it must be this idea, articulated within the play, that motivated Bond to fashion *Bingo* as a seemingly pessimistic drama. *Bingo* is a sombre, overtly tragic piece of work, its soundscape punctuated by isolated chapel bells and telling silences. Shakespeare himself is a largely silent, muted figure, spending much of the play sitting in isolation from the surroundings of his household, New Place, as if the weight of his experience and understanding has rendered him inarticulate. When queried by Ben Jonson about his current writing projects, Shakespeare asserts that he has '[n]othing to say' and acknowledges that he is '[w]ritten out' (43). The play as a whole resembles a character study of an artist whose voice and actions are stifled while around him life, his household, and history march on. In the play's conclusion he indicts himself not for his complicity with the Welcombe enclosure alone, but for his very existence as a beneficiary of early modern capitalism. There are no hopeful gestures, no humanizing last stands here other than Shakespeare's suicide, the tragic deed that may be his most self-humanizing gesture. That it is contained in his self-destruction makes this *pathos* a paradigmatic tragic action. Were *Bingo* to present some positive or progressive alternative to Shakespeare's silences, self-torment, and final self-mortification, one might be tempted to see him not so much as a tragic figure but as a deluded and paralysed member of the middle class faced with his own bad conscience in a clear light.[9] Yet most curiously, those who actively oppose the enclosure in the play are represented ambivalently: the gardener's son, a Puritan who is as harshly critical of the young transient woman as is Combe, and his labourer associates. In their superstitious Puritanism these characters are represented as somewhat fanatical, yet they are the only agents who actively oppose the enclosure by ruining the fences and filling in the ditches that Combe's men create. However, this activism, performed both in their own interests and in the interests of the poor, results in a tragic and absurd death. The gardener's son shoots his own father in the night, during the confusion of a mission to pull down another wall. The old gardener's death is a most tragic loss because he alone of all the characters in *Bingo* seems happy, even in his mentally damaged state: he takes pleasure in gardening, and in sex, even if there is an infantilism to his state of mind. The scene in which he is ultimately shot begins with him gleefully throwing snowballs at a drunken, morose Shakespeare, a delightfully comic undermining of the playwright's tragic seriousness.

The gardener's son rationalizes the death of his own father as the fault of Combe and the enclosers, and then rationalizes his personal part in it as part of God's plans for him, before finally persuading himself that perhaps it was not he who pulled the trigger at all. For all his righteousness and moral indignation at the greed and cruelty of the rich, the gardener's son represents the ambiguous status of Puritans at this moment of history: they serve what are overall humanizing social goals, but their own ends are morally conservative and thus have all the reactionary elements of religious morality. The misguided violence of the son against his own innocent father seems to indicate that these actions are not the solution to the historical contradiction any more than is Combe's enclosure. In effect, the play demonstrates the contradictions of history itself: the Janus-faced edge of historical change wherein means and ends are separated, long-term and short-term achievements of the same process are at odds with one another, and the large-scale instrumental alleviation of human suffering is predicated upon the small-scale intensification of human suffering. Beyond the scope of the play, the solution to this contradiction lies in the modern phenomenon of socialist democracy, but Shakespeare's tragedy is that he could see the problems of the present with utmost clarity yet could not conceive of the future.

Art, for Bond, is an essential component of human culture and absolutely necessary to our ongoing self-humanizations. At the same time, Bond yokes artistic activity closely to human rationality and progressive social change. Art affords its receivers a humanizing experience because, as in the example of *Bingo*, it opens a window onto the lack of humanity within the sphere of human experience. What Shakespeare sees is suffering, an overwhelming degree of dehumanization in his society. The inevitable conclusion of such logic is that art itself must be tragic in both form and content. Thus the companion piece to *Bingo*, Bond's play about John Clare, *The Fool*, is understandable as a distillation of the tragic into a seemingly pure form, free of hope, optimism, or any embedded metacommentary upon the play's themes or concerns. The play presents its action bluntly and mercilessly, and seems to resist with vehemence the temptation to *make* something of the drama. What elevates *Bingo* and offers an internalized element of affirmation is the ennobled figure of Shakespeare, his moving, poetic commentary upon the miseries and sufferings he has seen and the torment he himself has suffered as a result. His language and words in the second half of the play hint that his silences in the first half have been overcome by a welling up of emotions, which find manifestation in the beauty of Bond's simple yet evocative dramatic poetry. Shakespeare's self-castigation at the play's conclusion is one of the more moving passages of critical self-mortification in dramatic art, and in its earnest grandeur worthy of Sophocles:

I howled when they suffered, but they were whipped and hanged so that I could be free. That is the right question: not why did I sign one piece of paper? – no, no, even when I sat at my table, when I put on my clothes, I was a hangman's assistant, a goaler's errand boy. […] If the table's empty we blight the harvest. If the roof leaks we send the storm. God made the elements but we inflict them on each other. Everything can be stolen, property and qualities of the mind. But stolen things have no value. Pride and arrogance are the same when they're stolen. Even serenity. (62–3)

The reference to serenity hearkens back to an earlier attack from an envious and drunken Ben Jonson, commenting on Shakespeare's inscrutable serenity and his ability to seemingly walk through the world untouched and unaltered by all happening around him: 'Life doesn't seem to touch you, I mean soil you' (46). Perhaps this is a telling subtextual swipe at the idea that Shakespeare's plays take place at a fantasized remove from the quotidian troubles of daily existence, or a suggestion that Shakespeare's art, as an aspiration towards the ideal, eschewed the squalor of urban existence. Nevertheless, the idea of serenity is exposed by Shakespeare himself as stolen goods, as a transmogrification or sublimation of the suffering of others into his own comfort and security. His serenity is made up of other men's blood. The implication of such a possibility is that art's raw materials are always the material suffering of others, no matter how aesthetically elevated and pastoral the end result may seem to be. A socially conscious theatre within a capitalist society must therefore necessarily be a tragic theatre, consciously aware that suffering is its raw material.

The Fool

The Fool (1975), an acknowledged sequel to *Bingo*, concerns a pastoral poet whose verse elevates nature to the status of the aesthetic; in Bond's play, however, beauty is evacuated from the stage altogether. We meet John Clare the labourer struggling within the oppressive economic circumstances of rural England following the defeat of Napoleon and the beginning of industrialization. As in *Bingo*, it is a moment of historical transformation, as the old and the new come into conflict with one another and the disenfranchised prove to be the victims of progress. The draining of the Fens and enclosing of the commons, the building of railroads and factories all signal the end of a traditional mode of production and herald the ensuing awakening of class consciousness on the part of those who suffer the most from economic change. The play's most moving scene takes place on a night of mob looting, when Clare's labourer friends, finally driven by poverty to thieve directly from the rich, gleefully confront the local parson and strip him of his finery, only to find that the sight of the soft, pale, well-fed flesh hidden beneath the parson's clothes transforms a night of *ressentiment* into something larger: a growing dialectical consciousness. Clare's closest friend, Darkie Turner, represents the most assertively politicized awareness in the play: 'Our flesh. That belong t'us. Where you took that flesh boy? You took that flesh off her baby. My ma. They on't got proper flesh on em now. [...] Where you stole that flesh boy? Your flesh is stolen goods' (*The Fool* 24). It is an insight not far from Shakespeare's in *Bingo*, but from the opposite side of the class divide, thus resulting in anger rather than despair. The group is reduced to tears by their realization that this man literally wears their flesh, and that a woman's child died so that the parson might live. Darkie pays for his outspokenness with his life, sentenced and hanged as an example to the others. Clare, absent from this scene due to his obsession with a young servant named Mary, a woman who will haunt him throughout his life, is spared prosecution and goes on to a career as a poet.

Far grimmer and unrelenting that anything in Bond's earlier repertoire, *The Fool*'s plot has a notably unwavering drive and directness to its story. There is no moral or lesson to the narrative, no embedded commentary or even something resembling a message to be drawn from the events. There is no heroic figure to admire, like Len, Lear, or Shakespeare. There is only a plot, the dramatization of an action in which an artist is destroyed by the inescapable, tragic social contradictions of his existence. Clare's verse, which demonstrates a love of the English landscape, is what brings him to the attention of wealthy patrons, yet it is the members of this very class that praise his poetry while destroying the thing that Clare's poetry praises, and Clare's lines condemning the destructive forces of wealth and poverty earn him rebukes from his benefactors. Clare's artistic activities are presented in the play not so much as an escape from a field labourer's work as an irresistible drive to write, spurred by voices in his head, an unrelenting muse that is as much curse as blessing to him. For a time, he enjoys success and a brief respite from poverty, only to find once his verse has fallen from popularity that he is now in a worse situation than before: once more living in the country, but now with a family and without a source of income. Changed by his broadened horizons, he cannot return to the field labour that had inspired his earliest verse, and he cannot stop writing the poetry that no one will now pay to read. His poetry is his fate and his doom. His body and mind degenerate from poverty, drink, and the mental torture of his impossible circumstances, and he ends the play in a lunatic asylum, unable to speak and physically decayed into a '*shrivelled puppet*' (68).

The significance of the action is to be found in the forces of Clare's destruction and in their precise contours, which are illuminated in an angry, desperate tirade from his wife concerning the dire poverty to which they have been reduced:

> I'll tell you why you're ill: you're hangin' about atwix an atween. No mystery there. You on't know what you're supposed t'be at. No wonder you're sick. All that scribble scribble drive anyone sick. An' for what? For Chriss sake what? They on't even read it! Look at this child John Clare. Thass sick an' pukin since it come in the world – cause thass famished like its mother. An its father. An' we're famished for what? Scribble scribble scribble on bits a paper for rats t'eat! (51)

There is no inscrutable mystery to the tragic sufferings of this artist. He is torn between two irreconcilable demands for which he is the vehicle: the demands of poetry and the necessity of survival. He is, in his own words, unable to return to labouring and unable to stop writing (50). From one perspective, *The Fool's* tragic purity is found in the fact that it is not a cautionary tale; the drama lacks a moral. Naturally, the poverty of the rural working classes is not presented as an inevitable necessity in the play: the first half of the drama is careful to demonstrate clearly the ways that the rich control both the law and religious ideology as a means of maintaining their own wealth and privilege. The opening scene of the second half of the drama places a boxing match in the background in Hyde Park as a means of allegorizing the exploitation of the muscles of the poor by their wealthy backers, while in the foreground Clare is criticized for the traces of radicalism in his poems by his own patron, Admiral Radstock. Clare's responses, 'On't see no nymphs in our fields but I seen a workhouse' and 'They had a winter coat they on't perish' are a blunt materialist demystification of the idea that the plight of the poor is an unavoidable necessity (44).

Later in the play, as he is about to be forcibly institutionalized, Clare continues to speak the truth to those who control his economic predicament. Lord Milton, the landowner for whom Clare once worked and who drives the industrialization of the countryside, requests that Clare read him a poem. The poet refuses: 'On't write for you. On't be a poet then. No more'n his carpenter's a carpenter. He touch a piece a wood an' it turn t'coffin. His corn's grass. His men are animals – goo round an' round his house on a rope, on a path shape like a sover-in. [...] An' what I wrote was good. Yes. Worth readin'. Shall I step in line now? No' (57). He can see the deliberate dehumanization of workers by their exploiters for what it is. Clare is dragged away to the asylum under the guise of sympathy for his pains and mental anguish, leading to the actual deterioration of his mind and the silencing of his politicized and poetic voice. His rationality is destroyed by the capitalist society in which he lives, a society that is effectively insane because it is irrationally destructive and violent towards the human beings who live within it. It is not Clare who is mad, but the society in which he lives. Others understand his clear vision as delusion, and his rationality is therefore experienced by him as mental anguish. There is no alternative available to Clare, no choices or crossroads to which he comes. It isn't possible to find a mistake he has made or for which he takes responsibility.[10] In fact, his agency in the play is debatable. What happens to him is unavoidable and necessary because he is an artist, and art is the most essential thing for humanity's needs, even if or especially when that art comes into conflict with its society, as does Clare's, leading to his destitution and deterioration.

The Fool may mark a turning point for Bond, necessitating a step forward in his paratextual introductions to his plays. He includes with *The Fool* a complex theoretical apparatus explaining the social necessity of art, referring not just to Clare's verse but presumably to his own theatre as well. In a sense, the theory becomes an essential tool for reading the play's intense tragic negativity: 'In a culture, or the struggle for a culture, a cry, a tear, a death become rational. Art is beautiful only in the broadest sense because it can include death and ugliness. But it can never commit itself to despair or the irrational. Art is the human being claiming a rational relationship with the world, perhaps even especially when what it portrays might have otherwise seemed absurd or tragic' (Introduction, *The Fool* xvi). A compressed and itself poetic theory of the tragic is encapsulated here: mourning, artistically expressed, becomes a part of the hopeful, rational process of history, and this is the foundation of its claim to be beautiful: 'Art helps to create meaning and purpose in what is in many ways an apparently irrational world' (xvi). As a theoretical apparatus explaining the function of tragedy for a socialist aesthetic, Bond's introduction yokes the representation of negativity to a larger affirmative and humanizing process.

Missing from this critical theory is a precise definition of culture itself, specifically one that distinguishes between the different possible forms of artistic production that might make a claim to be included under a definition of culture. Bond's clearest definition of what he means by 'culture' comes in a poem of the same name, which accompanies his Brechtian play *The Bundle* (1978):

'What is culture?
Taking power from the owner
To give to the user
That is culture
The highest the human mind
Can aspire to!
The passing of power
From owner to user

Creates virtue and art
Nothing else raises
Men over the beast
Whatever hinders this passing of power
Is against culture
Culture is this change. (*The Bundle* 94)

It is easy to see how Bond can locate a play like *The Bundle* within the paradigm of culture that he describes in the poem: a play that teaches clearly about problems and offers socialist solutions, demonstrating how people can successfully change their world – such a play can claim an obvious place within a socialist definition of culture. Reactionary art is not culture, in Bond's definition. Yet a great deal of Bond's artistic output, specifically plays that fall within the definition of the tragic, refuse optimism and as such might be understood as reactionary in their pessimism. The place of the negative within a progressive culture is fraught and unclear, but this very problem of how the tragic serves socialist ends grows to become Bond's central concern in the 1980s.

An initial exploration of the problem is found in the critical materials accompanying *The Worlds* (1978). The poems, stories, and essays written during the rehearsal of this play and assembled under the title *The Activists Papers* indicate a growing awareness of the importance of dramatic form and style as themselves crucial bearers of political meaning in the theatre. *The Worlds* itself is an experiment with unusual character representations triggered by Bond's historicization of his own plays within the canon of progressive theatre from past eras, a canon in which he includes Greek drama and Shakespeare's plays. How, he wonders, can one create a contemporary equivalent of such art in the theatre while respecting the changed historical and political circumstances of the present? In the modern world 'political weight' (*Activists Papers* 135) belongs to the masses, but '[w]e can't use strikers in the way Shakespeare used kings. [...] An individual biography can't show historical movement or be a pattern for the historical understanding of society' (127). Bond uses this problem as a springboard for a speculative manifesto in which he outlines the possibility of a tentative new form of socialist theatre that would be such a contemporary vessel for history within the aesthetic.

Recognizable forms of socialist theatre include plays that 'show characters resolving a problem by using socialist consciousness. They may win a strike or decide to build a factory or hospital' (127). Bond calls such plays 'incident' plays, to be enjoyed by a socialist audience. Alternately, socialist propaganda plays present an agitational-propaganda, didactic message to an uninformed or unsympathetic audience, and as such must sometimes present class types, straightforward educational information, and generalizations. Bond outlines the possibility of a third type of socialist theatre, an Epic form that 'would be a poem. It would put history onstage as a dramatic reality' (128):

> History wouldn't be shown as immanent in an individual, individuality would be transcended by the historical pattern which it represented. Incidents would be chosen to show how historical problems arise and how they lead to resolutions. Movements spread over long periods and involving masses of people might be reflected in stories, often in simple stories. The characters wouldn't be moved by personal motives but by the forces of history. They'd be epic in analysis but not necessarily in size. (129)

History, for the idealist socialist, is the confluence and momentary identity of the abstract and the individual, the general and the particular. Historical abstraction would be represented in this theatre without cancelling the individual uniqueness of the characters themselves: 'So we'd show individual quirkiness. Indeed we'd show the power of historical forces by showing the individuality, ordinariness and human vulnerability and strength of the characters who live it' (129). This is a description of a dialectic in which the totality does not efface the unique human but becomes identical with it.

Although he does not specify a Hegelian terminology, Bond's vision of the function of art resembles Hegel's idea that the truth is concrete, as long as the concrete is understood only to be that which is mediated through both the general and the particular. For Hegel, such concrete theatre was Greek tragedy and the exemplary instance of *Antigone* and its characters.[11] Bond is inspired by this Greek model to envision a new form of poetic, political drama: 'And it may be that socialism needs and makes possible this other, poetic drama which impersonates history' (129). However, there are traces of a utopianism to such an artistic vision. The harmonious identity of individuality and totality is not an existing state but the anticipated endpoint of socialist historical change: 'Socialism could resolve most of the antagonisms between objectivity and subjectivity. It would let us live in the world as it is and so be our true selves, instead of living in the world as it is run for the benefit of a few' (142). An achieved socialist project would allow us to be fully human, but in the absence of this achievement our struggles with alienation and division are also struggles to achieve humanity. The completed resolution of social alienation, the gap between the subject and the objective, were it represented in theatre, would be a false utopia in the face of the present. Yet at the same time this new poetic drama must seek to refract history through itself and its characters, presenting not an unalienated unity of the totality of history and the humanity of individuals but rather, I will suggest, something necessarily more tragic in its contours: the ongoing struggle to become fully human within and as history.

The election of Margaret Thatcher in 1979 appears to have solidified a shift in emphasis on Bond's part, a turn in his artistic career that remains in effect to this day. Three key elements in this shift stand out: his theorizations become ever more complex and, moreover, focused on the importance of tragic experience; his impatience with the political atmosphere of the theatres with which he worked throughout his earlier career leads him into a self-exile from both the mainstream and the artistic theatre in England; and finally, his theatre abandons realism altogether and turns towards a remarkable poetic formalism as a means of achieving his political goals. My thesis here is that having laid out in his critical essays the project of a third form of socialist theatre, namely a poetic drama that serves as an impersonation of history, Bond continues to the present day to experiment with such a possibility. His pursuit of this project throughout the 1980s led to a number of radical theatrical experiments with style and form, at the heart of which lies Bond's major plays of the 1980s, the three-part *The War Plays*.

Restoration

As Michael Mangan discusses, Bond's most evident reaction to the election of Margaret Thatcher was his final production at the Royal Court, *Restoration* (1981), in which the impoverished aristocrat Lord Are kills his new bride, the daughter of a wealthy industrialist, and then convinces his servant Bob Hedges to take the blame for the crime with the false promise that he will have Bob pardoned. Instead, Bob is hanged. Bond compares Bob to the 'typical, working-class Tory voter' (qtd in Mangan 58). Mangan's observation that the story is as much tragic as it is comic (57) highlights the formalism at the heart of Bond's concerns. Ian Stuart notes that the two halves of the play are generically separated: the first half is a restoration comedy, but one, significantly, with a tragic ideology underpinning it. As Bond puts it, '[T]he first half makes the atrocities of society acceptable – its mottos are "You have only yourself to blame" and "God helps those who help themselves"' (Bond, qtd in Stuart 67). The comedy of the first half of the play embodies a tragic ideology of inevitability, while the working-class tragedy of Bob Hedges's death in the second half estranges this tragic ideology. Bond's creation of a new artistic language for a socialist theatre involves the manipulation of theatrical style. The key unit of this theatrical language is what Bond calls a 'Theatre Event.' Interrogating the received ideology of 'inevitability' associated with a tragic narrative, Bond inserts broad estrangement effects in order to dramatize the idea that these characters are responsible for their actions.

Bond's Theatre Event is the jarring clash of styles within a single play, which importantly reveals the larger material economic and social circumstances that puppet human beings. Bond calls these larger influencing social contexts 'metatexts,' and the function of Theatre Events is to illuminate such social metatexts: 'The TE makes metatext and character one. It points to a tragic social truth: often in real life when people think they are most utterly, profoundly themselves they are merely playing a metatext which is empty because they did not choose it. They are like puppets who tie knots in their strings to remind them when to dance' ('Commentary' 317). Thus, the penultimate scene of *Restoration* shows a situation where a community prepares one of its own to be hanged. Bond's concern is that this narrative should resist a tragic ideology of fate and inevitability, and throughout the play he uses bitter comedy in the representation of Lord Are in order to demonstrate the agency and culpability of those who collude in the murder of the innocent man. Yet in the penultimate scene what Bond uses is not farce but rather stark, tragic contradiction as Bob Hedges is prepared for his death with gestures of kindness on the part of family and associates, and for Bond, this kindness is itself the murder ('Commentary' 319). What matters in the scene is the economic situation in which the characters are embroiled, and how the material situation has the ability to refuse moral absolutes such as good and bad as a means of exposing the transformability of circumstances: '[T]he scene shows how good becomes bad, how sensitivity becomes callousness. A man drowns *because* he breathes; what keeps him alive in one situation kills him in another; the situation changes the meaning – drowning is another way of breathing' (318–19). What matters is not that Lord Are is evil for destroying the pardon that would save Bob Hedges's life; it is that the goodness of the working-class characters who help ease the end of Bob Hedges's life is a form of brutal murder.

Bond insists that despite how the script is written, the scene must be played with a direct and unrealistic presentation of the metatext: 'When the devoted wife forces alcohol down her husband's throat it should be as if she put the rope around his neck; and that is not done nicely – it is sick to imagine that it is. The priest prays as if he were drowning a basket of kittens' (319). Eschewing realistic or naturalistic impersonation of characters, Theatre Events are highly demonstrative and as a result 'graphic, direct, simple, theatrical and powerful' (318). They are only vaguely similar to Brechtian estrangement (or as Bond puts it, 'alienation') effects, in which the self-evident is rendered strange and unfamiliar so that we might question ideological assumptions. Theatre Events are closer to Brecht's concept of *gestus*, in which the particular phrase or action is used as a prism through which to refract the general determining social circumstances of characters' lives. Bond's critical response to mimetic theatre is to dramatize concrete human decisions in which the contradictions of human existence under capitalism are exposed. Theatre Events must stage the class and social contradictions that communicate themselves through human actions, and the dramatization of these contradictions is Bond's concern in *The War Plays*.

The War Plays

Composed of three plays dealing with the survivors of a nuclear war and the extremes of dehumanization to which they are subjected, *The War Plays* (1985) are most fascinating for the fact that despite the extreme stylization of the dramas, what unifies them as a trilogy also makes them the direct dramatic kin to *Saved*: each play is a dramatic iteration of a core event in which a soldier in wartime is ordered to kill a randomly chosen person on the street where he lives.[12] The soldier must choose between a neighbour and his own blood kin. There is no correct solution to this dramatic situation: it is a contradiction that, when acted out, serves as a crucial theatrical machine for rendering apparent the problem of humanizing oneself within dehumanizing social circumstances. Bond calls this situation 'the Palermo paradox,' since he developed it in improvisations with students at Palermo University: 'The paradox is never absent from our mind. It is the crux on which humanness is poised, an expression of the radical innocence which makes us human' ('Commentary' 251). In rejecting realism in favour of a new form of poetic drama that mimics history itself, Bond reveals that the murder of a child in *Saved* by its own potential father is a prototype for the key dramatic contradiction in his work. The concept of 'radical innocence' becomes, by the end of the 1980s when he publishes his commentary to *The War Plays*, Bond's ultimate materialist solution to the problem of nature and his entry into the realm of the postmodern. He overcomes what is essentially a bourgeois valorization of any kind of state of nature as 'foundational' in reference to human beings, and this overcoming of the value concept of 'nature' brings his theatre into a full Marxist fruition. For materialist thought the solution to this alienated, post-lapsarian state of existence is not found in nostalgia, retreat, or a discovery of authentic humanity at all, but rather in the process of reification itself and in the experience of dehumanization. This includes the violence that has been Bond's concern throughout his oeuvre, since violence is his key dramatic trope for the dehumanizing circumstances in which his characters struggle.

With the Palermo paradox we see a new dialecticizing of the problem of violence in Bond's work: the paradox makes apparent nothing less than humanness itself, as if Bond's dramatic project has been to gradually shed the superficial trappings of realistic and naturalistic theatre in order to leave standing only the most elementary of human situations, the worst, most dehumanizing events to which human beings can be subjected, for these will be the crucibles of struggle within which we can see the essence of the human itself, possibly because 'we can only be human in conflict with society' ('Commentary' 249). Out of this dramatic direction, Bond finds his escape from bourgeois thinking: 'We are born radically innocent, and neither animal nor human; we create our human-ness as our minds begin to think our instincts' (251). Radical innocence is the questioning, interrogating drive of human consciousness, the ability of the mind to confront ideology and destroy it. This capacity is liberated, in Bond's thought, from biology, foundation, or origins: it is the ongoing *process* of self-humanization: 'Our unconscious is not more animal than our conscious, it is often even more human. The unconscious sees through us and our social cor-ruption and sends us messages of our humanity, ingeniously and persistently trying to reconcile the divisive tensions in our lives. Our unconscious makes us sane' (250). Moreover, what matters now, in this maturation of Bond's philoso-phy, is not what we may have lost in our alienating socializations but the hope-ful possibilities in the reified condition of postmodernity itself, in which we are surrounded by our machines. Inhuman as this technology is, it is also a crucial repository of our humanness: '[W]e are more closely related to machines than to animals. [...] We speak and create machines in our image. [...] All the things we make are signs of culture and so they speak to us' (270). Technology, for Bond, is intimately related to the symbolic register of humanity as located in the abstractions of our languages. Machines are another form of language and function with the same structuralist ambivalence as do linguistic phenomena: created by humans as an expression of human consciousness, languages be-come autonomous structures, at once mutable and immutable, as de Saussure observed, and colonize their creators, as Lacan extrapolated. 'It is a circle,' Bond observes (271).

Machines are inherently progressive for Bond because they are not controlla-ble by their owners alone but speak to those who use them (271), and therefore are subversive of the existing state of class relations in a society. Machines and radical innocence are 'the two basic determinants of human life,' radical inno-cence because it offers 'awareness of mortality and loss' (268). Out of these neces-sities humans have the opportunity to take control of their own existences and create their own futures, since both machines and radical innocence force open human consciousness to doubt, questioning, and the rejection of social teaching in the form of ideology. From these two forces we have the possibility of free will: '[T]he first tools made the first humans, and made the first human psyche by giv-ing us free will. Perhaps the first tool was part of our body: perhaps to the first humans the opposable thumb was as mysterious as an object without a shadow, was the symbolic that pointed to nothingness' (277). The implications here are recognizably structuralist in their overtones: language and *techne* are the location of the human, and the symbolic register of consciousness is both an alienation of the ego and the domain of human agency. The animal foundation of the human, whether it is located in the unconscious or in biology, has been replaced by the ultimately progressive force of the machines: 'They are the phylogenetic and biographical foundations of our consciousness [...]. Machines stand irremovably between us and our animal origin' (278). Yet technology and language are not ends in themselves, and neither are they the only tools needed to allow humans to create a properly human world. This task requires art, 'the material production of the perceiving, analytical, symbolic mind.' In art, 'the mind's presence is visible' (274). The idea that our humanity is contingent upon our relationship to our technology implies that the condition of being human is a fundamentally tragic alienation, and this tragic alienation is also key to freedom and agency as a human being.

The Palermo paradox is a dramatic machine within which we find the performers subject to 'contradictory imperatives, and their resolution increases or diminishes our humanity' (315). Such contradictory pressures reveal the extent to which humans will go to hold onto their humanity. Such a use of contradictions within dramatic action is not new: 'The Palermo paradox raises questions theatre has dealt with from at least the time of the Greeks' (340). Accordingly, Bond's project to create a new form of socialist drama, poetic in its stylization and its use of Theatre Events, leads him to create a new form of postmodern, materialist tragedy. Of the three parts of *The War Plays* trilogy, the most significant for our concerns here is the third iteration of the Palermo paradox, *Great Peace*, which is the longest and most portentous of the three plays.[13] In the first play, *Red Black and Ignorant*, Bond creates a short agitprop Learning Play, direct in its teaching, as a means of educating the audience in how to interpret the paradox and decipher Theatre Events. In this iteration a soldier is sent home to kill someone on his street; he attempts to kill the weak old man next door but finds he cannot, and so shoots his own father. The lesson is declaratively presented in words worthy of Brecht's *The Measures Taken*: 'Praise this soldier / Why did he kill his father and not the stranger? / Under his scars the flesh was whole / Praise him as you would the first wheel / [...] We know ourself and say: I cannot give up the name of human' (38). The audience has been challenged to grasp in such a contradictory situation and its tragic resolution the expression of a fundamental humanity.

In the second iteration, *The Tin Can People*, the title characters are a group of survivors after a nuclear exchange, living in ruins and surviving off the tin cans that give them their names. They are an allegorical figure for the bourgeoisie within postmodernity: living in an alienated, dead world and perfectly at home there until an outsider enters their closed environment of mock affluence and disrupts the sense of stasis to which they cling. Deaths in their midst become signs that the stranger has brought a plague among them, and they attack him in an attempt to purge the pestilence. *The Tin Can People* also teaches how a new community can leave behind this alienating violence, take responsibility for the creation of history, and build a world that is just and human. They abandon the tins so that they can move beyond this dependence on the reified world of commodity fetishism: '[I]t means that at last we own ourselves' (96). In these two initial iterations Bond teaches the audience how to read his new form of theatre by using the existing forms of socialist theatre: the first play is didactic propaganda that confronts the audience with stark clarity, while the second play now assumes an informed audience and presents a socialist incident play, with an optimistic, problem-solving narrative.

The third iteration, *Great Peace*, is another type of drama altogether, Bond's new poetic form. *Great Peace* is infused throughout with a profound tragic negativity that evokes as do few other plays the wisdom of Silenus: it is better never to have been born, and having been born, next best is to return to whence you came with what speed you may. This tragic world view is voiced by Sophocles in *Oedipus at Colonus* and also holds a place of special importance in Nietzsche's *The Birth of Tragedy* (42), wherein the philosopher marvels at the ability of the Greeks to hold the wisdom of Silenus as a truth and yet live affirmatively and without pessimism. George Steiner describes this maxim as the 'pure tragic axiom' and ascribes it to the elegies of Theognis ('Tragedy, Pure and Simple' 536–7).[14] With *Great Peace* and subsequent tragedies in which the dehumanizing effects of war and genocide are explored *in extremis*, Bond seems determined to pursue the purest possible representation of this tragic postulate, while still holding to the possibility of humanization within a situation in which, for all intents and purposes, humanity as a whole is effectively extinct. Thus in *Great Peace* Bond gives this tragic maxim an unparalleled representation in what is nevertheless a piece of socialist theatre, indicating that the play is perhaps an attempt to turn this tragic negativity into an affirmative will not only to exist but to create a new and just existence out of the rubble of a nuclear holocaust. There is more than a superficial resemblance to Beckett's *Endgame* in this dramatic representation, but *Great Peace* is about those outside Hamm and Clov's bunker, out at large in the 'corpsed' earth, those who do not have the luxury of immobility and who are driven inexorably by their own humanity to survive. Thus the wisdom of Silenus, while stated flatly in the play, is given a small inflection that changes its meaning: 'Per'aps it'd think it was best not t'be born?' speculates the play's protagonist about the prospects that await a child born in the ruins of nuclear war (*Great Peace* 156). Later this becomes an angry assertion: 'Dead – not born – never thought of – that'd be best!/No kids to anyone!/But it was born – !' (174). Certainly the degree of despair given performative shape in *Great Peace* is enough to confirm this grim assessment: the play is effectively *Mother Courage and Her Children* transposed into a post-apocalyptic hell on earth, and we should note that the Palermo paradox is a distillation of the fundamental contradiction that Anna Fierling attempts, unsuccessfully, to resolve.

Yet that *Great Peace* is ultimately presented by the author as a political allegory for the consciousness of the Westerner today indicates a reading by Bond of his own play that is not dissimilar to Adorno's reading of *Endgame*, as a parable of the endpoint of the process of reification in the West.[15] The eloquence of Bond's expressionistic reading of his own play does not nullify the fact that his allegory of consciousness is a politicized interpretation: 'It is as if they had internalized their landscape and become the stories that wander over it. But that is how all of us live in a nuclear age, even before the bombs are dropped. Inside our head we browse through the maps of ruins' ('Commentary' 352). Bond is offering a tragedy in which the characters, wandering through ruins, are themselves ruins, and thus the human beings on display here, alienated and reduced to the status of the walking dead, are like worn-out skulls. The dark and optimistic revelation of the play will be the discovery of the human as allegory: human beings here will be shown to be forms of rhetoric, allegorical narratives who must write themselves through their actions in order to achieve humanity.

The unnamed protagonist of *Great Peace*, referred to as the Woman, is a version of Mother Courage with everything stripped away except the core contradiction of her dramatic action: Courage attempts to save her own children while surviving off war, but war consumes her children. The lullaby that Courage sings to her dead daughter Kattrin at the conclusion of Brecht's play is one of the most deceptive moments of the drama: if there is ever a moment when Anna Fierling will elicit emotions and sympathy from an audience, it is when she is reduced to this last, futile gesture of love for her child. Yet the playwright tempers such mawkishness by drawing attention to the content of the words: the song describes how this mother's child shall thrive and eat well while the children of other mothers will starve. In an unjust world, expressions of love are murderous sentiments. Bond might well have taken this final lullaby and magnified this single moment of Brechtian *gestus* into his entire play (and Bond indicates that *Mother Courage* is a reference point for *Great Peace* ['Commentary' 359–60]). The first section of Bond's play, which he refers to as 'the Greek Play,' is an iteration of the Palermo paradox: in the aftermath of a nuclear conflagration a soldier is ordered to return to his street and murder one young child in order to reduce the waste of food during a time of emergency. The soldier is unable to bring himself to kill a neighbour's child, and so he kills his own infant sibling. He then returns to his squadron, where in the final scene of 'the Greek Play' he is shot for refusing an order to pick up an empty cigarette packet.

As Mangan observes, it is a typical moment in a Bond play, like the futility of Lear's attempt to pull down his wall, where the small, 'ludicrous' gesture is nevertheless a 'glimpse of humanity' and 'simultaneously heroic and bathetic' (72). It is also an object-moment of the freedom-tragic. This silent and simple refusal of an order is an expression of Bond's theory of 'radical innocence' and the revised equivalent here of the Greek tragic protagonist's silent submission to the will of the gods, a submission that was humanizing for the Greeks because it constituted a paradoxical judgment of an inhuman fate: 'Submission to the Gods makes them less than human and the humans more than Gods. This is the way in which the Greeks transcended the Gods and gained their humanity' ('Commentary' 286). But the soldier's silence is not the acceptance of the order and of the social metatext that commands him. His submission is not defiance. Rather, it is closer to the truth to say his defiance is a submission to his radical innocence and to his own humanity: 'The silence of the soldier with the empty cigarette packet is also a chorus: the silence of radical innocence confronting the paradox, surrounded by the yapping of orders' (351). Moreover, and more challenging to our understanding, his murder of his own sibling is his only possible self-humanization within the paradoxical situation. The captain who has him shot for disobeying an order explains that he was already concerned that the soldier had shot his own sibling, thus showing signs of weakness and disobedience, and that the incident with the packet was the next step (*Great Peace* 150). These small gestures of defiance are Bond's revision of a classical tragic rubric: today, submission to determinism, fate, or necessity is not humanizing because fate today is actually economic and market forces ('Commentary' 298). Magnifying the tiniest gestures to the attention of the audience as a means of refracting humanization through these deeds, Bond uses the cigarette packet to bring together the most particular and mundane of actions with the largest and most portentous of matters in the play: 'War makes that little packet very big,' the Captain explains (*Great Peace* 148). The soldier is ordered by the captain to march to the packet, to mark time by it, to halt, and finally to kneel next to it. All of these commands are obeyed. Only the final one, to reach out and pick up the litter, is ignored. For the soldier's humanity, it is the most insignificant thing, the smallest gesture, that becomes the locus of the greatest significance.

Yet the play as a whole is not about the soldier's confrontation with the paradox but his mother's. The Woman is at first revolted when she learns of the order her son has been commanded to carry out, but when she calms she becomes fully complicit in the attempt to murder the neighbour's child, demonstrating a furious drive to do anything to save her own baby. As she considers how in not murdering her neighbour's child she is killing her own, she becomes violently steeped in the contradictions of the situation. She tells her own baby: 'You smile at me because yer don't know 'oo I am / These 'ands are killin yer but yer don't bleed / […] Im not fit t' 'old you in me 'ands / Im not cruel – cold – 'ard – cunning enough t'be a mother!' (132). It is a contradictory sentiment worthy of Shen Te in *The Good Person of Setzuan*. When the Woman fails to save her child, she is driven into a state of Lear-like madness. The second section of the play jumps forward seventeen years, where we find the Woman wandering the post-nuclear ruins, what Bond tellingly calls 'The Wilderness' (150). She believes herself to still be nursing her infant, cradling what is in fact a blanket that she shapes and folds into the sign of a child. This bundle is the mesmerizing, theatrical heart of the play: the Woman engages in a piece of theatrical fakery, the bundle being her dramatic prop, in order to become sane and create for herself her humanity.

Her bundle is the visual expression of her need to somehow remain or become human again and remain in confrontation with the paradox rather than simply accept its inevitability. Thus while she is 'mad' she expresses lucidity and human compassion in her madness, which are in fact reason and sanity. Bond compares the Woman's relationship to her bundle to an actual theatrical prop baby in the play, representing an orphaned newborn whom the Woman, in her madness, abandons while nursing her own 'fake' bundle. The 'real' newborn raises its fist and cries out faintly as she leaves it, a dramatic image to be achieved through mechanical effects. While the Woman needs her bundle to be real for her, the conscious theatricality or 'fakery' of her imaginary child establishes the '*theatrical reality*' of the abandoned newborn for the audience ('Commentary' 354). 'The audience need the baby-with-a-fist to be real so that they may carry it with them on the journey. […] They cannot let themselves abandon it as the Woman did' (355). Bond transforms the suspension of disbelief in the theatre into a Theatre Event by connecting the use of a theatrical effect to the compassion and self-humanizations we engage in when confronted by a child in need: 'The audience use the theatre in the way the Woman uses the sheet' (355). Ian Stuart phrases this admirably: '[T]he Woman's torn sheet is similar in function to the theatre for an audience; both provide necessary illusions that give access to reality' (128). As the Woman makes her bundle real because she needs it to be real so that she can become sane and human, so does the audience make the mechanical baby real for the sake of its own sanity and humanity: this, according to Bond, is why human beings go to the theatre.

The wasteland is a zone of illusions and a zone of theatre, but the two are not the same thing. The Woman encounters a group of soldiers, whom she does not know are the remnants of her dead son's squadron. These soldiers have convinced themselves that they, and everyone else remaining in the wilderness, are dead. This self-deception is their psychic means of managing their traumatic survival: it is too difficult for them to conceive that humanity has survived in this hell on earth. The Woman's arrival amongst them wreaks havoc with their self-deception, as they become confused about the ontological status of her bundle of rags. She insists to them that not only she but also her child still live, and that she must go on living for the sake of the child (*Great Peace* 167). Yet she also speculates that like the soldiers, she may in fact be dead: 'I don't mind bein dead as long as the child's alive' (173). This assertion is troubling for the soldiers, who long ago reconciled themselves to their status as ghosts or undead zombies, and find her affectionate gestures of love and nurturing towards a bundle of rags to be an effective unsettling of their confidence. The Woman's dramatic performance of her humanity provokes a confusion of fiction and reality amongst these men, and some of them begin to think that the bundle is in fact a child, even believing they have seen the baby.

Effectively, the play suggests that the child is in fact 'alive' because it satisfies an essential need on the Woman's part, as is evident in her behaviour towards it, which, in comparison to these men's delusions, is lucid sanity. The confusion the bundle engenders among the men when they begin to believe in it is effectively a kind of reluctant return to life: 'Yesterday we didnt know the difference between that an a bundle of rags / What does that make us? / We dont know what state we're supposed t' be in! / Are we dead or alive?' (180). Her theatre shatters their illusions, and they are worked up into a frenzy of confusion about their status as alive or dead that culminates in a kind of mass suicide: three of the soldiers badger their commanding officer into shooting them all, which he finally does out of frustration with their insubordination. Their self-destruction is an attempt to maintain their deluded conviction that they have been dehumanized to the point of being utterly inhuman. They cling to this in the face of the truth signified by the Woman and her bundle, which is the fact that humanity continues to live even within this wasteland. In attempting to remain untouched by this truth, the soldiers must perform a demented and hyperbolic parody of their already alienated states, holding to their dehumanized condition and making it a literal, material fact.

The Woman's journey to sanity constitutes a series of false recognitions, Bond's modernizing of scenes of *anagnorisis* in Greek tragedy. His interpretation of the social function of these Aristotelian scenes is political: 'In the confrontation and recognition, society's existing divisions – and the tensions in the psyche that maintained them – are developed into new, more humane divisions' ('Commentary' 289). The Woman's false recognitions are essentially theatre for her: dramatic scenes in which she plays herself and makes a stranger play a character from her life, all in the service of her growing sanity and her confrontation with the paradox once more. The Woman's journey towards her own humanity finally brings her in contact with a community whose members are building a new society while learning from the mistakes of the past; they are coming to terms with the need for technology while insisting that the bombs have no place in their world. A large part of their self-humanization involves the reclaiming and integration of isolated scavengers from the wasteland, a project that is challenged when the Woman refuses to leave the wilderness and join their city. The imperative need for them to bring her into civilization is conveyed to her by a Man whom she will integrate into her dramatic fiction: 'They wont go without yer / They'd feel they was dropping another bomb [...] we ain addin t' that misery – not even the little bits of cruelty that 'appened so often in your world they werent even noticed / If we did that we'd know we weren't 'uman! / That's *our* pain – an our good fortune' (*Great Peace* 218). Humanization is a conscious and ongoing activity on their part, both a blessing and a suffering, and this is what distinguishes them from those who lived before the nuclear war.

The Woman's final confrontation with the paradox that drove her into the wilderness in the first place takes the form of the false recognition of the Man as her son, and her expression of hatred for him: she struggles to articulate her frustrated attitude to the contortions of the paradox, which allows humans no correct actions. The grudge she still harbours against her son is only fumblingly articulated: confronted with his orders, anything he did would be a wrong action, so why not commit the crime she begged of him? (235). The Man who poses as her son counters her still-murderous sentiment with the truth of the paradox: 'If the men 'oo dropped the bombs 'd bin like your son they'd've dropped them on their own kids / Yer dont want sons like that / Yer want your sons t' be ordinary killers so yer can be good mothers' (236). Why, the paradox forces us to ask ourselves, do we find it acceptable to murder the children of others but not our own?

The Man offers to stay with her and try to determine why her son made the choice he did. The Woman's response to his offer tells us something of the structural, dramatic reason that she cannot rejoin the community: 'This isnt your place: the tears never reach the ground 'ere / The pain's so deep they leave the eye but never rest' (237). The Man replies with reference to the bundled sheet she still carries and how she speaks to it, but she counters him and explains that she knows it is just an empty cloth and that her baby is dead. It is the dead, she says, that she would like to question. The question she would ask them is: '[W]hy

I suffered an 'oo its for, an why we live on this earth an are buried in it?' (238). The Man insists no answer will come from the dead, and it seems that the asking of this crucial tragic question itself is the unceasing activity that animates her. She refuses to return with him, and when he visits her a year later he finds her desiccated corpse lying where he last saw her, still cradling the supplies he left her. It is a mute final image of the human as a decayed ruin, an image of literal mortification that allegorizes the shape of her self as an open question, formed around mourning and loss. Bond comments in reference to her refusal to join the city: 'It is a matter of the paradox. The paradox is demanding, but it is the foundation of our lives. […] She goes away from the city to be one of its foundations' ('Commentary' 363). The tragic is the basis for becoming human, and she serves, through her status as a tragic outsider, as the excluded centre of the society to come, a *pharmakos* figure, a taboo scapegoat that reveals the human as constituted upon loss, centred upon a confrontation with the paradox. Significantly, there are instances in the play when the tattered sheet that constitutes the bundle is referred to as empty (*Great Peace* 183, 238). This is precisely its importance as a crucial signifier of the human. Bond writes, 'The sheet shows the shapes of metaphors / The sheet is the great map of nothing on which we write' ('Commentary' 353). The sheet and its shape as a bundle demonstrate the crucial humanizing force of the symbolic order itself, the liberating and humanizing introduction of absence and loss into the register of human consciousness that allows humans to create themselves as dramatic characters and become the agents of their own history.

This is Bond's affirmative vision of the human as a tragic being: a dramatic theorization specifically placed in confrontation with the dehumanizing effects of late capitalism. For Bond, the human mind's central force is interrogation, and it pushes us towards philosophical contemplation of the outside horizons of our understanding, what we typically call 'the world' and what Bond refers to as 'the boundary – the cosmic world' ('Notes on Post-Modernism' 213). The boundary is by definition 'unknowable. Its mystery is analogous to the mystery people know as their "self"' (214). The boundary is Bond's term for the psychic confrontation with and interrogation of necessity, an action that is an essential part of our self-humanizations, yet that is endangered by the impoverishment of contemporary experience: 'But in post-modernity needs are met; or if they are not met it is a matter of mere interruption or shortfalls in organisation and not because meeting needs is sometimes impossible because the boundary (seemingly) does not will it. Post-modern society is a society of wants. […] The extraordinary consequence of this is that we can no longer have a utopian vision and so any mystery of any boundary cannot have any ethical content' (236). Although Bond does not use the word here, he describes the consequences of the death of what we would call 'metaphysical' thinking, although the term is obviously stigmatized today by the very same ideology that renders it increasingly impossible. In tangential terms, Bond's notes echo Steiner's argument about the death of tragedy in secular society. The problem of tragedy is itself tragic, and we will see this dilemma enacted again in the work of the so-called younger generation of playwrights. Bond surmises:

> In greek [*sic*] drama human suffering was enormous and served no natural, totemic purpose. It was – amazingly – endured for the purposes of the inner boundary, so that it might interrogate the outer boundary. [...] [P]eople achieved their humanity in defying the gods. Their ability to choose to submit to fate was a moral condemnation of its arbitrariness. A judgement on it. The radicalness of the greeks in doing this has not been surpassed. ('Notes on Post-Modernism' 219)

Bond does not yearn for the triumphantly Promethean existence signified by Greek tragedy, yet he suggests that that a new form of tragedy, one without 'catharsis,' will intervene into postmodernity. A new form of tragedy would enable 'the use of interrogation in post-modernity' (244). Tragedy, then, has the potential to disrupt ideological thinking and re-enable the mind's inherent capacity to interrogate.

Bond's concept of the human changes in his essays of the 1990s; we have already seen a significant shift from the early material related to *Lear* in which the human is an animal in a cage, alienated by social violence, to the concept of the human as defined by this capacity for violence, inasmuch as violence is an extension of the self, represented through technology, language, and machines. Both are visions of the human as tragically alienated, but the latter sees this tragic alienation as the condition of being human. By the 1990s, human beings are essentially, and only, stories for Bond, and there seems to be no remaining trace of nature, of the animal, or of biologism in his paradigm of the human:

> The self is the story that imagines itself. The self pays attention to the story because the self is also the valuer. [...] There is no homunculus in the brain, no 'ghost in the machine,' no soul in the imagination, no centre in the psyche. The brain is a complex nexus of relations to the world and itself. The brain structures a map not a person. There is no unified ego, instead there is a 'chorus' which is collectively the self. [...] Imagination, in the world, is theatre and its story is drama. ('Notes on Imagination' 97)

In the 1990s, Bond defines the human by the imagination. Bond argues that in drama, 'the imagination directly confronts itself, and when it does it is always drawn to an extreme because it remembers nothingness' (120). We inherit this capacity from childhood. Like a figure from Greek tragedy, a child comes into the world and immediately feels judged by it. The child turns this around: 'In its innocence the child judges its judges as guilty – it is a judgement not only against people but against the fact of the world' ('Commentary' 252). This inter-rogation of the world is for the child a ceaseless drive for justice and responsi-bility, because the 'child's radical innocence accepts responsibility for the world' ('Notes on Imagination' 121). It is a capacity for extreme responsibility, an imaginative sense of connectedness to the cosmos: '[T]he border with nothing-ness gives imagination its concern for the world. Imagination has the exuber-ance to endure and know tragedy,' he writes (121).

Bond credits children with a greater imaginative understanding than adults, an understanding characterized by the child's incessant questioning of its sur-roundings. The child's mind is a tragic consciousness: 'It is as if children pass freely in and out of death – the border is not barred to them – till the body claims the mind for life' ('Notes on Imagination' 121). The child's interrogating mind finds connections between the general and the particular, and art's func-tion can only be to engender a recurrence of this dialectical openness: 'Drama cannot instruct, it confronts, perplexes and intrigues imagination into recreat-ing reality' (121). Tragedy functions by putting us in the situation of the pro-tagonist, a figure facing a cruel, meaningless suffering, and throwing this cosmic judgment back in the face of the cosmos. For Bond, '[t]hese are situations in which imagination seeks its innocence and to take responsibility for the world; they are not situations in which it is easy to act humanly, and our imagination does it only at a cost to itself – really, at the cost of being ourself' (121–2). Bond evinces an unshakeable faith in the importance of the theatre, and especially of tragedy, because it replicates the childhood encounter with nothingness and dramatizes the radical innocent's tragic interrogation of the boundary.

Bond's playwrighting work in the 1990s and up to the present takes on a simple and straightforward uniformity while also becoming more esoteric and gnomic. In keeping with the model set by *The War Plays*, Bond organizes plays into trilogies and tetralogies.[16] Repeated situations come to dominate the scenes of his plays, echoing scenes such as the soldier's insubordination in *Great Peace*, and an ambiguous and abstract post-apocalyptic landscape serves more and more to represent Bond's vision of the ruins of the present. It is as if in his ma-ture work, Bond has become increasingly focused upon the dramatic demon-stration of one or two simple truths about the human being, to be repeated again and again in slight variations. A simple and easily comprehensible quality of the Theatre Event allows an initial route into our understanding of these recent, enigmatic dramas: Theatre Events in Bond's plays are refracted from

Theatre Events in life, moments where human beings dramatize themselves by playing a part or acting out a story and thus either increase or diminish their humanity through the dramatic act of self-imagining. Theatre Events in Bond's plays are moments of self-dramatization on the parts of characters, and of particular note are moments where authority figures are confronted or characters act out the ideological narratives imposed by authority and which they have unthinkingly internalized.

Olly's Prison

The focus upon the importance of small, domestic, familiar objects in the dramatic situations of characters, while ubiquitous throughout Bond's oeuvre, is revealed in the 1990s to also be a key component in his theory of the tragic. In the opening scene of *Olly's Prison* (written for television in 1993 and adapted to the stage in 1994), a man in his late thirties named Mike, recently returned home from work to the small flat he shares with his sixteen-year-old daughter Sheila, makes her a cup of tea, and becomes irate that she will neither drink the tea nor acknowledge his presence at all. She does not speak throughout the entire forty-five-minute scene, while Mike speaks continuously, eventually focusing all of his anger, energy, and attention on persuading her to drink the cup of tea. She responds only when he wraps his hands around her neck and strangles her to death, a deed that she resists to no avail. Mike's reasons for strangling Sheila remain nebulous to him throughout the rest of the play, and his attempts to understand his murderous action both trouble and drive him. Yet Bond wants to use the staging of the scene to make the deed's origin clear to the audience. In a criticism of the Berliner Ensemble's production, Bond gives us crucial instructions on how the Theatre Event in the play was to work. The strangling should not have been staged with 'unemphatic gestures' ('Modern Drama' 19) – an alienation effect allowing the audience to think coldly about the action and its underlying social causes, which this particular production suggested were economic (their class and living conditions representing the cause). Bond is at pains to point out that murdering someone for refusing to drink a cup of tea is already strange and doesn't need to be alienated. He wants not just to show *that* the killing was motivated by social factors, but *why* such things caused the action. Moreover, Bond suggests that the economic and social situations are only partial contributors to what happens. In other words, he cautions us against reading the scene as an instance of naturalism or social realism, although it is easily interpretable through the lenses of psychology and sociology. A formal, tragic analysis reveals the substantial contours of the play.

It behooves us to attend to the strangeness of *Olly's Prison* rather than to try to submerge its surreal elements within a realistic analysis. Mangan draws our attention to a peculiar aspect of Mike's behaviour: the morning after the murder Mike awakes and goes to answer the doorbell, having forgotten for the moment the crime he had committed. For Mangan, who also compares Mike's quest for understanding to Lear's, this forgetfulness is just as bizarrely noteworthy as 'the grotesque tragedy which arose out of what was initially an argument over a cup of tea' (Mangan 82). The momentary amnesia is symptomatic of Mike's self-hood: after he has served ten years in prison, he finds himself still unable to accept that he strangled Sheila. If anything, his unshakeable feeling that he is *innocent* becomes even more urgent now that he is out of prison and can think again (*Olly's Prison* 23, 52, 54). When pressed, Mike knows that he killed her, but he insists again and again that he didn't do it (48–52). He explains: 'I murdered my daughter. We rowed about a teacup. You dont murder over that. I loved 'er. I thought about it for ten years. I wanted it t'go slower so I could think. There was just three words: Im innocent' (54). Mike's humanity, what Bond calls radical innocence, will not be quashed. By the end of the play, Mike makes an even stranger conclusion: he attributes Sheila's death to her former boyfriend Frank, who went on to become a police officer and is responsible for brutally beating and blinding a young man named Olly in an attempt to frame Mike and send him back to prison. Mike does not claim Frank actually attacked Sheila; rather he falteringly connects all the violence of the play back to the social role that Frank plays.

Mike has stumblingly and partially solved the problem that has troubled him for ten years: the violence the characters inflict upon one another and upon themselves is an expression of the brutal force of social authority that they interiorize as ideology and assume as given thinking. This insight is offered to the audience through the non-realistic Theatre Event of Frank's assault upon Olly: Frank directs the dramatic performance, instructing Olly to wreck Sheila's flat, and then proceeds to beat Olly so viciously that Olly is blinded. What begins as a staged crime becomes a real crime, but it is when the attack becomes legitimately brutal and 'real' that Bond uses a Theatre Event to remind us that this is not real: the action shifts to a space Bond calls 'The Grey Room,' a non-distinct interior space where the furnishings and props from Sheila's flat remain the same and where the assault proceeds uninterrupted. The real act of violence is a social performance of violence. Bond's use of a non-realistic intrusion in the Grey Room isolates the act of police violence and removes it from the space of the uninterrogated given: our attention is focused upon it now not as something 'real' or 'normal' or 'natural,' and particularly not as inevitable, but as an event that is artificial and created. Exposed by this conceit are 'the fictions by which we live,' as Bond puts it (Author's Note 75). This insight is something more than is offered to Mike in the play, who sees that there is a connection but does not see what the connection is. The Theatre Event gives the viewer a clarity of perception that Mike yearns for but cannot articulate, and it allows us to look back at the first scene of the play with the Grey Room in mind and consider Mike's strangling of Sheila as a similar Theatre Event – a performance of a social role.

The cup of tea is the theatrical locus of what Bond calls 'a crisis of freedom-tragic' ('Modern Drama' 19), a moment when something very small focalizes something very large. 'He has made her a cup of tea (the object). He seeks pleasure. The daughter will not drink it. Pleasure is frustrated. As the father talks the cup becomes an "object-moment": a crisis of freedom-tragic. He uses the cup as a map of his life: his self-site and the world-site' ('Modern Drama' 19). The cup of tea becomes the unlikely but all-too-mundanely commonplace locus for Mike's basic humanity to attempt to express itself. A repeated comment that Mike makes throughout the scene must be mapped onto this conflict. 'Lad left t'day. No job to go to. Didnt tell his missus,' he remarks at the beginning of the scene (Olly's Prison 4). This unnamed young man has abandoned his job at Mike's work, and this may be the reason Mike now has to go into work the next day, a Saturday (6). Mike even finds a connection between the youth's mysterious abandonment of his employment and a missed opportunity to escape to Australia in Mike's own past (10). Mike keeps repeating the phrase 'The lad just left' (10, 11, 13) while trying to force Sheila to drink the tea. In this youthful expression of freedom and autonomy from the ideological narratives Mike himself has internalized, Mike finds a disturbing recognition of an aspect of himself that seeks expression.

His imagination is expressed in his questioning of the young man's actions and in the questioning that propels him through the rest of the play, but in this immediate situation with the teacup his questioning is incarnated in his smothering attempt to bend his daughter's will to his own as a contorted and dehumanized expression of his own autonomy. The radical innocence of the imagination appears here as the energy and drive to find pleasure or fulfilment in some small act of kindness accepted by another, but when blocked or refused, this energy expresses itself in the full guise of social authority: the patriarch, frustrated by the wilful child, then proceeds to spew at her a litany of parental clichés about order, obedience, and respect for one's elders – 'It's only right' (6) – while tellingly blocking the exits from the room with chairs. Mike's imagination has been corrupted by social authority, and thus his expression of his right to happiness leads him to terrorize his daughter and treat her as the equivalent of a terrorist. The cup of tea becomes the embodiment of all of his frustrations and lost opportunities, and her refusal to drink it is a cataclysm:

'You could've drunk the tea. It wasnt much to ask. No you wont. Too easy. Got to be the hard way. A tragedy. One cup of tea and the world's got to end' (10). For her part, Sheila's cryptic refusal is at once mundane and approaches the sublimity of Antigone's stubborn intransigence. It is a tragic silence that judges her interrogator most palpably because it is never broken and she never moves. Mike will even hold the tea to Sheila's lips and ask only the final gesture from her, echoing the soldier and the cigarette packet in *Great Peace*. Sheila's innocence collides with her father's corrupt innocence in the tragic crucible of a cup of tea, but Mike's innocence survives and carries him through the play.

With this turn in his work, Bond asserts that the human being is at its centre a tragic entity. Human self-consciousness, the folding in upon the self of reflexive thought, is the experience of time and consequently the arrival of imagination: 'Self-consciousness creates a future and so a sense of mortality. Imagination is the knowledge given by time that we live and die' ('Modern Drama' 15). From the experience of mortality comes the basic sense of the tragic, of negativity, loss, all of which impedes freedom; in other words, the force of necessity. Bond explains: 'The Tragic is the neonate's recurring mortality, which it meets on the other side of its skin. It lives its death and dies its life. It knows the Tragic and the tragic desire for pleasure. The child knows – *is* – this. It exists in this way until its skin becomes *time* and it enters the others' world' ('The Reason for Theatre' 115). This core of simultaneous loss and gain, pain and pleasure, freedom and necessity, remains a kind of purity at the core of the self even in adulthood: 'The first map, on which the Tragic gave meaning to our need to exist, is not obliterated. The Tragic watches over our humanness and no one can escape the tragedy which is their self' (117). This inevitable confrontation with one's tragic selfhood occurs to Mike in the most domestic of objects: within the cup of tea.

We are being asked to comprehend the scene between Mike and Sheila as a Greek tragedy distilled down to an immutable essence, like an X-ray of Creon and Antigone. Indeed, Bond contextualizes his reading of Greek tragedy within terms that are profoundly revelatory of *Olly's Prison*:

> Strictly the Greeks were right, it is better (or at any rate simpler) not to be born. But they were wrong in saying that once born it is better to die – because imagination seeks life. It seeks it even if it has to kill to get it, either because of ideological persuasion (I die for freedom) or ideological fear (I make a sacrificial offering of a life in place of mine) or through psychological compulsion: either the obsessive need to return to the original confrontation with the freedom-tragic and survive it or simply out of the desire to kill death and for a time be its master. ('Modern Drama' 16)

Most challenging to our understanding of the human in Bond's work is the idea expressed in this passage: we are potentially being asked to understand that all of his characters act from the same humanizing energy despite the heinous acts of violence that they commit, and on a fundamental level even the most common-place of situations or activities is in fact a tragic confrontation with mortality. We are far beyond problems of good and evil or of moralizing judgments of charac-ters, and much closer to an Hegelian reading of Greek tragedy, where the charac-ters are all equally right and wrong in their actions, both justified and partial.

Where Creon and Antigone have the unburied body of Polynices over which they collide, Mike and Sheila have a teacup as a grave. This analogy allows us to understand the significance of Mike's references to his late wife in the teacup scene. Sheila's dead mother is initially introduced into the conflict in the most colloquial and familiar of manners: 'You know I worry. If your mother was alive she'd talk to you. Table too big. Bargain. Couldnt afford to let it go. Sat here when she was ill' (Olly's Prison 7). It emerges shortly that mourning has filled this household in the recent past. Mike describes Sheila's profuse tears when her mother passed away, and then he expresses regret at having brought her mother up at all, as if this has pushed the situation past the point of no return: '[W]hy why why did I bring your mother into it?' (11). The reference to loss and the recent confrontation with mortality in their collective past seems, in Mike's mind, to be a tangible contribution to the transformation of the teacup into a tragedy. There is even an indication on his part, however faltering, that he sees the tragedy for what it is: 'Help me Sheila. You dont know what's happenin. People are cruel. O dont know why. They make you suffer. What we're in now – this teacup – that'll happen all your life' (11). Finally he links the teacup to the site of mortality and loss in no uncertain terms: 'No she wont the hard-faced little bitch – grinnin inside her head – she'd let it stand there on her mother's grave till it's colder than the corpse' (12). The cup of tea occupies, within Mike's psychic map of their world, the ineffable site of mourning and negativity and becomes a small material avatar of death within the dramatic situation.

At the Inland Sea

The narrative of Olly's Prison exists within a social situation that is easily adapted to the paradigms of realism, and moreover within the restrictive medium of television, and it is perhaps with that in mind that Bond's next two plays break violently with any realistic framework or trappings. In their formal strangeness they resemble nothing so much as Sarah Kane's Blasted.[17] It is perhaps signifi-cant that Bond's and Kane's plays were staged at roughly the same time. Blasted opened in January 1995 at the Royal Court, but Kane was writing the play as early as 1993. Bond's *At the Inland Sea* was commissioned by Big Brum in February 1995 and was first performed in October of that same year. *Coffee: A Tragedy* was published in 1995 and first performed in November 1996. Bond, who saw *Blasted* and was a vocal champion of Kane when the critical establishment vilified her and her work, is also one of Kane's influences, and it is tempting to imagine that Bond has been reciprocally inspired by a quality of *Blasted* that is alienating to critics: it is a deliberately broken-backed play, like two incompatible dramas forced together, in which a hotel-room tryst in Leeds is intruded upon in the second half by an indistinct and apocalyptic civil insurrection. Similarly, in *At the Inland Sea* and *Coffee*, Bond replicates this disjointed structure: a student at study finds the larger social world intruding into the bedroom, only to be removed from that interior, private space and through a purely dramatic conceit placed in a world-historical situation of cataclysmic proportions.

In *At the Inland Sea* an unnamed boy studying and writing exams is repeatedly confronted by the spectre of a woman trying to save her infant from a gas chamber in an unspecified concentration camp. She demands a strange form of help from the boy: she wants him to tell her a story, one that will save her child's life by giving momentary pause to the soldiers coming to take them away. This quest for a story is part of the play's dream-like, amorphous logic. The woman has faith that if the story is told, something will happen to save her child: the child will perhaps be hidden in a corner of the gas chamber and saved by the soldiers when they come to clean it out. She believes that the soldiers will do it because '[p]eople do things to show they're human! I heard – a soldier – saw a body with a wristwatch. They'd missed it, hadn't taken it. He bent down to steal it. The time was wrong. He put it right – and the body was buried with the watch telling the right time. Even soldiers have to show themselves they're human!' (12). In such tiny, seemingly pointless and insignificant moments, where the time on a corpse's watch is corrected, Bond locates an essential humanity. Like the soldier, the protagonist of this play is compelled by his humanity to set things right in the gas chamber. He shows himself that he is human as he confronts the disjointed fabric of human history and attempts to set this time right, to do justice to the past. Tormented by the woman's demand, the boy eventually travels with her to the gas chamber, which exists in the same space of the stage as his room, but when he is unable to tell the story she demands of him, he instead removes her child and brings it back to his room, deliberately stopping time, freezing the scene of the gas chamber in a moment of undying human torment, like a massive suspension of historical justice.

Having assumed responsibility for history, the boy now realizes this does not mean he can change or refute what happened: 'You were killed before I was born. What can I do? Take you back to die' (30). The boy has confronted necessity. He has experienced the tragedy of history. In this failure itself Bond stages an activity of humanization through the opening of a tragic consciousness. Once he has returned the child, the boy is finally able to tell the story, although it is told to his mother, the parental figure who has attempted to block his awakening historical consciousness. The boy's concluding tale mediates his surreal experience of the contradictions of history: a tired and hungry man, travelling through a dark forest, is lured to a hut by a beautiful and happy song emanating from within. Inside, he finds that the hut is cold and abandoned, with traces of a recent meal left on the table. Departing, he hears the song again but, knowing what would happen if he returned to the hut, he does not turn back. He has learned a lesson from this denial of hope, but the boy's story is cut off by his mother, just as he is about to describe what the man will do in the future when he meets those suffering or in need. The story allegorizes the freedom-tragic, the collision of the man's yearning for relief from his hunger with a magical situation in a dark forest where he is tormented by a taunting and false promise. The lesson the man learns in the story is allusive: the forest will torment those in need and never help them. Help will come from those who, like him, have faced this experience and learned from it.

The boy himself demonstrates the other facet of the freedom-tragic that Bond finds located in object-moments. The final words of the play are 'I made some tea' (34). When the spectral woman first appears from the depths of his bed, clutching her infant, the boy is holding a cup of tea, which he slowly extends to her in a gesture of offering, holding it there until the tea begins to spill slowly from the cup onto his pants and the floor. His mother attempts to take the cup from him and in the struggle it falls to the floor and breaks. Over the next two scenes, as the boy sits his exams and does well in all but, significantly, history, his mother brings up the matter of the broken cup. 'Is it the history? You got four As! Don't spoil it for me. I can't afford to be ill like you. If I let go I'd never get back. I have to fight. I use my fists. Now I can't even enjoy this. Everything I have gets broken. Like that cup' (16). The mother here is a deeply sympathetic figure in her contradictions. As the boy's caregiver she expresses constant concern and love for her son, but as a single, working-class mother who has accepted her society's ideology she has invested herself deeply in her son's examinations, seeing his success ultimately as her own, and seeing his troubled state as an obstacle to her own small moment of happiness. The teacup assumes the tragic status of all of the obstacles to her meagre happiness that she has faced in her life. When, at the end, her son tells her that he has made some tea, the gesture to his mother echoes the offering of tea to the doomed woman at the beginning of the play and summarizes the lesson of the story: those who are in need must be offered help, because there are great tragedies found in the denial of the smallest of objects. A cup of tea has been the site of a tragic crisis within the world of the boy and his mother, and his final words hint that he has found a correlation between the cataclysm of the Holocaust and the apocalyptic conflict over tea that occurs in the first part of the play, a struggle that is over-shadowed at the time by the hallucinatory figure of the spectral woman but is available to our attention through the uniquely theatrical language of objects on the stage.

Coffee: A Tragedy

Yet the mediation of the general through the particular in such theatrical object-moments will not always serve the same dramatic purpose from play to play, and while it is not uncommon for Bond to inflect the hopeless situations in his plays with a stubborn and optimistic gesture in their conclusions, his dramas are equally concerned with the refusal of false hope. The particular can illustrate the trivialization of the general, and Bond will also occasionally re-mind us that theatre's proper subject matter is the gravest and most monumen-tal of human failings: 'Theatre begins at the gates of Auschwitz and in the ruins of Hiroshima and if you don't know what I'm talking about, then I'm wasting my time' ('Theatre begins,' *The Independent* 21 May 1997: 4). *Coffee: A Tragedy* explores the radical potential for dehumanization. The thematic tension of *Coffee* is to be found in the referent of its title and in the relationship between mass genocide and the preparation of a pot of coffee. This paradoxical connec-tion reveals the contradictions of humanity, the truth of the human always be-ing found in its paradoxes. In the play's central scene, soldiers prepare a pot of coffee at the end of a day of mass murder over a ravine. The protagonist of the play, an engineer and mature student named Nold, has become one of these soldiers through a purely theatrical conceit: he has simply fallen into the role much as the boy in *At the Inland Sea* has travelled, theatrically, to the gas cham-ber. Orders come that there is one last group of victims to be machine-gunned. The dramatic conflict of the scéne arises from two facts: they have run out of machine-gun bullets, and they are supposed to be finished for the day. Ordered to proceed with the mass slaughter using their rifles, one soldier expresses his disgust with the work by scattering the percolating coffee across the ground.

This gesture is bookended by telling silences; framed, so to speak, for its dra-matic importance. Bond explains that this action is drawn from survivor testi-mony of the historical genocide at the ravine of Babi Yar in the Ukraine: a woman waiting on the ledge to be killed looked across the ravine and saw a soldier scatter his coffee in this manner. 'Why does he scatter his coffee like a child?' Bond asks. 'This little gesture contains all the paradox of the last century. An entire century rests in that moment, and if you can understand that, you can understand what it signifies to be human' ('Theatre begins,' *The Independent* 21 May 1997: 4). The contradiction of this moment is an expression of the contradictions of history in the twentieth century: in the background, a mass killing field placed just out of view of the audience, while in the foreground, a pot of coffee is overturned and poured on the earth. In the space or gap between those two locations are the soldiers who dehumanize their victims through the activity of mass slaughter and dehumanize themselves through their willing participation in it. The humanity of the soldier is put on display in a situation where he struggles, and finally fails, to be human. In the scattering of the coffee we see the struggle, and in the second pot of coffee that is subsequently brewed and consumed by the soldiers as they go about their mass murder we see the abandonment of their humanity. That the act of negation is frustrated, nearly petulant, seems to be the only glimmer of possibility that Bond will allow here: 'Our social order is chaos, we live in a death culture. Evil is our attempt to be at home in this world – to earn our coffee and drink it in peace' ('Notes on *Coffee*' 167). In a fundamentally alienated world the attempt to escape this alienation is itself dehumanizing.

Following the incident at the ravine involving the pot of coffee, Nold finally kills his Sergeant rather than murder one more victim. At the end of the play, in a brief, enigmatic scene, Nold then confronts the daughter of the Sergeant whom he has killed. Nold flatly reveals that he has killed her father. In response to the daughter's numbed question, 'What did yer do?' Nold replies: 'I survived, I survived' (*Coffee* 216). What does it mean that Nold survived? As much as it means that Mother Courage has survived. Both Courage and Nold demonstrate that they can choose, that they have options, yet within the conditions of war there are no right choices. Nold chooses to save his potential victim and kills the Sergeant and another soldier instead. Yet he reveals that the woman he saved died in the end, all the same – shot by soldiers. Nold can choose but he cannot make the right choice, a humanizing choice. Survival here means the same thing as does the throwing away of the pot of fresh coffee: survival mean losing one's humanity unhappily, rather than obediently. War's contradictions do not allow humanity to exist. Survival is not noble or tragically elevating in a classical sense. Bond's tragedies push us towards the painful, conscious experience of this state through their formal qualities: bereft of context, of narrative groundings, of *sense* in any traditional manner, they present to the contemporary audience a form of suffering for the mind.

Coffee and *At the Inland Sea* are enigmatic and challenging plays because they are deliberately severed from narrative or historical context. In both cases, young men studying in closed rooms are intruded upon by phantasmal figures that compel the protagonists to travel, theatrically, to historical sites of genocide, where they are forced to confront their own inability to prevent the deaths of the victims. In both plays we are presented with a strangely closed work of art that we will not be able to place socially or historically, yet that uses recognizable historical events and represents them as concrete atrocities. In interpreting these dramas, reviewers have taken them either as representations of historical events, or as using historical events to comment, allegorically, upon contemporary contexts. What is sought is a referent in a mundane historical sense. What is then missed is the potential fact that the referent is not an historical event because theatre is not an historical record. The referent, so to speak, is History itself, inasmuch as history as we live it today is a failure. This referent is both concrete and abstract. Thus in *Coffee*, Bond explains that his inspiration is the historical massacre of 34,000 Jews at the ravine of Babi Yar outside Kiev, Ukraine, in 1941, by the Nazis. This leads to problems of interpretation: one reviewer of the original production by the amateur company Rational Theatre in Wales suggested that the point of the play was to draw analogies between the Holocaust and the destruction of communities in the Welsh valleys. Yet *Coffee* itself does not document the murders at Babi Yar in an antiquarian manner or search for transparent analogies between genocide and other historical catastrophes. Instead, Bond's goal is similar to Brecht's in *Mother Courage and Her Children*, a chronicle of the Thirty Years' War that is actually not overly concerned with this historical referent as such, but rather with what happens to a human being's humanity within the situation of war. By providing a concrete historical context, Brecht found himself compensating with attempts to redirect critical attention to the play's essential action: namely, the attempts by a woman to remain human in a situation where this is not possible. Bond solves a problem in Brecht's historical plays: he eliminates historical context and deliberately gives us the situation of war in a strange artistic vacuum. The result is something much closer to Brecht's Learning Play *The Measures Taken*, or even more appropriately, Heiner Müller's revision of *The Measures Taken*, *Mauser*, in which the contradiction of revolution, the substance of History, is represented freed of specific historical context, which would only distract us from the essence of the dramatic action: the attempts by Müller's executioner to remain human in a dehumanizing situation, working in the service of revolution, the goal of which is paradoxically to create a just society where everyone can be more fully human. 'The paradox of history is tragic,' Bond writes, 'we have humanness only at the cost of inhumanness' ('Freedom and Drama' 216). Within an unjust social totality, the only access to humanity is through acts of inhumanity.

The Crime of the Twenty-First Century

In Bond's work, this tragic humanness finds itself manifested in acts of violence with such frequency that the cumulative effect is a seeming valorization of crime as an expression of humanness in an inhuman society. Crime is an expression of radical innocence, the right to exist. In a recent piece of writing that is perhaps his most refined, concise, and clear articulation of the imagined function of his plays, Bond relates the radical innocence of the child to a telling classical forebear. In correcting Aristotle's class-based distortion and misinterpretation of the nature of tragedy, Bond engages in a revision similar to that performed by Nietzsche in *The Birth of Tragedy*, where the philosopher exposes Socrates's inability to understand the tragic. Bond asserts that *hubris*, for example, is only a failing of character from the perspective of the ruling class: 'In fact, *hubris* is insubordination against authority, either divine or state. It asserts the Promethean imperative to be human – and that is why Aristotle, the owner of slaves, needs to destroy it' ('Freedom and Drama' 219). It is the use of the concept of the Promethean that is most curious here, as the phrase immediately situates Bond's tragic characters within a Nietzschean framework. Nietzsche speculates that the rational philosophers failed to grasp the pre-Socratic, irrational power of Dionysus at work within tragedy: 'Because of his titanic love of man, Prometheus must be torn to pieces by vultures; because of his excessive wisdom, which could solve the riddle of the Sphinx, Oedipus must be plunged into a bewildering vortex of crime,' Nietzsche writes in *The Birth of Tragedy* (46). Such titanic overreachers are, within Nietzsche's aesthetic philosophy, avatars for the Dionysian: '[A]ll the celebrated figures of the Greek stage – Prometheus, Oedipus, etc. – are mere masks of this original hero, Dionysus' (73). In the myth of Prometheus, *hubris* expresses the essence of the human itself: 'The Titanic impulse to become, as it were, the Atlas for all individuals, carrying them on a broad back, higher and higher, farther and farther, is what the Promethean and the Dionysian have in common' (72). Bond's radical innocence is a secular version of this Promethean impulse to life and to affirming all that exists, without asceticism, negativity, or renunciation.

Thus we find ourselves, somewhat curiously but perhaps not surprisingly, arriving at a Bondian tragic that will have strong parallels with that of Barker, and also, as we shall see, with that of Caryl Churchill, as if the many varied paths of these playwrights lead them each towards a single Dionysian destination, reached by dissimilar routes. One of Bond's most Promethean characters is Sweden in *The Crime of the Twenty-First Century* (2001), but he is also one of Bond's most overtly Oedipal characters, sending echoes back to *Lear* and even *Saved*, and dramatizing the connections between the Dionysian/Promethean and the Oedipal that are essential to the play's attack on authoritarian, ideological thinking. There is an intensely compressed dramatic power to *The Crime of the Twenty-First Century*: in the razed, flattened ruins of what was once a vast city, an ostracized and alienated woman in her mid-fifties, Hoxton, finds her isolation intruded upon first by Grig, a man in his sixties who has fled his suburban life, having abandoned his wife as she dies of cancer. This initial intrusion is followed by the arrival of Sweden, a young man of twenty who claims to have fled the army and who usurps Grig's place in Hoxton's bed. Thus Sweden begins as a recognizably Oedipal figure, but will soon reveal this to be a mask for the Promethean impulse.

Sweden is an unquashable life force in this Oedipal triangle, too human and too in love with living itself to be conceivable to those around him. Sweden explains how he has avoided recapture by the army: he has dug the electronic tag worn by all soldiers out of his chest, from behind his ribcage. He recounts the experience with overtly Promethean imagery: 'Cut me 'eart out! Rupture me gut! Slice me liver! An threw it over the river! Over the other side! The other side! I should 'a bin dead 'n I felt immortal!' (227). As he tells this story his frenetic gestures turn into a dance, the ecstatic overtones of which we should not overlook (227). Later, he will confess that he was first pursued by the army because he was a pyromaniac obsessed with setting automobile showrooms ablaze, another Promethean image of the life force that institutional authority wants to apprehend and shackle. By the end of the play Sweden will have endured physical mutilation to rival that of Prometheus, and while he does not lose his liver to a vulture, he crawls offstage into the wasteland in the penultimate scene, blind and without feet, yet indefatigable in his energy.[18] To survive, he explains, he will live like a dog and forget that he was ever human (268).

The violence to which Sweden is subjected during the dramatic action is both an attack upon and an affirmation of his radical innocence, a testing of his Promethean right to live. His energy, enthusiasm, optimism, and skills at cuckoldry are an affront to Grig, who refuses to believe that Sweden could have dug the tag out of his own chest, and so betrays him to the army. Sweden returns to Hoxton's hovel blinded and indomitable. He recounts how even in his mutilated state he slew a dog that came sniffing around him: 'Sacrifice the dog so I could live – show I 'as the strength. If they come t' bury me now I'd grab the sides a' the grave 'n drag the world in with me – I got a right' (246). His right to live even extends, it turns out, towards blinding himself. The soldiers, like Grig, refuse to believe Sweden removed his tag himself. As representatives of social authority, they are fascinated by the energy of humanity and by what innocence will do to live. In order to make him prove his fortitude, they force Sweden to dig out his remaining eye himself. He could do it, it turns out, because he cannot escape his desire to live at all costs: 'I couldn't die, out there a week – crawl – things growin in the rubbish brush me face – I ate – I couldn't stop meself – I ate' (248–9). This will to live also extends to murder, as Sweden becomes convinced that Hoxton is a force blocking his survival: when his attempts to persuade her to travel with him to a fantasized utopian oasis that he imagines is beyond the ruins delay him and draw him back to her hovel, he finally stabs her to death (251).

After the soldiers catch him again and cut off his feet, Sweden, by his own reckoning, must now abandon all pretenses at humanity and become the feral animal he has feared he would eventually be. Sweden becomes an abject figure stripped of all the trappings of civilization, a raw exposure of the right to be that is implicit in thought as such, and which is the radical innocence of the self, though it seems like savagery. '[I]n psychoanalysis radical innocence is guilt. [...] Freud cannot deal with the Promethean in humankind, yet without the Promethean we are not even decent,' Bond remarks ('Freedom and Drama' 211). If Sweden has been stripped down to a figure of what is more commonly known as the id, the impulse to crime and the elements of the self that are managed by guilt, then Grig's fate reveals a demystified version of conscience, because to make a claim to humanity in this place is worse than inhuman acts of innocence. Sweden claims that for Grig to place a blanket on Hoxton's corpse is a human ritual of respect for the dead that has no significance here: 'I kill 'er, 'e's worse: 'e pretends we're still 'uman this late, in this place' (*Crime* 261). Grig is finally consumed by remorse when he sees Sweden's physical degradation. As Sweden crawls off into the ruins, Grig is transported by the play's theatrical imagery into Bond's Grey Room, a bare grey space with a stone block at its centre, a kind of existential hell where Grig stands and stares vacuously, mentally enfeebled, moving slowly and in small, pointless gestures, and finally howling seven times. This Theatre Event exposes the social script of guilt as a humanistic value: a madman in an institutional smock, bereft of either reason or freedom due to the inhumanity to which he has clung in the guise of humanity, reduced to the status of a ghost or a zombie in a hellish grey prison because the fictions he has adopted as truth have finally abandoned him. Thus we are left with two alternative subjectivities at the end of the play, neither of which is immediately recognizable as a possibility.

The extremity of Bond's dramatic situations, throughout all of his work but particularly in his most recent plays, is motivated by a clear theoretical premise. Ideological thinking will always seek to reduce the contradictory and inconceivable to something comprehensible by rational conceptual thinking, thus into mere ideas. The Promethean innocent at the heart of the human, what Bond calls our 'core self,' is not understandable within the terms of rational thought. In fact it is not, technically speaking, understandable at all; rather, it is perceivable or detectable within moments of paradox and impossibility, the special reserve of drama:

> Drama must be extreme so that it drives the contradictions beyond the point where ideology can control them. Then the self confronts the core self. This produces the paradox – which appears as non-reason because ideology has made reason irrational. The paradox comes from the confrontation of humanness with ideology, radical innocence with corruption. In the Tragic humanness always prevails. ('Freedom and Drama' 220)

And so Bond's continued dramatic project entails the exposure of contradiction and paradox in an assault upon the ideological corruption of human reason, and the site of such contradiction and paradox remains the most mundane of human locations. Drama is found in the particular, when the particular becomes a site of crisis. In those object-moments, the sudden infusing of significance within the insignificant also serves as such a challenge to ideological thinking, which cannot overcome the opposition of general and particular: 'What seems irrelevant may become most relevant of all. In drama this is the devastating play of the relevant and irrelevant which reopens the ideologically closed world. Then the cup may "contain" the universe because it is cathected with it' ('Freedom and Drama' 213). Thus for Bond, drama is the opposite of fiction. Fiction is the ideology that we live every day: 'We live these fictions on the street just as actors play fictions on a stage. [...] We are fictions because we live the logic of ideology' (212). Drama is reality, 'because it enacts the core self, which is the means by which we entered into reality' (209). Thus we must understand Bond's dramas as concrete interventions into human reality through the internalization of reality itself onto the space of the stage. What we see on-stage is the Promethean within ourselves, enacted within the action of drama.

Chair

This theory is refined into recent plays of elementary simplicity and starkness. There is, in works like *Have I None* (2000), *Chair* (2001), *Existence* (2002), and *The Under Room* (2005) a bleak and grim hopelessness on display. The settings are closed rooms in private flats, at the heart of impersonal, alienated cities, sometimes located in the present (as in *Existence*) and sometimes in the arbitrarily designated year 2077 (as in *Chair*, *The Under Room*, and *Have I None*). These are urban spaces blighted by the most profound and irremediable disconnect between citizens. In the futuristic dystopias that Bond portrays, humanity

seems to have gradually wilted and died under the weight of capitalist democracy's slow, incremental erosion of human rights, replacing society with institutional apparati and transforming authority into military force. A permanent
state of alert has suspended human rights. This corruption and decay has expanded to the point where compassion has become not just a liability but a
crime, such as in *Chair*, where the possibility that the protagonist, Alice, might
have felt pity for a criminal places her life at risk.

The action of *Chair* is simple and brief: Alice harbours in her home Billy, a
twenty-six-year-old man with the mind of a child, whom Alice found abandoned as an infant and committed the crime of keeping, thus meaning that she
would forever have to hide him in her small flat. One day Billy suggests to her
that she might take a chair out to a soldier who is escorting a prisoner and waiting for a bus on the street. Alice, in her curiosity about the prisoner, does so, but
the chair proves to be a deeply destabilizing object when introduced into the
situation. The prisoner becomes agitated and uncontrollable, seemingly enliv-
ened by an incomprehensible gesture of compassion, and the soldier, panick-
ing, shoots his charge. Alice is subject to an interrogation about the incident
that concludes with a decision to transfer her to a smaller flat away from any
bus stops. Realizing that she will not be able to conceal Billy's presence any
longer, she arranges for her own cremation and hangs herself, but not before
instructing Billy to scatter her ashes in a car park, where the wheels of automo-
biles will disperse her utterly, erasing all trace of her existence. She plans this
death in order to escape the institutionalized euthanasia that awaits all undesir-
ables in this society: death by choice of tablet or injection in a clinic, followed
by cremation, a short, empty funeral rite, and a memorial in the form of 'a block
of marble resin and a thornless rose bush' along with a generic floral arrange-
ment in a garden of remembrance where the Prison City wardens eat their
lunch (*Chair* 137).

From this perspective, *Chair* is a play about the ancient tragic theme of funeral rites. It concludes with a scene of sparse and hopeless mortality that serves
as the only possible resistance against the dehumanized emptiness of false humanism in the face of human mourning. Alice explains to Billy that he must
scatter the ashes in the box that is brought to him because she will not be owned
by this society: 'There'll be no flowers. No music. No speaking. No people
standing in lines. No grass. No stone. Nothing they can get their hands on and
say it's theirs. Nothing. I was never here. I was never anywhere. I never was. I
was nothing. Not even a piece of dust' (141). Billy himself must go out into the
world alone, utterly without resources. It is difficult to articulate exactly why
the ending of *Chair* is so profoundly life-affirming: for a full day, Billy stands
and observes the sights and sounds of the city he has lived in for twenty-six

years but has never seen. Utterly alone in the universe and wrenchingly innocent, he seems to experience a lifetime's days, perhaps because the experiences
are all the more precious for their rarity. At the end of this day, he finds a car
park and scatters Alice's ashes into the sky. He is seen and perfunctorily shot
dead, and his corpse is sprinkled with falling ashes. The play's hopefulness is
located in this image: a dead man who has lived only one day is gently shrouded
by the ashes of a dead woman, and in their deaths they express the freedom of
the human from the oppression of an unjust society. It is a purely theatrical moment deeply saturated with human mortality.

   Chair returns us to Len and his chair in *Saved*. It is clear that Bond cannot be
reduced to social realism, or to the Brechtian estrangement of ideological
thinking. Instead, Bond's formalism is the refinement of the project of socialist
tragedy: as an assertion of the contours of the core self, the tragic human, within
late capitalist postmodernity, itself an economic landscape of reification in
which existence is characterized most fully by the image of an undead wasteland. What seems most pessimistic in these profoundly negative plays is in fact
the most optimistic. The expressions of Promethean will, acts of violence, and
negation at the heart of situations of endemic, institutionalized social violence
are in fact tragic affirmations of humanity. What appears to be most abstract
and existential in these late plays (and their sparse, gestural titles hint at such
existentialism) is, for Bond, what is most material about them: the drama of the
core self, what emerges as a Promethean assertion of self within tragic situations. Yet looking back at earlier plays we can observe this Promethean figure,
this 'radical innocence' emerging in the paradoxical struggles of Len, Lear,
Shakespeare, John Clare, the Woman in *Great Peace*, Mike in *Olly's Prison*, and
Nold in *Coffee*. The politicized formalism of Bond's plays finds expression in a
new theatrical language of material objects as locations of emancipatory tragic
experience. Learning this new language is Bond's challenge to ideological
thinking, not just to Englishness but to the ideology of capitalism itself. The
object-moment of the freedom-tragic is a challenge to see dialectically on the
part of an audience: to grasp totality in a teacup, to see the social contradictions
of contemporary existence expressed in desperate conflicts over mundane domestic objects. The impulse to justice, the work of being human, is invested in
chairs, shovels, cigarette packages, teacups, coffee pots, and a bundle of cloth
shaped in a humanizing, theatrical mimicry of a child.

Caryl Churchill:
The Dionysian Möbius Strip

The inclusion of Caryl Churchill in this analysis of contemporary English tragedians may seem, at first glance, unexpected. With the exception of works like *Fen*
and *A Mouthful of Birds*, Caryl Churchill does not write plays that are recognizable as conventionally tragic in dramatic form. Nor does she philosophize at great
length about theatre or theorize about her own work as tragic, although she does
preface her work with references to the philosophy and theory that have influenced her plays. Nevertheless, I feel she has a crucial place in the present study.
Churchill, born in 1938, has proven a remarkably elusive playwright to classify
over the course of her career. While she is most readily categorized as a feminist
playwright with strong socialist commitments, this is largely due to her own statements in rare interviews.[1] Despite her declared politics, she rarely intervenes in
public or scholarly interpretations of her own work.[2] Attempts to investigate her
plays as examples of a transparent political stance or even of a single theoretical
underpinning founder on Churchill's shapeshifting qualities as a playwright, one
who is constantly reinventing dramatic form and frustrating past expectations.
Moreover, Churchill's plays do not conform to the clichés of what is expected of
'political theatre' in that they rarely offer positive images of socialist or feminist
progress.[3] Most recently, there have been thoughtful attempts to find a unifying
concern throughout Churchill's career without forcing the plays to conform to
pre-existing templates for political theatre. Elaine Aston and Elin Diamond
('Introduction: On Caryl Churchill') suggest 'distinctly anti-capitalist' with a focus on 'gender concerns' (4), and this reading of a chiefly critical, oppositional
stance is consistent throughout their *Cambridge Companion to Caryl Churchill*.
Therein, Diamond argues separately for a 'unique dramaturgy of terror' as a coherent thread running through Churchill's career ('On Churchill and Terror'
125) and discusses how, in the case of *Thyestes*, 'the cosmology of tragedy gives
Churchill rein to explore the spatial simultaneity of contemporary terrorism'

(138). New ways of appreciating Churchill are emerging, readings that enhance rather than reduce our understanding of her political theatre.

Three further recent assessments establish key concerns for this chapter. Dan Rebellato posits that Churchill's abiding concern is the conflict between 'the authoritarian, rational, repressive form of power and the playful, non-rational, irruptive force of dreaming' ('On Churchill's Influences' 168). Elin Diamond asserts that Churchill has a kinship with Samuel Beckett because 'Churchill's characters have always been lonely, even on a stage full of people. [...] [B]oth are dark and precise poets of a suffering that is comically and self-consciously inflected. Both locate the human subject in interstices, not positivities' ('Beckett and Caryl Churchill along the Möbius Strip' 287). Finally, Amelia Howe Kritzer connects Churchill's recent plays to her earlier concerns through 'the possibility of a non-objectifying love transcending ego and reaching out to all being,' fuelled by 'the strength and completeness of an alternative subjectivity and the non-possessive love potentiated by such a subjectivity' (*Political Theatre in Post-Thatcher Britain* 78). I want to connect all three assessments: dreaming implies the force of the unconscious, the locus of alienation, suffering, isolation, and subjectivity, but also of desire – a desire that, as Kritzer's point implies, contains utopian possibilities for subjectivity within collectivity. The tragic figure who unites these concerns is Dionysus.

Churchill's abiding interest in the place or non-place of desire within the human subject makes her plays pieces of philosophizing in their own right, and her dramatic exposure of the vicissitudes of the subject locates her work within a tragic rubric, as long as we continue to maintain a place for the Dionysian within contemporary tragedy. Dionysus and his theatrical power appear most forcefully within *A Mouthful of Birds*, Churchill's collaboration with David Lan, but the influence of the bacchic is detectable elsewhere. The human is tragic in Churchill, but the contours of this tragic change throughout her oeuvre. Churchill moves, over the course of her playwriting career, from grappling with the problem of subjectivity as articulated within traditional paradigms (the Freudian, the Marxist-socialist, the feminist) towards overcoming those paradigms by means of a passage through them. The problem of the human as defined through lack, through negativity, through loss or absence is given a post-structuralist revisioning, so that what appears as lack and alienation is rewritten, dramatically, into difference, and the tragic paradigm of the human as self-divided is emancipated into an affirming, if impossible, vision of the human as a Möbius strip. The unlived life becomes the life of dreams, the unconscious transformed into the underside of everyday life, but with the added twist of the Möbius strip itself: the underside is merely the same side at a different point in the unending surface.[4] However, we should remember that the Möbius strip is an impossible object that can nevertheless be imagined: as such, it constitutes an impossible promise, but a promise made nevertheless. This promise is of a unity with one's desires, a one-ness with Dionysus.

Seven Jewish Children

A very recent piece of theatre frames this discussion, modelling how Churchill's playwriting constitutes a simultaneous intervention into the pathologies of human psychology and the pathologies of modern history. While Churchill's 'solution' is Dionysus, the problem of Dionysus is that he is at once everywhere and nowhere, ubiquitous and utterly unlocatable, an absent presence.[5] This is nowhere more in evidence than in *Seven Jewish Children: A Play for Gaza* (2009), a play examining the effects of historical events upon the individual psyche and the effects of the individual psyche on historical events. It is arguably the most obviously 'political' play Churchill has ever written, provoked in response to the Israeli Defense Force's attacks upon the Palestinian territory in December 2008. In seven short scenes that play out onstage over a total of ten minutes, Churchill shows us seven groups of Jewish adults, debating and arguing strategies for explaining historical events to a child. We move from the Second World War and a family who must conceal a female child and discuss what to tell her in order to maintain her safety, to a post-war series of historical snapshots in which adults discuss how to explain the Holocaust to a child, then how to explain why they are moving to Israel to a child, then how to explain who the Arabs are who are being displaced from their homes, then how to explain the victorious war in which they have acquired land (presumably the Six Day War in 1967), then how to explain the bulldozing of Palestinian homes and the terrorist bombings of cafés, and in the final scene, how to explain the violent incursion into Gaza and the massive death toll in Palestinian lives.

This culminates in a long tirade of anger and loathing spoken by one character, who concludes: '[T]ell her we're chosen people, tell her I look at one of their children covered in blood and what do I feel? Tell her all I feel is happy it's not her' [6]. As Tony Kushner and Alisa Solomon put it in their deeply insightful and sensitive assessment of the play, 'The play stages the return of the repressed, an explosion of threatened defensiveness that, unexpressed and unowned, has turned into rage.'[6] Thus in its content, the hate-filled rant demonstrates a typically Freudian reflex of the psyche, the alienation from emotions and thoughts that return violently and unbidden, both at the level of the private subject and in the wider context of violent historical tragedy. Yet this rant is followed by a reply: 'Don't tell her that. / Tell her we love her. / Don't frighten her' [6]. The text of the play was made available free of charge at the websites of Nick Hern Books and of the Royal Court Theatre, and this accessibility has garnered an enormous amount of attention for the play. Detractors who accuse the text of anti-Semitism and of being 'hate speech' focus upon the long monologue quoted above while eliding the response that comes afterwards, three short lines that I will argue are much more important to consider, although in their simplicity and subtlety they are also much easier to overlook. However, Churchill prepares us to attend to these final, gnomic words, not just in this play but throughout her work: the phrase 'Don't frighten her' is repeated in the first, third, and sixth scenes of *Seven Jewish Children*, while a permutation, 'Tell her not to be frightened,' appears in scene 4. Those familiar with Churchill's work will naturally recognize the key repeated word from the conclusion of *Top Girls* and from the conclusion to the short play *Abortive*. In Churchill's work, to be frightened, the special capacity of children, is to be openly thinking about and anticipating the future.[7]

The return of the repressed is not all the play has to offer, and it is at the level of form that the play promises an alternative to such a violently and tragically alienated subjectivity. The text of *Seven Jewish Children* does not assign roles and explains that it can be performed by any number of actors. It might be a single actor onstage or a pair of actors. It might conceivably be twenty. In the performance I saw at the Royal Court in February 2009 it was nine. The play can be as monologic or dialogic as is desired by the company performing it, and as is evident, this will affect profoundly the meaning of the play: the more characters there are onstage the wider may be the disagreement and dissent among them, the less confident they may become in their assertions, the more isolated will be the penultimate, hate-filled rant. This lone monologue thus sits couched within a larger framework of Bakhtinian heteroglossia and dialogism.[8] This authorial openness on Churchill's part is a familiar tactic, echoing the doubling of roles in plays like *Cloud Nine* and *Top Girls*. As with all of her plays, Churchill enacts strategies that leave some of the meaning to emerge only in performance, resulting in a unique plurality of sense in her plays. There can be no final interpretation of a Churchill play because multiplicity is part of these meanings. As I will suggest here, this relaxed authorial attitude is key to the meaning and effects of her plays, which more than any other contemporary oeuvre are texts for *live* performance, and will find their meaning within the instance of performance.

Watching *Seven Jewish Children* in performance at the Royal Court, what was unexpected were the moments of humour: the statement 'Tell her she can take her toys' receives the reply 'Don't tell her she can take all her toys' [3]. Through an emphasis on the word *all* the moment evoked the laughter of recognition. Yet this evocation of laughter is also integral to the structure of the drama, which is predicated on a series of responses and counter-responses. The humour emerges when a character suggests, 'Tell her maybe we can share' with the Arabs who are losing their homes, which elicits the contemptuous reply 'Don't tell her that,' spoken in a tone indicating that such facile nonsense is insulting to a child's intelligence. Such a moment draws laughter from the audience because it evokes recognition of what the audience member is thinking, just as does '[T]ell her she can watch Friends' [5]. A simple moment of banal familiarity, the name of a well-known television program, has the ability in live performance to draw the audience into the situation depicted onstage. At the heart of what is essentially an historical tragedy, the collective moment of performance brings out unexpected laughter.

Through this familiarity of response, Churchill devotes most of *Seven Jewish Children* to rendering recognizable and sympathetic characters that immediately elicit acknowledgment. They are, after all, adults trying to decide how to introduce children to the painful realities of the world, and this is a simple and ubiquitous commonplace. It is an evident distortion for critics of the play to accuse it of villainizing Jews or of portraying them as quasi-Nazis. To the contrary, Churchill avoids any facile stereotyping and in fact counters the traditional 'othering' of Jewish characters according to mannerisms or behaviour. I am not even convinced that the play rehearses the familiar argument that Jacqueline Rose attributes to it: 'The point is to make us think about how trauma transmutes itself into ruthless self-defence' ('Why Howard Jacobson is wrong,' *The Guardian*, 24 February 2009). While I agree with Rose's assessment that the play portrays an historical tragedy, her reading of it as a transparent and pointed critique of specific Israeli policies renders it into a political tract rather than a piece of theatre. While she is a defender of the play, she focuses to such a great degree on the particulars of its content that she treats it as do its detractors: as a content-bearing message. Yet it is not a public speech, a letter to the editor, or a piece of researched political analysis, and while it bears a particular message it must also be respected for the general meaning it expresses.

From the perspective of this study, the eloquence and simplicity of Churchill's play is to be found in its rendering taut of an historical contradiction embodied in the condition of war and modernity, one that is a constant refrain here: this mother's child must thrive at the expense of other mother's children. This simple ideologeme, famously given shape in Mother Courage's lullaby to her daughter, is more forcefully and controversially expressed in the ranting monologue at the climax of *Seven Jewish Children*. *Seven Jewish Children* rehearses the same tragic social contradiction that Bond dramatizes in the Palermo paradox. I choose to interpret the play not as an accusation against Israel or its populace, but rather as the articulation of an utterly banal and tragic truth: all over the world every day children die so that other children might live. Quite simply, in trying to love and protect their children and secure their survival, the adults in this play gradually find themselves compromising the lives of other children. In demonstrating this contradiction, *Seven Jewish Children* has the eloquence and stark simplicity of a *Lehrstück*. If this Learning Play is experienced by the mind *as* a real contradiction, it is because the shared humanity of the children, as children, is recognized and accepted, and the unacceptability and incoherence of the contradiction avowed. These children who die are your children just as much as those of your nation or family. As a good Learning Play, the contradiction dramatized here has no existing solution.

This helps us to understand why Churchill feels it necessary to stipulate from the outset in her published text what should seem self-evident: '*No Children appear in the play*' [1]. The demand that something remain absent forces us to attend to the compelling power of absence, particularly in live performance. The play's form is specifically simple and repetitious: a series of dialogues or arguments that never come to a conclusion or an agreement, but rather constitute a series of statements and contradictions, a seemingly stunted and directionless, unproductive series of exchanges, the exact opposite of a dialectic. Yet in the midst of this disagreement the presence of the titular characters is conjured, the figures for whom everything in the play is in fact at stake. If the adults wish to protect the children from being frightened, it is because the children have the potential to be frightened, because to be frightened means to imagine circumstances and consequences, and that is children's progressive potential. By demanding that children not be present in the play, Churchill at once excludes such hopeful figures from the content of the drama, and yet at the same time exploits the power of theatrical form to conjure them virtually, as absent presences. They embody, in a virtual sense, the contradiction, the incoherent gap or unsolved problem, at the heart of the play.

It would be too simple to state that owing to the remorseless logic that plays out through the scenes, this is therefore a pessimistic play, or a nihilistic political play without a positive vision. Or even to state tritely that the play leaves its audience to find solutions to the problems, constituting a 'negative dialectic', although it does do this. Churchill confronts, I think, the familiar artistic problem that Adorno articulates with respect to committed art: how to suggest change and alternative visions without embodying them directly, which would always constitute a compromise to the present.[9] For Churchill the playwright, the challenge of theatre is how to unleash Dionysus upon negativity and repression, and through artistic intervention affirm the negative into multiplicity and joy. How to wear repression as a theatrical mask, and in so doing reinterpret it from Oedipal alienation into Dionysian difference. How to repeat the tragedy of history into tragic joy. This strategy, I will suggest, accounts for the morbidity, negativity, and open-endedness of much of her theatrical content. In Churchill, tragic joy is found not so much in the content of her plays as in their unique experimentation with dramatic form and theatrical possibility; her style and her unique theatrical conceits. Multiplicity and affirmation are found in the materiality of her plays in performance, and in *Seven Jewish Children* this affirmation is given its most tangible shape in the conjuring of the titular characters out of theatrical nothingness. It is a telling instance of the Dionysian: the affirmation of pure negativity into pleasure. The children are the avatars of the Dionysian here: they cannot in fact be located anywhere but in the mind of the perceiver. This creates what I will call tragic joy, or a joyful tragic. Dionysus here is multiplicity in the openness of theatrical staging.[10]

Lovesick

The collision between alienation and difference is staged to bleakly comic effect in one of Churchill's early works, a play that confronts the clinical repressiveness of Oedipal thinking with a Dionysian, bacchic overturning. In the very first lines of dialogue in the earliest play that Churchill cares to put into print, *Lovesick* (radio 1966), we find the compressed and evocative vision of the self that animates her writing: 'When Smith raped he didn't find what he was looking for, so then he dissected with a chopper and was left with a face and meat to stuff in a sack' (3). This radio play takes as its central figure a psychiatrist, Hodge, who experiments with Pavlovian treatments for modifying human behaviour, in particular for redirecting the arc of human desire. Hodge identifies with the murderous dissection performed by his psychopathic patient Smith: Hodge lays bare the human mind with the sharp instrument of reason. He sees love as no different from illness, to be treated in accordance with a clinical yardstick of health. Having stumbled into the midst of the dysfunctional middle-class Zolotov family, Hodge immediately diagnoses them with a series of standard neuroses, but he himself becomes obsessed with Ellen McNab, who is unhappily married to and in love with Kevin Zolotov, who is gay. Hodge, applying instrumental reason to the situation, hatches a scheme to use Pavlovian techniques to 'cure' Kevin's homosexuality, and to 'cure [Ellen] of Kevin' and 'addict her' to Hodge himself (16). Desire is a sickness, and easily cured by science.

Meanwhile, Robert Zolotov reveals that he enjoys a sexual relationship with his own mother, Jessica, comically frustrating Hodge's attempts to diagnose Robert's unconscious incestuous impulses. This key revelation signals a reversal of circumstances and is Churchill's playful, Dionysian overturning of Oedipal, Freudian paradigms of neurosis and repression. In Hodge's absence, Robert sabotages the aversion therapy, with the result that Kevin now loathes himself and loves Hodge, and Ellen discovers herself to be a lesbian. Hodge's friend Max Brown, who has been having an affair with Jessica, is provoked by the revelation of incest to finally find happiness with his wife Lucy when he starts wearing her dresses, and Lucy in turn buys six trouser suits. The play concludes with Hodge about to administer the aversion therapy to himself so that he can stop thinking about Ellen.

Lovesick is a grimly humorous play: its comedy arises from the satiric confrontation provoked by cold reason's attempts to apply terms like 'cure' and 'addiction' to the unpredictable arrows of human desire that elude rational discourse. At the same time, the play does not shirk the violence inherent in instrumental reason as applied to the human, and in the terrors of desire when it is yoked by reason. Hodge suggests to Ellen that if she smacks her child before it wets itself this will serve as a better deterrent than hitting it after it does something wrong (12). The psychiatrist describes himself as akin to an axe murderer, while Kevin ultimately commits suicide when finally spurned by Hodge. The Pavlovian aversion therapy has strong Freudian overtones: Hodge's cure for Smith the rapist and murderer is described as an effective alternative to castrating the criminal, and Hodge's technique functions as a kind of symbolic castration of his subjects, a redirecting of insubordinate desires into socially acceptable channels through repression and the internalizing of negativity.

Robert plays a subversive Dionysus to Hodge's Pentheus authority figure. The final turnabout, where the revelation of healthy, untroubled Oedipal love effectively overturns Hodge's medical discourse of illness and cures, heralds a kind of bacchanalia of blissful incest, celebratory homosexuality, and gleeful gender subversion. Significantly, when Kevin and Ellen are subject to the Pavlovian treatment, they insist that they have *always* been this way: 'I've always loved you,' Kevin insists to Hodge. 'I used to be so annoyed by your knowing talk and now I see that was just a defence against my true feelings' (18). In its comic manipulation of Freudian cliché, this hints at the potential for a steady continuity of experience between conscious and unconscious, desire figured as eternal and unchanging and within the grasp of the self. If we take the characters at their word, in becoming one with their desires they have not been changed by aversion therapy at all. They have simply revealed that one's true self lies not in the past, the future, or beneath the surface of conscious agency, but in the moment of realized desire. The Oedipal mask of repression and neurosis is not pushed aside, but discovered to have been wearing a cunning smile all along, sign of the god lurking within the mask itself.

The joke is on Hodge, who himself is decentred by the events: 'I've homosexual tendencies like anyone else, but well suppressed, and it was most inconvenient to have them stirred' (18). Churchill here begins to gently mock and displace the alienated self of Freudian paradigms, the ego divided from its desire by social repression. Owning one's desire is both the key to the problem of knowing the self and also the potential bar to the subject's completeness. Hodge, the play reveals to us, does not know or understand himself because of the dislocating force of his own desire, which he narrates as a haunting fear of a childhood fall that never took place. Ellen McNab's beauty reminds him of a youthful experience: a tall boy at school who dressed in dirty clothes one day pushed Hodge into the canal. Upon his climbing excitedly out, a passing dog almost knocked Hodge back in, and this moment of being off balance, of being at risk of stumbling and falling again bred a feeling of fear that now returns to him in dreams or when he misses his footing. The attraction to beauty is a manifestation of the fear of falling.

As Hodge reveals, being frightened connects Churchill's characters to the life of dream and figures significantly within her developing expressionism. In its negative aspects, to be frightened is to be tortured by some aspect of one's own selfhood, but somewhat more elusively, to be frightened is also a symptom of how desire – here the attraction to beauty – engenders an open, apprehensive consciousness. Thus the capacity to be frightened hints bleakly at unrealized possibilities for the realization of desire. When Hodge was pushed into the canal, he was filled with excitement and, it seems, attraction for the boy who pushed him. It is only when the experience risked being repeated with the dog that trepidation entered the situation, and fear was erected as a screen barring him from his desire. In a Churchill play, being frightened is an anxiety with a particularly strong symbolic weight. It represents an ambiguous potential residing within selfhood, one that serves as a warning or anticipation but that also serves as a portentous presentiment. Fear is an anxious mask for Dionysus.

Abortive

While the importance of being frightened would later be given a politicized inflection in *Top Girls* and *Seven Jewish Children*, in these early plays being frightened guides us primarily to the contours that define the Churchillian self. Consider the conclusion to another radio play, *Abortive* (1971): 'I do find I'm afraid to go to sleep. Just as I'm going off I get that feeling like in a nightmare but with no content. I'm frightened something's about to happen' (36). While it is evident that *Abortive* has a more obviously politicized sensibility than does *Lovesick*, it also, perhaps inevitably, makes a more traditional statement about middle-class subjectivity. This tension between the impetus to articulate alternative subjectivities and the onus to offer coherent political interventions establishes a productive and telling contradiction that runs throughout Churchill's work and provides a potential motivation for her formalism. In *Aborted*, an upper-middle-class couple named Colin and Roz watch the dawn rise outside their country house and discuss the impact upon their lives of a thirty-seven-year-old man named Billy, a charming, intelligent transient whom Colin met on a train platform one night and brought home to stay with them for three months. Eventually, bored with him, the couple ejected him from the home, but not before Roz became pregnant with Billy's child in a sex act that she maintains, somewhat feebly, 'started as rape' (23). Colin maintains that it was not rape. It has been three weeks since she had the fetus aborted. Billy's class status is subtly but clearly delineated: part black, with an Irish stepfather, the homeless man charmed both Colin and Roz for reasons that remain allusive and unclear.

Billy, who does not appear in this radio play, is the absent presence here, and he gradually takes on certain Dionysian qualities: ambiguous, unreliable, of mixed racial origins but equally fascinating to both men and women, possessing an understated erotic energy that eventually motivated the couple to send away their flirtatious au pair girl and ultimately led to Roz's impregnation. Yet Billy serves not as erotic liberator but rather as a disruptive and innocent outsider figure. Billy-as-catalyst reveals the massive cruelty of a privileged and insular middle-class couple who forcibly evicted the man when they tired of his presence. Reacting like the return of the repressed, Billy, however, stayed in the local area, following Colin and Roz around and telephoning them incessantly, having clearly formed a strong emotional investment in the couple, one towards which they are alternately oblivious, dismissive, or insensate. They project their own resentment upon him, suggesting that he stalked them not out of love, as he claimed, but because he hated and envied them (29). Gradually such accusations, combined with the uncaring veneer that inflects their assessments, reveal that the idea of such obsessive love is unfathomable to them and that they themselves see things only in terms of class resentment, perhaps because this loathing is the only way they have of thinking about others.

As a Dionysian figure Billy represents both the possibility of an escape from middle-class alienation and their disavowed and unconscious desires. Colin attributes his initial kindness towards Billy to abstract and half-forgotten philosophical origins: 'I did have inklings in my youth of the unity as it were of things. If such indeed exists I appear to be excluded from it. My efforts to join take the form of pity' (25). Roz describes her sexual seduction by Billy as analogous to Colin's decision to bring him home in the first place: 'You'd had this moment of feeling close to him and rational considerations dropped away. They were your words' (30). Billy contains a potential for Roz and Colin to overcome their own alienation in an experience of oneness with the 'unity of things,' but they eventually dismiss him with contempt when such oneness entails actual receptiveness to another human being. It is the degraded tragedy of the middle class that its attempts to be a part of something larger than itself can take no more productive form than pity, because it can never escape its own bad faith and resentment.

Churchill's political intervention is to fashion this class intruder as an absent figure of affirmation and love as a contrast to the resentment of the bourgeoisie. Billy has granted this middle-class couple some glimpse into their own disavowed unconscious lives, but the subjectivity that is on display for us is one still dominated by negativity, as indicated by the title: what is abortive here are the selfhoods of Colin and Roz, in their attempt to abort Billy from their lives. This is a recognizable paradigm: the working class represents the disavowed other, the unconscious of the middle class, one strenuously denied and repudiated by the bourgeois mind. The play shows us two people who, despite their callous protests that Billy was an inconvenience they would have been better to avoid, seem to have been profoundly unsettled by the visitor they welcomed into their home. Roz now sleeps poorly and is haunted by the idea that she has aborted a child, even as she describes the eight-week-old fetus as '[e]ven less of a person than Billy' (36). Moreover, the play's action is triggered by a failed attempt at lovemaking that indicates a lingering divide between the couple, combined with a sense of something now being absent that they were previously unaware of: 'I do miss something,' Roz laments, before breaking into tears (33). Colin suggests that it is the child that she misses and that she regrets aborting it, but the undercurrent of the scene suggests that it is Billy himself who is missed now, even as they assert energetically that they are glad to be rid of him.

Nevertheless, Billy has given them something, summarized by Roz's final words: Roz feels, at the verge of sleep, that she is in a nightmare and she is frightened that something is about to happen. He has discomfited them, disrupted the hermetic routine of their lives, invaded, perhaps, their dreams and forced a small sense of dreams into their waking lives. Being frightened in *Abortive*, then, constitutes the ambiguous gift to consciousness that this Dionysian guest leaves behind him. Being frightened, this undirected fear or anxiety, also resides at the liminal non-space between the conscious and unconscious selves. Within a Lacanian vocabulary, this experience constitutes the *tuché*, the missed encounter with the unsymbolizable real, traumatic object-cause of desire, and the ultimate object of all anxiety. Tellingly, Lacan illustrates the *tuché* through the example of consciousness caught in the moment between sleep and wakefulness, sleep intruded upon by a knock on the door, an accidental noise that is integrated into dream even as one wakes (*The Seminar Book XI* 56–60). It is the location of Roz's fear: the feeling of possibility located between sleep and wakefulness.

Owners

It is particularly with Churchill's early work for the stage that we can appreciate the ongoing challenge of balancing the emerging expressionism in her situations with the growing politicization and social content of her concerns. Churchill's campaign to estrange given social assumptions about gender and sexuality is articulated through recognizable comedic strategies in *Owners*, her first play for the Royal Court (1972). What is noteworthy about the play is the stylistic tension between social realism and the exploration of inner psychic life akin to that portrayed in the two radio plays discussed above. The dynamic of the action is driven by the struggle between two couples (Alec and Lisa, and Marion and Clegg), previously acquainted when younger, whose lives have taken them in different economic directions but who reconnect in a conflict over property development. The deft dramatic strategy of the play is to begin with a recognizably social realist situation in which Alec and Lisa, a poor, pregnant couple living with an aged mother and two children, are intimidated by a property developer's agent, who wants them to move out of their apartment so that the building can be gentrified and sold. Yet the play's actual concerns are how concepts such as ownership and property have analogues at the level of psychic investment and erotic desire, and *Owners* asks us whether the human is ultimately defined by want or lack, an absence in the self for which the desire for possession and consumption is the inevitable palliative, or whether this pathology is an historical symptom of capitalism's effect upon human relationships.

In retrospect, *Owners* seems productively mired in the realist aesthetic that we saw in early Barker plays for the Royal Court. *Owners* similarly writhes against this style through its employment of social satire, which is ultimately where its politics are located. Using acerbic gallows humour, Churchill presents us with a series of pathological and eccentric British characters from different class backgrounds, and through their conflicts again forces the question of whose desire is 'sick' and whose is 'healthy' or 'normal' in Western society. The play's arch-capitalist property developer, Marion, is a figure of avarice: the modern woman as relentless consumer of food, property, and others, driven by desires that have metastasized into the epitome of capitalist achievement: real estate. Marion portrays human history as a long narrative of pure capitalist consumption. She explains to Alec, whose family occupies the flat she wants to renovate and sell, her justification for her competitive, acquisitive drive and frenetic energy to fight and succeed: '[T]he animals are ours. The vegetables and minerals. For us to consume. We don't shrink from blood. Or guilt. Guilt is essential to progress. You'll tell me next you don't feel guilt. I don't know how you know you're alive. Guilt is knowing what you do. I see the children with no shoes and socks in the houses I buy. Should I buy them socks? It would be ridiculous. But I feel it. That gritty lump is the pearl. Swine. And what would happen to work without guilt?' (30). She offers a powerful image of bad conscience as the motor of productivity in Western society. Guilt is figured not just as the tool of cynical reasoning used by the middle class as a means of justifying competition and rapaciousness (one justifies being callous with the rationale that one knows it and feels bad about it); Marion describes it as the *pearl*. Curiously, guilt itself is the valuable commodity created by all of this productivity, and it allows Marion, faced with children who suffer so that she can gain, to profit happily from her confrontation with this version of the Palermo paradox. In *Owners*, the material is only a support or foundation for the human psyche: at stake are libidinal and psychic economies.

As a counter-image to Marion, *Owners* offers Alec, a passive, self-contained, and unmotivated man who, after a long process of becoming detached and alienated from his work, surroundings, and his family, seems to have simply dropped out of society's values one day after fulfilling a powerful and unexpected longing to see the sea in winter (47). We first encounter him with his wife Lisa after their apartment has been robbed. He prefers not to call the police: 'If he wants the things that much, perhaps let him have them' (13). Alec seems to have come to a point in his life where he wants neither things nor people, not because he is satisfied but rather because he has transcended the experience of wanting altogether. Jean E. Howard asks, rhetorically, 'Is Alex [*sic*] a saint or a mutant whose suffering has made him no longer fully human?' (38). The answer seems to be that he is both. Alec skirts the realms of the possible: he tests not only the patience of the other characters, who find his seeming indifference frustrating, but also the credibility of the play itself.

Yet Alec only seems indifferent to the world around him; *Owners* deploys his zen passivity as a pretext for exploring a decidedly Brechtian problem, centred, as it is in Bond's paradox, upon children. Alec asserts that he does feel love but has no need to feel that anyone belongs to him. Marion finds this inconceivable, because she can only conceive of the value of *being* loved and of love as possession: 'It's no use being loved like that. You love your children more than someone else's,' she says. Alec replies, 'Not necessarily' (47). Within the same scene, a few moments after Alec makes this profound and simple assertion, he demonstrates the agency that his freedom from possessiveness grants him when he unhooks his comatose mother from a life support machine and allows her to die. Later he tells his own wife that he is happy for his child to be adopted by Marion, an exchange securing their tenancy, as long as the child is being cared for (49). It is the key problem explored within the final major group of plays by Brecht: the love of children within a capitalist society, and the degree to which such love is marred by the psychic deformations of reification, which transforms the relationships between human beings into the relationships between commodities and graphs such relationships onto family relations. Children, lovers, spouses, parents: all become property. Our investments in them become forms of possession. Children in particular have a special place within this problem because of the productive manner in which this investment creates self-division. Alec is a powerful intervention into the received understanding that love must inevitably be embroiled with possession.

Alec's suggestion that he does not love his own children more than the children of other people is not a denigration of his paternal affection, although it might seem as such until the conclusion of the play. He eventually dies in a fire in their home deliberately set by Marion's agent Worsely, because he re-enters the burning building to save the neighbour's child. It is his unflinching willingness to enter a burning building that reveals the truth of Alec as a figure of unconditional love for humanity. He becomes a tragic figure in the form of a burnt offering, one that must be mediated by language rather than perceived directly by the audience. The sublimity of the event remains tied to the fact that it must be imageless, must transcend the imaginary and reside in the realm of abstraction. Contrast this with the actual final visual image of the play: Marion's agent Worsely, whose attempts at suicide throughout the play are prone to comical failure, raises a pistol to his forehead and fires it, missing. This representation of a self-destructive subjectivity, a pathological, ego-bound self founded in lack and denial, is banal and obvious, the source of comedy, sharply contrasted with the egoless and thus imageless figure of Alec. That we cannot see what happens to Alec makes it all the more important as an image of the escape from ego: his death is described by Worsely, who first characterizes the fire not as an act of consumption but instead as a process of transformation: '[I]t was the house turning into fire because of the high temperature it was reaching rather than a fire consuming the house.' Alec, entering the house calmly as it incinerated, 'rose as if climbing the stairs. Turning into fire quite silently' (66). Here is a quasi-Buddhist image of the cleansing, transformative power of fire, mapped onto the utopian productive and transformative possibilities for a subjectivity not bound by the negativity of consumption, ownership, and possession. This possibility is conjured through the absent presence of Alec.

However, at the same time we must note how traditional is the manifestation of this utopian selfhood in the play: it can only be rendered negatively, as an image of holocaust and self-sacrifice to be hidden from the eyes of the audience, literally unrepresentable. In contrast, the most legitimately utopian figuration of Alec's experience of the world is found not in his demise but in his moment-to-moment encounters with selfhood. He rejects the idea that he is the same person that Marion was in love with seven years earlier. To her insistence that he is 'not someone else altogether' he replies simply, 'I think it might just as well be. You talk about the past and the future but it doesn't apply. Here I am now' (31). To be free from want or lack means to necessarily be free from the negativity or absence of past or future, to be affirmed into an eternal present, a selfhood without obverse or underside, which is perpetually *now*. 'Here I am now' is an early, linguistic image of Churchill's self-as-Möbius-strip.

Traps

It was presumably the playwright's desire to explore the theatrical (im)possibilities of such liberation from the temporal that led to *Traps* (1977), a play that is at once one of the most overlooked in Churchill's repertoire and increasingly one of the most striking. *Traps* is an attempt to create a play, an object in four dimensions, that realizes the impossible geometry of a Möbius strip as a theatrical metaphor for an unalienated subjectivity at one with its desires. *Traps* anticipates the later theatrical experiments *Blue Kettle* and *Heart's Desire* (performed together as *Blue Heart* 1997) in its representation of theatrical impossibilities and alternate realities, while maintaining a striking emotional and political core that is, arguably, absent from the later plays. This core is most visible in the play's concluding few minutes, in which a meal is collectively prepared and eaten while one after another, the play's six characters, a group of twenty-somethings, take turns bathing in a metal tub, openly sharing their nakedness and being washed by each other. This communal activity is momentarily stifled by the shame and embarrassment of one member of the group, Reg, who is finally cajoled into the bath and sits in it, enjoying the warmth and eating his dinner. Gradually their increasing happiness brings smiles to all their faces, and the action closes with Reg's joyful laughter.

This conclusion is a simple and beautiful image of a moment of collective bliss in a nascent rural commune.[11] It does not follow chronologically from anything that has been seen before: one of the characters, Albert, has been referred to as long dead by suicide earlier in the scene. A little later he enters casually from working late in the garden, just after Reg gives his wife Christie a brutal beating, leaving her badly bruised. No further mention of the beating is made, and when Christie disrobes to bathe she is no longer bruised. The play contains a multitude of such details, large and small, that contradict attempts to assign a temporal direction to the events. In Act 1 three characters – Albert, Syl, and Jack – living unhappily together in a collective flat in the city are visited by a stranger named Reg. Reg is looking for his wife Christie, who left him the night before and who shows up at the flat shortly to see her brother Jack.

Midway through the scene an estranged resident of the collective, Del, arrives and subjects his roommates to an angry tirade about their treatment of him. The first act of the play is characterized by misery, entropy, and dissonance. Albert, who works in some kind of factory position, appears to be a paranoid schizophrenic and a hypochondriac; he fears he is getting the flu, that he is being followed by a mysterious man in a raincoat, and that his fellow employees believe him to be some kind of labour agitator. He expects to be handed his cards soon, but he is the only member of the flat who brings in an income.

Traps thus paints a picture of the malaise and despair of English life during the mid-1970s that is at once dystopian and utopian, seeming somehow to move towards both entropic social decay and utopian psychic revolution. The play achieves this by engaging in purely theatrical conceits and by suspending all realism and causality. It is as if the characters in the play are purely theatrical beings who, since they have no existence outside of the representation, can reconfigure their personal realities through sufficiently robust acts of will. Syl, for example, is responsible for a newborn. Her profound unhappiness at her maternal duties is stressed from the outset: she whines about the tedium of being left alone all day and the lack of support for childbearing that she receives, and complains about the traditional housekeeping responsibilities she is forced to endure. The first overt challenge to narrative coherence arrives when Syl unexpectedly starts discussing her frustrations with her dance career. She is ambivalent about her talent and wonders if she should stop taking the pill and have a child instead (82). Suddenly, without warning or indication, the play has presented an alternate life possibility for Syl, one with clear social and political significations, particularly for second wave feminism in this decade: the two different possibilities for Syl highlight the fact that women are expected to choose between family and career, particularly if it is an artistic career. Near the end of Act 2, Syl will talk about how hard she is working and that she is happy with her dancing at present, and then ask the men how the baby is sleeping. Albert and Del then discuss the minutiae of preparing infant formula (122). An alternate reality has stepped onstage.

What this attempt at narrative coherence is responding to is the fact that the emotional and collective wellbeing of the characters improves visibly over the course of the play. Act 2, for instance, takes place in the country, where they are just starting out their rural farming adventure, and it seems at first glance as if the characters have abandoned the misery of city life in Act 1 for the simplicity and communal openness of a farm in Act 2. Of course, this reading overlooks the fact that at the beginning of Act 2 Syl is pregnant for the first time and ignores the repeated references in Act 1 to how much better it was when they lived in the country and how things went wrong when they came here (83, 89).

It is just as logical to assume that Act 2 takes place earlier than Act 1 as to assume the reverse. At times it seems as if Act 1 takes place the next day, and the passage of the sun suggests that the two acts cover twenty-four hours over a single day. Yet the group is, by the play's conclusion, happy together, living collectively and cooperatively. A search for narrative coherence will then assume that either they were happy in the past, living in the country (as is stated in Act 1), or happy once they leave the city for the country. In the former possibility, the chronological narrative represents a fall from grace or expulsion from Eden; in the latter, a romance narrative of collectivity that resolves the action happily.

The play introduces the image of the Möbius strip as a means of suturing this circular dramatic action into a single unbroken surface. Midway through Act 1 Del bursts into the room and interrupts the scene, haranguing Albert, Syl, and Jack for shutting him out of their collective and for deceiving him: 'You have all lied to me. Sometimes together, sometimes separately. You don't correlate. I've made lists. [...] Coming back down a Mobius [sic] strip motorway ever since I left. You thought I was on the other side but all the time I was ... Mobius strip, right?' (86). Del arrives as a frustrated and confused outsider who has struggled to integrate himself into the group and failed. He is, in this sense, a momentary audience surrogate, experiencing the same confusion as the attuned audience member: 'From the middle of July I was squeezed out. There was every kind of alliance. Albert and Jack. Jack and Syl. Syl and Albert. Albert and Jack and Syl. But no Del. Where was Del? When I think what expectations. Never again. Utopia means nowhere, right?' (87). Del has been unable to adapt to the transitory and shifting relationships in the flat, although he has sought to fit in with what he calls their 'Way' (88), which seems, mysteriously, to involve a constant act of self-creation: 'I can't continually wake up every day as if the day before hadn't happened. Sometimes, yes, but not every day' (88). Del's reference to the Möbius strip as somehow embodying the situation in the flat should be combined with his devoted attention to a plant once he is settled back into the group: 'It doesn't ask where I was yesterday. Or if I'll be here tomorrow. It doesn't ask if I love it more than Jack does or more than I love Jack or anything. Totally here, every time, all the time' (93). Albert comments that meditating upon the plant 'kills time like a crossword' (96). It is Del, too, who refers to 'Albert's pamphlets and meetings' and asks if membership is rising, if consciousnesses have been raised, or if anyone has been transfigured yet (89). This, combined with Jack's insistence upon his psychic powers, creates the presentiment that the group is engaged in a kind of cult experiment in collective self-overcoming. The ultimate goal that the group seems to be striving towards is the escape from past and future into an eternal now, figured by the temporal impossibility of the Möbius strip's geometry, where time and space can be imagined to blur into or transform into one another.

R. Darren Gobert, in an eloquent exegesis of the play, argues that 'the bathing scene resolves the fractured ontology of *Traps*' by concluding the play with an image of corporeally grounded bodies bathing and eating in 'the baptismal present of performance' (114).[12] For Gobert, *Traps* is a play about 'the impossibility of imagining a self outside of its spatial and temporal locations' (113). Subjectivity, he surmises, is relational, and as such is constituted upon material grounding in time and space, thus in a sense of difference and distance, and he argues that the conclusion of the play shows this to the audience by resolving the non-causal and non-linear logic of the rest of the play. Yet I would add that just because the Möbius strip is impossible does not mean it is not important. It offers a utopian promise latent within the present, an escape from time, space, and selfhood, which are sources of anxiety and fear for the characters, the locus of being frightened in this play (*Traps* 94). The Möbius strip is the promise of a perfection that, due to its impossibility, allows the characters to pass through these anxieties and arrive at the play's conclusion, affirming their existences. The play suggests that the experience of the impossible is crucial to their subjectivities and to the transfiguration of the historical present. In this sense, the Möbius strip is an image of the Absolute or the sacred that allows for the possibility of a sanctified experience at the play's conclusion.

Thus, while Albert says, 'I don't want perfection. Just changes' (97), *Traps* nevertheless shows us changes with utopian inclinations, a gradual refining and amelioration of circumstances. The jigsaw puzzle, which all the characters are expected to work on at random points in the play, comes to represent the collective activity in which they are engaged, as does the card game of Patience (Solitaire), which is played at different moments (85, 113). Reality is a puzzle or game, to be solved by trial and error, by trying different permutations and combinations of relationships. The action of the play is then the setting and resetting of character relationships, repetition with differences, growing closer and closer to a harmonious unity. The action is not simply random changes that move accidentally towards harmony. The action is driven, we must presume, by the will of the characters, which draws them towards one another. Will power and the attractive force that draws them together occupies much of their conversation and can be understood as the energy that perpetuates the changes in situation. What their wills drive them to do, by drawing them towards one another, is to create a perfect family, an extended family where they can find belonging, something that none of them feel they have (92).

The only logic followed by the play is the logic of the character's desires. The energy that drives the play is love, and the conflicts between the characters are expressions of love trying to find its full utopian expression, eschewing the social forms into which it is commonly forced. This energy is Churchill's Dionysian force of the multiplicity of desires, which engenders diffusion and possibility even while offering the potential for utopian oneness. This energy finds uniquely theatrical expression in Churchill's artistic experimentation. Jack and Christie, they mention casually at one point, tried incest together: 'It's not the solution to me and Christie, Del. More something you get out of the way' (107). Merely violating taboos is not the solution; what is needed is something altogether new. The final bathing and eating sequence is triggered by the surprising return of Albert; that a supposedly dead man reappears signals the miraculous tenor of this final dramatic shift. Throughout the bathing, Reg, the formerly priggish outsider, watches the others with discomfort and growing embarrassment. His final triumph over his own shame is both simple and profound: the act of will, the self-overcoming that allows him access to the collective, is achieved by conquering the self-mortifying divisions of self-consciousness. It is thus appropriately Dionysian that the affirmation of love and will irrupts into collective joy and laughter. *Traps* dramatizes a utopian, collective, Dionysian energy that struggles to manifest itself within the tragic decline of English life in the mid-1970s.

Light Shining in Buckinghamshire

Churchill's immersion in collective theatre workshops with Monstrous Regiment and Joint Stock in the late 1970s resulted in stylistic changes in her work, resulting in theatre forms that are generally acknowledged as Brechtian in their use of estrangement effects and formal experimentation. Yet if we approach these plays with the present analysis in mind, a continuity of concerns emerges in Churchill's development. Ostensibly about a missed moment in English revolutionary history and the hijacking of the English Civil War by the propertied classes, *Light Shining in Buckinghamshire* (1976) is profitably approached in view of the suppression or demonizing of the libidinal other. Without depoliticizing the historical events, *Light Shining* nevertheless asserts that a political revolution walks hand in hand with a revolution in the self, an inner overcoming of the nihilism with which Christianity mars consciousness. At the same time, we must note the unique Brechtian stylistic strategy of *Light Shining*: there are no characters in this play, if in the sense of character we mean a figure that represents a single continuity of consciousness or self as signified by the icon of an actor's form. While there are characters designated in the written script, they are to be played by different actors throughout the play, and the names are thus mere conveniences for the purposes of rehearsal. This allows each scene, in good Brechtian fashion, to stand as its own independent episode, but it also radicalizes the tools of the Epic theatre by distancing the audience from attempts to track character arcs through the dramatic action. Instead, we are offered the experiences of depersonalized and interchangeable human beings: these individuals are metonyms for the English masses and their shared experiences during the confusion and tumult of the Civil War. It is as if we see, over the course of the play, different people going through the same story.

A productive contradiction then emerges when this stylistic innovation is applied to the inner struggles experienced by these figures: *Light Shining*, while a play about the masses during the Civil War, is also a play about the private, agonistic relationship between individuals and their monotheistic Christian God. As if to bookend this thematic emphasis, the play begins with fervent prayer, first by the entire cast (singing from Isaiah 24:17–20) and then by a single character. In contrast, the long penultimate scene of the play is a striking gathering of disenfranchised revolutionaries who form an impromptu prayer group of Ranters and embrace the idea of a personal, profane god that transforms the experience of the present. The multiple role playing, in a manifestation of this thematic emphasis, presents the diffusion and dispersal of selfhood amongst the players, and thus we grasp the presence of Dionysian multiplicity (the erotic, profane god) in the theatricality of the play itself, which becomes the drama's most political content.

The contradictions of Christian consciousness are dramatized in the second scene of the play: a young gentleman, Cobbe, seeks forgiveness for an existence in which sin seems to be as ubiquitous as taking a breath: 'Lust when the girl gave me meat last night, not keeping my eyes on my plate but followed her hand. [...] What is worst, I am not praying to you about the worst sin. I sin in my fear of praying about that sin, I sin in denying my fear' (191). Over the course of this long, earnest plea to his God, Cobbe's mind moves through a convoluted and contradictory logic of self-negation. His loathing of the upper classes and the blaspheming officer class emerges, as does his sympathy for a beggar he saw whipped in the street. He condemns the privilege of his wealthy family and fantasizes about overturning their dinner table during grace. His consciousness is left in a state of pure self-loathing: 'Not to honour my father is sin, and sin to honour a greedy, cruel, hypocritical – Is it sin to kneel here till he leave the house? I cannot go down to him. It is sin to go down' (192). All actions and thoughts, it appears, have been infused with culpability, resulting in irreconcilable contradictions for Cobbe's morality. The result is mental suffering without visible solution, but we should keep in mind the articulated contradiction itself: for Cobbe, it has become a sin *not* to sin.

As these characters are portrayed by different actors in each scene, the sense that emerges is of different individuals who all experience the same struggle with their ideological beliefs, but this struggle is not to overthrow their faith through a turn to atheism or materialism. Rather, the struggle is closer to a Nietzschean act of overcoming, in which Christian religious beliefs are *fully* inhabited, bringing to consciousness the untenable inconsistencies of the same, with a transformative effect. The characters always claim to be Christians, even and particularly when their Christian fervour disrupts the precepts of monotheism. For instance, a woman named Hoskins speaks up in church, disrupting the Calvinist doctrine of the preterite and the elect by asserting that all human beings are saints, none are damned, all are chosen by God, that '[t]here is no pit, there is no snare' (201), and that God speaks directly through her. When the preacher quotes St Paul in an attempt to get her to shut up, she fires back at him a verse from the book of Joel, which states that the Holy Spirit will fill all humanity, male and female alike. The Christianity that manifests itself in the pre-revolutionary moment is not simply that of the radical, politicized Christ who rejects parents, family, and home in favour of the community of all mankind. It is also, as becomes more apparent as the play proceeds, a carnal, profane, feminist Christ.

The second act demonstrates the corruption of the revolution's goals by the emergence of capitalism, and the contrasting attempts by the Levellers, the Diggers, and finally the Ranters to fulfil the yearning for universal freedom and equality that fuelled the Civil War. At the same time, the characters' inner struggles to resolve the contradictions of their religious beliefs continue. Both are portrayed as fuelled by the same Dionysian, libidinal energy. Claxton becomes an itinerant wanderer driven by a personal sense of freedom and spiritual inspiration: 'I felt myself moving faster and faster, more and more certainly towards God. And I am alone, because my wife can't follow me. I send her money when I can. But my body is given to other women now for I have come to see that there is no sin but what man thinks is sin. So we can't be free from sin till we can commit it purely, as if it were no sin' (221). Here, in the transformation of spiritual beliefs within the moment of the interregnum, the characters begin to resolve for themselves the negativity of their Christian indoctrinations. As was implied by Cobbe's opening prayer, the setting of sin against sin is the passage into a self-overcoming.

The Ranters describe their relationship to Christ as one that is joyfully anti-Christian: 'Now is just a strange time between Antichrist going and Christ coming, so what do you expect in a time like this?' (233). They proclaim that it is Christ the Leveller that they await now, but this is a God that is in the whole of creation and affirms everything, allowing for a perfection within humanity through communal living and the renunciation of private property. At its most frenetic, this rhetoric makes of human beings gods themselves: 'perfect men, perfect Christ in the street, I've seen them' (235). Cobbe rants about Christ's carnal body: 'Christ's arsehole. He had an arsehole. Christ shits on you rich. Christ shits. Shitting pissing spewing puking fucking Jesus Christ' (230). A logic of dialectical reversibility, of the utopian identity between opposites, comes to dominate their frenzied rants. The ultimate fulfilment of the logical contortions of sin is found in the embracing of the profane and the sinful as a passage into godliness itself: 'We don't want any filthy plaguey holiness. We want base things. And the baseness confounds the false holiness into nothing' (236). They encourage a woman not to be frightened by her sinfulness, but to '[s]in again, do the same sin as if it were no sin' (237). In sinning to God's glory she shall be free of sin (237). This reversal wears the mask of Christianity and embodies its discourse while betraying its precepts. It embraces all of creation and all of humanity, affirming even the most negative. This Christ is deeply Dionysian: somehow both an absence and a presence, merging the sacred with the profane and infusing both the material and the metaphysical realms with jubilant fucking.

However, this drunken revelry is portrayed as a missed moment – whatever potential seems to have irrupted spontaneously in this bacchanalia is subsequently lost, gone to ground, scattered, or *sparagmos*, to pursue the Dionysian imagery to its logical conclusion. The world is not transformed. A crucial counterpoint to the Ranters is the presence of the soldier and Leveller Briggs, who serves as a grounded, all-too-clear-eyed materialist contrast to the Ranters' unbridled utopianism. Throughout the scene he negates their assertions that Christ has come, is coming, or will ever come. For Briggs, this is naive idealism that his bitter experiences as a soldier and a Leveller have rendered impossible for him. He expresses a cold historical truth for the contemporary audience: 'England will still be here in hundreds of years. And people working so hard they can't grasp how it happens and can't take hold of their own lives, like us till we had this chance, and we're losing it now, as we sit here, every minute' (233).

However, Briggs represents the last glimpse of political energy in the play. While the Ranters appear to fall back into quotidian existence after the Restoration, Briggs does not. He speaks at length about his inability to re-enter society. He is fired from his job in a shop because he kept giving things away and wouldn't stop thieves. He subsequently decides to personally drive the price of corn down in order to benefit the poor, but his strategy is absurd: he stops eating it and eventually gives up food altogether, foraging for nourishment and eventually weaning himself of everything except grass, which he has learned to eat and has subsisted on for two years, living in a field like an animal. This is not simply a humbling image of human derangement and alienation, it is a staggering vision of unquashable socialist energy that transforms its vessel into a figure of abjection when this passion for justice has no productive outlet.

The futility of Briggs's actions is entirely the point: they emerge as a desperate idealism. Jean E. Howard describes Briggs, compellingly, as 'a holy fool who has negated desire [...] for all those things that elsewhere in the play drive human beings to turn themselves into beasts' (42). This is obviously not a solution to any problem, but it nevertheless cannot be dismissed as meaningless. I am persuaded by the image of Briggs as a sacred figure, simultaneously high and low, a tragic *pharmakos* caught between the profane and the saintly. Briggs is an expression of humanity all the more visible for being unproductive, and while it is tragic it is also deeply hopeful, inasmuch as it is an image of the utopian, Dionysian energy of revolution that, bereft of productive avenues of expression, manifests itself in madness. Churchill dramatizes an historical moment of tragic failure but infuses it with a liberating, libidinal energy: pessimistic in content, affirmative and progressive in its formal dispersal of character throughout the cast. It is somehow a portrait of a messianic moment of redemption that does not occur, yet somehow also does, due to the ambivalent, absent presence of the Dionysian.

Cloud Nine

Libidinal energy and its Dionysian facets function in Churchill's work in a manner not dissimilar to Barker's employment of sexuality and the unconscious as a political affront to a repressed English consciousness, but the key difference is how Churchill diffuses this energy throughout the collective ensembles of her plays: desire, for her, exists as a kind of collective Dionysian id lurking beneath the surface of social life. This approach gives a new inflection to what is Churchill's best known and perhaps most overdetermined play: *Cloud Nine* (1979). *Cloud Nine* confronts directly the larger subtext of her earlier plays: the profound repression and denial of life in England. *Cloud Nine* is most commonly understood as a feminist deployment of Brechtian *Verfremdungseffekte* as a technique for estranging ideological assumptions about gender and sexuality. However, the cross-dressing that dominates Act 1 of the play can be understood merely as a theatrical metaphor for the disconnection from one's desire characteristic of English life in the post-war generation immediately preceding the 1970s. Churchill points out quite directly that the cross-dressing is a rehearsal of stereotypes: 'Edward' is a repetition of the hackneyed and particularly English stage convention stemming from Barrie's *Peter Pan*, 'of having boys played by women' (Preface 245). Meanwhile, it is evident that the performance of 'Betty' in Act 1 is not in the least undermining of gender identity; rather, it is nothing more than a comic drag performance. Thus I think that these dramatic strategies are quite deliberately reiterations of the conventions of English stage comedy, and taken on their own they do nothing much to trouble an audience's ideological assumptions. I would even go so far as to suggest that these seeming estrangements of sex, race, and gender are in fact performances of the dramatic conventions of Englishness itself, stemming from the nineteenth-century British stage. For hundreds of years on the English stage, white men played Othello, women played men, and men played women. Thus James M. Harding is correct in pointing out that the first act of *Cloud Nine* does nothing more than repeat and retrench a series of stereotypes, but I think that this is entirely the point. The cross-dressing is all a deliberate evoking of traditions of English theatre.

And so *Cloud Nine* is most fairly assessed as a play about gender and sexuality within the texture of Englishness.[13] To suggest that the play's referent is Englishness is also to argue that the sexual and gender identities that are performed within the play are staged within a national framework and cannot be excised from it. Yet this is also, I think, what *Cloud Nine* suggests, because it begins and ends with reference to England. In the play's opening, the Union Jack hangs from a flagpole on a verandah as the characters sing, 'Come gather, sons of England, come gather in your pride' (*Cloud Nine* 251). In the play's closing moments, the oppressive Victorian patriarch, Clive, returns and condemns his wife for her long-delayed, awakening sexuality: 'You are not that sort of woman, Betty. I can't believe you are. I can't feel the same about you as I did. And Africa is to be communist I suppose. I used to be proud to be British. There was a high ideal. I came out onto the verandah and looked at the stars' (320). Since English national identity was, and remains, fundamentally a discourse of Empire informed by heterosexual and racist ideologies, this does indeed mean that in attempting to 'stage' Englishness, *Cloud Nine* is inevitably imbricated with those heterosexisms and racisms. Victorian colonial Africa here is not a literal location but an expressionistic psychic landscape, and Africa is indeed a metaphor for the repressed other of European consciousness,[14] or rather, for the idea that sexuality must be embodied in a discourse *as* a repressed other: 'Women can be treacherous and evil. They are darker and more dangerous than men. The family protects us from that, you protect me from that. [...] We must resist this dark female lust, Betty, or it will swallow us up,' Clive explains to Betty (277). Sexuality is portrayed as feminine, savage, and demonic, as in need of policing through Christian ideology of sin, and as rooted within a cultural otherness: it is, in other words, Dionysian, and the attitudes of the two acts of the play towards the otherness of desire also fall along appropriately Dionysian lines.

In Act 1, the repression of otherness results in the return of the repressed in the form of a violent African uprising, while in Act 2 the acknowledgment of otherness results in a communion and an ecstatic transformation of present experience, as is described by the play's title. In the second half of *Cloud Nine*, when the characters are living in a more open, permissive society rather than a repressive, Victorian one, the purported *Verfremdungseffekte* of Act 1 are largely put aside as the characters become more at one with their varying desires and senses of self, thus indicating that the cross-dressing does not function as an estrangement effect at all, but merely as a sign of the disconnect between the characters' desires and how they are taught to behave by society. In Act 2 they are living on 'cloud nine,' experimenting with the multiplicity of possibilities for desire that are available to them. These two relationships with desire replicate precisely the two attitudes towards possession by the god that Jean-Pierre Vernant observes in his analysis of Euripides's *The Bacchae*. The Thebans who deny the god find themselves the subjects of violent and terrifying hallucinatory possession (the return of the repressed), while the bacchae who submit to otherness are rewarded with a transfigured and theatricalized existence: a relationship to the other, and a revelation of life itself as a Dionysian mask (398–400).

The utopianism in the second half of *Cloud Nine* also marks a point of closure for Churchill's 1970s project. As it did for many playwrights, the election of Margaret Thatcher provoked a change of attitude and emphasis in Churchill's work. We will not see any more utopian extended families in Churchill, and the techniques of the Epic theatre are retired in favour of a shift into a politicized expressionism. Churchill pushes to the forefront of her stage a series of tragic subjectivities, selfhoods defined by loss and failure. The representation of the tragic becomes a political tactic used to counter Thatcherite neoconversative ideology, because it is the tragic aspect of the human that is foreclosed upon by the dominant public discourse in England in the 1980s. To some degree, this results in an apparent depoliticization of content in Churchill's plays. Confronted with a reactionary turn in society itself, there appears to be a return to more traditional forms of dramatic representation and a focus on more normative forms of characterization.

Top Girls

For example, I see little that is importantly Brechtian about *Top Girls* (1982), although other critics have argued at great length for its interpretation within such a rubric.[15] Despite the innovative ahistorical and imaginative surprises of the dinner party scene, and the reversal of chronology involved in the third act, *Top Girls* is by and large a realistic play and works effectively through such realism.[16] What *Top Girls* also offers is remarkable character studies within the framework of such realistic theatre, and as realism is of course its own style, we are being asked to consider the vision of the human that such realism offers to us. Specifically, we are being asked to attend to character *subtext*, investigating the silences, elisions, and parapraxes of characters as evocative of an underlying meaning and motivation. This results in a play that quite deliberately makes itself out of the trappings of neoliberalism: coherent, individuated characters with recognizable relationships to their agency and discretely privatized relationships to their desires.

Reading subtext is an essential factor to be considered in relation to the character of Marlene, who has proved a problematic figure of interpretation because of the fact, revealed very late in the play (and the melodramatic significance of such a dramatic discovery should not go unremarked) that as a teenager Marlene gave up her newborn daughter to her elder sister and allowed Joyce to raise Angie as her own. This has led to any number of interpretations of the play and has allowed critics and commentators to draw particularly anti-feminist conclusions about Marlene and *Top Girls*.[17] It is all too easy to simply conclude that Marlene has abandoned her maternal instincts or responsibilities and cut herself off from an essential aspect of her self by 'abandoning' her child. A conservative reading of the play can conclude that there is a social problem on display here, namely women who walk away from their traditional roles in the home. Churchill herself notes such a reading of the play: 'They felt the play was obviously saying women *shouldn't* go out to work' (Interview 82). It is a particularly reactionary message, but one that the structure of the play does little to dispute. The apparently reactionary attitude towards childrearing, while clearly in contrast to the progressive vision of the extended family in *Cloud Nine*, is available to an audience member because there is no alternate vision presented in the play. Joyce is portrayed as bitter, having sacrificed her own happiness to care for Angie. The sisters are estranged and Marlene seldomly visits the working-class town she has left behind. *Top Girls* is certainly a play that resists solutions to the problems that it represents, but this has clearly proven to be a risky strategy in a drama that offers to its audience many of the comfortable theatrical signifiers that playwriting of the 1970s sought to displace or disrupt.

The problem of reading the play as anti-feminist is resolved when we attend to the representation of tragic experience in the play, and the tragic aspects of *Top Girls* emerge if we approach it as an instance of realism and attend specifically to issues of subtext and character. Here too will be located the political heart of the play: while *Top Girls* is a very funny play, it is also one infused with a profound mournfulness, and there is political substance to such joyful grief. *Top Girls*'s dinner party scene is a raucous and ribald celebration of the extremes of suffering, loss, grief, and mourning. It is little wonder that Churchill added a stage direction at the end of the scene that states explicitly that Lady Nijo is '*laughing and crying*' (83). Such an ambivalent emotional response challenges not only representation but also critical discourse. Critical responses to this first scene have been famously incoherent, because they seek a simple black-and-white coherence in the characters represented. The historical and fictional women who meet and dine are expected to be either quasi-feminist role models or cautionary examples of women who sacrifice their feminine difference to make their way in a man's world.[18] Instead, they are multifaceted and complex individuals who spend the entire dinner reminiscing on the death, suffering, and loss that they have experienced over the course of their lives. Marlene, importantly, evades all of this, often quite pointedly avoiding the subject by turning to the menu and ordering more food or drink.

Gradually, the women's stories show more and more in common: they have all, save Isabella Bird, lost children, through difficult decisions or through sheer necessity. Many have dead lovers (64). But most apparently, they are all willing to speak of their painful losses, not without emotion or residual suffering, but volubly and energetically voiced nonetheless. There is a communion of grief and avowed loss, heavily leavened with comedy and laughter. The ambivalent qualities that unite the women at the dinner party offer us *Top Girls*'s vision of the human. The fabric of women's history, inasmuch as such a dramatic tapestry is woven artfully out of the bravura mimesis of the dinner party scene, is a tableau of tears and mourning celebrated with collective laughter. Marlene is the exception to this. She shares nothing of her own experiences, but hints occasionally that she relates to the unhappy pasts of these women: 'Don't you get angry? I get angry,' she states, but when asked what she gets angry about she avoids answering and orders more wine (60).[19] When Lady Nijo speaks of becoming a Buddhist nun and wandering Japan on foot, she describes herself as having dedicated what was left of herself to nothing because she felt she was dead already, following the death of her father and her rejection by the Emperor of Japan, whose courtesan she had been (61). While the other women relate to the sensation of one's life being over in such a metaphoric fashion, Marlene begins to articulate her own experience of first coming to London, or of returning from America, and then truncates her account once more (61). Marlene has also had experiences of death, despair, emptiness, and loss: she hints, very briefly, that she has travelled extensively as a response to this impression of her life being over. Moreover, we eventually learn that she too has lost a father to whom she has deep antipathy, and that she gave up her own daughter to her sister. But she says nothing of these experiences to her friends. As the dinner party scene takes place after the final scene of the play in the chronology of events, Marlene's behaviour here indicates that despite the climactic confrontation with her sister, she has not come to terms with her past. Marlene is a classic instance of Freudian repression.

Dull Gret, who ends the dinner party with her narrative of a descent into hell itself, summarizes the underlying content of all of the women's stories: 'We'd all had family killed. My big son die on a wheel. Birds eat him. My baby, a soldier run her through with a sword. I'd had enough, I was mad, I hate the bastards. I come out my front door that morning and shout till my neighbours come out and I said, 'Come on, we're going where the evil come from and pay the bastards out' (82). Gret leads an army of women against a multitude of devils as a means of fighting back against the suffering and loss that they have endured throughout their lives. The suffering of existence is still portrayed as a metaphysical evil, but no longer one to be endured passively. Gret's tale reveals something about these historical women: they have each experienced a lifetime's worth of pain and death, but with the exception of Patient Griselda, the fictional character presented as a clear contrast to the rest of them, they have not accepted it passively. Necessity is certainly present here, but so is agency that arises from the apprehension of necessity itself. Life is a process of fighting back against suffering and loss. The scene actually ends with a description by Isabella Bird of her final adventure, at the age of seventy, in severely ill health but determined to travel in any case: 'What lengths to go to for a last chance of joy' she remarks (83). Joy, here, is manufactured out of the acknowledgment of and confrontation with pain, not in spite of it. Joy injects Dionysian laughter into a scene saturated with grief: the laughter, such as it is, arises from the affirmative embracing of loss rather than the denial of loss. As we discover at the end of the play, Marlene has denied her own loss, and this, subtextually, is what separates her from the other women at the dinner party.

The scene as a whole is nothing more or less than a series of such intimate and compelling character studies in which women have been humanized by their losses and drawn affirming strength from tragic experiences. The three historical women, and Marlene, are also travellers, and share their common experiences of homelessness and homesickness, while also acknowledging their awareness that to return to the home would have been a dismal failure. While they are wanderers, alienated, often melancholy, and dedicated to nothing (61), they also seem to acknowledge that this questing has no object: they will not arrive at any destination. Isabella Bird will travel until she drops dead. This appears to be the price of an individuated subjectivity: to be both homeless and permanently at a distance from the object of one's desire. In other words, the dinner party scene presents a highly familiar image of tragic subjectivity and prepares us for the representation of character in the subsequent acts of the play. It is *homelessness*. Travelling signifies agency. It is a tragic vision of the human as fundamentally *Unheimlichkeit*, an Oedipal subjectivity, the self defined as a trajectory on a quest to avoid a homecoming, to maintain an alienated, distanced relationship with the origin, one that nevertheless brings about an ironic return.

Such a tragic, Oedipal return to the home is the function of the third and final act of the play: the fact that this scene takes place at a chronologically earlier point than the previous scenes merely highlights the fact that we witness here Marlene's return to her origin. That it happens accidentally, through a kind of slip or parapraxis, is also crucial: Angie has lied, contacting Marlene by telephone and telling her Joyce wants her to return home to Suffolk for a visit. Angie thus steps into the function of the id or of fate here, articulating the unconscious yearnings that will assert themselves at the level of consciousness through double-voiced or deceptive messages. The fact that Marlene accepts the deception and responds to it indicates that she does want to come back, even if (or particularly since) it has been six years since her last visit. Like Oedipus, Marlene is forced by her accidental homecoming to revisit her family history: a violent working-class home and an alcoholic father she despised, and the adoption of Angie by Joyce, the elder sister, who has raised the girl as her own. Marlene seems never to have looked back and has rarely visited the town she came from. Yet the scene is full of tantalizing hints of a Freudian process of repression of the past: Marlene reveals that before coming to see Joyce she spent the day visiting Ipswich and going to see their mother (132).

It is only here, in this traumatic encounter between sisters, that the play becomes overtly class conscious. The bitterness and class resentment of both sisters emerges over the course of the long scene: Marlene speaks with loathing of the poor environment she grew up in and now despises, while Joyce expresses venomous and spiteful hatred for the class signifiers of the wealthy (139). The women become unexpectedly and vocally politicized: Marlene praises Thatcher and pours bile upon trade unions while Joyce hopes angrily that the 1980s will see some violent reaction against the capitalist class (140). The social contradictions of the moment are wrested wide open, but the political energy of the exchange is given a crucial salting by the sisters' occasional gestures of love and affection towards one another. Here, however, the sisterly bond has the ultimate purpose of allowing the class contradictions to finally assert themselves. When Marlene apologizes for her words and asserts that they are still friends anyway, Joyce replies, 'I don't think so, no' (141). As Lizbeth Goodman discusses, the tone of the exchange here between Marlene and Joyce is crucial to the conveyance of the meaning of the scene. It would be possible to play the scene as a long relentless fight, but Deborah Findlay, who played Joyce in Max Stafford-Clark's 1982 and 1991 productions, notes how the second production tried to emphasize the underlying love between the women rather than the surface strife of the exchange (see Goodman 85–7). It is the subtextual bonds between the women that matter most here, but what the subtextual bonds of love communicate is that they are not friends, and that they have nothing in common. Class divides them.

The sudden and violent assertion of class conflict here places it in the position of the repressed past, and must be connected to Angie as the avatar of Marlene's working-class history. It is not anything that Marlene has done in the past that is at issue in *Top Girls*, it is what she does in the present of the play, and what Marlene does in the present of the play is refuse to talk about her past. While Marlene has typically been understood as a negative representation of middle-class, individualistic, capitalist feminism in the 1980s, she is also, importantly, a typically repressed Englishwoman, incapable of expressing her emotions, who has found that this attitude in the 1980s makes her an exemplary role model. It is this in particular that distinguishes her from the women in the dinner party scene: they have all experienced grievous loss and pain in their lives, but they speak of it and narrate it into present experience. They turn grieving into a socially progressive activity. Marlene has disavowed her past, and keeps Angie, the child she lost, a secret. If Angie plays the id to Marlene's ego, then it is Marlene's attitude towards that id that is at issue here: she behaves as if she does not have one.

And it is here that *Top Girls* asserts a traditional psychoanalytic paradigm of the human as a counter to the reactionary political turn in England: the women here are defined by loss and grief. They are tragic selfhoods. Marlene, as a modern woman who models herself on the Thatcherite vision of the human, cannot grieve or mourn or even avow the existence of her own child. She cannot give voice to her history, to her background, and particularly not to a mistake that she made when she was seventeen, because loss, grief, and mistakes are all psychic conditions that undermine the coherence of the liberal-conservative self. To avow the negative is to undermine agency through a submission to necessity and to admit an ultimate failure of agency as determinative of the self. It is to accept one's mistakes as an essential facet of the self. A tragic selfhood describes the idea that we are the sum total of our accidents and mistakes, our grief and our losses. Discussing the death of their father with Joyce, Marlene's disavowal of loss is palpable: 'I got drunk. You were just overcome with grief,' she remarks, and when Joyce says she still maintains their father's grave with flowers, Marlene is surprised. 'Why wouldn't I?' Joyce retorts (126–7). For Joyce, the process of mourning is, potentially, interminable, while Marlene appears not to have considered the idea that grief never ends.

It is within this discourse that Angie must be situated. Angie is that which not only Marlene but all of Thatcher's England disavows and refuses to grieve for. *Top Girls* has a central emotional function as part of its dramatic machinery, namely to allow the audience, over the second act of the play, to apprehend the character of Angie with all of her peculiarities. The force of the writing is found in how effectively Angie is humanized in her quirks and oddities. If sympathy is generated for her, it will be because of, not in spite of, her disconnected and alienated behaviour. In this sense *Top Girls* engages the full arsenal of social realism, asking quite simply and loudly where there is room in society for a girl of sixteen who has dropped out of school, has as her only friend a girl of twelve, and seems to be seized with a desperate and perhaps violent energy for something more than her working-class existence has to offer her. She is intelligent but uninterested in the education she has received. Neither smart nor talented in a way that anyone around her can recognize, she nevertheless wants something more from her life, an aspiration that she finds embodied in Marlene. If one is moved by Angie, it is quite simply because she is recognizable in her humanity. She wants and yearns for something from life. 'If I don't get away from here I am going to die,' she tells her friend Kit (90). When she runs away from home to see Marlene in London, the humbling energy of her humanity expresses itself through the demand she embodies: 'That was the best day of my whole life,' she tells Marlene (110), referring to Marlene's visit to Suffolk in Act 3, one year earlier. Twice the question of what will happen to Angie is asked, at the end of Act 2 and then again at the end of Act 3. She is, within the rhetoric of the time, a loser, a write-off: she is the disavowed. 'She's not going to make it,' Marlene comments dismissively (120). She's 'stupid, lazy and frightened,' Joyce insists, 'so what about her?' (140). The action of the play is to avow her and, perhaps, to mourn her. The play's final word, as is well known, goes to Angie. She enters the living room after Joyce has gone to bed, calling for her mother. She has had a nightmare, and seems to still be half in and half out of it: 'Frightening,' she utters, twice (141). Moments earlier, Marlene has expressed her contempt for those who are stupid, lazy, or frightened and who will therefore be left behind in the 1980s. Angie enters in a state of abject fear.

The significance and the object of Angie's fear has been the subject of great critical speculation. Although a common surmise is that Angie is traumatized because she has overheard Joyce and Marlene, both Churchill and Stafford-Clark assert that she has not overheard the angry conversation and its revelation that Marlene is Angie's mother, although Churchill admits that in performance the question of whether or not Angie has overheard remains open (Goodman 97). Alicia Tycer summarizes the interpretations that have been made of the word 'frightening,' many of which seek to politicize it by divorcing it from any literal referent and making the words a premonition of the future that awaits Angie in Thatcher's England (Tycer 66–7). However, the word does not necessarily need an object in order for the moment to maintain its political force. In the play, the word has no referent. If Angie has overheard the argument, she has done so while asleep, because she enters the room in the mental space between sleep and wakefulness, caught in the nightmare, so to speak, and enacting the Lacanian *tuché*, the encounter with the real.[20] Her response is an objectless fear, in other words a manifestation of anxiety.

This is the source of her power as an image at the end of the play: she is a vision of the real, that which resists symbolization absolutely, as mediated through anxiety and fear, the radically other that must nevertheless be avowed as other by consciousness. Angie, we have seen, lives close to the borders of abjection and seems, in her strangeness, ready to cross over them at a moment's notice: the moment in Act 2 when she licks menstrual blood from her friend Kit's finger shows us a selfhood that is profoundly open to otherness. This offers to us a further possible political reading of the end of the play. If Angie serves as an avatar of the real here, then the intimation of the impossible that irrupts in the final moment may be related to the social substance that has been evoked in the conflict between Marlene and Joyce: the bedrock antagonisms of class contradiction, which Slavoj Žižek will argue is a facet of the real in the social (*Sublime Object* 161–4). 'I don't believe in class,' Marlene spits out moments before Angie, haunted, enters (*Top Girls* 140–1). Angie's fear reminds us that it doesn't matter whether or not you believe in it, the unsymbolizable antagonism of the real works on the self through its effects, here visible in the vitriolic *res-sentiment* that both Marlene and Joyce demonstrate towards the social classes to which they do not belong. Marlene may not believe in class, but it obviously believes in her.

Fen

If *Top Girls* is dedicated to the embracing of the accidents, mistakes, and fail-ures that make up our lives, then *Fen* (1983) insists on the place of desire, as the force that dissolves our agency and locates us at a distance from ourselves. *Fen* is a deeply anachronistic play. If *Top Girls* deploys a strategic realism, then *Fen* goes even further, resuscitating dramatic naturalism for tactical purposes, as if Büchner or Zola had awakened in England in the 1980s, sought out the most overlooked and out-of-step citizens in the country, and then written a socialist tragedy about them, one shot through with streaks of Strindberg's expression-ism. A Joint Stock workshop in the town of Upwell in the fens of East Anglia led to Churchill's play, which follows a tight dramatic arc over ninety minutes with-out an intermission. In the most traditional sense, we are witness to a tragic *action* here, established in the opening minutes of the play as the character of Val abruptly stands up from her work in a potato field, seized by the realization that she must change her life, but within circumstances where she has no fea-sible options. The play shows us, with relentless energy, the final outcome of her standing up from the field: death. But this is not the kind of death with which

Ibsen might conclude a play; it is rather as if Strindberg in his post-inferno period had rewritten the ending of *Woyzeck* so that death became the revelation of Woyzeck's private mental landscape. The emergence of Val as a ghost, in the final tableau of the play, within a landscape of ghosts, dreams, and nightmares grants to expressionism a political valence. Although the fen dwellers are imprisoned within an existence that defines them entirely by physical labour, the play insists that alongside this material work the psychic labour of desire is an equally substantial substratum of their selfhoods. While a utilitarian, work-oriented vision of the human has no room for desire, *Fen* reveals that yearnings, wants, and unfulfilled desires are necessarily definitive of the human.

The tragic here functions through the plot as nowhere else in Churchill. Val's story is simple: torn between her lover Frank and her love for her two children, Val goes back and forth between them throughout the play, unable to separate her children from their father but unable to live apart from Frank. Her first scene with Frank serves the dramatic function of persuading the audience away from the liberal humanist ideology that the middle classes will inevitably apply to such a story: if she doesn't like her life in the Fens, Val should simply leave. It is precisely this action that she undertakes, packing her bags and gathering up her children. She tells Frank she is going to London with them to start a new life and that he should follow. By the time their conversation is concluded, Val's ill-thought-out plan has been abandoned as unfeasible. She takes the children home to her husband and goes to live with Frank. We are offered, from the beginning, a lesson in necessity and the lack of choices available to the working-class residents of this rural environment. Unhappiness as endemic to their lives is a constant refrain throughout the play. Torn between two loves, the irreconcilable contradictions of Val's existence drive her inexorably towards death.

In this sense the action is classically tragic, revealing the fatality of this situation through the exposure of social contradictions. However, its political nuances are unique: while the harsh working conditions and lack of unionization that the fen dwellers endure are portrayed as a profound part of their general unhappiness, the contradictions that Val's plight exposes are those of a woman rather than those of a worker. Her tragic struggle emerges through an attempt to escape the social unhappiness dictated by the general lifestyles of the fen dwellers, and being torn between two loves is actually an emancipatory experience for her. While the topic is never broached directly in the play, the fact that Val is being divided painfully in two is in fact a sign of progressive, if incomplete, social change: a situation where a woman can actually conceive of leaving an unhappy marriage. An older man named Geoffrey admits as much when he blames her situation on changing times: 'I don't hold you personally responsible, Val. You're a symptom of the times. Everything's changing, everything's going down. Strikes, militants, I see the Russians behind it' (169). From this perspective, the social contradiction that Val's personal conflict brings to light is the profoundly anachronistic lifestyle of these characters. Her decision to leave her husband and live with Frank is a perfectly modern and progressive decision, but it is the deeply conservative environment of the fens and the reactionary, rural ideology that saturates the place that make it impossible for Val to maintain her maternal relationship with her children. This ideology, in turn, is a manifestation of the undeveloped economic circumstances where women work as potato pickers and onion sorters: it is simple, menial, uneducated labour. Whereas in a more uniformly modernized social situation she would be able to bridge, however tenuously, the imperfect tension between loving motherhood and her right to love and desire whom she likes, social pressure and peer judgment dictate a strong moral imperative to sacrifice her own happiness. As a woman, she is expected to put motherhood before her selfhood and not leave her children (164). Even her own mother, May, ultimately passes such judgment on her, claiming she would never have left her children and would have passed through fire for them. 'What's stronger than that?' she asks (160). The question, rhetorical in its immediate context, is nevertheless given a literal answer in the play's conclusion.

Eventually both Val and Frank consider suicide as the only solution to the problem: if one of them is dead, they surmise simply, there will no longer be a conflict pulling Val apart. Here, the ideology of liberal agency is exploded by a dialectical conflation of opposites: Val's ultimate submission to the inexorable necessity and lack of agency in this situation is, from her perspective, a passage into freedom. While she has no other choice she feels that she can make, this realization in and of itself is a liberating assertion of agency: it makes her happy, no small feat in a social environment where the older generation insists that unhappiness is the normal state of affairs and no one has any right to expect otherwise (170).

After Frank reluctantly kills Val with an axe and puts her body in a wardrobe, she unexpectedly reappears as a ghost, but her specific ontological status is ambiguous and deserves special attention: she can see and communicate with Frank, can see a multitude of dead people and apprehend their histories, and can also see the dreams and nightmares of the other characters in the play. As a revenant, Val enacts the idea that death is a crucial part of this world rather than life's termination, but this expressionistic landscape qualifies the initial impression that it is simply the afterlife that Val describes. Moreover, Val is not the first ghost to appear in the play. Earlier, an angry ghost working in the field confronts Mr Tewson, the landowner in the process of selling the fenland to a multinational capitalist concern. Val sees this woman at the end of the play and describes this ghost's story of misery and death. Moreover, the play opens with a pantomime, to be performed while the audience enters the theatre: a boy in nineteenth-century rags chasing away crows in a field until he is hoarse and it grows dark. We are being introduced into a theatrical reality where, from the beginning, ghosts and the living cohabit within the misty landscape of the fen.

Ghosts, here, are not simply representative of the antithesis of life. Ghosts are a part of life, and by haunting the fenland they merely highlight the ontological status of the living here. *Fen*'s ghosts signal the abiding unhappiness that haunts all the characters in the play. Subject to material conditions that ultimately bar them from pleasure and joy in their lifetimes, the play suggests that they are themselves spectres, living at an agonized and permanent distance from their desires. Thus the final tableau of the play shows us a series of tragic subjectivities figured through the dramatization of the *tuché* itself, the liminal space where consciousness and dream overlap, an encounter with the impossible real. The real is broached through this properly tragic action, where a lack of choice leads to the submission to fate and death. Thus another way of understanding what we are shown at the end of *Fen* is the unconscious itself: it is not just a space of ghosts and nightmares, but of wish fulfilments. The final image is of Val's mother, May, a sixty-year-old woman who cannot sing and regrets this lack of talent: 'My mother wanted to be a singer. That's why she'd never sing,' Val says (190). In response to these final words in the play, May appears and sings a beautiful piece of opera, yet it is to be performed with a recording, in order to highlight the sheer impossibility of such artistic liberation within their lives.

The tragedy of desire in *Fen* reflects back upon and reveals the tragic contradictions of late capitalism by exposing the inconsistencies of the economic transformation affecting the fens. Uneven development is one crucial reason for their misery and alienation from their desires, but uneven development is central to how capitalism today works. As Terry Eagleton remarks, this contradiction is both central to capitalism's functioning and its key weakness: '[T]he modern-day scapegoat is essential to the workings of the very *polis* which shuts it out. It is not a matter of a few hired beggars or gaolbirds, but of whole sweated, uprooted populations' (*Sweet Violence* 296). The fen workers are such *pharmakos* for capitalism, the excluded sacrifices for economic progress who, in their abjection and in the nullification of their happiness, reveal the limits of capitalism and of so-called social progress. The play portrays the modernization of what is essentially a nineteenth-century work environment, yet in no way is this represented as an improvement in working conditions or the granting of opportunities for the workers. Tewson's selling of the farm to international capitalist concerns will not change anything: '[E]verything will go on the same,' he explains to the angry ghost, who replies, 'That's why I'm angry' (162). The unique circumstances of the fens serve to expose the reality of uneven development that is so essential to capitalism's functioning, yet that is contrary to the capitalist ideology of rational progress as something that is inevitably ushered in by economic change. International capitalism here is portrayed as thriving off the very undeveloped and uneducated labourers who are excluded from its benefits.

For Eagleton, the crucial political importance of tragedy and tragic thinking is that it induces dialectical thinking, which in turn opens avenues for exposing capitalism's inconsistencies and weaknesses. Eagleton articulates a political message surmised from his analysis of the tragic dialectics of capitalism, one that I quote in full for how accurately it speaks to the concerns of *Fen*:

> In this context, Lacan's 'Do not give up on your desire!' becomes a political injunc-
> tion. It means 'Be steadfast for death': don't be fooled by 'life' as we have it, refuse
> to make do with the bogus and second-best, don't settle for that set of shabby fan-
> tasies known as reality, but cling to your faith that the deathly emptiness of the
> dispossessed is the only source from which a more jubilant, self-delighting exist-
> ence can ultimately spring. (*Sweet Violence* 296)

I would be hard-pressed to find a more apt description of the structure of feeling conveyed by the conclusion of *Fen*. The characters' desires are indeed wedded to a deathly survival, an undead or spectral persistence that is resolutely hopeful because it refuses to capitulate to the meagre reality of their existences.

The fen dwellers are a disavowed social unconscious, the labouring, undying id that is excluded as a condition of social coherence. Eagleton writes, 'Such fig-ures represent a truth which the system must suppress in order to function; yet since they therefore have the least investment in it of any social group, they also have the strange, hallowed power to transform it. They incarnate the inner con-tradictions of the social order, and so symbolize its failure in their own' (*Sweet Violence* 280). The fen dwellers are, in this sense, all in the position of Angie in *Top Girls*, and like Angie, they live in a state of anxiety and fear, an incoherence in the self that is an ambiguous avenue into an authentic agency. A brief scene between Val and Frank is dedicated simply to the question of fear. Val was fright-ened, she says, when she left Frank, and Frank explains that he was frightened when she came back to him. He is also frightened of going mad, of heights, and of beauty (*Fen* 177). It is a curious and effective little scene, suggesting that they live in a state of constant insecurity, an insecurity that is spawned by their mar-ginal, uncertain status. While this fear is the result of changes to their lives that open up unexpected and unsettling possibilities, the fear is also, as Frank's refer-ence to beauty highlights, a means of appreciating experience. Fear is ambiguous because while it is a form of anxiety and thus an abrasive towards the ego, fear is also a symptom of an open and receptive consciousness.

A Mouthful of Birds

Churchill's overt assertion of Dionysian energy in the 1980s is a far cry from the utopian collectivity in her 1970s plays. At first glance, the most Dionysian quality of Churchill's collaboration with David Lan, *A Mouthful of Birds* (1986), is the often humorous and sometimes joyful affirmation of women's capacity for violence. The assertion that women have an ability that is stereotypically associated with men is also the play's politicized estrangement effect. Violence is not 'natural' to either gender, but neither is violence moralized here as unnatural or a contortion of human nature. The purpose of this overturning of gender stereotypes is to argue for the human capacity for conscious responsibility for one's actions, regardless of gender. One message we can read in this is that the capacity for violence is definitive of humanity. This violence is one aspect of Dionysos (as it is spelled) in the play, but this is not an argument that Dionysos is the natural or animalistic quality that expresses itself in humanity through the antisocial impulse to violence.[21] Dionysos here is first and foremost *dance*, and this activity of embodied, corporealized meaning contains the recognizably deconstructive connotations associated with dance. Dance is the play of meaning that is most tellingly expressed in vacillation, equivocation, ambiguity, and duality.

Dionysian dance is the play's image of the tragic human as inhabited by difference. To be human is to be 'not at home' within one's self, is to be 'decentred,' and this is where *A Mouthful of Birds* reveals its other Dionysian quality, located not at the level of content but of style: the play breaks significantly from the expectations of dramatic form and is a highly collaborative, workshopped venture between the actors, Churchill, Lan, director Les Waters, and choreographer Ian Spink. The play contains elements of movement, mime, and dance interspersed throughout the seven stories that constitute the play's structure. Occasionally, dialogue from *The Bacchae* interrupts the narrative, and the modern characters are described as being momentarily 'possessed' by Pentheus, Agave, or the Bacchantes. The play enacts, in its style, this Dionysian decentring. This, I think, is what is most Dionysian and jubilantly tragic about *A Mouthful of Birds*: the liberation of meaning from the monologic strictures of text into plural forms of expression. Meaning is dispersed in an artistic *sparagmos*, replicated by the scene of *sparagmos* that the play borrows from *The Bacchae*. *A Mouthful of Birds* asserts its creativity as an act of force exerted upon Euripides's play, a strong misinterpretation of the earlier Greek interpretation, one that overcomes and consumes the text by which it has become possessed. Violence at the level of content and artistic creation at the level of form are both expressions of *difference*, of cruelty, within the human, apprehended as such.

As an affirmation of cruelty the play is unflinching. The simple narratives are replete with dialectical ambivalence. Lena, a woman who is squeamish around dead animals, is continuously berated by a spirit that describes her boorish husband to her in abject, nauseating terms and threatens Lena with the possibility of becoming unborn. The spirit's harangue bears all the qualities of a schizophrenic hallucination. Lena eventually drowns her child in an attempt to silence this inner voice. When we see Lena in the play's epilogue, she has become a caregiver for the elderly, where her newfound power over life and death is omnipresent: 'I remember I enjoyed doing it. It's nice to make someone alive and it's nice to make someone dead. Either way. That power is what I like best in the world. The struggle every day is not to use it' (51). This knowledge of her own abilities is empowering: she is no longer repulsed by abjection, nor is she afraid of anything any more.

Other characters pass through experiences that enact a similar affirmation of the creative power of violence. Dan, a vicar, questions the idea that God is necessarily male and becomes a serial killer who murders with pleasure, seducing his victims with a dance that is, the stage directions tell us, precisely what they long for: when they are the beneficiaries of Dan's dance, they die, presumably fully satisfied. Dan's philosophy, recorded in a diary and read out loud by a prison guard, explains that these are deaths designed to feed and replenish the earth, from which humanity has taken so much. Dan asserts that he neither makes nor destroys anything, but simply does man's work: 'I transform' (25). This word serves as a dialectical identity between creation and destruction: both are simply aspects of transformation itself. What is most unsettling about this imagery is not the literal idea that murder feeds the earth's regeneration, but rather the possibility of the dissolution or dispersal of human consciousness beyond its centred psychic boundaries, beyond its imagined walls, barriers erected as a means of self-definition. Dan, for instance, fantasizes about being dispersed into nature himself: 'I want to be milked from the udder of a cow. I'd like a pine tree to grow inside me. I want to rest the tips of my fingers on the peaks of two mountains so my muscles tear' (26). The force of these images finds anchor in the fate of the 'I' within the rhetoric of the sentence, dissolved or scattered to the four winds.[22] It is an anticipation of the transformation that the seven characters experience by the play's conclusion.

While Dionysos is dance in this play, Dionysos is not a utopian oneness preceding individuation. What all the characters are left with in the play's conclusion is a sense of openness, permeability, and multiplicity. This is alternately comforting, joyful, or deeply discomfiting. Derek, an unemployed man who redresses a crisis in his masculinity by bodybuilding, is possessed by the historical hermaphrodite Herculine Barbin. A newly transgendered subject by the play's conclusion, Derek is the beneficiary of a comfortable sense of self that is only partially located in a feminine body: 'My shoulders are still strong. And my new shape is the least of it. I smell light and sweet. I come into a room, who has been there? Me. My skin used to wrap me up, now it lets the world in. Was I this all the time?' (52). The gift of Dionysos here is not so much a simple trans-gendering but an exposure of the self to the world, a heightened consciousness of the transience of the boundaries of selfhood and the potential dissolution of those apparent psychic walls.

Doreen, the final character and one who bears particular importance in the play, wants only peace and quiet. She lives in a rooming house with several other people and struggles with her rage at the close quarters and the constant intrusions her housemates inflict upon her. Finally, Doreen's rage manifests it-self in telekinesis: she slams a man against a wall through the force of her voice, and then makes objects fly across the room. When, following this narrative, the characters are all possessed by figures from *The Bacchae* and act out the rending of Pentheus, it is Doreen who becomes Agave, and following the *sparagmos*, Doreen/Agave refuses to return to her old life: 'There's nothing for me there. There never was. I'm staying here' (50). Her decision inspires the other women, who were about to go home or to work, to remain as well. Yet while the other women are empowered by this decision, Doreen's embodying of carnal knowl-edge is more curse than gift: 'I can find no rest. My head is filled with horrible images. I can't say I actually see them, it's more that I feel them. It seems that my mouth is full of birds which I crunch between my teeth. Their feathers, their blood and broken bones are choking me. I carry on my work as a secretary' (53). Habitual life continues with this carnal, visceral feeling now as an under-current: Dionysos dances to conclude the play.

This is the ambivalence of Dionysian multiplicity: the scene of *sparagmos*, the rending into pieces of Pentheus, is also the death of the god and the scattering of divinity in all directions. The *sparagmos* is represented in the play by a dance re-peating *'moments of extreme happiness and of violence from earlier parts of the play'* (50). The *sparagmos* is the ultimate expression of jubilant cruelty: a joyful dispersal of sense away from any origin. Dionysian cruelty is difference, the sense of being open, inhabited, and dispersed, dispossessed of one's self in some way, but beyond this, it is the apprehension of self *as* difference or dispersal. The final seven short speeches from the characters dramatize how this cruel sense of dif-ference, of being decentred from one's self, is experienced by different characters: there is no single, monologic form of experience of the god. The scene of *sparag-mos*, however is also the most self-reflexive aspect of the play, where this play's characters are 'possessed' by other characters from Euripides's play. The image of the *sparagmos* is a rhetorical image for the activity of misprision, the violent assertion of force upon pre-existing meaning exercised by one artistic object upon another, and the ensuing dissemination of sense that the victorious object exerts as a triumphant, strong misreading of the historical object: it is renewal through destruction.[23] The work of art here is an example of overcoming, and serves as a rhetorical trope for selfhood as an energetic and affirmative expression of desire. Yet Doreen's concluding speech, evoking the titular image, demonstrates that such a self-overcoming is fraught and imperfect.

It is tempting to suggest that within England of the mid-1980s, the emergence of Dionysos is as close to an experience of alienation as it is an embracing of difference. Notably, both Derek and Lena make specific reference at the end of the play to no longer being frightened. Dionysos, it seems, is a possible means of overcoming the ubiquitous anxiety that Churchill scatters throughout her plays, but Doreen's state at the end of the play seems unsettlingly close to such a perturbed condition. What all seven characters have in common at the beginning of the play is a marginalized psychic state, an inability to follow the routines of quotidian life that breaks into a crisis. They are *anxious*, and this in itself is the avenue through which Dionysos arrives. The embracing of difference and the overwhelming experience of fear are not opposites but, appropriately, related aspects of the same continuous process.

Lives of the Great Poisoners

Churchill's work of the 1970s is characterized by the exploration of utopian possibilities for affirming desire, the unconscious, and the Dionysian as the underside of the human Möbius strip. The work of the 1980s pragmatically forecloses upon the utopian and explores instead more traditionally tragic subjectivities characterized by mourning, the division from desire, and the energizing terrors of Dionysus. Her 1990s work raises the possibility that tragic experience and a relation to the unconscious are no longer possible. While Churchill's plays are always characterized by an intelligent and subtle humour, an essential part of their energy, there is at the same time in her work of the 1990s a disquieting focus on the spirit of revenge that seems at first to be oblique and only tangentially related to the present. However, if we translate this spirit of revenge back to the terms we have considered so far, then we can see that it is as if the playwright indicts the cultural moment as having been, in the post-Thatcher years, reduced to nothing more than the expression of *ressentiment*: this is all human beings are capable of thinking because this is all they have been reduced to thinking and being.[24] What was once a tragic dialectic has become its negative image: no longer a negation that achieves something affirmative or positive but a stultified form of negativity. Consider the opera *Lives of the*

Great Poisoners (1991), which begins with the image of Medea as a *pharmakos*, restoring the dying Aeson to life by draining his blood and pouring a potion into the wound: 'Hurting you I heal you / Killing you I cure you / Secrets of death and new life / Poisons that heal / Fill your blood fill your breath / By my skill / I kill you and give you new life,' she sings (191). What begins as a dialectical reversal, a poison that cures, will be shorn of its dialectic in postmodernity. Over the course of the opera, this by now recognizable dialectical figure of the tragic *pharmakos* is inverted until it becomes a condemnation of an entirely toxic modernity.

While there are three separate stories in *Lives of the Great Poisoners* dealing with sensationalistic murders through the application of poison, what unites them all is the figure of Thomas Midgley Jr (1889–1944), the enterprising American industrial chemist who conceived of putting lead in gasoline and who created chlorofluorocarbons (CFCs). Midgley's 'cures' are now known to be two of the worst environmental toxins of the twentieth century. Midgley follows the action of the opera, an anachronistic time traveller who serves as an ironic counterpoint to the tales of murder he witnesses. The doubling of characters creates a dramatic continuity throughout the narrative: Medea, the healer, becomes Cora Crippen, who was famously murdered by her husband, Dr Hawley Harvey Crippen, in 1910. Cora's disembodied head swears revenge and then becomes, in the second story, Medea once more, the healer who cures the sick and brings the dead to life. When she learns that her husband Jason plans to marry Creusa for political purposes, Medea is corrupted by hatred, rage, and revenge, poisoning Creusa and Creon with the famous dress. Medea becomes one with her rage, and in the final story becomes Marquise Mme de Brinvilliers (1630–76), a notorious French poisoner. Having murdered her father and brothers to gain the family fortune, the Marquise attempts to slowly murder her dissolute husband before he can squander her hard-won estate. When we meet her, she is murdering the hospitalized sick in order to test her poisons: 'Healing you I hurt you / Curing you I kill you / Secrets of life and new death' (218). Hatred and revenge have transformed the *pharmakos* into its reverse: the healing power of the tragic figure has been inverted into pure negativity.

Thomas Midgley moves from story to story in a state of benign ignorance, always thinking the best of the poisoners and unable to grasp their sinister intentions. He falls in love with the Marquise; she confesses her crimes to him and then tries to poison him in order to silence him. Midgley is appalled to discover the ubiquity of poisoning within this society. The simple facts are explained to him by the Marquise's mentor in crime: 'Come on, Midgley. And it's not just love affairs. The whole political life of the country depends on poison. [...] Don't worry. Everything's pointless anyway. People are vile. Death doesn't matter' (231).

It is a sobering diagnosis: this violence is meaningless, because it is omnipresent. The Marquise is caught, beheaded, and her ashes scattered to the winds, where she is inhaled by all the characters: 'Now we all breathe her in so we'll all catch a mania for poisoning which will astonish us' (236). This breath of toxic inspiration seems to give Midgley his final idea, one that in reality he did not live long enough to implement: 'To control the growth of crops by increasing the ozone in the earth's atmosphere' (237). The legacy of the opera's cycle of revenge is Midgley himself, whose purportedly benevolent inventions are expressions of the purest *ressentiment*: destruction masked by the best of intentions.

There seem to be two interrelated political diagnoses happening at once in *Lives of the Great Poisoners*. Most evident is the environmental message about the earth, which will come to occupy Churchill in *The Skriker*. This human neglect of our living environment is linked to a general expression of irrational human loathing, found in a human world where poisoning is an essential part of the fabric of the social dynamic. But poisoning here also means revenge, and the ubiquity of poisoning also figures the general dominance of the spirit of revenge upon human consciousness. We are shown a dramatic movement wherein the tragic *pharmakos* is corrupted by betrayal and becomes the Marquise de Brinvilliers, the spirit of revenge, cast upon the four winds and inspiring humanity's self-destructive decline in the twentieth century. What was once the meaning of the tragic – the affirmation of negativity – seems to be no longer possible here. *Live of the Great Poisoners* thus casts doubt upon the possibility of tragic experience within the condition of postmodernity.

The Skriker

Such a context helps us to understand the convolutions and apparent obscurities of *The Skriker* (1994). On one level, the titular character is an Erinyes, or Fury, a chthonic revenge spirit meant to redress an imbalance incurred by a human deed – typically, as in the *Oresteia*, a crime against blood. On another level, the Skriker is a creature out of faerie, a changeling spirit who seems to have bodied forth into the human world because of an altered relationship between the human and spirit realms. The change is due to the process called 'thinning,' a term literary critic John Clute uses to describe the passing away from the human world of elements of magic and faerie: 'Thinning is a sign of a loss of attention to the stories whose outcomes might save the heroes and the folk' (Clute 942). While the figure of the Skriker has been read in a number of ways,[25] I find Sheila Rabillard's figuration most compelling: she offers that the Skriker and the realm of faerie are instances of Freudian projection: 'not so much [...] representations of nature as dramatizations of the human relationship to nature,' and thus what is at stake is 'the psychic structure of projection governing human perception of the non-human world' (98–9). I would add that another word for this projected human relation to nature is the unconscious, and Ann Wilson's trenchant analysis of the Skriker as the return of the repressed, the permanent absence that haunts consciousness, is apposite here (Wilson 186). Combining the two readings, this image of the id can be historicized; thus *The Skriker* is also about the damaged human relationship to the id within a toxic postmodernity. The Skriker travels to the human world and plagues two teenage single mothers. One of these two girls, Josie, has killed her newborn infant, and the other, Lily, is pregnant and gives birth over the course of the play. While is it clear that the Skriker wants something from Lily and Josie, what she wants is at first unclear. She claims in all earnestness that she is a good fairy and has come to do good, but this is not necessarily a human good (257). She also speaks of the changed human attitude towards faerie: 'They used to leave cream in a sorcerer's apprentice. Gave the brownie a pair of trousers to wear have you gone? Now they hate us and hurt hurtle faster and master. They poison me in my rivers of blood poisoning makes my arm swelter' (246). A crime, it seems, has been committed against the chthonic, and 'Revengeance is gold mine' (246). The Skriker's revenge comes about through the offering of wishes, which, when indulged, give the Skriker something of the human in return.

The human destruction of the natural world is a strong source of ire for the Skriker. She is, Churchill remarks, '*damaged*' (243), and Josie articulates her sense that something seems to be wrong with the supernatural spirit (250). 'You people are killing me, do you know that? I am sick, I am a sick woman,' the Skriker tells Lily in a humorous exchange where Lily tries, unsuccessfully, to explain the mysteries of television technology to the fairy (256). It is possible that the Skriker is starving due to the effects of the toxic poisons released into the planet by the technological advances of the twentieth century. The Skriker explains this using the punning run-on sentences that have sometimes left both audiences and critics baffled as to the significance of the play:

> the nation wide open wide world hurled hurtling hurting hurt very badly. Wars whores hips hip hoorays it to the ground glass. Drought rout out and about turn off. Sunburn sunbeam in your eye socket to him. All good many come to the aids party. When I go uppity, follow a fellow on a dark road dank ride and jump thrump out and eat him how does he taste? Toxic waste paper basket case, salmonelephant-iasis, blue blood bad blood blue blood blad blood blah blah blah. (271)

In language designed to render strange not only the realm of faerie but also how that realm perceives the mortal world, the Skriker describes world wars, drought, the failure of the ozone layer, HIV, and the increased toxicity level in human beings.[26] Once, human beings tasted delicious, and the Skriker remembers with nostalgia tearing delicious English flesh limb from limb. Now there is '[p]oison in the food chainsaw massacre' (271). Josie, hearing this, realizes that for the Skriker, 'no one tastes any good' (271), an intuition perhaps connected to Josie's apprehension when she is in a mental hospital that '[t]he food's not healthy' (247). In one of her many shapeshifting disguises, late in the play, the Skriker muses philosophically about global changes that appear to have unsettled a fundamental balance in the world and serve as portents of cataclysms to come:

> Earthquakes. Volcanoes. Drought. Apocalyptic meteorological phenomena. The increase of sickness. It was always possible to think whatever your personal problem, there's always nature. Spring will return even if it's without me. Nobody loves me but at least it's a sunny day. This has been a comfort to people as long as they've existed. But it's not available any more. Sorry. Nobody loves me and the sun's going to kill me. Spring will return and nothing will grow. (283)

Nature, as a concept and as a phenomenon, is at risk of grinding to a halt. If the destruction of the environment is the crime that has caused an imbalance, then the Skriker, as a fury, should seek revenge that will pay back the blood crime against the natural world and restore equilibrium.

It seems to be such payment that she wants from Josie and Lily, and the Skriker seeks to extract it through traditional fairy means: the offering of wishes, which, when indulged, bind the Skriker to her human host. The logic of the Skriker's contract is found in the nature of wishes themselves, particularly the wish fulfilments that abide within human beings but that their best interests dictate they not act upon. It is this very human paradox that the Skriker exploits and feeds upon, and the paradox is, aptly, embodied most evidently in fairy tales such as the story of Bluebeard's bloody chamber (245). These stories constantly portray a human desire to perform a forbidden act, and then a will to outwit the consequences of that action: 'Tell them one thing not to do, thing to rue won't they do it' (245). The Skriker knows well that if human beings are forbidden to do something, then some irrational aspect of them will be compelled to that very action, and her wishes are bound to the same logic, for the possibility of wishing for whatever one wants risks unleashing one's heart's desire, something that one would never, in life, practically seek to fulfil: 'Whatever you do don't open the do don't open the door' (245). What the Skriker wants is the totality of human desires; by offering humans whatever they want, she receives what she wants (268). So it is not surprising that in the underworld the Skriker has fed on Josie's 'Jung men and Freud eggs' until there is nothing left but scraps (272). She wants not only blood from Josie and Lily, but psychic material too: dreams and wishes. The blood that feeds the Skriker here is the energy of the unconscious.

If we are to maintain this easily recognizable metaphor of blood for the fluidity of the id, then the environmental message of the play must coexist alongside a philosophical one. In poisoning the earth, and thus themselves, and in failing to give due reverence to fairy folk, the human race has at the same time disavowed the unconscious and failed to respect this Otherness. The destruction of the earth is nothing more or less than the unleashing of an unrestrained and omnivorous ego upon the planet, a ravenous, hubristic, and narcissistic self driven by an illusion of its own complete agency and omnipotence that licenses it to consume its surroundings and master its reality without fear of consequences: the ego sees nothing outside of itself and finds in its surroundings only a mirror for its own identity. The stylistic strangeness of *The Skriker*, frequently considered to be the key weakness of this play, is an essential affront to this ego. Not only does the Skriker open the play with a remarkably long speech full of challenging puns and convoluted wordplay, throughout the entire play the realm of faerie is represented onstage all around the Lily and Josie. The fairy folk act out their own bizarre and surrealistic narratives wordlessly, performed by dancers. There is no relationship between the main plot of *The Skriker* and these oblique fairy narratives: the audience is quite deliberately being offered something that it cannot understand, something resolutely Other.

By the end of the play the Skriker is so starved of healthy blood that she compares herself to a domesticated cat that, fed only on tinned food, was frightened when it smelled fresh bloody meat. In an attempt to appease the Skriker, Josie begins to perform disturbing acts of violence and promises to do terrible things if only the Skriker herself will do nothing (287). However, it is finally Lily who revitalizes the Skriker with energy when she offers to go with the Skriker to the underworld if her sacrifice will protect humanity and help the Skriker be good. Like a character from a fairy tale, Lily is hoping to outwit the logic of faerie; she remembers that while Josie spent a lifetime in the underworld, no time passed on earth. She hopes to be restored to her newborn daughter, having missed nothing of the child's life. Naturally her plan is thwarted by the Skriker: Lily is handed a lighted candle and holds it until it goes out. So much time has passed in this brief interval that the earth is dead, a vast cemetery, and the only two remaining humans are an old woman and a deformed girl. The old woman is Lily's granddaughter, and when the child realizes Lily is from the 'distant past master class,' she bellows her wordless rage at what Lily's generation did to the earth (290).

The play concludes with two grim images: Lily takes a piece of food to eat, which according to the traditional fairy tale will return her to the mortal world and cause her to age and crumble to dust (246). At the same time that Lily reaches for the fatal food, a fairy who has been dancing in the background for the better part of the entire play stops. We may presume that the death of humanity is the death of faerie, and the death of the dance is the death of Dionysus. This suitably bleak conclusion to Churchill's fairy tale breaks from the traditional tragic logic of the fury: the Skriker's revenge does not redress a balance or regenerate the earth. This is not an image of a post-human Eden but of a dead, post-apocalyptic planet, and the Skriker's revenge leads to a literal dead end, as if the self-destructive resentment humanity expresses towards the earth and, by implication, towards itself leads to a similarly cataclysmic act of revenge on the part of the fair folk. The conclusion of *The Skriker* is a curious inversion, demonstrative again of the potential death of the tragic within postmodernity, where nature has been extinguished and therefore regeneration through violence, sacrifice, and submission is no longer possible. Lily's attempt to offer herself has no redeeming effect: the human race will not be saved by her gesture, and the fury will not be made 'better than she should be' (290). When the id lashes back at humanity now, it is so slighted and damaged by our massive neglect of it that it destroys us utterly. No healthy relationship to the unconscious, the Skriker's world of faerie, is possible in this play.

Churchill's most striking inversion in *The Skriker* is in her location of fear. Fear is a major concern here, but the figure that experiences it is unexpected: it is the Skriker who is afraid of humanity (257). Josie, who is fearless in the face of the nature spirit, knows this well (267). The Skriker's reply is to mock Josie for her fearlessness: 'Josie's not frightened' she repeats (262, 268). Yet Josie has experienced fear. Her mental state is ambiguous in the play. She has killed her ten-day-old infant and appears to have pathological tendencies. She eventually achieves a moment of lucidity about the murder when Lily wishes her sane: 'Why did I? It should have been me. Because under that pain oh shit there's under that under that there's this other [...]. Don't let me feel it. It's coming for me. Hide me. This is what. When I killed her. What I was frightened. Trying to stop when I. It's here' (279). Josie has killed her baby out of fear of something traumatic, huge, and apparently ineffable. This draws our attention to the two young protagonists of Churchill's fairy tale: two young single mothers who seem to have only each other to depend upon. Their attitudes towards their newborns, while seeming different, may be connected. Josie's fear may, perhaps, have been quelled or averted by the death of her child, because the child then would not have to face whatever it is that frightens Josie. Being frightened in this world is an appropriate, perceptive response to the conditions of their lives. When Lily, suffering from worry and fear, finally decides to try to appease the Skriker, she has become a new mother and her personal world has been reoriented by the arrival of her child. Her offer to go with the Skriker seems to be, in part, motivated by an awareness of the needs of her child, and by implication other people's children too. She wants to save everyone. Fear is an expression of apprehension, and a reminder of individual agency and responsibility. Fear is the aim, too, of the grim tales that *The Skriker* draws upon in its narrative. A moment, early on, when a dead child sings a macabre refrain indicates that these traditional stories are being drawn upon with a renewed, politicized effect: 'My mother she killed me and put me in pies / My father he ate me and said I was nice' (259). Children remain a key locus for the activation of dread and anxiety, and the most hopeful gesture that Churchill makes in *The Skriker* is when she demonstrates that fear is still a means of communication with the unconscious world of faerie, at least for young women and mothers.

Thyestes

The visceral image of a child in a pie being eaten by her father connects the content of the fairy tale with the tradition of the tragic and reveals the social content lurking within Churchill's translation of Seneca's *Thyestes* (1994), performed only a few months after *The Skriker*. At the heart of the narrative of Thyestes is just such an image of a father consuming his children: this is the origin of the curse of the house of Atreus, as is played out in the *Oresteia*. Churchill's lean and poetic translation is of the only existing dramatic version of this part of the myth: a Roman revenge tragedy, which in form has far more in common with Elizabethan tragedy than with Greek. Roman tragedy is rarely considered within analyses of the tragic, not only because as a poetic form it is generally considered unplayable but also because the emphasis upon the bare bones of revenge exclude it from considerations of the tragic in the same way that Raymond Williams separates the Elizabethan and Jacobean from the Greek form in *Modern Tragedy* (28–32). By offering *Thyestes* for our consideration, Churchill evidently finds contemporary relevance in its content: 'I don't think it's just because I've been translating Thyestes that the news seems full of revenge stories. Seneca could have brought a god on at the end of his play, but he's made a world where gods either don't exist or have left' (Introduction, *Thyestes* 301). This is indeed what is most striking about Seneca's cosmos in *Thyestes* and what allows Churchill, in a remarkable and understated *léger-de-main*, to make a stunning comment upon the condition of the present: in response to Atreus's numbing crime of killing his nephews and feeding them to their father, Thyestes, the gods go silent: 'but earth is / unmoved. Heavy and / still. The gods have left' (*Thyestes* 340). There is nothing redeeming or humanizing available within this narrative, nothing within which the primordial act of revenge against Thyestes for usurping the kingdom and cuckolding Atreus might be contained. *Thyestes* is about the potential death of tragedy.

Most notable about *Thyestes* is the character of Atreus, whose dedication to his revenge is so complete that he attempts the worst crime of which he can conceive, and after he has executed it is disappointed that he did not do worse. The deed is described by the messenger in the most horrified of terms: 'The way things take turns/in the world has stopped./There'll be no setting/any more and no rising. [...] No winter, no spring,/no moon racing her brother, planets/piled together in a pit' (334). Nature has ground to a halt in response to the act of revenge, and fear is the natural response, one that is, at this point, without purpose: 'Let's not be frightened./You'd have to be really/greedy for life/if you didn't want to die when the whole world's/dying with you' (335). We are led by the play's rhetoric to understand Atreus's deed as a ne plus ultra of human agency on earth: the ultimate, final crime. Yet the comic irony to come is that Atreus realizes too late that he could have done better: 'Even this is too/little for me. Hot blood/straight out of the wound/into your mouth while they/were still alive, yes,/my anger was cheated/because I was hurried' (342). It would have been a much better crime, Atreus realizes, had the father and the sons all been conscious of the act of cannibalism as it took place.

The cannibalism itself rather than the actual deaths of the sons is the most horrifying aspect of the crime: Thyestes, shown his children's heads, is emotionally restrained and measured in his response. He realizes he has been betrayed but he also understands that this is revenge for his past betrayal of his brother: 'I ask as a brother./Let me bury them./Give what you'll see burnt./I'm not asking for/what I'll keep, just/what I'll lose' (340). Seeking calmly to gather his boys' remains together so that he can perform due funeral rites, he is only then informed that he has eaten them. He will not, now, be able to lose them properly, to bury his sons like a father should, unless he himself is cremated (343). The extent of Atreus's crime is such that it arrests mourning itself, grinding to a halt the human work of lamentation. *Thyestes*'s answer to the seemingly rhetorical question 'Is there any/limit to crime?' (341) appears to be a resounding 'no,' an answer so thunderous that it drowns out both nature and the gods. As in *The Skriker*, the ongoing work of humanity has reversed the order of things: 'Atreus stands unmoved/and frightens the gods/who thought they'd frighten him' (330). As the Skriker is frightened of humanity's achievements, so too are Seneca's gods, who ultimately absent themselves altogether. In Seneca Churchill has found an image of postmodernity. Here, I think, we come to the heart of the matter in Churchill's work in regards to what is frightening. We do not fear the gods, we do not fear the Other, and this lack of fear is, or should be, frightening in and of itself. What is frightening is the very condition of postmodernity: our creation of a completely secularized, reified, rationalized human world, where humanity is in charge of its own destiny and our agency is complete. There is no crime we are not capable of, and no crime that cannot be bested with a worse deed. There is no limit beyond which human beings cannot pass, and god is either dead or has fled in terror. What is frightening is the death of tragedy.

Far Away

It is through these recent explorations of the philosophical problems of post-modernity that Churchill continues to convey her political messages. It is ironic that at a point when her political theatre has become more abstract and philo-sophical in its tactics, critics should insist on reading her all too literally, as creating instances of realism. *Far Away* (2000), for example, quickly became described as a prescient play when, less than a year after it opened in London, the events of September 11, 2001 took place. When the play premiered in New York in November 2002, it seemed ready made to mirror the American sense of self. However, the premise that *Far Away* is trying to make some kind of mi-metic political commentary upon world events is also what has allowed hostile critics of the play to dismiss it as irrelevant: the play concludes with a descrip-tion of a surreal, farcical, and nonsensical world war, where not only have ani-mals taken sides in a global conflict but every conceivable object one might imagine has been mobilized in a total conflict, the defining lines of which are utterly arbitrary and shifting. Weather, pins, heroin, petrol, chainsaws, hair-spray, bleach, foxgloves, grass, gravity, noise, and light have been recruited and have taken sides. For individuals who felt vulnerable and under attack after the terrorist events of September 11, this seemed to somehow mirror their fear and paranoia. Yet the total ludicrousness of this imagery was also a handy lever for critics to claim the play had third-act problems that undermined the first two parts of the play, which are more readily understandable as pieces of dystopian political satire than is the final scene.

In the first scene, Joan, a young girl staying with her aunt in the country-side, has just seen her uncle beating unknown people, including children, in a shed. When she queries her aunt about this, she is given a series of lies, which she counters with more questions until finally accepting the older woman's deception: 'You're part of a big movement now to make things better. You can be proud of that. You can look at the stars and think here we are in our little bit of space, and I'm on the side of the people who are putting things right, and your soul will expand right into the sky' (20–1). The child is persuaded, and we next meet her as a young adult living in a vaguely defined totalitarian society, working as a designer and creator of preposterous hats that are used in ambiguous and frequent parades. When we see one such parade, it is a group of ragged prisoners, wearing these ridiculous and grotesque accoutrements, being marched to their executions and incineration. Joan is oblivious to the apparently inhuman treatment of these individuals but is particularly righteous about the possibility of graft and corruption in her workplace. Her idealistic indignation concerning bribes and low pay fosters a budding romance with her fellow milliner, Todd. The two of them are portrayed as smug, naive, and self-satisfied stooges: Joan wins a hat competition and is impressed that Todd has voiced his concerns about corruption to his superior. Todd, in turn, is inspired by Joan's demonstrated fervour: '[W]e could expose the corrupt financial basis of how the whole hat industry is run, not just this place' she speculates (32). The ineffective hollowness of their rhetoric renders them laughable in relation to the mass executions of which they are a part. When we meet them again in the third act, Todd is on leave from military service and Joan has deserted her post, following him to her Aunt Harper's home once more. 'The cats have come in on the side of the French,' Harper explains in one of the scene's more notoriously humorous lines (35).

They sound like paranoid lunatics, and the credibility of what they describe is stretched beyond acceptance. This is entirely the point, I think: we are not shown this global strife and I do not think this vision of a world divided every which way against itself is meant to be a feasible description of world events in the new millennium. I find the suggestion that this is a vision of the breakdown of the 'natural contract' between humanity and the globe unpersuasive (Chaudhuri 132–4). Where does such a thesis leave the pins and gravity? There is also no causal link established between the police state hinted at in Act 1, the totalitarian dystopia of Act 2, and the cartoonish apocalypse of Act 3. With the significant exception of the parade scene, this play is a series of small, intimate exchanges between individuals. We are meant, here, to attend to what we are shown, particularly in Act 3, which opens with the apparently innocuous words, 'You were right to poison the wasps' (*Far Away* 34). What matters here is less the fact of poisoning wasps than the connection of poisoning to moral righteousness: the toxic state of postmodernity is a symptom of a toxic consciousness. The play is about a certain ubiquitous way of thinking, one that throughout this discussion has been referred to as *ressentiment* and that Nietzsche describes in *On the Genealogy of Morals*: '[I]n order to exist, slave morality always first needs a hostile external world; it needs, physiologically speaking, external stimuli in order to act at all – its action is fundamentally reaction' (37). Joan is persuaded by her aunt that they are righteous and serving a greater good; Joan and Todd fall in love and ignore the circumstances within which they live by holding to and seeing in each other an idealistic sense of self-righteousness; and Harper, in Act 3, explains that 'Crocodiles are evil and it is always right to be opposed to crocodiles. Their skin, their teeth, the foul smell of their mouths from the dead meat' (38). The thinking of *ressentiment* is essentially negative and finds its own sense of goodness and righteousness through the location of an enemy: '[H]ere precisely is his deed, his creation: he has conceived "the evil enemy," "*the Evil One*," and this in fact is his basic concept, from which he then evolves, as an afterthought and pendant, a "good one" – himself!' (Nietzsche, *On the Genealogy of Morals* 39). *Far Away* shows us not so much the growth or flowering of such *ressentiment* as it performs a comedy of *ressentiment* for us, seducing us through a recognizable premise only to take this away from us in the play's final scene. The desire to be on the side of what's right, to define oneself as right and good in opposition to 'evil,' is rendered into a hyperbolic comedy in the play's final scene, a laughable and ludicrous display of nonsense. What matters in the end is Harper's display of pathological thinking, not the crazed and improbable world that she describes. Her 'us vs them' thinking is, of course, reflective of the dominant American rhetoric after September 11, 2001, and this is the play's political commentary: this form of thought – vengeful, sick, and righteous – is not a reflection of reality at all. It has lost the ability to perceive reality.

It is in this sense that Peter Brook, who directed the play in France, was certainly correct when he insisted that it was 'unmorbid and positive' (Paul Taylor 'An open Brook,' *The Independent* 30 Jan 2002: 9). This affirmative gesture comes from the arrival of Joan at the play's conclusion. She has deserted her military post and describes her voyage to Harper's home. Joan seems indifferent to her own participation in the violence: 'I killed two cats and a child under five' (*Far Away* 43). The only indication that she is not entirely subsumed within *ressentiment* is found in her confrontation with a river: 'I didn't know whose side the river was on, it might help me swim or it might drown me' (44). Forced to cross it, she enters the cold running water despite her uncertainty about its allegiances: 'When you've just stepped in you can't tell what's going to happen. The water laps round your ankles in any case' (44). These are the final words of the play; its final image is of an uncertain girl, and this uncertainty is the understated lever with which *Far Away* seeks to undermine the zealous confidence that is its subject matter.

Perhaps the play's ultimate joke is that if you accept the vision of strife in the third act as reflecting reality in some way it is because you find it persuasive; and if you find it persuasive it is because you think like Harper does. Moreover, the play manipulates the audience's impulse to take some instinctual moral high ground: we never see the people being beaten in the shed in Act 1, and we don't find out why people are being executed in Act 2. We never learn why any of this is happening; the typical response will be to assume that these fascistic and violent actions are morally questionable. Beating children and mass executions are morally heinous acts, as is the condoning of them. The audience will naturally assume that Joan, her Aunt Harper, and Todd are morally wrong to approve of these events, and that the audience is in a morally superior position to judge them for it. But positions of moral superiority are just what the play is out to expose and question, and it is all too easy for the audience to take just that superior position.

Far Away is thus subtly antagonistic towards an audience that is willing to take its paranoid vision of global warfare literally. This guides our attention back to the only time in *Far Away* that we actually see any of the events going on in the background of the story: the parade of prisoners wearing extravagant hats. It is not just a dramatization of a moment of morbid pageantry, it *is* a moment of morbid pageantry. Churchill asks for a group of somewhere between twenty to a hundred people, suggesting that the more the better. Critical response to this scene is invariably that it is the play's show-stopper: a tour de force, the great theatrical coup at the heart of the performance, a big visual surprise that critics are reticent to ruin for the audience. In a perversely calculated move, the script demands exactly the kind of pageant of individuals parading across the stage that it is condemning as an extravagant, inhuman spectacle. When Joan laments the waste of the hats, which are incinerated along with their wearers, Todd replies, 'No I think that's the joy of it. The hats are ephemeral. It's like a metaphor for something or other. [...] You make beauty and it disappears, I love that' (31). It is, of course, a wry description of the transience of theatre, and it is hard to imagine a more vitriolic satire of theatre's oblivious pageantry and waste.

A Number

Just as *Far Away* is not a piece of transparent political propaganda for the post–September 11 moment, *A Number* (2002) is not a play about cloning. Cloning is a simple narrative device used in the play to explore the question of what a human being is: like a clone, a human being is a repetition, a difference. *A Number* offers two different visions of the tragic human: one as defined by loss and alienation, and one who affirms and embraces difference. This latter figure is an optimistic return to the utopian figures of Churchill's 1970s work, indicating that she has made a passage through the remarkable pessimism of the 1990s and finds new potentials for the human.

A man of thirty-five, Bernard discovers accidentally that he has been surreptitiously cloned many times by an unknown scientist. He asks his father, Salter, how this might have happened, and his father admits reluctantly that Bernard's original died as a child and that Salter wished to have him again. Bernard learns that he in fact is a clone of the dead boy. This turns out to be a lie when the original, forty-year-old Bernard finds Salter. The original Bernard, we learn, did not die but was given up by Salter at the age of four. Salter explains that the suicide of his wife left him a broken alcoholic who neglected his two-year-old son, ignoring the boy's cries for attention and even going so far as to abandon him for long periods. After two years of abuse, Bernard was deeply traumatized and severely dysfunctional, and so Salter gave him up to foster care and, after dealing with his alcoholism, had a clone made whom he could raise anew. This clone is the Bernard who has grown up as Salter's son. The original Bernard, now a violent, working-class criminal, is so enraged to discover that he has been cloned that he tracks down his replacement, confronts him, and then later murders him. After telling Salter about the murder, the original Bernard commits suicide.

Although the theatrical impact of *A Number* is weighted towards the opportunity for the actor playing the sons (Daniel Craig in its premiere) to fully distinguish between the different characters, it is Salter's tragedy that grounds the play's emotions. Salter spends the first few scenes of the play lying cravenly and evading an admission of the truth, but once the full narrative of his past actions emerges, then the character we see in the final scene of the play takes on remarkable contours, and his subtextual motivations suggest the opportunity for more sympathetic connections to be made with him. Now that the original Bernard has killed himself, Salter is finally confronted with the experience of loss he has avoided for thirty-five years, if not longer: 'I can't put it right any more' (61). He has, it appears, spent forty years running from the experience of loss: the loss of his wife, perhaps the loss of his marriage, or perhaps even something more ephemeral, which was the source of his despair and his neglect of his son.

The creation of a second child may be understood as a part of that flight from his error: having damaged his son so deeply, Salter attempted to erase this history of trauma and loss by creating a child who would not be touched by the after-effects of the wife's suicide. It is a recognizably tragic narrative: the attempt to thwart history and fate doomed, by this very action, to fulfil fate. When Salter, informed of the murder of the second Bernard, spews a long litany of bile at the first Bernard as an expression of spite and revenge, there are echoes of an old narrative: 'I could have killed you and I didn't. I may have done terrible things but I didn't kill you. I could have killed you and had another son' (51). The failed act of Oedipal infanticide and the inevitable return of the repressed circulate as ghosts in the background of the play. Salter has fled the experience of grief only to find that he is inevitably returned to the loss and grief he has been evading.

In the final scene, we see a man who is consumed by his emotions: 'I miss him so much. I miss them both' (62). Salter is a classically tragic figure, defined negatively by his losses and his mistakes, but he is set against an unexpected contrast: a man without an origin, *Unheimlichkeit* man, who embraces this state of existence not as alienation but as joyful difference. Salter visits one of the numerous unauthorized clones of Bernard, a man named Michael Black, a happy and well-adjusted family man and teacher of mathematics, and Salter seeks from this man some confirmation or reflection of his own unhappy state, as if it is the cloning itself that in some way is the source of Salter's loss. First, he asks Michael to describe something unique to himself, and when Michael's charming responses fail because they are all references to his family, or to aspects of himself that are perfectly commonplace, Salter presses him on his feelings about discovering he is a clone. Michael's disarming response is unsettling to Salter: he is fascinated, amused, delighted by the prospect: '[A]ll these very similar people doing things like each other or a bit different of whatever we're doing, what a thrill for the mad old professor if he'd lived to see it, I do see the joy of it' (61). Salter is tragic man defined by the anxiety of loss, and what Salter wants to hear is some sense of that anxiety and loss: he wants to hear that Michael is 'frightened' of 'losing [his] life' (60). Michael, however, has no such fear and still has his life, even if it is one that is now defined in relations of difference to other clones rather than in reference to a sense of originality.

The elegant simplicity of Churchill's play finds its fulfilment in this gentle confrontation between two men who have completely different world views: Salter's tragedy is that he thinks tragically, and throughout the play he grasps desperately at the concept of uniqueness as a measure of value, speculating that someone might be sued for the illicit cloning and money received as recompense for the loss of worth suffered by Bernard. In a subtextual manner, Salter's fear of loss is bound up with his fear of being similar to others, an anxiety aroused by the existence of the clones: 'what does it do what does it to you to everything if there are all these walking around, what it does to me what am I and it's not even me it happened to' (60). For Salter, the loss of the loved one and the loss of a sense of identity are commingled into a single inevitable crisis of self. His attitude towards loss is negative and perhaps pathological, but ultimately futile. Fate dictates that it shall be a part of his life. What Salter has perhaps failed to grasp is that the very concept of value is contingent upon the possibility of exchange, and exchange demands relations of difference: similarity and distinction are both necessary. Michael, in contrast, affirms loss as a joyful part of existence. He has no fear of a lack of uniqueness and finds the value of existence not in a sense of uniqueness but in the experience of difference. He defines himself not in relation to an origin but with regards to the multiplicity of existence itself: he enjoys the feeling of belonging that comes from knowing that he has 99 per cent the same genes as anyone else on earth and 30 per cent the same genes as a lettuce. It is a delightfully Dionysian image, reminiscent of the intrusion of the natural world into consciousness in *A Mouthful of Birds*. *A Number* is a suitable précis for Churchill's tragic vision of the human, where the passage through Salter's tragedy of alienation and loss is finally and comically affirmed into Michael's joyful tragic difference.

Churchill's plays embody a promise, contained within the open potential for theatrical staging. Here I have called what is promised Dionysian multiplicity, sometimes figured in an impossible object like the Möbius strip. We see this in various guises in both content and form. This promise is often an absent presence, the absent presence of desire, and its trace is the anxiety of fear: in *Lovesick* it is the inversion of Freudian theories of repression with the promise of a multiplicity of desire. In *Abortive* it is Billy, the absent presence in the minds of the characters who leaves them with a haunting fear, while in *Owners* it is the unalienated selfhood of a man who incinerates himself while trying to save a child. In *Traps* the promise is the self as the Absolute, at one with its desire in an unending Möbius strip, within the bliss of collectivity, while in *Light Shining in Buckinghamshire* the promise is embodied in a failed moment of revolutionary overturning, which nevertheless finds its expression in the multiple playing of characters by the ensemble, itself an image of the escape from repression and negativity. *Cloud Nine* offers Churchill's most utopian manifestation of this promise, suggesting that England in the 1970s contains the seeds for the escape from Victorian repression through the embracing of desire: the absent other made present. The 1980s saw Churchill confront the English repressive consciousness with that which it disavows: its own unconscious, the repository of mourning, loss, and desire. Angie's notorious fear in *Top Girls*, the expressionistic landscape of desire in *Fen*, and Dionysos's dance in *A Mouthful of Birds* are the avatars of this return of the repressed. The 1990s saw an even more pessimistic social diagnosis in *The Lives of the Great Poisoners*, *The Skriker*, and *Thyestes*: the toxic state of capitalist postmodernity has rendered traditional tragic experience fragile and perhaps impossible. The redemption of negativity through a dialectical reversal, and thus through the embracing of loss and suffering as emancipatory and humanizing, leads only to toxic destruction rather than to renewal and growth. *Far Away* seems to diagnose this plague as a global catastrophe of *ressentiment*, the spirit of revenge, infecting Western thought. From this tragic stalemate or deadlock, Churchill negotiates an escape by returning to a joyful, Dionysian image of the self in *A Number*. Michael Black's affirmation of difference in his social being is presented as an optimistic alternative to the despair of alienation. Finally, to return to the play with which we began, in *Seven Jewish Children* it is the children themselves who are the play's promise. They are both the absent presence and the avatars of fear, fear tellingly projected onto them by the anxious adults. The hopefulness of this play is found in these figures and in the openness of staging possibilities: both are signs that for Churchill the absent presence is still ubiquitous and has not been rendered mute by postmodernity. Giving voice to the Dionysian, to the children who are, from the adult's perspective, embodiments of all that adults are not and thus the locus of anxiety, is revealed to still be a matter of pressing political importance in Churchill's ongoing work as a playwright.

New English Tragedians:
The Tragedy of the Tragic

Paul: I am the dirt that needs to be destroyed so you can be purified.
Stephen: That's so ... old-fashioned.

– Mark Ravenhill, The Cut (51)

Mark Ravenhill (born 1966) and Sarah Kane (1971–99) are the most high-profile young dramatists to have emerged out of the Royal Court Theatre in the mid-1990s. Both were quickly deemed representative members of the 'in-yer-face' generation that came to prominence at this time, along with Patrick Marber, Joe Penhall, Anthony Neilson, Martin McDonagh, and Jez Butterworth. This designation was based on Aleks Sierz's diagnosis that their graphically violent, sexually explicit plays 'had become the dominant theatrical style of the decade' (*In-Yer-Face Theatre* 4). The critical prognosis at the time focused on the confrontational quality of these playwrights' work, which seemed designed to shock rather than to communicate. Both Ravenhill and Kane are the subjects of growing bodies of scholarship, and more complex and nuanced assessments of their artistry continue to emerge.[1] My argument here is that the perceived popular thesis – that the violent and disturbing aspects of these plays have, as their chief purpose, a kind of pure phenomenological impact – is a misinterpretation of the tragic elements in their plays. Instead, I suggest that the tragic aspects of their work contain the 'experiential' qualities of the plays within an ongoing debate about the possibility of tragic experience within the condition of postmodernity. This is not necessarily a radical thesis on my part.[2] What the argument here stresses is that the perceived moment of a break, of an avant-garde shift having taken place with the emergence of a younger generation in the mid-nineties, is more apparent than real.[3] With Bond and Churchill we have seen, in their work of the 1990s, the awareness that the possibilities for tragic experience have been endangered, if not foreclosed upon altogether. Their committed socialism is apparent in their insistence on theatre as a means not only for exploring and articulating this degradation of human experience within postmodernity but also for countering it with the promise of the tragic within the aesthetic. Ravenhill and Kane are of a generation that emerged into this degraded condition, and their artistic responses to this bankrupt birthright are the subject of this chapter.

I am not alone in considering Kane and Ravenhill as part of a continuum of English tragedy. Recent critical assessments stress continuity and dialogue between the older and younger generation of playwrights, with particular emphasis, either explicit or implicit, on the importance of the tragic for understanding this new generation. Graham Saunders sees *Blasted* as a continuation of *King Lear* ('"Out Vile Jelly"'), while Karoline Gritzner compares Howard Barker to Kane, discussing first how 'Barker locates the possibility of authentic individual experience in the realm of the tragic' ('(Post)modern Subjectivity' 332) and then how Kane's late plays question 'even the minimal self that Barker appears to accept' (335). Yet Gritzner suggests that in 'aestheticizing the failure of the subject,' Kane's work, paradoxically 'preserves subjectivity' (337). Kane's plays, then, within the perspective of the present study, can be understood as explorations of the survival of authentic tragic subjectivity within late capitalist postmodernity, as Hare, Barker, Bond, and Churchill's plays have been seen to be. Amelia Howe Kritzer compares Kane's plays to Caryl Churchill's work in the 1990s as a form of 'inter-generational dialogue,' although Kritzer's analysis risks superficial sentimentality: 'Churchill allies her viewpoint with that of Sarah Kane in suggesting that loving another creates the basis for meaning even in the extremes of chaos and threat' (*Political Theatre* 75). While Kritzer claims that Churchill is more traditional and optimistic, she, like Kane, 'finds the impulse for a better world in love that puts the welfare of another before that of oneself' (78). Kritzer too turns to Howard Barker as a means of understanding the playwriting of the 1990s and suggests these are plays without *catharsis*, much as Barker discussed the Theatre of Catastrophe's refusal of reconciliation (Kritzer, *Political Theatre* 65). For Kritzer, this signals that these are not tragedies, yet as we have seen, Barker's concept of Catastrophe was transitional, and his more persistent concern is precisely tragedy without reconciliation.

Kritzer's argument about the new generation speaks directly to the concerns of this chapter, although her conclusions are at odds with my own. For her, the morbidity, violence, and suffering dramatized in the plays of the 1990s is both a comment upon, but also more troublingly, an unmediated reflection of, the depoliticized, dehistoricized society out of which the works emerge. Traditional humanizing concepts and categories have been dismantled: 'Freedom appears to be an almost meaningless concept because of the difficulty or impossibility of determining what constitutes choice' (*Political Theatre* 63). Yet Kritzer does not appreciate that this impossibility is a classically tragic problem of agency. She argues, 'The plays do not contextualize their immediate and intense, though ephemeral, experience of pain within a structure of value or beliefs, or even within a stable and complete narrative' (64). Isolated, privatized, and bereft of meaningful context within a social fabric, 'even death loses its defining power. The absence of moral and historical definition negates the potential for tragedy' (63), Kritzer writes. In other words, her analysis agrees that the postmodern condition has rendered tragic experience impossible. Yet I will stress that this impossibility is itself a form a tragic experience.

In contrast to Kritzer's assessment, consider that of Elizabeth Kuti, who reads Ravenhill's *Shopping and Fucking*, Kane's *Blasted*, and David Hare's *Stuff Happens* as solidly traditional instances of tragic plotting. Kuti's analysis, while Aristotelian in its method, is underpinned by Raymond Williams's study of modern tragedy, and she presents her argument as a specific countering to both the ideology of 'in-yer-face' theatre that dominates the understanding of *Shopping and Fucking* and *Blasted* and the larger political implications of this labelling, namely, 'the consequent misleading categorization of plays into po-litical versus non-political, public versus private, big versus little stories' (458). Kuti's reading is deliberately traditional, following the (perceived) protagonists through these plays on quest narratives and observing how the plots of the plays allow the audience to connect the personal to the political, the particular to the general. Ken Urban, too, insists upon the tragic as a valid mode of analy-sis for the new generation but couches his sense of the tragic in Nietzschean terms. This places Ravenhill and Kane within a continuity of the tragic we have seen with Barker, Bond, and Churchill: 'The tragic, for Nietzsche, is that which turns suffering into an affirmation of life. [...] Active nihilism, therefore, is a stage that one passes *through* in order to achieve what Nietzsche variously calls the "Dionysian," the "tragic," or the *Übermensch*, and that same, perhaps ro-mantic, desire to move *beyond*, while also remaining *bound* to this existence is found in these plays: an impossibility which art strives towards even in its im-possibility' (369). Yet despite the sensitivity of Urban's understanding, this idea of the contemporary tragic is merely asserted rather than argued, applied to the new generation of plays without analysis in rhetoric that supports rather than challenges the ideology of 'in-yer-face' theatre.[4]

Into this dialogue arrives Mark Ravenhill himself, who in a lecture in 2004 makes a diagnosis of the 'in-yer-face' generation that is at once thoroughly de-mystifying and remarkably obscurantist, offering an alternative explanation of the mid-nineties phenomenon. Ravenhill identifies the infamous murder of two-year-old James Bulger by two ten-year-olds in 1993 as a moment of collective British loss and grief; in short, a tragic experience in which loss was transmuted into a collectivity-in-sorrow. It is a structure of feeling that Ravenhill connects to his early plays, all of which have young victims in their teens, but this is a common pattern that he was only able to diagnose after the fact, in 2004. The incomprehensible and sadistic murder of Bulger stands for Ravenhill as a cultural signpost within British consciousness in the 1990s, a moment of rupture in a social and historical fabric, the end of Enlightenment, and with the benefit of hindsight he realizes that it is, indirectly and perhaps subconsciously, what provoked him to begin writing plays. The act brought into question the potential meaningless of the human endeavour and thus signalled the death of history, raising the question for English society of whether or not English society as such actually existed. But Ravenhill also qualifies this reading of a moment in recent history as symptomatic. What he thinks of when he thinks of the murder of James Bulger is not the literal event but a feeling. In 1993, Ravenhill lost his boyfriend to AIDS-related complications, and his grief found an expressionistic outlet in the death of Bulger. He suggests this may have been a common, even *national* response:

> Maybe many people, most people, didn't absorb the facts but projected into that image of the boy being led away in a Bootle shopping centre lost babies, babies never conceived, the loss of their parents, the loss of their own innocent selves. Maybe any striking image will do: the murder of a child, the death of a princess – anything to draw out the pain of our own personal grief.
>
> I'm sure this had some part to play in the nation's response to the murder. [...]
>
> But I also think there was a sort of public grief projected onto that case – grief and guilt for the decade that had passed. For the greed and neediness, the divisiveness, for the communities consigned to the underclass. For the anxieties about our homes, our low mortgage rates, our low taxes, that had meant in the previous two general elections a significant proportion of the population had operated on double-think: ticking the Conservative box in the polling booth and emerging only minutes later to tell the exit-pollsters that, yes, they had voted Labour. People who in the secrecy of the booth could only bring themselves to vote for their self-interest, but back in the outside air said – and probably wished, hoped – that they voted for the public good. And so there were not only personal griefs for the murder of James Bulger to draw out, but a national sense of grief as well. ('A Tear in the Fabric' 309)

Ravenhill's retrospective diagnosis of the traumatic events that sparked his playwriting career extends to his peers as well: the whole generation of young writers of the mid-nineties who seemed to define a watershed moment without in any way constituting a movement or a school, the purported 'in-yer-face' generation. Yet because Ravenhill himself is the most high-profile and prolific playwright to emerge from this moment his authorial position also risks, perhaps deliberately, the possibility of having the final word and closing all further debate. He has just explained for all time not only the meaning of his own work but also that of his peers: it was a mournful expression of lost hopes and ideals, a lament for the passing of the socialist promise of English society, a tragic dirge for the dismantling of English society by Thatcherism.[5]

And it is perhaps as a counterpoint to this comfortably demystifying analysis that Ravenhill couches it within a larger, somewhat less easily rationalized discussion of the concept of evil, along with the surmise that his own plays may have been about evil without his knowing it. Ravenhill's broader concern is with two instances in which he is confronted by the rhetoric of 'evil': the first instance in discussion with a young novelist who uses the term to describe the protagonist of his own novel, and the second while speaking with a university professor and a group of students, during which time the professor insisted that the abiding theme of Ravenhill's oeuvre is 'the metaphysics of evil' ('A Tear in the Fabric' 313). In both situations, Ravenhill is perturbed by the use of the term, as it potentially absolves one of the necessity of political and social analysis. Particularly in relation to his own writing, Ravenhill insists fruitlessly to the academic that his plays are firmly situated within the situation of late capitalism and that this 'is not a world of metaphysical absolutes' (313). Tellingly, '[t]he author was unable to convince the reader of his reading of his own work' (313). As a result, Ravenhill is left troubled and self-questioning, considering the influence of the Bulger murder upon his writing, and is finally open to the possibility that the crime may have been evil – 'somewhere beyond poverty, somewhere beyond brutalization, somewhere beyond desensitization' – and that accordingly, there perhaps are events represented in his plays that are evil even if he is not aware of it (313). In support of this, as a political playwright, he insists that he has never been a moral relativist, and that he has always tried to construct situations that force an audience into a position of judgment, of active moral decision-making. He is left, then, in a contradictory situation, caught between the need for materialist analysis and the unavoidability of morality, the latter of which hinges upon the possibility of the absolute, the potential existence of the phenomenon that will only answer to the concept / name of 'evil.'

Ravenhill, thinking he is a political, materialist playwright, is surprised and intrigued to find that this may have included a metaphysical vision all along.[6] He aptly describes the dominant structure of feeling in the generation of new English playwrights through the contradiction that he outlines above but which he cannot (and in fact justifiably makes no effort to) solve. He is caught between materialist and metaphysical world views, appreciating the need for both within the condition of postmodernity. Ravenhill has described this contradiction elsewhere in terms that broaden its scope and relate it specifically to questions of aesthetic form: 'I spotted two contradictory needs in contemporary audiences. We still have that urge for an epic narrative that draws us to the *Oresteia* or *Paradise Lost* or Shakespeare's history plays. But also we are the children of the sound-bite age, able to absorb information and narrative in a few quick seconds from the various screens that surround us. [...] I think this reflects the age we live in, an age in which we yearn for a grand narrative even as we suspect it is dead' ('Introduction' *Shoot/Get Treasure/Repeat* [5]). Ravenhill's self-diagnosis of his own writing articulates the social contradictions that he and this entire new generation of playwrights grapple with: they are caught within the contradictions of postmodernism itself, and their work articulates this at the level of content and of form. Having been told that they were born into and are living in the postmodern condition, they explore fully the inconsistencies and the ultimately untenable status of this claim. What unites the most representative members of the younger generation of English dramatists is their concern with the potential impossibility of tragic experience within the condition of postmodernity: what has been lost is the value of loss itself. It is an expression of a tragic historical attitude within the condition of postmodernity: the demise of metanarratives signals the death of history and the demise of the tragic, but this demise is itself a tragic narrative, a loss, mourned, out of which gain can emerge. We mourn the death of the tragic and in this grief maintain tragic experience. These playwrights use theatre as an attempt to evoke the tragic within the moment of the death of tragedy, and they do this through the exploration of metaphysical absolutes within the condition of their demise.

Thus Ravenhill's fascination with the possibility of evil in his own plays provides us with another means of finding some continuity with the older generation of playwrights. Hare has explored the possibility of spiritual experience with his saint-like, tragic characters; Barker has evoked the yearning for a kind of postmodern sublime through his romantic, Nietzschean Antichrists; Bond's project has been to dramatize the Promethean 'radical innocence' of the core self, the absolute purity and honesty of the human untouched by ideological contamination; and Churchill promises an impossible oneness with the unconscious. In a similar vein, Kritzer makes a remarkable, enigmatic comment with regards to Kane: 'Kane's plays deal with a politics of the soul' (*Political Theatre* 38). This refreshing phrase is fascinating in its ambivalence, emerging from Kritzer's analysis of the redemptive power of love in Kane's oeuvre. Kritzer sees this as an incomplete political project, truncated by Kane's suicide. I disagree, and in the second half of this chapter will present an argument regarding the representation of love in Kane's oeuvre, although I will argue against the idea that love is redemptive in Kane. That the idea of the soul is a political issue speaks directly to the concerns of this book, as all along we have seen political playwrights who have surreptitiously slipped the idea of the human soul into their playwriting in various guises. The new generation, influenced by the older, in turn reveals new aspects of these influences. What is provocative and noteworthy about Ravenhill and Kane is precisely their interest in metaphysical absolutes, the conditions of the soul, within the condition of postmodernity. In Kane it is love, while in Ravenhill it is evil.

While the references to capitalism and postmodern crises of subjectivity dominate the content of Ravenhill's plays, this risks overshadowing another content: his first three plays contain simple, stark social tragedies. At the heart of the po-mo philosophizing and irony are three young men who are doomed within their societies. Gary, Donny, and Phil meet ends that are 'evil' and thus tragic, because they are presented as having no hope, no possibilities, no alternatives available to them within their social contexts. A consideration of them as tragic figures will lead us to an understanding of the concept of evil in these plays.

Shopping and Fucking

If a key metaphysical concern in Ravenhill's work is the location of the human soul within postmodernity, we can locate it through its key symptom: emotion. The interpretive problems in Ravenhill's work embody the social contradiction regarding emotions that is our concern here, and that it is indeed a real contradiction is made apparent in one of the central narrative ideologemes of *Shopping and Fucking* (1996): the animated Disney film *The Lion King*. This is a film that I have never actually watched, nor have any interest in watching. In this sense, I am in accord with Ravenhill's representation of Lulu, who can deduce key elements of the movie's plot without ever having seen it: it is, presumably, a litany of narrative clichés, and within the postmodern condition one doesn't need to watch it to have already effectively seen it. However, undergraduates with whom I study the play admit freely to being emotionally moved by the very moments in the film described by *Shopping and Fucking*'s enigmatic businessman Brian, who is brought to seemingly sincere tears by key aspects of the movie. Nevertheless, the play appears to satirize Brian's profound emotional investment in the lessons and affective content located within a children's cartoon, one ruthlessly assembled and manufactured by an international capitalist corporation.[7]

However, the play may instead be simply observing the peculiar postmodern condition, within which the fraudulent commercial products of cynical capitalist mass production and consumption become the last redoubts of authentic human emotions: are micronarratives simply symptoms of our sound-bite culture, or are they aphoristic fragments of meaningful metanarratives? The humour and satire of *Shopping and Fucking* (humour much too overstated and emphasized in the original production) challenge the attempt to locate earnest representations of human sentiment. Consider that within the same scene Brian demonstrates himself to be moved to speechless tears by Olga's concluding lines from Chekhov's *Three Sisters*, which are, however, performed by Lulu topless. Olga's words about the meaning of suffering and the need to work seem all too well-suited to Ravenhill's play, but when Lulu reluctantly strips off her blouse to perform her audition speech the sense of portentous significance is undercut. In the final scene of the play, Brian plays a video of Lulu performing this same speech, and the Chekhovian imperative to work in the name of the future is firmly and finally divorced from its pre-revolutionary Russian context and situated in relation to Brian's didactic lesson that money is civilization and civilization is money: work is no longer located within a metanarrative of historical progress but is instead the means to fiscal ends alone.

Is this a bathetic satire of the uselessness of traditional dramatic sentiments within a contemporary context? Are Brian's tears meaningless? Ultimately the problem must be framed within a larger metanarrative: that of the human soul, of which Brian appears to be the proprietor. When values themselves have become goods and commodities, does that mean that values no longer exist? It seems to be one of the deliberate ironies of the play that Brian, the character who demonstrates the deepest well of traditionally recognizable emotional responses, the person who fashions himself as the emotionally correct spectator of art, has the least depth as a character. Alternately, Gary, an emotionally damaged and sexually abused teenager who refuses all emotional ties with others, who seems to have no interest in feelings at all, and is driven by a literal death wish, is the most fully rounded, vulnerable, and sympathetic character in the play. Gary is the subject of the play's social tragedy, but Gary does not answer to the descriptor of the traditional human.

The problem, then, is about what happens to feelings within postmodern capitalism. 'I want to find out, want to know if there are any feelings left' is a simple statement for a character to make (34). However, the underlying implications of Mark's stark inquiry are not so simple: the direct reply that comes to this plea is a choice of instant noodle flavours: 'Beef or Nice and Spicy?' Feelings here may have the ontological status of junk food. The only person who seems to find any nourishment from emotions is Brian, who can afford healthy ones.

Shopping and Fucking's criticism of the traditional tragic is most clearly evident in Brian, who is ultimately offered to us as a satiric caricature of the tragic ideology, reminiscent of J. Pierpont Mauler in Brecht's *Saint Joan of the Stockyards*, the man of great, Faustian emotion and self-division.[8] In a later scene in *Shopping and Fucking*, Brian plays a video of his son performing at a cello recital and explains that the tears he weeps profusely are drawn from him by the beauty of the music: 'You feel it like – like something you knew. Something so beautiful that you've lost but you'd forgotten that you've lost it' (45). It is a glimpse of paradise, he remarks, a small reminder of the prelapsarian state of innocence that we have lost, and he is ennobled, humanized by his melancholy feelings. He then points out that what supports this humanizing appreciation of our collective fall from grace is money, which is what is found 'behind beauty, behind God, behind paradise' (48).

What is particularly Brechtian about this satire is the fact that this seeming demystification isn't an invalidation of emotions at all. It is simply the argument that emotions, and the attendant humanistic values that accompany them, are property like everything else in this world. Upset that he has trusted Lulu and Robbie with three thousand dollars worth of designer drugs that they subsequently lose, Brian offers himself as the paradigm of the human: 'I don't like my mistakes. And now you tell me I've made a mistake. And so I hate myself. Inside. My soul' (49). The violent gangster-businessman is the locus for the traditionally tragic human here. Brian is Faustian man, and emotions are portrayed as possessions that allow their owner to shore up the foundations of his soul. While the play is highly invested in the importance of human relationships, it is highly suspicious of human feelings, which are private, individualized commodities. The feelings aroused by traditional tragic experience don't allow you some sympathetic contact with other human beings and they don't make you a better person. They simply make you a better capitalist.

Beyond Brian, the degradation of human experience is portrayed as a seemingly ubiquitous, dystopian condition in the play. *Shopping and Fucking* begins with the disintegration of a social triad of educated, middle-class twenty-somethings for whom the mundane routines of day-to-day existence have become unmanageable. Their flat, once a sign of their social background, is denuded and bare. The habitual has become frustratingly impossible: eating, for instance, has become a gargantuan, anxiety-inducing task and a venture in which their bodies will no longer cooperate. Lulu and Robbie sit, trying to feed Mark (the eldest of the three) as if he was a child, offering verbal expressions of love, support, and affection, and they all behave as if regressing to an infantile stage (in the 1998 West End transfer to the Queen's Theatre, Lulu sucked her thumb.) 'It's not working,' Mark remarks as explanation for why he decides to leave Lulu and Robbie (7). It isn't clear why their lives have fallen apart: this isn't realism, and we will find out very little about these characters' histories. Heroin is mentioned, but on a less specific level what seems broken is the general ability of human beings to make meaningful connections with one another.

Accordingly, the trio fragments and they spend the rest of the play trying to recover their equilibriums, trying to make the assumed forms of human social interaction functional once more. By the final scene, they have reunited and are now successfully feeding each other, sharing the microwave supermarket-ready meals to which their diets have descended. Yet this quietly optimistic reunion is marred by the price paid for it: "You've got a bit of blood," Robbie observes of Mark (90). The blood on Mark, we must presume, belongs to Gary, the fourteen-year-old teenager and gay hustler (he was also Scottish in the 1998 version) whom Mark has recently raped and murdered with a knife. While Gary emphatically asks for this action to be performed upon him, Gary's prom-ised payment will allow Lulu and Robbie to pay off the businessman-gangster Brian. Killing Gary gets Mark's friends out of trouble and reunites them. In the final instance, Brian lets them keep their hard-earned bankroll; he magnani-mously surmises they have learned their lesson: that money is civilization, and that the first words in the Bible are 'Get the Money First' (87). He offers them positions working for his home shopping channel. Naturally, it is the moral ambiguity surrounding the murder of Gary that matters most here, particularly because it is so understated in the script and in the original production: we do not see Gary's murder, and he simply vanishes.[9] The violence perpetrated against Gary seems disturbingly regenerative to the trio: it is difficult to shake the sensation that what they are nourishing each other with, in the final mo-ments of the play, is Gary himself. While the play's evoking of class issues is not forceful, the image of three educated, if down and out, adults prospering off the murder of a dispossessed, working-class Glaswegian is easily interpretable as a vicious commentary on the perpetuity of class disparity within 1990s England.

It is the trace of Gary's blood on Mark that troubles the conclusion of the play, reminding us that legitimate *catharsis* finds its energy from the violence of *pathos*. Thus Elizabeth Kuti's reading of Mark as a liberal tragic hero in the manner described by Raymond Williams is apposite (see Kuti 462). For Kuti, Mark is on a quest to escape his degraded, fallen world, a reading identical to Finlay Donesky's analysis of Susan Treherne in *Plenty* (*David Hare* 86). Yet Kuti sees the death of Gary as Mark's final failure to escape this existence. In con-trast, I think that Mark's world – the world of Mark, Lulu, and Robbie – is re-deemed and validated by this death, and this is thus a satire of the liberal tragic subject, just as Brian is a satire of Faustian man. Their ability to authentically re-immerse themselves within their false world is contingent upon a real loss.

In other words, Mark's attempt to escape his false existence appears to be a symptom of that false existence itself rather than an indication of inner integrity. The play troubles critical acts of interpretation because it is deliberately ambiguous on the subject of false and true experience or authentic and inauthentic emotions: just because feelings are mass-produced in postmodernity does not mean they are illegitimate; they are simply artificial and depersonalized. 'Listen, this stuff is happiness,' Robbie insists, preparing to sell Ecstasy tablets at a gay nightclub (*Shopping and Fucking* 20). Mark replies, 'It's not real.' Yet this is an easy criticism to make, and one affected by Mark's ongoing attempt to kick not only heroin but other forms of addiction, such as emotional dependencies on other people like Robbie (17). Robbie's reply is to exclaim, '[I]f this, this … planet is real,' and then start popping E: he implies that the totality of human reality is no more or less dubious in authenticity than an E tablet. This ambivalent discourse surrounding authentic experience leads, in turn, to interpretive dissent amongst critics. Caridad Svich, taking the characters as spokespersons for authorial point of view, argues that 'Ravenhill at heart seems to be making a plea for a world in which love can transcend the violence and hatred' of consumer society, thus revealing 'a suspiciously bourgeois sentimentality' (82). Yet in marked disagreement with this reading, David Alderson is justly suspicious of characters like Mark, whose rhetoric of addiction reveals that 'the subjective depthlessness of commodified existence is merely confirmed by expressions of interiority which ironically undercut their own claims to authenticity' (865). The characters themselves are sometimes inconsistent regarding the rhetoric of emotions. Mark explains to Gary that his happiness was once simple and clear: he was a trader whose happiness was directly indexed to whether or not he was making money. Now he is unsure if there are any feelings that exist that aren't chemically or drug-induced. He wants to try to locate a feeling he can consider real, but at the same time he tells Gary that he is avoiding emotional attachments to others because he finds them addictive and he loses all sense of himself by defining himself in terms of others. Mark wants to know if there are feelings left or if anything is real, but he also shuns emotional investments. Later, after Mark has spent a week with Gary, he seems to manifest some self-insight, perhaps moving beyond the rhetoric of addiction in relation to others and appreciating a definition of love: 'Now, here, when you're with me I feel like a person and if you're not with me I feel less like a person' (56). But it is at this point that Gary's own paradigm of human relationships is forcefully asserted in contrast to Mark's, and, as we shall see, Gary stands out as the incontrovertibly real and authentic in this play.

Thus to claim that Mark is the tragic protagonist in this play is to overlook the legitimate suffering endured by Gary. However, to even argue for the legitimate in *Shopping and Fucking* is a problematic venture: in fact it is very hard to find anything in Ravenhill's oeuvre that can be held up to light as unambiguously 'real,' and blood might be the only sign that asserts its privileged status as incontrovertibly literal.[10] Accordingly, it is blood that potentially nourishes human emotions and the possibility of substantial connections between humans. When Mark first meets Gary he wants to pay the young man for sex, to make sure that their interaction is an impersonal transaction and not a meaningful experience (25). This fails when Mark discovers that he has blood on his face: Gary is bleeding from his anus, an injury sustained from the sexual abuse that drove him out of his home in the first place. Blood makes the transaction personal and meaningful, and despite himself Mark stays with the young man for a week, finds out too much about Gary, and falls in love with his vulnerability. Lulu discovers blood on her face in the scene directly following Mark and Gary's initial encounter: she tells Robbie that she was buying a chocolate bar in a convenience store and witnessed a customer attack the young female clerk with a knife. In shock, Lulu just ran away, appalled to find herself stealing the bar of chocolate rather than offering help.

Blood, then, is a sign of trauma, that which disrupts or negates the indifference of the exchange-based transactions that Lulu and Mark would prefer to hide behind. But even these traumatic, bloody events aren't invulnerable to co-option. Late in the play, while performing phone sex to make money, Lulu finds herself on the line with someone who is using a tenth-generation copy of the security video of the convenience store attack as snuff-porn. Elsewhere, Lulu makes a telling inquiry when Robbie recounts to her the story of how he got fired from his job at a fast food restaurant. A customer came near to tears when asked if he wanted cheese on his burger, and Robbie confronted the numbed victim of capitalism's illusive offers of agency with the need to make a real choice for once in his life. In response, the customer attacked Robbie with a fork. When Lulu hunts fruitlessly for the resultant wound, Robbie explains that the utensil was plastic. She seems disappointed that the encounter has left him unscathed, and later, when Robbie is beaten badly at a nightclub, she admires his bruises and starts to masturbate him (34). The 'wound,' as she puts it, suits him. By disrupting the system of transactions and exchange that dominate social interactions here, blood and trauma have the potential to regenerate more vital and lively forms of human contact, but those meaningful connections themselves can always be reintroduced into the system of transactional exchange. This is not an easy or unambiguous solution to the postmodern condition, since Lulu's fetishization of the idea of a bruise or a wound seems to be the first step into commodifying it (as we shall see in Ravenhill's *Product*, below).

Gary, as the repository of authentic trauma in the play, yearns for an alternate economy of the self that will express his tragic subjectivity outside of the system of commodities that dominates the play. Gary is an emotionally damaged fourteen-year-old, but he is also portrayed as assertive, confident, and strong-willed. He is unmoved by Mark's declaration of love and asserts instead his own desire to be owned by a big, older man who will keep him, take him home, protect him, and most importantly, be cruel with him. Gary's use of the word 'cruel' is evocative – this man will also be kind (26). This man will fuck him hard but it will not be the rape he has suffered from his stepfather. It will be 'a good hurt' (56). While on the one hand pain and suffering have been reduced to sound bites from Chekhov to be enjoyed by Brian and used to reinforce the capitalist work ethic, on the other hand the play offers Gary, and the cruelty that he seeks, as a set of values that stand in sharp contrast to those of both Mark and, I think, Brian. Gary's rhetoric of slavery, while potentially understandable as kin to Brian's capitalist ethos, sounds more like a comforting Nietzschean phantasy of a clear, unambiguous relationship of cruelty, of owner and owned, a fundamental apprehension of difference as a ground to a stable selfhood. Gary also wants to feel that someone is watching him: 'I want a dad. [...] All the time, someone watching me' (33). It is the internalization of cruelty, that 'good hurt,' that may engender superego and stable socialization, thus allowing Gary's survival.

The legitimate tragedy of *Shopping and Fucking* is that this compensating phantasy of affirming cruelty is not available to Gary. When Mark takes him to meet Lulu and Robbie, Gary mentions his imagined owner, this man he is convinced is out there in the world waiting for him. Robbie, in jealousy of Mark, offers to act out Gary's story with him, for payment. The end of this story is not the comforting dream Gary has claimed it to be. It ends with him being raped with a knife, and he demands, angrily, that they provide the service for which he is paying. The tables have been turned on Robbie and Lulu: 'I thought you were for real. Pretending, isn't it? Just a story' (85). Gary's traumatized feelings are presented as incontrovertibly legitimate. He knows that the man he seeks does not really exist. 'I've got this unhappiness. This big sadness swelling like it's gonna burst. I'm sick and I'm never going to be well' (85). The traumatic wounds for which blood is simply a metaphor are the wounds in the self. For Gary, this pathology is his fate. In the midst of a play in which choice is generally presented satirically, as the illusion of agency within the capitalist market, Gary's troubling assertion of will is singular. Gary's desperate cries for help to social support agencies have been ignored and his attempts to stop the abuse failed. The only agency and control he can find in his life is by ending his existence according to the story he himself imagines, and he asks Mark to do this for him. It is the tragic persistence of a tragic narrative, and while Robbie earlier offers an elegy to traditional metanarratives, the big stories of the 'Powerful Hands of the Gods and Fate' (66), it seems that such a narrative manages to creep back into the play as a forceful negation of the postmodern condition, disguised as Gary's small, private narrative: it is a small story that is also a big story.

Yet even this negation is problematized in the final scene of the play. Mark again tells the comforting fable of ownership that began the play, this time setting it far in the future. However, the crucial change in the story is not its science fiction setting but the fact that Mark buys his slave only to then set him free, despite the slave's tears and pleas that freedom is terrifying and he will be dead in a week. Mark is prepared to take that risk. Lulu and Robbie like the story, but whether or not they actually appreciate the terrors of agency and freedom themselves is doubtful. While Gary has lived and died according to his own agency, the trio of Mark, Lulu, and Robbie are immersed in their comforting triad, their microwave-ready meals, and, potentially, a home shopping channel, all of which have been paid for by Gary's blood.

Faust Is Dead

The numerous references to the classical canon of literature that Ravenhill scatters liberally throughout *Shopping and Fucking* are deployed primarily for purposes of satire, specifically satire of humanist values. When Lulu and Robbie get jobs performing phone sex, they interperse phantasies set in the Garden of Eden and involving the Tower of Babel with a recitation of lines from *Romeo and Juliet* that ends in a perfunctory 'Dirty fucking cunting fucker' (52). The comedy emerges from the gap between dramatic narratives of a fall from grace and the bathetic sexual ends to which the narratives are put. Here, classical narratives are reified clichés and cannot be employed to humanize experiences or redeem those who engage with them. They are instead useful for making money from all the 'many sad people in this world' (52). This satiric gesture is inverted in *Faust Is Dead* (1997). Now it is not the ideologemes of humanism that are portrayed as out of touch with reality, but the clichés and catchphrases of postmodernity that are represented as bereft of experiential weight. Moreover, this satire is dramatized not comically but through the repetition of what may be the paradigmatic ideologeme of humanism itself, the Faust legend. It is telling that without some knowledge of the canon, and of course without the gesture of the title, it is unlikely that any audience member to this play would be able to deduce that it is a recalibration of the Faust story: this divide between titular reference and dramatic content replicates the play's chief theme, and we must actively bridge that divide in order to escape the problem of postmodernity. The tragedy of *Faust Is Dead* is found in the gap between abstract thinking and lived experience, but the abstract thinking here is postmodern, posthumanist thinking. The numerous triumphant declarations of the death of man in *Faust Is Dead* are not the message of Ravenhill's play. Rather, the disastrous effects of this intellectual, distanced thinking about postmodernity upon actual people are the dramatic interest here. This reified thought is a tragic separation of general from particular, of conceptual from material, of mind from body, of soul from blood, and finally of title from play.

Faust Is Dead follows the aimless adventures of a French philosopher on a road trip across an apocalyptic American landscape of television talk shows, deserts, designer drugs, impersonal gay sex, random beatings, motels, riots, MTV, and Internet websites for amateur masochists. The philosopher-academic Alain is a humourous caricature of a French poststructuralist. Obsessed with abstract parables of violence meant to dialectically complicate the nature of concepts like 'seduction' and 'cruelty,' he has his head in the clouds and a naive, hedonistic appreciation of America as a zone free of the lingering ghosts of history, as an ahistorical utopia of voluntaristic freedom.[11] Alain is a hodgepodge of a caricature: he has the general contours of Michel Foucault but he spouts philosophical sound bites borrowed from Jean Baudrillard. As the play's Faust figure, he has quit his academic position and decided to immerse himself in the vitality of experience that his European sensibility associates with America. We first encounter him on the David Letterman show, dabbling in the highly mediated fabric of American culture, where celebrity is presented as the substance of everyday life. Trying to explain the ideas within his book *The Death of Man*, Alain sits next to Madonna, who mentions that she liked his book on sexuality. Letterman meanwhile protests that he doesn't feel dead. American culture, it is announced from the start, consumes everything, literalizes it, and turns it into television comedy.

Alain finds his Mephistopheles in a young man named Pete, a sexually ambiguous hustler with links to pop stars who is building his own video website. Pete initially mistakes Alain for a music producer and offers to sleep with him as a favour to a musician friend. When he realizes his error, the two of them make a Faustian deal: Pete is intrigued by Alain's philosophical parables of seduction, while Alain wants sex. Pete will get access to Alain's mind (his soul) in exchange for Pete's body. At first the deal seems one-sided: Faust wants to experience the realm of the corporeal and he gets this from Pete, yet Pete has an unexpected and surreal aspect to his background that reverses the relationship with Alain. Pete is on the run because he has stolen a computer program from his father, a major software mogul named Bill who is recognizable by his first name alone. Bill's plan for his software is deliberately vague in its contours: the program is Bill's vision of a human millennium dominated by chaos, and also his guarantee that his software alone will be in every home. Bill wants to be omnipresent: 'Bill, Bill, Bill. Like God, God, God' (111). The precise details of this project are never made clear, so the content remains allegorical. At the end of the play Pete shoots Alain to retrieve the software disc and then visits Alain in the hospital. He reveals that he has stolen Alain's ideas embracing the end of history and progress and celebrating the death of man, and advocating suffering and cruelty in 'this new age of chaos' (120–1). Pete thus receives the part of the deal he was promised: Alain's soul in the form of his abstract ideas.

But Pete has done this not so that he can endorse these sentiments but to oppose them, because they offer nihilism and despair: 'And it may be true, but it doesn't get us anywhere' Pete says (140). Pete has teamed up with his father, and now his father's visionary image of the new millennium takes on literally apocalyptic proportions. Instead of the manufactured chaos of the stolen software, Pete reveals, his father has created something new: a house. 'And in my father's house, his vision of the future, of perfection, is realized' (139). This plan, deliberately evocative of Christ's words in John 14:2, is a banal commercial parody of the kingdom of heaven. Within Bill's world, what was once religious apotheosis is now the fulfilment of the capitalist dream: a phantasy of complete agency where the walls of the home around you are programed with digital images of famous and valuable works of art, displays of masterpieces licensed exclusively to Bill, images that change to suit the homeowner's mood. The solution to the fact of postmodern despair is a virtual reality that offers an illusory freedom from the strictures of necessity; it is an apocalypse of heaven that reveals the ultimate end of history to be the freedom to have whatever you want here on earth. This satire demands our attention: this is simply the inverse side of Alain's facile 'embracing of suffering.' It is the disavowal of suffering and unhappiness through the mirage of complete control over one's surroundings, here in the form of canonical works of art – repositories of traditional humanism, envelopes for the human soul – rendered bereft of aura by the miracle of mechanical reproduction.

Alain's callous, pseudo-Nietzschean rhetoric, demanding that humanity embrace suffering and chaos, speaks once more to the issue of what is 'real' in this world. Alain is fascinated by an Internet video of a self-destructive teenager named Donny, whom Alain glamorizes as a modern primitive: 'A testament of suffering upon the body. [...] A moment of power, of control over the self as he draws the blade through the body. [...] An initiation rite for the end of the twentieth century' (124). Alain's impersonal, abstract rhetoric is immediately undercut by Pete's blunt response: 'Or he hurts real bad inside and he wants the outside to kinda match' (124). One sees the general and one sees the particular. Alain insists on imposing his metaphors upon experience while Pete's determination to be resolutely literal in his interpretation of events seems to be clear-eyed and demystifying, but they are still watching an image on a screen, one that Pete insists is faked with ketchup and that Alain is convinced is real. In contrast, Pete shows Alain his own recent scars, inspired by Alain's prophetic rhetoric of cruelty. Pete has latched upon the self-mutilation of his body, the cruelty to the self, as the one real thing in a fraudulent world: 'The food, the TV, the music … it's all pretend. And this is the one thing that's for real. I feel it, it means something' (126). There are in fact two meanings emerging from Pete's assertion: cuts are real because they are corporeal, and viscerally painful: he feels it. They are grounded and traumatic and bloody and of the body, and thus appear to be unmediated. Yet Pete immediately conflates the concept of the real with the idea of the meaningful. Everything is mediated in some way here, but the question to pose is whether the mediation of an event renders something more concrete, and thus 'meaningful,' or simply abstracts from the event and demonstrates the perceivable distance between experience and significance. In scars and self-mutilation, an imagined identity between corporeal and meaningful is conceived.

Thus when they determine to solve the problem by meeting Donny, it appears to be Alain's postmodern rhetoric that is viciously satirized in the encounter. Pete and Donny compete to see who can be most real, while Alain videos the self-lacerations. However, unlike Pete, Donny is not the wayward child of the American ruling class but a deeply emotionally damaged teenager from a lower working-class background. He is the figure of social tragedy in this play, standing in marked contrast to Faustian man's self-absorption. As a result of his background Donny suffers from a severe behavioral disorder (the result of a junk food diet), has a mother whose harsh work environment gave her terminal cancer, and is driven by a mental image of Christ's martyrdom as an image of his own self-mutilation. Donny cuts his throat in front of Pete and Alain, who desperately try to stop the bleeding. When they fail, Alain retreats behind a new rhetorical ploy, one rendered grimly absurd by the dead boy. Alain asserts that at some point near the end of the twentieth century, reality ended and humanity entered an all-encompassing simulacrum, in which the purity of the actual 'event' is terminally compromised by pre- and post-mediation: 'the event itself is just a shadow, a reflection of our analysis' (133). Despite the brutal disconnection between the death and Alain's commentary, subsequent events seem, ironically, to support Alain's thesis: Donny's death ends up on the Internet, and the story is disseminated across the American talk show circuit, even inspiring Donny's musician friend to write a successful song about it that plays 'three times an hour on MTV' (135). Alain ends up being right about American reality, since Donny's actual body, the heavy materiality of which asserts itself imposingly upon Alain's consciousness, is mysteriously disposed of by Pete, and Donny's death becomes a media event.

This ambivalence is paradigmatic of Ravenhill's work: he satirizes the intellectual rhetoric that celebrates the end of history while at the same time observing social phenomena indicating that history may in fact be over. The difference that needs to be parsed is as follows: on the one hand there is the seemingly observable fact that history in a traditional sense no longer seems to be happening, and progress in a grand sense therefore is no longer an operative category of social discourse; on the other hand, there are those like Alain who celebrate the death of history and the so-called death of man for its seemingly liberatory effects but completely overlook how the rhetoric is put to use ideologically and politically. America is conveniently manufactured as the paradisal end point of history, the kingdom of heaven on earth courtesy of the software magnate's apocalyptic vision of virtual reality.

The intermittent choral figures who speak throughout the play, American teenagers who are seen on video screens and whom we learn are the subjects of Pete's ongoing camcorder recordings for his website, communicate something different to us than the hollow sound bites of Alain's post-philosophy. These teens represent a collective sorrow about the present: the first choral speaker talks about experiencing an inability to sleep as a child and constantly weeping at night, induced by a youthful awareness of how terrible the world is combined with a guilty yearning for an apocalyptic catastrophe to bring the world to an end (137). Assured by her mother that the world would get better, the teen resolved to cry more quietly at night (97). The platitudes of social progress fall flat before the young person's clear-eyed emotional awareness that she is inheriting a world bereft of hope. These choral voices, however, are also presented as fully immersed in the mediated postmodern simulacrum: they talk about how stealing a VCR during a riot is more important that stealing food because it is pointless to have food in the house unless you have something to watch while eating it. Moreover, an awareness that the world is neither ending nor improving but simply 'going on, on and on and on' induces no feelings whatsoever in the young adult, who feels so detached from reality that she can stand in the middle of an earthquake and suffer no affective response. She wonders, absently, what made her that way (137).

What is missing is a dialectic, an understanding of the relationship of the poles of this contradiction between the material and the mediated, and this seems to be what the open-endedness of Ravenhill's work potentially enables. The ghost of Donny has some function here. Donny's absence presses heavily upon Alain when the boy bleeds to death. He takes the boy in his arms, and finds himself making a philosophical observation of a different kind: 'A person, you know, there is so much. So much skin and bone. And brains and eyes. What do you do with a person with no life in them?' (134). Donny has a presence, one made tangible by his absence: he is a person, but a person with no life in him, as if the absence of life, the fact of mortality, is actually what drives home to Alain the personhood, the Being, of Donny. He serves as the Gretchen figure to Alain's Faust, the person who pays the ultimate price for the intellectual's adventure in the sensuous world but who nevertheless returns at the end of the play to save Faust from damnation. Pete gets rid of Donny's body (and apparently uploads the video of his death to the Internet), but this callous disposal of a human being engenders the final split between Faust and his demon. Donny's ghostly return, eyeless (his eyes are in a shoebox, a macabre final gift from Pete to Alain), reminds us that Donny's death has changed Alain in some significant way. He has perhaps been seduced by the young man's humanity, humanized by the loss of life.[12] The ghost is a gain in loss: Donny's ghost has returned to save Alain from hell and to nurture him back to life in his hospital bed. If Alain deserves this redemption it can only be because he himself has projected Donny's personhood from the mute fact of his mortal remains. In effect, the ghost is hopeful not because he represents life after death but because he represents life-in-death, the human as a ghost in the inhuman postmodern machine. Donny thus represents something real in a dialectical, concrete sense: material because metaphysical, and metaphysical because mortal. Through his sacrifice, it seems, Alain gets to keep his soul.

Handbag

The tragedies of characters like Gary and Donny, neglected young people who fall through society's cracks and whose deaths benefit those of a more privileged social class, should not happen but do. This is not just a tragic waste of youth, it is also a disavowal of the working-class queer youth's humanity. Ravenhill's materialist approach to this tragic social loss takes a new direction in *Handbag* (1998), wherein he presents once again a central, sympathetic figure in a Scottish rent boy, this time named Phil. Ravenhill also offers a counter-narrative to Phil's tragedy, set in Victorian England, dramatizing the antecedent action of Oscar Wilde's play *The Importance of Being Earnest* and showing us just how infant Jack Worthing managed to get left in a handbag at Victoria station and adopted by Mr Thomas Cardew, who runs a foster home for gay youths.

Phil is deeply conscious of his own failure as a father: he reveals that when deep in the throes of heroin addiction, he eventually let a dealer rape his five-year-old daughter in exchange for drugs (200). Phil and his dysfunctional girl-friend Lorraine abduct a newborn from a middle-class quartet (two lesbian women and two gay men) who are trying to establish a non-heterosexual family. This crime is both Phil's attempt to imaginatively correct his failure as a parent and his attempt to assume a personhood as such. Throughout the play Phil moves, figuratively, through infancy to adolescence, and finally to adulthood and the status of parent. In his first encounter with David, one of the quartet, he reveals his complete inability to take care of himself and even wets his pants. His affair with David gives way to a more heteronormative (and thus purportedly 'adult') relationship with Lorraine. Finally, however, there is no one in Phil's world who is willing to tutor him in how to become a person, a citizen of society, and so when the abducted baby stops breathing Phil can think of nothing more than to burn it with a cigarette again and again, finally scorching its eyes and placing the corpse in a plastic garbage bag.

There is, however, someone who is willing to care for and mentor Phil and who attempts, unsuccessfully, to do so. This is Thomas Cardew, who encounters Phil when *Handbag*'s two narratives briefly overlap and commingle. Cardew, searching desperately for one of his young wards who has gone astray, finds Phil, as if Cardew's passionate avuncular drive propels him across time and space to the person who needs him the most. Cardew offers love and acknowledgment of Phil's humanity, but he fails to mentor Phil successfully because Phil cannot be socialized within a Victorian environment. Despite his appreciation for Cardew's kindness and help, Phil cannot be like his mentor, cannot love him in return, and so returns to 1990s England, where he will attempt to complete his own socialization. From Cardew he seems to have received a positive benefit: 'I'm ready now. To be my own person. [...] I'm gonna find out who I am' (205–6). Lamentably, the subjectivity that is available to Phil is tragic, finally: he is left wailing pitifully on the stage, having reproduced the destructive parenting that he was attempting to efface the second time around. Like Oedipus, he finds out that he is exactly the person he does not want to be.

But the disavowed possibility of which he has had a glimpse in his time-travelling episode is also present on stage at the end: Cardew is given the infant who will eventually grow up to be Jack Worthing because no one else wants to be responsible for the child. His nanny, Miss Prism, deliberately arranges to lose him so that she can concentrate on her three-volume novel: 'You were born in quite the wrong family, were you not? Neither father nor mother to care for you. So, why should I? (224). Jack Worthing, unlike Phil, will grow up to happily find out who he is, and this is Wilde's inversion of the Oedipal plot. Jack discovers himself to be Ernest, namely, the man he has been pretending to be all along. The real tragedy of *Handbag* is that uneducated working-class characters like Lorraine and Phil are left to try desperately to build their selfhoods without social support. They cannot live earnestly, in good faith with the person they feel or imagine themselves to be, they cannot develop their souls, so to speak, and as a result of this tragic gap within their subjectivities an infant dies. The event is evil in the sense that we have dis-cussed here, in that it is a symptom of tragic social failure.

Some Explicit Polaroids

The tragedies represented in Ravenhill's first three plays all take place within the context of a particular all-encompassing social situation. The vision of con-temporary Britain that Ravenhill portrays is not just one where metanarratives have been rendered defunct; he also shows us a completely depoliticized soci-ety, the result of Thatcherism's dismantling of both the social safety net and socialist values. Where there are no great narratives left, there are no causes, no meanings to human events, and finally there is no political consciousness avail-able. The election of a Labour government in 1997 led Ravenhill to craft a cau-tiously optimistic play, one widely observed to be an unexpectedly traditional 'state of the nation' play from a member of the shock-value 'in-yer-face' genera-tion. Yet he also now articulates explicitly what is implicitly indicated in his earlier work: the vital importance of tragic experience as both a humanizing activity and a critical intervention into a depoliticized social environment. Moreover, he portrays tragic experience as that which has been deliberately and purposefully excluded from late capitalist society. *Some Explicit Polaroids* (1999) is about the completely depoliticized society that is the legacy of 1980s conservatism and the detrimental psychic effect of this social decay upon the minds of England's citizens within a situation of triumphalist international capitalism. Ravenhill, however, is not a traditional socialist who laments the demise of leftist politics. In his plays there is detectable as much an acknowl-edgment of the appropriateness of the end of history (in the revolutionary sense) as there is an observation of the problems inherited by those who follow this demise. *Some Explicit Polaroids* makes this contradiction clear, and thus outlines England in the 1990s as a fundamentally incoherent society: socialism, history has proven, is impossible, but capitalism is unstable.[13] In between the poles of this problem, Ravenhill's characters attempt to find some traction for agency, affect, and connection with others.

An unexpected and deliberately theatrical conceit, similar to that of *Handbag*, animates the action of *Some Explicit Polaroids*. Into the fabric of Tony Blair's 'Cool Britannia' arrives a different kind of time traveller: a hard-left socialist named Nick who has been in prison since 1984, when he tried to beat an arch-capitalist asset-stripper to death. The conceit is easily dismissed as 'unrealistic,' which is perhaps the point. Nick is both anachronistic and deliberately theatri-cal, having a kind of wry allegorical resonance around him: 1984, the year of the miner's strikes and Thatcher's final triumph over unions, heralded the death of socialism in Britain. Nick, apparently the last hard leftie in England, seems to have spent fifteen years in jail with his head in the sand and hasn't the slightest modicum of cultural knowledge to draw upon in this strange new world. Most importantly, he hasn't changed in the least and arrives on the doorstep of the comrade for whom he committed his crime expecting her to still be driven by the same righteous anger and class hatred that he espouses. Instead, Helen is a local councillor who aspires to become a member of Blair's cabinet. Ravenhill offers us a very playful suggestion of how to understand the character of Nick when a young table dancer named Nadia applies a package of frozen food to her fat lip. She explains that this object was in the fridge when she moved into her flat two years earlier: 'And I thought: It's got to be good for something. Obviously I wasn't going to eat it. I mean "Best before December 1984," [...] But I thought: Hold on to it. Everything has its value. Everything is of use' (247). Nick is far past his expiry date and his traditional function is long gone, but the presentiment remains that he has something to offer to the present.

In the absence of socialist politics, the recently defrosted Nick seems largely useless and can only offer abrasive critiques of the world he wakes up in. For Nick's old comrade Helen, politics in any proper sense is over: 'Bit by bit, you do what you can and you don't look for the bigger picture, you don't generalize' (236). She devotes her efforts to coordinating the bus timetables in her constituency, rendered chaotic by deregulation. In other words, she micromanages the detrimental effects of capitalism's privatization of the social fabric of England. Nick sneers at this, but he has nothing to offer other than the stale and defunct revolutionary rhetoric that got him sent to prison in the first place. We are presented with a contemporary England where there still seems to be a large problem called capitalism, but there are only small forms of fitful management available to deal with its effects.

One of those forms of management is to insist that everything is perfect and everyone is happy, in other words to act out the ideology of 'Cool Britannia' and ignore anything that doesn't fit this template. Nick, homeless and lost, finds himself caught up in the lives of a group of young adults attempting desperately to fulfil the Thatcherite mantra that insists that there is no such thing as society. Nadia insist that she is a peaceful, happy person despite the fact that throughout the play she is constantly getting beaten up by an unseen boyfriend. She also lives in a state of the perpetual present: shortly after she brings Nick to her flat she walks out of the room momentarily and is then surprised to find that he is still there: 'I'd just filed you away. In here. Past tense' (247). Nadia's flatmate Tim is HIV-positive, but his medical treatments allow him to avoid this brutal fact and instead embrace a hedonistic lifestyle. Tim has just 'bought' a Russian sex slave named Victor, whom he saw on the Internet, by paying for Victor to travel to

London. They attempt to live the empty, affirmatory master-slave relationship narrated by Mark in *Shopping and Fucking*. Victor and Tim espouse a rhetoric of 'trash,' which they celebrate as a blissful and meaningless state of happiness.

In other words, in 'happy world' as they call it, the negative itself has been disavowed from consciousness and the result is what Horkheimer and Adorno call 'positivist decay,' which is the end result of Enlightenment thinking that takes place once the determinate negativity of dialectical thought is yoked to the project of the absolute and totality (*Dialectic of Enlightenment* 18). This positivism is objectified, reified, rationalized thought, living in a state of the perpetual present, without negativity. Positivism reproduces the mechanism of capitalist exchange at the level of thoughts themselves. That this 'happy world' is a fulfilment of both Thatcherism and capitalism becomes apparent when the young characters rebuke Nick for the irrelevance of his ideals: 'We're all responsible for our own actions, okay? We don't blame other people. That's very nineteen eighty-four' (*Some Explicit Polaroids* 269). What they assert as the 'right to be happy' is a numb and inert state of existence that is bolstered by chemicals such as Ecstasy: 'Everyone is the same when you take this. Everybody loves everybody' (275–6). As Nick points out, they're 'not connected with anything' (273). Helen describes the situation more bluntly: 'Start out with a society and end up with individuals fighting it out' (280). Thus 'happy world' also describes Helen's world view: micromanagement without generalizing mediation, without larger connections or conclusions. The young people are advocates of positivist individualism and instrumental reason, products of the privatization of social reality.

As a catalyst to the disruptions of the psyches of the other characters, Nick serves as the return of the repressed: not socialism, or activism, or even a politicized sensibility, but emotions, particularly fear and anger. I would venture to offer him as something more: an avatar of the object-cause of anxiety, in other words negativity itself in the shape of mortality and history. He is, metaphorically, a ghost of the past, and thus is it appropriate that one of his legacies to the current situation will be a literal ghost, the ghost of Tim. Negativity, here the bitterness of Nick's class *ressentiment*, is the energy behind productive human endeavour, and what Nick forces everyone around him to see is the fact of conflict as a vital part of life. As Nick says to Tim: 'Inside you there's chemicals fighting virus fighting your body fighting' (273). Fear and anger, rather than numb happiness, are a healthy signs of such struggle.

While Nick flails helplessly around in this situation, trying unsuccessfully to find a positive focus for his anger and directionless energy, his very presence nevertheless disrupts the illusion of 'happy world.' Nick seems unable to do anything productive in this new world, but his frustration alone changes the situation. His abrasiveness provokes Helen to reflect upon the gradual erosion of the social fabric of England and admit her unflagging desire to 'pick up the pieces. Trying to create a few possibilities for the bits of humanity that are left. I've seen those bastards fuck up the country all these years. Now I want to do something about it' (281). Nadia falls in love with Nick despite herself, and Tim refuses to take his AIDS medication, suddenly abandoning 'happy world' and confronting his need to feel in control of his life. Victor, in turn, abandons his 'trash' rhetoric and tries to care for Tim, urging him to take his pills.

It is not Tim's illness that is metaphoric here, but the treatment of illness that slides into the denial of the fact of illness itself that serves as a metaphor for the denial of negativity in life. HIV-positive since he was nineteen, Tim has lost the sense he once had that his life 'was a fucking tragedy. My life was a tragedy and that was frightening and sad and it used to do my head in. But I knew where everything was going' (288). He had a tragic awareness of his own mortality, and the indefinite, unending present of his current existence lacks this sense of loss: 'I used to know everything and that's what those fucking pills have taken away from me' (289). Tim looks back nostalgically to a time of 'communists and apartheid. I want the finger on the nuclear trigger. I want the gay plague' (288). These are all fearful things that Tim associates with Nick, who represents for Tim and Nadia a particular 1980s-related anxiety that they seem to have dis-avowed from their lives. They observe disparagingly and repeatedly that Nick is 'frightened' (250, 269). Nadia, without insight, points out that '[t]hey're very often linked. Fear and anger' (251). What has been repressed in this society is anxiety and affect, and what anxieties like fear avow are the terrible and tragic facts of existence.

Nick brings an emotional thaw into this situation, itself the first step towards tragic experience. Tim dies, and the detrimental effects of 'happy world' upon Nadia and Victor are no more apparent than in their struggle to grieve for him. 'I wish we knew what to do,' says Victor. 'I think maybe inside us, if we were allowed feelings we would know what to do. [...] Maybe it's fall to our knees, sway, beat our chests. Maybe wash his body. Maybe that's inside us' (294–5). The possibility that Tim's death will be the salvation of their emotional lives risks a cloying and potentially disingenuous redemption of the situation through Tim's apparent sacrifice, and the play has been read in such terms. Patrice Pavis gleans the message that the human body must 'be nourished by love and not [...] reduce[d] to a mask hiding true feeling and human spiritual-ity' (14). Kritzer argues, 'Through his death, Nadia and Victor acknowledge love and loss, and discover an ideal of Tim that persists beyond his death. Strengthened by this ideal, they risk experiencing life without the "happy world" myth' (*Political Theatre* 45). David Alderson is dubious about redeeming experience in this play. He questions how Nadia and Victor are changed significantly (873–4) and flatly denies the idea that the play has any time for spiritual questions (873). In contrast, I suggest that the play is sceptical about redeeming experience *because* it is deeply invested in a 'spiritual' problem, namely, what has happened to humanizing experience within late capitalism.

Instead of redeeming tragic experience, what Nadia and Victor perform is the very damage wrought by capitalism upon emotions. Nadia rejects Victor's attempts to locate gestures of mourning: 'Maybe you just saw that in a film somewhere' (*Some Explicit Polaroids* 295). She has met Jonathan the capitalist, and from his jubilant philosophy of unending disaster, transformation, and chaos she has learned that she is finally alone in the universe; she resolves to accept this as her fate. Victor, in contrast, mourns Tim so energetically that Tim, dead, nevertheless replies to him. The outcome of this act of mourning is that Victor expresses his love for Tim and Tim, after Victor leaves, realizes too late that he too loves Victor and resolves to haunt him. In a rejection of realism, the act of redemptive love and grieving belongs not to Victor but to Tim. In contrast, Victor clearly is not humanized by his experiences. While he abandons 'happy world' as a 'big fucking lie,' he instead advocates the constant transient movement and sameness of international capitalism (302–3). Nadia and Victor have gained self-insight into their illusions, yet they are left in a situation of individualistic nihilism, human symptoms of the truth of capitalism itself. It creates a world entirely homogeneous in its sameness: 'the same music, the same burgers, the same people' (303). This world is populated by privatized, depersonalized individuals, constantly travelling but never arriving anywhere new and without any sense of home: 'Nothing is fixed any more' (303). The only lingering shadow that mars the emptiness of Nadia's and Victor's situation is Tim's ghost, which leaves a fleeting trace on a Polaroid that Nadia takes of Victor. This ghost is a more ambiguous blessing than Donny is in *Faust Is Dead*; a small trace of loss, grief, and haunting that vanishes from a developing photograph.

It is such an experience of grief and loss that is the potential ground for individuals to move beyond themselves and make connections with one another, connections that, for Victor and Nadia, will be predicated on absence and loss as such, that from which they flee. Loss is the result of conflict, of people arguing and fighting and disagreeing, forms of disruption out of which change can emerge. Ravenhill offers an uncharacteristically hopeful conclusion that finds Helen and Nick reunited. Nick's anger has reminded her that managing the problem is not enough, and she hopes to be fuelled by his emotional energy. She longs for a fight. Nick has met Jonathan, the only character in the play who is described as a traditional human being. Nadia calls him noble, strong, spiritual, powerful, and carrying an air of authority (290). Yet Jonathan reveals that he has been fantasizing about a violent, agonistic encounter with Nick and is disappointed to find someone weak and lost rather than 'angry and threatening' (309). It makes Jonathan nostalgic for the past, for the struggles he experienced, and when his self-satisfied pomposity finally manages to coax from Nick's eyes 'a flash of the old hatred,' Jonathan reveals that it is just this that he enjoys about his benevolent capitalist philanthropy in developing nations: sometimes he catches a glimmer of hatred in those who praise him (312).

This longing for antagonism and strife speaks to the metaphysical concerns of this chapter. As Ravenhill himself observes, it is somewhat unexpected for him to suggest that there are evil deeds in his early plays. Perhaps the point is not that the characters who commit the acts are portrayed as evil – which makes no sense in the context of his plays – but that the events are understandable as 'evil' in a particular sense: evil is that which both demands and resists a materialist analysis, both frustrating practical solutions and inspiring continuous human endeavour, and thus the idea of 'evil' certainly has a place within an analysis of the tragic. Calling an event 'evil' is to suggest that it was incomprehensible and thus unavoidable, but also, perhaps less evidently, that it should have been comprehensible and should have been avoided. 'Evil' is a contradictory word used to describe contradictory and incoherent situations, deeds, and events, and as such is an uneasy signifier, the persistence of which stands as a testament to the ongoing presence of real contradictions within human life, events about which no properly coherent response is possible. Nick went to prison for fifteen years for attempted murder, and the man he tried to kill was once described by Helen as 'the scum of the earth' (234). It was she who encouraged Nick to attack Jonathan because he mercilessly destroyed her father's career (235).[14] Nick's return into a situation of flat positivism provokes those around him out of their stasis precisely with his reminders of hatred, anger, and fear, anxious responses to the agonistic incoherence that underlies social existence and in fact constitutes the social as such, but which has been repressed throughout the 1990s. *Some Explicit Polaroids*, in its diagnosis that English society has become 'happy world,' suggests that it has become stagnant precisely because of its disavowal of the negative, its refusal to allow the concept of absolute 'evil' to intrude into the rationalized positivism of its world.

Product

Nick is also a reformed terrorist, a one-time advocate of kidnapping and firebombs through mailboxes, strategies of violent class war (232). He is a reminder of something terribly, violently, apparently 'real' that cuts unhappily through the self-delusions in the lives of those around him. Ravenhill repeatedly employs a constellation of familiar tropes in his work as signs of the real: blood, bruises, wounds, illness, and death. His working-class characters are deliberately designed to be his most sympathetic and well rounded, more grounded in "reality" by virtue of their suffering. Pain, grief, and loss are portrayed as the traumatic disruptions of sense that provoke a renewed sense of significance. This is never far from a traditional sense of the tragic, and as such it is never immune from the possibility of being yoked to ideological ends. Ravenhill is thus appropriately sceptical about the fetishizing of authentic tragic experience that his own work risks.

On this subject, the title of *Product* (2005) tells us something crucial that might be overlooked by attention to the monologue alone. The nature of commodities and the ability of capitalism to commodify anything is the subject here. *Product* vacillates back and forth between honest emotions and hollow products, between *pathos* and *bathos*, between trauma and trauma-as-product. Most of all, it comes across as Ravenhill parodying his own playwriting aesthetic, which is perhaps why he wrote the monologue for himself to perform. While it is ostensibly about a Hollywood executive who pitches a ludicrous film about a woman who falls in love with a terrorist, called 'Mohammed and Me', to a young ingénue, it is implicitly about something much closer to home for Ravenhill: the presentiment that his own theatrical language might become commodified. Ravenhill's fear is that he might become a commercial parody of himself.[15] *Product* dramatizes this possibility, and the specific theatrical trope that Ravenhill satirizes in the play is the traumatic psychic wound.

The plot that the executive describes to the actress is so absurd it is not hard to imagine it actually being filmed: a young woman named Amy, who bears deep emotional scars because her husband died during the September 11 attacks, meets an attractive Muslim and falls in love with him, only to discover that he is a member of a London cell of al-Qaeda. When Osama bin Laden arrives in her stylish loft apartment, Amy finds herself volunteering for a suicide bombing on Disneyworld Europe because she can't bear to lose the man she loves a second time. She comes to her senses and reports the entire cell to the authorities, and her lover is shipped to Guantanamo. Amy is left an emotional wreck, and when she sees Mohammed being tortured on TV, she resolves to rescue him. She transforms herself into a movie action hero and storms the detention camp, liberating the prisoners and telling Mohammed she is now devoted to his cause. He is killed while they try to escape, but Amy in her bereavement is instantly transformed into a devoted Muslim who swears to Allah that she will avenge his death.

Thus the film script that is pitched describes a secular Westerner, a capitalist whose work furthers corporate globalization by outsourcing call centres to developing nations and who takes a voyage through pain, loss, and grief only to emerge transformed into a person of unshakeable Islamic faith. However, what is most political about Ravenhill's short play is not the timeliness of its overt content regarding terrorism. For the most part, this story is presented through the lens of vicious satire, but it is also a character study of a woman's inner journey from a pointless Western existence to a life filled with faith, meaning, and purpose. Within this character study, Amy's traumatic past is pointedly portrayed as Hollywood's most valuable commodity: 'Amy is wounded. She is … to each of us the wound, to each the wound is different. It sounds classical but it's me, it's my note to my writers … show me the wound,' the executive explains (157). The traumatic wound that circulates throughout Ravenhill's work as a mark of tragic experience, which within a classical tragic paradigm is both isolating and ennobling, which individuates and humanizes, is here the locus for a litany of laughable narrative clichés, the signs of class privilege and romantic isolation.

Moreover, the wound is a product, perhaps the key product that dramatic narrative has for sale: the romance of the bourgeois subject, locus of interiority, of alienation through loss that offers a more substantial presence in the world. The wound engenders classical interiority. The entire sales pitch is presented as an inner monologue, an exploration of Amy's thoughts and inner turmoil from her point of view exclusively. What is for sale here is tragic ennoblement, ideologeme of the tragic ideology: humanization through suffering and bereavement, elevation through debasement, the discovery of meaning within meaninglessness. This satiric take on interiority of character perhaps explains why Ravenhill is so often considered to be short on character development: he is conscious of the politics of such dramatic representation. *Some Explicit Polaroids*, for instance, while resembling the 'state of the nation' play, is brief, fragmented, and sparse in its characterization.[16] One could easily imagine it being expanded into a verbally heavy work virtually identical to a play by David Hare.

Ravenhill's work demonstrates an understanding of the politics of dramatic form, and he refuses to present character as a protective refuge from the issues at hand, since character interiority, the locus of the soul in the classical sense, is the ultimate commodity. The executive describes Mohammed's death to the actress: 'There is actually a moment. We're going to need a fantastic lighting-cameraman, but there is actually a moment when the soul leaves the body. [...] If we can get that on celluloid then … they can fucking kiss my arse' (*Product* 177). Traditional humanist values are once again satirized as the property of the privileged, and with this in mind I think we need to understand the conclusion of Amy's story as a double irony: it is not despite her status as a Western capitalist with a converted Docklands loft, Gucci luggage, Jimmy Choo pumps and a Versace suit that Amy ends up believing in a righteous faith and a cause. Those signs of affluence are merely accessories to her most precious possession, her wound, which allows her access to a depth of grief, affect, emotions, and inner experience unavailable to others, and which eventually leads to her devoted faith. It is precisely because of Amy's status as a privileged member of the upper middle classes and the owner of a soul that she is able to become a terrorist.

If the traumatically real is something that can always be turned into a product and thus subject to the tragic ideology, at the same time the 'wound' (as it is fetishized in *Product*) only has value as a commodity because the fetishized object has been abstracted from its real use value. This is perhaps what is most comically obscene about *Product*: its satire also draws attention to the commercial fetishization of aspects of the self that also answer to terms like 'authentic' and 'real': personal, individual trauma arising from massive social trauma, namely 11 September 2001. The fact that Amy carries around on her cell phone the final recording she has of her husband dying in the World Trade Center, a message that ends in him screaming in agony, highlights the transformation of the tragic *pathos* into an obscene instance of *bathos*.

The Cut

Thus Ravenhill's plays are constantly at pains to parse the gap between tragic experiences and the mediation of said experiences through ideological lenses, of which aesthetic representation is one such lens. Ravenhill's next play, *The Cut* (2006), explores this ideological divide over the question of the wound. This divide is finally a social difference, one ultimately determined by class. *The Cut* is an abstract political parable, whose uncertain time and place indicates an increasing formalism in Ravenhill's work. The society at hand is seen indirectly, represented through the story of a state apparatchik named Paul who is in charge of administering 'the cut,' a painful and socially stigmatized activity performed behind closed doors. The cut is balanced tenuously between surgical operation and state torture, carefully administered and managed, deeply unpopular with the current government, and avoided if at all possible in favour of other humane 'solutions' to the problem of social control and organization: namely university, the army, and prison.

Yet the young black man named John who shows up for the cut in the opening scene of the play has a different attitude to this activity: for hundreds of years everyone from his class of rural society, all of his ancestors, received the cut, and he has studied and prepared for it carefully. As Ian McKellen, who played Paul, puts it, the cut is 'whatever society has devised to keep the underclass in place' ('Making the cut,' *Western Daily Press* 6 April 2006: 38). While for Paul it is barbaric and causes him enormous guilt to perform, for John the cut is traditional and a cherished rite of passage: 'very old and beautiful … it's a ritual, a custom, […] To actually leave your body' (*The Cut* 189). Paul reveals that the government is thinking of eliminating the cut because it contradicts their 'core values' of progress and humanity (189). Paul hates to administer the treatment because while John would be in enormous physical pain, Paul would suffer 'spiritual' pain (191), something he hints is worse: 'Have you any idea of the burden for a man – of my class?' (201). John admits that he does not, but is relentless in his demand that he be given the cut.

The play is a counter-humanist parable, testifying to the persistence of and need for absolutes, of which the cut is the representative, within a secular, Enlightened society. John affirms the traditional violence of the cut as a humanizing activity of cruelty and suffering. The cut will liberate John: 'I want to be Cut away from this body. Yes – and this history and this wanting and this busyness and this schooling and these, these ties. I want to be released' (192). John sees the cut as 'Liberty. Freedom. Nothingness,' and he has been preparing for this psychic liberation by practising 'little moments of emptiness' (194). He shows Paul how to free himself with a meditation technique that liberates the subject from the burden of physicality and allows him to 'Feel the darkness. Feel the void' (195). Darkness has been vilified, John insists, filled with imagined evil, horrors, and terrors, and portrayed as a negative place to be filled with light, or avoided altogether in the name of society, history, and progress. John celebrates this darkness, a symbolic place of counter-Enlightenment that for the enlightened, progressive mind is populated by 'monsters […] witches […] paedophiles' (196). These are all lies: 'Darkness is light. Void is everything. You are truth' (197). This is the first time Paul has heard someone interpret the value of the cut this way, and he is both troubled and reluctantly persuaded, but only because he interprets this from his own class perspective. For John this is a liberating apprehension of a negativity that underlies existence, while for Paul it is the locus of a despairing truth, one linked to his own unhappiness, his lack of faith in the current political regime, and his constant contemplation of suicide: 'Everything's shit. Everything's fucked up. There's nothing worth crap' (198). When Paul pulls out a gun and threatens to shoot himself, John pleads with him instead to administer the cut. John receives exactly what he wants: the cut is performed with old tools, well-cared-for instruments evincing 'classic craftsmanship,' but Paul is left 'broken' by the encounter (202).

The cut is 'evil' as both deed and apprehended experience, but the cut is also class conflict. Denying the cut is false, but only those who are cut can benefit from it. John, it seems, gains traditional spiritual experience: a soul. Social antagonism is a real contradiction here, a division wedged deep in the foundation of society, but for the underclass the experience of the cut is humanizing while for the ruling class it is a source of bourgeois guilt and suicidal despair. The second scene of the play sees Paul at home, struggling with his unhappy consciousness in a domestic situation that makes the class divisions that plague his society repugnantly clear. While for most of the play the cut serves as the signifier of this class antagonism, by the play's conclusion it has taken on new contours.

The final scene sees Paul in a political prison in the aftermath of a vaguely Maoist social and cultural revolution. His son Stephen, a university student and fervent supporter of this new regime, visits Paul in jail and denounces his father's work as administrator of the cut. This is now a world of tribunals, more prisons, and the optimistic rhetoric of positive social change. The cut has been abolished and society is more honest and transparent. Paul insists vehemently that he is evil, and Stephen agrees with this estimation. There is a 'Ministry of Forgiveness' available for Paul, who refuses it: 'I want to be paraded and scourged and feel the blood in my eyes and see the blades before me. I want to know that everyone sees my rottenness and is ready to Cut it out. [...] I am the dirt that needs to be destroyed so you can be purified' (231). While Stephen insists that such 'old-fashioned' rituals of tragic scapegoating and purgation don't happen any more, Paul insists that sooner or later things will change back to the way they were: 'Any moment now that light's going to go blink and then there's going to be total blackness' (231). His commentary stands as a scathing critique of the socially progressive society that disavows the negative as barbarous and uncivilized.

If the cut and the man who administered the cut are described as 'evil' by the play's end, then finally the title of the play also serves as just such an uneasy signifier, serving to unanchor the concept of evil as something clear and unambiguous. Instead, the cut is incoherent, ambiguous, and contradictory, clearly a cruel material torture but also an immaterial psychic activity, equally dehumanizing and, as a persistent reminder of the flawed fabric of society itself, a humanizing wound. The cut is the trace of counter-Enlightenment that rationality and reason disavows from itself. The cut troubles the progressive, open, and transparent society but it also provides something traditional, vital, and deeply meaningful, spiritual even, for the young man to whom it is administered, even if the administrator himself finds it barbaric and torturous and his administration tries to avoid using it as much as possible, preferring other forms of socialization such as the university, prison, and army, which are presented as more humane but no less oppressive forms of social indoctrination.

The Cut can also be read as an allegory of New Labour: within moments of the play's beginning Paul talks of the new performance indicators his government has put in place to avoid any unnecessary brutality. If Thatcherism was happy to exacerbate class contradictions – letting the cut that divides society fester and grow – then New Labour was simply an embarrassed inheritor of this legacy, with tools to manage the problem but without any real ability to resolve the contradiction. Paul's regime inherits the old regime's systems and attempts to be more humane and progressive, but the same tools of control and the same class contradictions exist, and this regime has no intention of eliminating them, simply of managing them in a less barbaric manner as a means of minimizing their effects, as an expression of liberal guilt. The final scene takes a further step and represents the Stalinist-Maoist fantasy of the post-historical society where class differences and antagonisms have been eliminated. This is the end result of the dialectic of Enlightenment, where transparent reason and rationality finally eliminate the aspect of Enlightenment that would save it from totalitarianism: negativity, the 'dirt' that generates purification and light, the mark of counter-Enlightenment that goes by the name of 'evil.' The inevitable return of this repressed trace, the smear that reason cannot digest or transform into itself, is the sign that History is not over.[17]

pool (no water)

One response to living in the dehumanizing end result of Enlightenment would be to offer traditional humanizing experience, of which the tragic is the exemplary theatrical paradigm. Yet Ravenhill's work, while entertaining such a possibility, is both suspicious of nostalgia for classical paradigms of selfhood and also aware that art does not stand outside of commodification. In other words, the commercial fetishizing of the tragic always risks the pornographic, the prostituting of suffering and mortality. The question inevitably turns back upon artistic representation itself and demands an interrogation of the politics of tragic art, the politics of the poetics of tragedy. While Ravenhill's work has never conformed to the dramatic paradigms of realism, the increasing formalism of his dramaturgy indicates a growing self-consciousness of the politics of aesthetic form. It is a problem that any self-professed political playwright grapples with on an ongoing basis: the political play necessarily makes a claim upon social reality, the objective, which is always rendered particularly problematic by theatre's unique materiality, its embodied phenomenological weight. The result is an imperative to fetishize the authentic, either the authentic voice or the authentic experience, as a more politically legitimate artistic praxis within a subsidized and ultimately middle-class theatrical institution.[18] Ravenhill's work is balanced precariously on the divide between commerce and art, and the tragic sits uneasily in this tension. The content of tragedy emphasizes the centrality of blood, pain, death, mortality, suffering, illness, necessity, and poverty, and it can be easy to forget that none of these 'authentic' aspects of human experience are ever actually present in art, despite the physical presence of the human actor in the theatre.

Complicating this is the fact that trauma is by definition a kind of absence – in life it is detectable only by its effects and is no more graspable by material existence than by artistic representation. It is the absence of meaning which, when mediated, grants to life general significance and experiential weight. When theatre makes an unproblematic claim to represent the real, to find the authentic in the midst of the fraudulent or the commercial, then theatre falls prey to the ideology of realism and the delusions of mimesis, which is always a temptation within live performance. Content alone is left responsible for the problem of the real, and trauma becomes a product, offered up for sale. Formalism then returns to address this particular problem, to allow art to re-flect or mediate life rather than to succumb to imitation. Formalism forecloses upon the possibility of a mimesis of the real, a mimesis that would inevitably descend into the pornographic.

Ravenhill's *pool (no water)* (2006) is about the politics of tragic art as such and addresses the pornography of suffering through Ravenhill's deliberate use of formalism. Written for physical theatre company Frantic Assembly, *pool (no water)* is also, perhaps surprisingly, a Brechtian *Lehrstück* in both style and con-tent. The play calls for an indeterminate number of speakers (four performers in the original production) and takes the form of a story that this group tells about a member of their artistic collective who was elevated above the group by artistic and financial success. This successful individual is not a character in the play but is represented indirectly throughout by the other characters. She thus resembles the absent presence of the Young Comrade in Brecht's *The Measures Taken*, and like this seminal *Lehrstück*, *pool (no water)* addresses the uneasy tension between the impulse to individuality and the hostility of a group dy-namic towards the individual.

The speakers, a group of politically committed bohemians for whom artistic dedication and social conscience are welded together, tell the story of their suc-cessful friend, who vaulted to artistic fame through art pieces that made use of 'blood and bandages and catheters and condoms,' the artifacts of one of the collective's unsuccessful struggle with HIV/AIDS (295). The resentment of the collective towards their successful friend is a murky combination of moral judgment over her use of such raw material in her art, their own righteousness regarding their artistic work in creating 'murals for heroin babies,' and simple envy that she has become both internationally revered and wealthy (296). When another member of the group dies of cancer, the group reconnects with the successful friend at the funeral and accepts her invitation to visit her and swim in her new pool. They go for a midnight skinny-dip, not realizing the pool has been drained: after diving into the empty pool, their hostess ends up near death, comatose, and in hospital. Their response to her accident is a resentful manifestation of the tragic ideologeme: 'I'm sorry you had to suffer, I'm sorry there's this pain – but there is justice in this. Something is shaping our ends. [...] You see you flew – yes – you reached out your wings and you flew above us. [...] And now you've crashed right down' (303). They accuse her of *hubris* and revel in a brutal image of poetic justice as they stand over her agonized and broken body.

The group then proceeds to surreptitiously photograph her slow recovery, turning her terrible wounds and bruises into the same kind of dubious aesthetic project that she herself flew to success on. They thrive off her suffering like vampires, reaping a psychic and physical health and regeneration from the photographing of her flowering bruises. When she regains consciousness and sees the photos, she assumes they were done for her benefit and decides to continue the project of visually recording her recovery. There is nothing they can do: 'It was lost then. It was her body. She had dived into the pool. It was her act. And we thought we took the images but she was the work' (315). Slowly the collective begins to feel sapped of strength and will as they realize that she is growing from the experience and will continue her successful career. When many of the digital photographs are wiped from a computer by a virus that one of the group may have introduced deliberately, they take this as licence and hold a drug-addled bacchanalia where they meticulously erase all of the photographs and burn the hard copies. When the artist walks in on this violent act of destruction, it is as if they are rending her body in a virtual act of *sparagmos*: '[W]e have snapped her neck and we have broken her legs and we have trodden on her skull. And finally. Oh finally she is absent no longer. She is totally ... there' (322). The friend, who has been subtly absent to them ever since her success, finally becomes a fully manifest presence. They claim to have created her by destroying her.

Here the form of the play demonstrates itself to be inseparable from the content. The group claims to be able to hear her as she calls them small and insignificant, full of jealousy and hatred, and weak compared to her strength. The friends who died were too weak to live and create art, and the successful artist is the only strong one among them. Yet this litany is an unknowing projection of their own minds: '[I]t's as if we can hear her say – her mouth is closed, but still I, we, I we, heard' (322). If the group has performed a bacchanalia, then her appearance at the end has the resonance of an apotheosis, much like the appearance of Dionysus at the end of Euripides's *The Bacchae*. What is revealed at the end is what is implicit in the style of the play: the successful friend has been a projection of their minds all along, entirely a matter of how they perceive her.

The imagined castigation that they receive is exactly what they want and grants to them the ability to return to the mundanity of quotidian life, absolving them of both their envy and resentment of the successful friend, and their own collective artistic aspirations.

Thus this interrogation of the pornography of the tragic turns its eye upon the impulse in artistic representation to consume those aspects of the world that seem to negate the virtual and the mediated: the bruise, the wound, and the cut (313). The value of such raw facets of experience is precisely that they apparently resist or refuse consumption and digestion by mediation and representation: they are the shock that the 'in-yer-face' generation makes claim to as its unique currency. Yet the style of *pool (no water)* serves as an estrangement effect levelled at the very idea of raw, immediate experience, which is revealed to be caught up in consciousness's inevitable dialectic between absence and presence, one to which the audience of this play has also been subject through the narrative conjuring of the character of the successful artist. The presentiment of the 'absent' that characterizes the successful artist for the group, 'that quality in her work that sells' (295), is as much as projection of consciousness as is 'presence.' The tragic ideologeme of poetic justice that the group articulates, namely, the narrative mediation of human pain and suffering, is transformed into a cautionary tale of *hubris*. The story of overarching pride that predicates and necessitates a subsequent fall, accompanied by the mantra that claims that misfortune is weakness, is revealed to be a psychic purgation on the part of a collective, a *catharsis* that serves their own ideologically normative ends.

Thus the play is not primarily about the collective's resentful relationship to the successful artist at all, but about their fraught relationship to mortality itself, the authentically real, the non-identical that follows them through their lives, that troubles their group, and that they resent the artist for making the subject of her art. While their resentment begins with her apparent exploitation of the AIDS-related death of one of their group, and is exacerbated by her absence when a second member dies of cancer, their grief and mourning over dead friends turns into spite towards the individual as such: 'It was you who killed Sally. [...] Because none of us was meant to be wealthy, none of us was meant to be recognized, none of us was meant to fly' (298). They make of her a scapegoat, as if the negativity of death can be absolved by this purgation, when in fact throughout the narrative it is their own mortality from which they are in flight: 'Oh yes the sad sad rot to the grave has already begun' (301). They are aging and the enjoyment they take from seeing their successful friend near death, covered in wounds, serves to stave off their own awareness of dying. Their *ressentiment* is most of all inflamed when the friend makes her own mortality, the inarguable authenticity of her own traumatic suffering, the subject of her work, and thus returns them to their grieving emotional states prior to her accident: 'I call it grief when the bones of dead friends are banging against your head and drowning out the sounds of life' (311). Their eventual scapegoating of her is ultimately a displaced, pathological form of mourning provoked by their turn to drug and alcohol abuse.

It is not tragic art that is subject to a critical gaze here, it is the ideological attitude towards tragic art that sees it as inevitably pornographic and exploitative within a capitalist situation. This ideological attitude is demystified, ultimately, as a symptom of the postmodern inability to mourn, itself provoked by the ability of capitalism to rationalize and reify all experience: 'The fate which befalls all feelings, the ostracizing of what has no market value, is applied most harshly to something which cannot even contribute to a psychological restoration of labor power, mourning. [...] Therefore mourning, more than all else, is disfigured, deliberately turned into the social formality which, for the hardened survivors, the beautiful corpse has always been' (Horkheimer and Adorno *Dialectic of Enlightenment* 179). Tragic experience, while not necessarily eliminated altogether from contemporary life, is caught up in this continuous loop of commodification, and so potentially compromised in its integrity. This leaves tragic art in a permanently fraught position, with no choice but to reflect this contradictory situation at the level of form itself.

Blasted

In its overt formalism and choral structure, *pool (no water)* is the play by Ravenhill that most resembles the later work of Sarah Kane. The play can also be read as a commentary on the censorious public attitude towards seemingly 'pathological' or 'pornographic' work like Kane's and the entire 'in-yer-face' trend in theatre: the public vilification of such experiential theatre as pornographic is a social symptom of the postmodern disavowal of tragic experience. Kane's work seethes with antagonism towards the postmodern condition. This antipathy is most apparent in the unflagging dedication to ideals of honesty and integrity that are the hallmarks of Kane's tragic vision. Love, ultimately, is that which postmodernity renders impossible and is that which Kane's plays assert as an unlivable tragic ideal.

Yet while recent assessments have stressed the important of love as a proto-political emotion in Kane's work, they do so at the cost of reading the plays through the lens of social realism and imbuing them with superficiality. Kritzer, for instance, locates a series of hopeful gestures throughout Kane's first three plays and abstracts from these gestures the idea that 'extreme pain may transform the sufferer and that powerlessness may open him or her to a supreme experience of love' (*Political Theatre* 37). Kritzer argues that this love is offered by young women, and the gesture 'effects change in a violent and hate-filled world.' This is Kane's 'politics of the soul' (38). If this is so, then Kane's work offers only a naive and grotesque pornography of the tragic, the ideological myth that love redeems humanity, an expression of the tragic ideology. Kritzer's analysis is silent on the subject of Kane's last two plays, works that mitigate such an idealistic heroization of love.

Yet the idea of a 'politics of the soul' is a productively contradictory way of approaching Kane. I have argued elsewhere that the politics of Kane's *Blasted* (1995) are ultimately located at the level of its form, both as a tragedy and as a deliberate rejection of realism and the creation of a formally 'broken' play.[19] This was a 'symptomatic' reading of *Blasted* that focused less upon authorial intention than on an analysis of the play as a social symptom of contemporary historical contradictions, particularly the contradiction of postmodernity and the failure of metanarratives, such as have been analysed here with reference to Ravenhill's work. The two disconnected halves of *Blasted* are, in this analysis, an instance of generic discontinuity, the expression, at the level of form, of incoherence at the level of the social. This reading was an attempt to account for the widespread sense that *Blasted* was a 'political' play, although it has no clear political message, deliberately avoids contact with social situations, and eschews the conditions of social realism.[20]

This reading was fixated upon Ian's undead head at the end of *Blasted* and upon the surmise that the best way of understanding it is as an instance of what Lacan, in his analysis of Sophocles's *Antigone*, describes with the Greek word *atè*. The word is typically understood to describe the fate of the tragic protagonist and is translated with English equivalents such as ruin, misfortune, doom, bane, or mischief. In Lacan's analysis, however, *atè* describes the peculiar position of Antigone in a space beyond the limits of the human, in a 'zone between life and death' (*The Seminar Book VII* 280). Yet where the present analysis parts from my earlier analysis of *Blasted* is in its surmise about how Ian arrives at *atè* himself, which I initially argued was an expression of the larger social context of politics and war, a murky sense of situation that circulates vaguely and nebulously throughout the play. This was an attempt to assert the concrete politics of the play, something that *Blasted* itself attempts rigorously to disavow. Here, I want to draw attention to another possible cause behind the undead, 'corpsed' universe that arrives on stage at the end of *Blasted*. Ian arrives at *atè* at the end of *Blasted* for the same reason that Antigone arrives at *atè*: out of the terrible and unavoidable fact of love within social conditions where it is impossible. While such a message certainly seems banal, I want to attempt to tease out the larger political implications of such a metaphysical crisis.

The importance of love is more self-evident in Kane's later plays, but recent criticism helps us confront the disagreeable fact of love in *Blasted*. Graham Saunders, for instance, has suggested recently that Ian and Cate in their codependency resemble Vladimir and Estragon in *Waiting for Godot* ('The Beckettian World of Sarah Kane' 69). Kane herself makes the uncomfortable subtext of her play starkly apparent for us: 'It was about violence, about rape, and it was about these things happening between people who know each other and ostensibly love each other' (qtd in Sierz, *In-Yer-Face* 101). This is an issue that would be easier to overlook silently. Kane's plays are frequently focused upon rape, and *Blasted* is a central instance of this, but the challenge the work offers to us is to understand rape happening within a relationship of love. It would be simple to dismiss this contradiction as false by emphasizing Ian's negative qualities, which are so very prevalent in the play: his racism, his selfishness, his violence, his moments of emotional cruelty. Finally, the extreme age difference between Cate and himself places him in a potential position of moral turpitude – he is forty-five and she is twenty-one, but it appears to have been a couple of years earlier that they were actually in a romantic and sexual relationship with one another. All of these things allow us to dismiss the possibility that there is love between them. If one wishes, Ian's drunken rape of Cate between scenes 1 and 2 can be read as the final indication that he does not love her in any legitimate sense.

Recent critics argue otherwise. Elaine Aston argues that *Blasted* criticizes a misogynistic social situation where attempts to love and be loved are thwarted by masculine power dynamics. Aston suggests that it is a sign of Kane's atypical feminism that she shows the rapist as an 'unlovable love object' who circulates within a situation where love and affection are corrupted by a violent and pervasive masculinity ('Reviewing the Fabric of *Blasted*' 24–5). I too am going to argue that love and rape coexist in Kane's work, in order to establish a premise for the analysis of *atè* in Kane's plays as articulations of the tragedy of love within the postmodern condition. However, I am not convinced that the threat to love is a result of social conditions. It may be a metaphysical condition of Kane's theatre that love is corrupted and debased.[21] Kane's characters are *atè*, can neither live nor die, because they are in love within a postmodern situation where love as such is impossible and thus takes on the form of rape. If this is a social condition, it is one that has become ubiquitous as a symptom of the condition of postmodernity, and as universal, this condition takes on the guise of the metaphysical and therefore may be read as another facet of the contemporary existence of 'evil.'

The very problem of determining whether or not Ian is in love with Cate is at the heart of this interpretation. Rather than making such a determination, we should focus instead on why it is a problem at all. It is an interpretive undecid-ability because love implies honesty, sincerity, and integrity; love as such can only exist within a situation of good faith, trust, and truth, a place where good faith without *ressentiment* is possible. When we ask the question of whether or not Ian is in love with Cate, we implicitly demand a dramatic situation where consistency of character can be asserted, thus where an unproblematic concept of *truth* can be apprehended. When Ian and Cate arrive in the hotel room to-gether we may think ourselves to be in such a place of social realism, where truth and falsehood can be determined. Ian wants, with seeming integrity, an emotional and sexual experience with Cate, something that he can no longer have because she no longer loves him and they are not a couple any longer. He asserts throughout the scene that he loves her and craves sexual contact with her. She has come to the hotel room out of care and concern for him: she says he sounded unhappy, and he is clearly in severe ill health. He tells her he is dy-ing of lung cancer and cirrhosis of the liver, and his constant wracking cough testifies to this. His attempts throughout the scene to initiate a romantic and sexual situation are awkward, manipulative, and embarrassing, and his narrow-minded racism makes him repugnant. Nevertheless, he seems to have a core of emotional sincerity located in his insistence that he does love Cate: the scene ends bathetically, with his re-assertion of love, her denial that she loves him, and his pathetic offering of the room's decorative bouquet of flowers to her.

In between scene 1 and 2, overnight, we learn that he has raped her. The de-tails are sketchy and emerge piecemeal; he was drunk and doesn't remember it well (*Blasted* 43). He performed a forced act of cunnilingus on her that left her bleeding (32). She is pissing blood and her anus hurts (34). Cate has remained in the room and slept there, but she is furious with him when she awakens. She clearly feels betrayed, both emotionally and physically, but she is also much more self-assertive than she was in the first scene. The situation resembles the post-coital situation of *Miss Julie*, where the sexual encounter results in an af-termath where the brutal divisions between men and women are brought to light. Before sex there are declarations of love; after sex there is hate and vio-lence. But the interpretive challenge here is the same one found in Strindberg's play: within the paradigm of realism or naturalism, the post-coital situation seems to be the honest, demystified truth of the relationship, which makes the man's claims of love and sincerity nothing more than attempts to get the woman in bed. Yet Strindberg is neither a naturalist nor a realist and his characters have no such consistency, something he warns us of in his infamous preface to the play, where he describes them as patchwork quilts. We must accept that Jean and Julie are just as integral before the sex act as they are afterwards, which is to say that they are contradictory and inconsistent.

There is a certain moment in scene 2 of *Blasted* where both Ian and Cate break sharply from any sense of psychological consistency, demonstrating the same Strindbergian vacillation that characterizes the wild energy of the second half of *Miss Julie*. Very shortly into the scene, Cate has torn the arms off Ian's jacket, has physically attacked him, and has held his own gun to his genitals before passing out and having one of her quasi-epileptic fits. During this fit, Ian holds his gun to her head and starts to rape her again. All of this is perfectly consistent with the violent betrayal that took place during the night. Yet after Cate awakens from the fit the dynamic changes. She asserts that she wants to go home immediately, and Ian locks the door, telling her he loves her and needs her to make him feel safe. A car backfires, and he panics, crawling onto the floor. In response, Cate becomes uncharacteristically amorous: she soothes his fear by kissing and licking him all over his body, undressing him, massaging him, scratching and biting him sexually, and finally performing oral sex on him.

An unconvincing psychological explanation of this sexual aggression on her part would claim that she is doing it out of selfless concern for his extreme emotional distress. A further, unconvincingly blunt rationalization would deduce that she is doing this only so that she can bite his penis (as she does) and thus subject him to the same type of abuse to which he subjected her. A more subtextual interpretation of the moment would suggest that she is initiating a sexual encounter for her own reasons, in order to relax Ian and get him to talk about things that he has adamantly refused to discuss with her in the previous scene: namely, the reason for his paranoid fears, why he carries a gun, and most importantly, why he terminated their original romantic relationship and stopped calling her. It is just this information that he confesses while she seduces him: he is not just an exploitative shock-journalist, he is an undercover intelligence agent working in counterterrorism and he became paranoid that his relationship with Cate was putting her life in danger. Since then he has, he claims, become a killer. However, none of this is going to grant consistency to Cate's behaviour here: it remains perfectly contradictory that she would suddenly have sex with a man whom she consistently refused contact with throughout scene 1, and who then raped her in the night.[22] Moreover, Ian's confession that he is a killer, which culminates in Cate biting his penis, is such an unexpected announcement that it jars the credibility of the play. Cate is suddenly a sexually assertive woman and Ian, the tabloid journalist, is a counterterrorist agent. It is as if we have walked into another play.

In short, we as an audience no longer know what to believe, and very shortly a knock comes at the door heralding the unexpected arrival of the soldier: all realism is abandoned.[23] One way of describing this is to say that from the perspective of realism, the play is destroying itself. Or that it is poorly written, and makes no sense. Another might be to say that the play has betrayed us: following the rape in the night and Ian's betrayal of Cate, the play's very fabric has become one of betrayal. *Blasted* abandons all claims to truth, good faith, or consistency, and its characters are forced to exist within this landscape of bad faith and infidelity. Thus the play's other significant rape needs to be mapped onto this situation, a rape notable for the fact that it is performed in front of the audience rather than offstage. The soldier rapes Ian, but the specific details of this act are laden with ambiguity. The soldier's lover, a woman named Col, has been raped, murdered, and savagely mutilated by soldiers. The soldier still experiences a profound emotional and sexual longing for her and is, as he puts it, 'dying to make love' (42). When he holds his gun to Ian's head and forces Ian to submit to the rape, the soldier weeps profusely and smells Ian's hair, which smells like Col because of the cigarettes Ian smokes. When, following the rape, the soldier sucks out Ian's eyes and eats them, it is both because the soldier is hungry and because this is what happened to Col. The contradictions of this act of sexual assault serve as a theatrical X-ray of the act that took place during the night. The soldier's expression of love for his dead girlfriend is at the same time a violent act of rape, but the fact that it is a rape does not cancel out the expression of love: they are forced to coexist within the same action, even though it is inconceivable that a man would rape a woman that he loves. The soldier imagines himself not, finally, as Col's lover but as Col's rapists.

This depraved expression of love is a symptom of a metaphysical condition. Next to the expression of love, the other dominant discourse that circulates throughout the play is, as mentioned earlier, the afterlife, and I want to suggest that these two topics are in fact the same topic. Love and the afterlife only overlap once. Ian describes how his love for Cate makes him feel: 'You take me to another place.' Cate replies, 'It's like that when I have a fit' (22). Earlier, she analogizes her fits to a spatial displacement into a zone of death. She supposes her fits are like death: 'Feels like I'm away for minutes or months sometimes, then I come back just where I was' (10). While for Cate mortality does not represent an imagined terminus, Ian is terrified by the '[n]ot being' of death (10). Later in the play when Ian wants to commit suicide, they argue about the afterlife again. Ian insists that there is no afterlife, there are no ghosts, and there is no God. Cate demonstrates a devoted religious attitude to the contrary: 'Got to be something. [...] Doesn't make sense otherwise' (55). The conclusion of the play proves them both to be right or both to be wrong: there is an afterlife, but God does not exist. In the end Ian and Cate are together in *atè*.

There is such an afterlife, I surmise, because Ian loves Cate, a feeling that, as he puts it, takes him to another place. At the end of the play, he finds himself there. The existence of love as such demands an afterlife, God, a heaven, or an

Eden, somewhere that love, good faith, and fidelity can exist in untrammeled metaphysical integrity, a location of perfect truth and bliss. Love for Ian feels like a transport into someplace outside of the material, mundane world, a place where there is only Cate. But God does not exist, Ian expresses his love for Cate by raping her, and therefore the place that Ian's love for Cate takes him is *atè*. The redemption of Ian's love for Cate is impossible because there is no God; or alternately, his love for Cate redeems him into an undead hell. What Ian does to Cate is 'evil' in the sense Ravenhill describes in his discussion of James Bulger's murder, because Ian's love for Cate indicates that he should be protecting this young, child-like woman from people like himself. Nevertheless, Ian's love exists, but like the soldier's rape of Ian/Col, it is a form of betrayal, a rape, because in the absence of God everything, even the form of *Blasted* itself, is a betrayal. Betrayal is, paradoxically, a metaphysical absolute in Kane's universe. Love, accordingly, may be evil.

Phaedra's Love

Thus Kane's cosmos is not a secular one, it is one where God has either left, died, or worst of all, doesn't exist yet (as in Beckett's *Endgame*). Nonetheless, God has left humanity with the gift of love, which, in the absence of the possibility of redemption, is the most profound of curses. All of Kane's other plays are attempts to negotiate a relationship to this tragic burden. *Phaedra's Love* (1996) is at once a brutal social satire of England in the 1990s and a metaphysical picture of a completely corrupt cosmic order, debased by a pervasive and ubiquitous bad faith. Perhaps appropriately, the play by Kane that looks most superficially like a tragedy is in fact a satyr play, a comic burlesque of tragedy that only ostensibly takes its inspiration from Seneca's version of the myth. Once again, at the centre of the play is a highly visible and highly ambiguous rape, an act that disrupts the coherence of the society represented in the drama and precipitates the violent scapegoating with which the story culminates.

　　Phaedra's Love is stylistically unlike Kane's other work: it is a thoroughly comic play, as if the Pythons had decided to stage a parody of the Royal Family by starring them in a Roman tragedy. But the joke is also a serious one: when life itself is a cosmic jest, then existence isn't funny but is instead meaningless. The satyr at the centre of the play, Hippolytus, knows this and behaves accordingly. There is no place in Kane's sordid drama for a Hippolytus representative of chastity, virtue, or integrity, not when the world itself is shown to be hypocritical and dishonest. The only scrupulous way to behave is to be honestly and openly corrupt and depraved: in the opening scene of the play we are presented with a Hippolytus who seems kin to Brecht's anti-hero Baal, the debased creature of appetite who stands counter to all humanistic values, particularly those to be found in classical tragedy. Kane's corpulent Hippolytus eats hamburgers on a couch and watches violent American television while masturbating absent-mindedly into a dirty sock. Tragic representation has been dragged down beyond the level of the body and into the realm of soiled underpants and junk food.

Much of this is legible as justifiable contempt for what tragedy in a classical sense signifies. The idea that the descent of a tragic protagonist – a man of noble blood who is drawn down into the realm of the bodily and the commonplace – in fact further elevates and ennobles said man through his struggles and travails is teasingly parodied: 'Women find me much more attractive since I've become fat. They think I must have a secret. […] I'm fat. I'm disgusting. I'm miserable. But I get lots of sex. […] Therefore. I must be very good at it' (77–8). Hippolytus insists that he isn't mysterious, that his corporeal debasement – in other words, his physical suffering – hasn't humanized him or made him a better person, and that he has no redeeming qualities at all. In other words, he denies that he is human. The play doesn't entirely agree, hinting that his past love for Lena, about which he gets very angry and refuses to speak (83), may be the secret pain he keeps inside him and which will give him a trace of *pathos*, but otherwise he is resolutely, unapologetically bathetic. The only person in the play who doesn't know she is in a parody of tragedy is Phaedra, who is earnestly tormented by her inexplicable, burning passion for her revolting, spoiled stepson: 'You're difficult. Moody, cynical, bitter, fat, decadent, spoilt. You stay in bed all day then watch TV all night, you crash around this house with sleep in your eyes and not a thought for anyone. You're in pain. I adore you' (79). Like a proper character in tragedy, Phaedra interprets his wretchedness as inner torment and loves him for his suffering.

The rape in this play is not apparently a rape when it takes place. Phaedra is someone painfully serious within a situation where seriousness is not possible. It is not simply that Phaedra as a character seems out of place in this environment, but that her love for Hippolytus comes across as inconceivably naive and ultimately incredible, not just because he is so unpleasant but because no one loves anyone in this situation, they just fuck. As Hippolytus has discovered, existence is boring. Phaedra, desperately seeking to express her love for her stepson, gives him a birthday present she thinks will convey her feelings: oral sex. He watches TV throughout the act, holds her head down, ejaculates in her mouth, and then proceeds to express his full contempt for her self-loathing behaviour, concluding with the admission that he has gonorrhoea.

What Hippolytus does not know is that Phaedra actually loves him: he assumes she is no different from the self-loathing hypocrites who surround him on a daily basis, celebrating his royal birthday and adoring him. When news comes from Strophe than Phaedra has accused Hippolytus of rape and has hanged herself, Hippolytus muses that '[s]he shouldn't have taken it so seriously,' and is genuinely surprised to learn that her love for him was real (90). In her accusation of rape, false from his perspective, Phaedra has given him a real birthday gift, something to make life worthwhile. While Phaedra's love will not redeem an irredeemable universe, she offers to Hippolytus the ability to take a paradoxical stand against the hypocrisy he so loathes, by assuming his fate as a rapist and a criminal. As he explains to the Priest who comes to hear his confession, because there is no God there is no one to forgive him, and moreover, because there is no God, there is no such thing as love: 'A non-existent God can't forgive,' he remarks, which doesn't mean forgiveness isn't necessary, simply that it won't happen (95). He accuses the Priest of the crime he finds loathsome in all men: 'You think life has no meaning unless we have another person in it to torture us. [...] You have the worst lover of all. Not only does he think he's perfect, he is' (93). Love for Hippolytus is just a form of bad faith, a betrayal of the self, and it is magnified in the self-loathing love of the clergy for God.

Hippolytus's public lynching begins like a piece of satiric sketch comedy: the gathered crowd includes a working-class family from Newcastle who have come down to jeer at the rapist and have brought their barbecue and their dog. Hippolytus is efficiently disemboweled and his guts are roasted, at which point the police disperse the crowd. Hippolytus, happy at last, dies, and a vulture naturally descends upon his corpse.[24] In the midst of this broad and vulgar satire it would be easy to forget that of which the title of the play reminds us: the violent exposure of the bad faith woven into the fabric of this society, the social hypocrisy that is expressed visibly in the contradictory destruction of the Royal Family, supposed repository of divinity and morality on earth, has all been made possible by the authentic love of Phaedra for someone undeserving of it.

It is perhaps for this reason that her accusation of rape is not incorrect. '[P]erhaps rape is the best she can do,' Hippolytus muses while wondering why she used this word (87). Phaedra wasn't forced into the act by Hippolytus, but as he realizes later, she was forced into it by her love for him. The encounter was a betrayal and a violation because Hippolytus betrayed her love for him, a trust that is the only instance of innocence and good faith in this universe. Love exists, but in a godless universe of ubiquitous hypocrisy, when love expresses itself honestly it finds this expression within the vehicle of a rape and is subsequently expelled into death. But even this death does not redeem Phaedra's love or ennoble her, because there is nowhere for it to be redeemed. Simon Critchley argues something similar in a recent analysis of Jean Racine's *Phèdre*:

If Phaedra's existence is defined by malaise, then this malaise will continue after her death. Which is to say that death is not death, but simply a deeper riveting to the fact of existence and its eternal curse. Phaedra's discovery is death's impossibility. [...] Which raises the following question: if Phaedra does not die, then of which subject is this play the tragedy? Who or what dies in this tragedy? In my view, the corpse on stage at the end of the play is not that of Phaedra, but that of the city, the state, the world. The moral of the tragedy is that life in the world is impossible. (179)

It is tempting to adopt his observation here as even more relevant to Kane than to Racine. Life is a fraud and thus impossible either to endure or to escape, and while the fraud cannot be redeemed here or in an afterlife, the tragedy can expose the corpse of the world as such, just as Kane does at the end of her play. This is to make the world something of a farce, Critchley observes, and he notes that it is contemporary versions of the myth such as Kane's that appear to have captured this essential point about the tragedy (189–90). The meaning of the play seems to inevitably or necessarily contaminate its formal or stylistic qualities, resulting in grotesque *bathos*.

Cleansed

Cleansed (1998) does not skirt around this issue but instead announces from its opening moments that death is not an escape from the hell of life. 'I want out,' Graham tells Tinker, and demands a heroin overdose in order to effect his exit. Graham's sister Grace wants something from him, something that Graham seems unwilling to offer to her or live through, and despite Tinker's warning that '[i]t won't end here' Graham begins the play by committing suicide (107). *Cleansed* begins in the zone where *Blasted* and *Phaedra's Love* end: the space of *atè*, between life and death. As shortly becomes apparent, *Cleansed* takes place in an entirely expressionistic environment where the literal and the figurative, the material world and the inner landscape of the self are indiscernible from one another. The metaphoricity of language, the fact that the simplest of statements such as 'It's just the beginning' (108) evoke at once both transparent and deeply opaque senses, serves as the most tangible sign of this indeterminacy. The return of Graham to the play four scenes later may be read as the literal presence of a ghost or as a projection of his sister Grace's emotional investment in him: the play upholds both interpretations. The play has the fragile logic of a dream: Grace comes to an ambiguous incarceration centre, what was once a university campus, to attempt a rite of mourning for her brother, dead six months. His body has been cremated and so her grief finds a vehicle for expression in her donning of his clothes, now worn by another resident. Since the director of the institution cannot allow any objects to leave the place, and Grace, who loves her brother very much, will not part with the clothes, she insists on staying. It is a critical commonplace among reviewers, academics, and even Kane herself to understand *Cleansed* as a hopeful drama about the redemptive power of love within a situation of extreme dehumanization.[25] To the contrary, I am going to argue that the indestructibility of love in the play is precisely what makes this place hell on earth.

Certainly the dynamic tension between love and dehumanization is obviously at the heart of the play, and more than in any of Kane's other works the thematic importance of love is apparent as the central dramatic image here. The location of the play is an institution of reason and knowledge that has been transformed into a concentration camp for incarcerating drug addicts, schizophrenics, and homosexuals. This prison is located at the heart of a social situation that can be deduced from auditory hints beyond the university fence: the sounds of a cricket match or children singing a Beatles song indicate that quotidian English life is proceeding just beyond the perimeter of this place. We are in a kind of prison of the unconscious, the place of the id that Englishness disavows, and despite the fact that he is in charge here, Tinker, in his unhappiness and his obsessions, seems as much an inmate as the other characters. The instruments of the university are still in Tinker's hands, namely, the application of cold reason to the question of human feelings, as if the situation is a laboratory whose primary purpose is the reified, fascistic dissection of human emotions under controlled experimental situations. English reason performs a vivisection of the aspects of the human that said reason represses and puts behind bars: feelings. Love is the object of study for Tinker, attacked not so much because he wants to destroy it but because he wants to understand how it works, particularly in himself.

This is a terrifyingly material, godless world, which is why something as metaphysically absolute as love is both out of place and so fascinating to Tinker. Grace's devoted love for her brother summons up the ghost of Graham or possibly an idealized fantasy of Graham: this Graham is not a junkie, and unlike the Graham in scene 1, who seems to have some vague fear of Grace's intentions towards him, this Graham is more than happy to teach Grace to emulate his voice, stance, and movement, and also to confess his secret sexual fantasies about her before making love to her. When she unites with this all-too-perfect Graham, Grace's love is fulfilled in a peculiar kind of utopian plenitude. For Grace, mourning the loss of her brother also means having her brother as a lover and as a love object, which in turn means being her brother, or having her brother's Being. Love, completed, for Grace becomes a feeling of ingesting him as a part of herself, of experiencing love without loss. Grace doesn't believe in heaven or hell, and she has no desire to wish Graham back to life, because she doesn't 'think of Graham as dead' (125). She is perfectly happy with her relationship to Graham as it is. She suggests, idly, that the only thing she might improve is her body: 'So it looked like it feels. Graham outside like Graham inside' (126).

Tinker, meanwhile, has fallen in love with Grace, seemingly moved by her loving devotion to her brother's memory, but when he overhears this particular wish, he decides that he must save her from this pathological investment. First he has her tortured and raped, and then, while trying to convince her that she is a woman rather than a man, he lobotomizes her. When her love for Graham proves to be resistant to this treatment, Tinker tries to give her what he thinks she wants: he cuts off her breasts and attaches Carl's penis to her in a clumsy and poorly performed surgical operation. 'I'm sorry. I'm not really a doctor,' Tinker apologizes bathetically (146). Tinker realizes his misjudgment of Grace's situation too late: 'I think I – misunderstood,' he confesses to the unnamed stripper upon whom he has projected his love of Grace throughout the play, a woman who, like Graham for Grace, may or may not be a projection of Tinker's mind (147). Ironically, Tinker receives exactly what he wants from this figure, just as Grace initially received exactly what she wanted from Graham. Tinker is granted absolution for his error by the dancer who has pretended to be Grace for him, and now that Grace herself has been transformed physically into 'Graham,' Tinker is finally able, it seems, to see this nameless woman for who she actually is and to experience a reciprocal love with her. Yet when she tells him her name, it is, surprisingly, Grace. We are left with a Tinker deeply, happily in love with a person who seems to be both actual and entirely a projection of his mind.

Love, then, is revealed to be a powerful form of projection that constructs an idealized image of the loved one rather than an actual material relationship with another person. In the case of Grace, Tinker mistakes the metaphysical for the material, or misunderstood that within the state of love they are indiscernible from one another. Graham is a ghost: both an imaginary figure in Grace's mind and a corporeal entity that exists within the fabric of the play. *Cleansed* will not allow us to decide on one or the other interpretation. Thus the surgical, corporeal literalization of Grace's love is a grotesque misinterpretation of her emotional investment in her image of her brother. In the final scene, Grace gives every sign that in becoming her brother in every way, she has in fact lost her brother and her love for him altogether. Graham is no longer present to her, she can no longer hear his voice, and most importantly she can no longer feel, inside, the love that was also a form of perfect identification with him. 'And when I don't feel it, it's pointless.' The word 'pointless' is repeated six times, culminating in 'Think about dying only it's totally fucking pointless' (150). Even death will not resolve this loss. If she has received a gift from Tinker, it is the opposite of what he meant to give her. He has given her not her heart's desire but the pain of loss and grief, the depression of melancholy, and the tangible experience of absence that her love affair with Graham has postponed. The significance of Grace's final words, 'Thank you, Doctor,' are to be found in the punctuation of the sentence, which subtly emphasizes the sarcastic vitriol behind this clinical designation (150). She curses the surgeon whose attempt to heal what he saw as her pathology leaves her wounded and damaged.

Yet there is also a potential sincerity to her thanks, an awareness of the gift of loss. Finally, this gift may be mourning, may be the understanding that Grace cannot love the loved one and also be the loved one: love cannot be fully fulfilled, perfected, or completely realized. Love must always be tragic in some way, flawed by a sense of loss, distance, or dissonance. In the play's final, deeply ambivalent image, the sun comes out, which brings a smile to Grace's face, reminding her of Graham, who always called her sunshine, but the light becomes blinding, echoing the shaft of blinding sunlight that concludes the scene of Grace's lobotomy.

Crave

It is stylistically appropriate that Kane abandons not only character and plot in her final two plays, but exteriority altogether. The point of such a stylistic fluidity is that selfhood never really addresses anyone but itself, and the worst manifestation of this illusion is the experience of love, which is the greatest possible betrayal of one's self, since love deludes you into thinking you actually perceive the other. Yet the interpretive challenges of *Crave* (1998) should not overshadow the predominant clarity of the piece, which presents two asymmetrical and unbalanced relationships as a means of illustrating the inability of love to ever hit its mark. Here, the two older voices seem to terminate the relationships and leave the two younger voices with broken hearts. The depersonalization of the narrative – its diffusion or dissemination across the multiple voices and perspectives – ultimately has the effect of universalizing this condition.

Early on in *Crave*, a younger female voice in the play, 'C,' rebukes an older male voice: 'You've fallen in love with someone that doesn't exist.' This older male voice, 'A' replies sardonically: 'Tragedy' (158). At the end of the play, however, this tragic situation is reversed. 'You've fallen in love with someone that doesn't exist,' is now spoken by this older man, and he directs this at the younger woman, who tries to deny this painful fact with declarations of 'I love you' (190). He has finally become fed up with this damaged relationship and ends it. The young woman appears to be a victim of childhood sexual abuse within her family, and this trauma has left her damaged and incapable of loving others. The older man with whom she speaks describes himself early in the play as not being a 'rapist' but rather a 'paedophile' (156), a troubling admission that becomes understandable when we learn that he is in love with a woman who is emotionally damaged by childhood experiences that she can neither remember nor forget (158). She is still in some way the damaged child, and his love for her is unhealthy for him, and impossible. Comments like 'Tragedy' serve as much to mock the foolishness of this affective state as to elevate it.

Throughout the play the mental state on display, particularly in the two younger characters, is analogized to the state between life and death that is now a familiar condition in Kane's work. 'You can only kill yourself if you're not already dead,' and 'If you commit suicide you'll only have to come back go through it again,' are two representative sentiments (183, 188). There are many interjections and non-sequiturs throughout the play, an accumulation of vaguely related observations and comments that only tentatively cohere. The young woman is at the heart of the play in that her emotional duress is most clear and coherent. In her state of ungrounded, unresolvable grief, she makes references to being caught between life and death: 'I write the truth and it kills me. [...] I hate these words that keep me alive / I hate these words that won't let me die' (184). She describes a profound and pervasive unhappiness, the result of mournfulness, which in turn internalizes a death-bound trajectory. The play hints strongly that the reason she denounces her mother appears to be because her mother allowed the sexual abuse to happen: 'if she'd left – [...] None of this would have happened. [...] None of it. [...] None' (157). However, the narrative explicitly describing this abuse is spoken not by the young woman but by the older man in reference to a 'small dark girl' (157). In the first production, this would have evidently been the young woman because of the actress who played the role.[26] However, it is not necessarily the young woman who has been raped. Rather, rape may take on metaphysical contours here.

Rape may be a kind of foundational suffering inherited by subjectivity as a condition of existence. Consider that the young man talks about how he inherited a broken nose from his father: 'Genetically impossible, but there it is. [...] And don' t you think that a child conceived by rape would suffer?' (162). He is speaking these lines to the older woman, who wants him to father her child, although she has no interest in him. He wants it to be 'an act of love' (167) but fears that the older woman is going to rape him (163). The younger woman echoes the young man's fears of rape, but speaking to the older man (163). It is the older man who describes, in a third-person narrative, the image of the 'small dark girl' being sexually abused, and then comments: 'And though she cannot remember she cannot forget.' The young woman herself adds: 'And has been hurtling away from that moment ever since' (158). The play tempts us with the possibility that the young woman's trauma is metaphysical rather than material, an existential state that manifests its origin in an image of childhood abuse – a vivid non-memory – that can only be described in the third person.

This dictates that all relationships with others will be doomed to be projections of a primordial trauma – a rape – that is still only virtual: 'Still sleeping with daddy,' she says of the man she is sleeping with (180). Near the end of the play the characters will make a more telling assertion: 'This never happened. [...] None of it, [...] All of it, [...] None. [...] I am an emotional plagiarist, stealing other people's pain, subsuming it into my own until [...] I can't remember [...] Whose [...] Any more' (194–5). The rape that seems to lie at the foundations of this selfhood is at the same time not a rape that can be said to have happened to this selfhood. The betrayal is virtual, though substantially so. The sentiment becomes metatheatrical, and the young woman's inability to discern her own trauma from that of others is reflected in the inherent falseness of tragic theatre's exploitation of human suffering. Theatre as such is a betrayal, a pornographic lie about the truth, and if this is evil, it is so no more than is the playwright: 'God has blessed me with the mark of Cain' (195). This mark of evil now comes to describe two things simultaneously: the pure bad faith that the young woman's attitude towards trauma, and thus her psyche, constitutes; and tragic theatre itself, which takes up into its fraudulent representation the substance of pain. Art, as sin, is an image of existence.

The result of this impossible genetic inheritance of suffering, the sense that one's unhappiness is preordained as one's fate renders the fabric of this play, once more, a tragic zone of *atè*. 'I'm evil, I'm damaged, and no one can save me,' the young woman explains to the older woman, who performs the role of her therapist (173). The play eventually enters the realm of the clinical and raises the question of psychopathology, only to dismiss the idea of treatable illness and affirm staunchly that this misery is the state of being human. We are, finally, in the realm of the paradigmatic tragic sentiment: it is best never to have been born, second best to go back where you came from as quickly as possible. 'Why did I not die at birth [...] Come forth from the womb [...] And expire,' the speakers lament, mourning, it seems, the loss of the young woman's mother (193). It is a properly tragic state of existence, one projected as universal because utterly private: 'The outside world is vastly overrated' (189). While there may be a world beyond the self, the tragedy here is that despite the pain of being human, pain that should be a tangible sign of engagement with something larger and perhaps metaphysical, the only potential vehicle for any proper contact with the outside world – love – is demonstrated as an autistic loop of trauma.

4.48 Psychosis

This enclosed, hermetic envelope of the self resists representation through the dramatic vehicle of character. The idea of character is a theatre figuration that, no matter how abstractly and expressionistically it may be envisioned on stage, always implies some basic interaction with social reality, simply as an offshoot of theatrical form and specifically through the presence of the actor on stage. The body is not the mind, and this seems to be the tragic problem in *4.48 Psychosis*, a dramatic monologue that announces itself as a play about a mind severed from a body: '[M]y mind is the subject of these bewildered fragments' (210). The play is not, however, a series of incoherent fragments, but an all-too-coherent explanation of why existence is intolerable. The play is also impossible to stage, because it is about the gap between consciousness and existence; *4.48 Psychosis* can no more be embodied on stage than it can be lived. This is not to say that it should not be staged. It is not a poem, it is a play: while it has no plot, characters, or story, it has, I think, a dramatic action. A suicidal woman who claims that she was '[b]uilt to be lonely / to love the absent' (219) resists clinical treatment for her condition, is motivated to mutilate herself by her obsessive love for a fantasized woman who does not exist, agrees with reluctance to drug therapy, and suffers such severe side effects from the drugs that she refuses further treatment. She then suffers psychosis, depression, self-destruction, insomnia, stark lucidity, and finally commits a carefully premeditated suicide. Nevertheless, the impossibility of staging the play is essential to its identity between content and form. This impossibility renders theatrical form inherently tragic: a futile, doomed gesture, to be performed without hope, as an enactment of a promise that will not be fulfilled.

While *4.48 Psychosis* is usually performed with two or more actors, my own sense of the text is that such a decision inevitably seduces the performance into the comforts of realism. There are passages in the play that break from the monologue form and present a dialogue between the suicidal voice of the play and a psychiatrist. To embody this dialogue with two actors inevitably removes us from the realm of the mind and places us in social reality, introducing the possibility of politicizing the text as an indictment of psychiatry.[27] Suddenly the psychiatrist is a 'character' intruding from the exterior world, and we are consoled by the recognizable contours of dramatic form. We are released from the enclosed space of the mind into 'reality.' This misses the refusal of realism within the dialogue itself, specifically the hints that this is an inner argument that projects one pole onto a psychiatrist figure. In the end, this persona is revealed to simply be an aspect of the woman's self-loathing when the psychiatrist unprofessionally, and unrealistically, confesses that he hates his job and can't stand being around the mentally ill (237). The point of this dialogue is not that it challenges the suicidal woman's pre-existing views but that it confirms them utterly. She projects a figure who reinforces her anger and her understanding of her situation, which is that despite the fact that she has many friends, there is something about her that bars her from loving and being loved. She denies that she needs a doctor; she insists that she needs a friend, despite the fact that she already has friends. To the non-suicidal mind, it is this paradox that is so incomprehensible and leads to designations of mental illness. This harsh apprehension is highlighted by the repetition, in the dialogue with the psychiatrist, of the passage that serves as prologue to the play: 'You have a lot of friends./What do you offer your friends to make them so supportive?' (205). The question is un-answered, and as a self-accusation it is both a rhetorical positioning and also a launching point for the play's apologia for suicide.

The play begins in the realm of unmitigated *atè*, a sense of being doomed, articulated in a melancholy withdrawal from reality that expresses itself in a long litany of self-castigations and contradictions: 'I do not want to die/I have become so depressed by the fact of my mortality that I have decided to commit suicide/I do not want to live' (207). Consciousness is torn between intolerable imperatives towards life and death, and there is a specific reason that the voice is caught in this undead state: '[M]ost of all, fuck you God for making me love a person who does not exist, FUCK YOU FUCK YOU FUCK YOU' (215). This lacerating attack is readable in two ways: it is God who does not exist, and the speaker, forced to love a non-existent God, is also in love with a non-existent person and thus suffers from a need to love and be loved by someone who can never actually be embodied by another. Long passages surrounding this section of the text describe an obsession with 'a woman who was never born' (218). This curse is the result of a non-existent God who nevertheless burdens hu-manity with the blessing of love. The need to be loved and to love, as a recipro-cal and perfect harmony of selves, is described in a passage that mockingly repeats the clinical, psychiatric checklist of human needs that require satisfac-tion as a means of avoiding suicidal urges: 'to form mutually enjoyable, endur-ing, cooperating and reciprocating relationship with Other, with an equal.' The clinical description is immediately demystified by the female voice: 'to be for-given/to be loved/to be free' (235). The sentiment remains sincere and press-ing. This promise of a healthy existence is the means of avoiding suicide.

Yet the promise is false. This voice feels that she was '[b]uilt to be lonely/to love the absent' (219). She describes having fallen in love with the one junior psychiatrist who expressed kindness and humanity to her, and then explains her feeling of betrayal when she decides that the emotions and seeming honesty of this person were hypocrisy: 'I loved you, and it's not losing you that hurts me, but your bare-faced fucking falsehoods that masquerade as medical notes. [...] [Y]ou were covering your arse too. Like every other stupid mortal cunt' (210). We are entirely within her mind here, without access to this relationship. For her, the world as such is unlivable, a place of betrayal, and the speaker is bereft of faith. This is the reason life is intolerable, and it is clearly and starkly delineated by a voice that demands to be heard and not be pathologized by the psychiatrists who scrutinize her: 'I shake without reason and stumble over words and have nothing to say about my "illness" which anyway amounts only to knowing that there's no point in anything because I'm going to die. And I am deadlocked by that smooth psychiatric voice of reason which tells me there is an objective reality in which my body and mind are one' (209). Being suicidal is not a mark of mental illness here but rather the mark of consciousness, and this is what is so intolerable and unlivable within the play. This melancholy consciousness is also expressed, crucially, in what at first seems like an insurmountable divide between selfhood and the body: 'Body and soul can never be married / I need to become who I already am and will bellow forever at this incongruity which has committed me to hell' (212). It seems, at points, like a simple problem of disconnection between self and bodily existence, but at the point of extinction, the voice's penultimate line expresses something other than such alienation: 'It is myself I have never met, whose face is pasted on the underside of my mind' (245).

The critical tendency with such bleak and remorseless work is to search for a glimmer of hope somewhere near the conclusion. This line signifies such a possibility: at the moment of the disintegration of the self, the self apprehends the painful dissonance of identity not as an unbridgeable gap between soul and body (what she calls 'a tale of sense interned in an alien carcass' [214]) but as the inherent experience of difference within the self, unendingly pursued along the contours of a Möbius strip of mind. The promise of healthy psychic wholeness, a cure implied by the experience of inner alienation, may be comprehended as an impossible promise, never meant to be fulfilled within the self. Such an image perhaps helps us to understand the persistence in Kane's plays of the non-existent, alienating God who burdens humanity with a curse of love for a non-existent other. I would intervene here and suggest that this other is an avatar of the Other, whose language is the unconscious, and that in Kane, God is the Other. '[T]he true formula of atheism is not *God is dead* [...] the true formula of atheism is *God is unconscious*,' Lacan surmises (*The Seminar Book XI* 59). Kane's plays, driven into the zone of *atè* by the inexorable curse of love, articulate the voice of the Other, the lack in the self, with a terrible clarity. In contrast, the image of an unmet self whose face is pasted on the underside of the mind offers a hopeful apprehension of the self that knows that division is not from the outer world, not from a God or an impossible loved one, but is within, and that the tortures of love and of an absent God are mere projections of this inner difference.

This reading may or may not have something to say about the actual final words of the play: '[P]lease open the curtains' (245). Interpreted in the original production as vocalized stage directions and as an opportunity to bring a hopeful note into the world of the theatre, director James Macdonald had the window shutters of the Jerwood Upstairs opened to admit into the performance space the light and sounds of the outside world.[28] It was the comforting return of social reality into the expressionistic world. More recently, in a production I saw in Montreal, I was surprised by the director's decision with regard to this stage direction. This production took place in a small studio space surrounded by white curtains.[29] The audience of twenty patrons was lined up on either side of the small rectangular runway space, claustrophobically contained by the clinical enclosure on all sides. The curtains stayed closed at the end. When I asked the director why she had done this, she explained: 'There is nothing behind the curtains.' It is a simple and inarguable point, and the distance between these two productions is the distance between social realism and tragedy. The original production was, perhaps inevitably and appropriately, about Kane's death and thus about social reality. Subsequent productions must avoid the use of the play as obituary or suicide note and attend to its substance as art. In the latter production I saw, the curtains refer not to the outside world but to the space offstage. There is no exit into death, which makes the world Kane represents unlivable but also presents a glimmer of something affirmative about the here and now. It is the afterlife and all that it communicates to the conscious mind that is the unbearable false promise and the ultimate betrayal here: 'It's fear that keeps me away from the train tracks. I just hope to God that death is the fucking end' (211). Sarah Kane herself committed suicide because she was clinically depressed, but the voice of *4.48 Psychosis* articulates a tragic condition without exit or solace, doomed in advance to a ruin that is, horribly, the only promise that can be fulfilled.

Far from a depoliticizing gesture, the insistence on metaphysical absolutes in situations where they are impossible is precisely where Kane's political vision lies. It is fitting that it is the new generation of tragedians, represented by Ravenhill and Kane, who dramatize most directly the idea that we live in a fallen world. Our world takes on the guise of a fallen world not because we have been exiled from Eden or because God has abandoned humanity, but because we are left with the burden of such metaphysical thinking within the condition of postmodernity. Within postmodernity, the social and historical appears as the metaphysical, because alternatives to the current conditions of existence have been rendered systematically unthinkable. As Ravenhill diagnoses, what is called for now is dialectical thinking, which is itself, as I have argued, the most humanizing vision of the tragic. In this paradigm of the tragic, our alienation within the world is rewritten as our difference within the world. In contrast, within the postmodern condition, a dialectical view of reality, a vision affirming transformation and change, has been dismissed as paradox and irrationality in favour of the late capitalist phantasm of utopia: smooth, reified positivism, without flaw or fissure, harmonious and transparent, 'happy world.' The logic of contradiction has been effaced; there is only the management of problems left. But this image of a utopian present is simply the capitalist image of apocalypse and apotheosis: heaven on earth. Capitalist utopia is merely the rational endpoint of the image of a postlapsarian fall, which promises a return to Eden and then falsely delivers on that promise. To insist on the (im)possibility of metaphysical absolutes, on evil and love, which, as we have seen, are both present in Ravenhill's and Kane's plays, is to engage in just such a dialectical intervention into the flat, rationalized positivism of the postmodern condition. Tragedy is an aesthetic refusal of 'happy world.'

Conclusion:
Late Modernism in *Jerusalem*

In this conclusion I wish to highlight the productive contradiction that has emerged in the argument of this book: a political playwright is typically understood as a materialist and a humanist of some kind, an artist whose representation of the human avoids metaphysical issues and insists instead on the here and now. Thus, for a political playwright to create tragedy is to immediately engage in a contradiction in terms, since tragedy, even as we have seen it here, seems to constantly risk renouncing the here and now in favour of some aspect of human life that transcends the present through a metaphysical claim. This is so even if this renouncing of the material is made through a confrontation with mortality, the negativity that lies outside of material existence. This, as we have seen throughout, is a fundamental aspect of the tragic.

But what I want to draw attention to here are the unique paradoxes of these playwrights' projects. There is a formal impulse in all of these playwrights towards stylization, towards a break from realism, towards experimentation and innovation. Yet there is also a strong impulse towards content that is 'social,' recognizably uplifted from reality and injected into formal stylistic edifices. The following argument highlights the fact that these plays are inheritors of late modernism (Beckett and Brecht) and as such manifest a productive, contradictory, dialectical tension between political, realistic content and tragic, aesthetic form, a tension that cannot be resolved. Thus they are not making authentic, tragic claims to the Absolute, as in high modernism, but they are nevertheless making an important tragic claim to the absolute, one that is deliberately wrecked by the contradiction between form and content in the plays. The result, I want to argue, is a paradoxical claim to the absolute as the human-as-historical, the material as the metaphysical, the profane as the sacred. I will analyse Jez Butterworth's *Jerusalem* as a manifestation of this contradictory, productive claim to the sacred within postmodernity: a powerful piece of formal tragic drama located in a squalidly realistic setting.

The seemingly defeatist renunciation of the present has been a theme through-out this study. If we were to consider the plays discussed here as first and foremost responses to their particular historical moments, then we can discern a rough historical narrative that begins with the failures of the post-war affluent society in the 1960s (*Saved*). This failure is then looked back at dramatically from the perspective of the 1970s (*Teeth 'n' Smiles*, *Light Shining in Buckinghamshire*), with an artistic focus upon the demise of the post-war dream and the lie of consensus (*Plenty*) along with a theatrical exploration of the failures of socialism generally (*Claw*, *Fair Slaughter*, *That Good Between Us*, *The Power of the Dog*, *Lear*) and even the failure of humanism in the face of capitalism (*Bingo*, *The Fool*, *Owners*). These largely bleak diagnoses of the 'state of the nation' are, however, leavened with some tentative explorations of 1970s possibilities of reanimating the promise of the 1960s (*Traps*, *Cloud Nine*).

Thatcher's election and the 1980s foreclosed upon socialism in England and led to fuller dramatic explorations of the tragic effects of unrestrained capitalism upon human beings (*Top Girls*, *Fen*, *The Secret Rapture*, *Red Black and Ignorant*, *The Tin Can People*) as well as the tragic effects of a repressive social climate upon English subjectivity (*The Castle*, *A Mouthful of Birds*, *Top Girls*). Meanwhile, in the 1980s there were also hopeful explorations of a tragic subjectivity not determined by repression, negation, and denial, but rather by the difficult Nietzschean task of self-overcoming, of affirming existence as a model for a new subjectivity within a period when a socialist revolutionary promise had been squashed by a counter-revolutionary moment (*Victory*), and using the moment of catastrophe or apocalypse as the ground for a rebirth (*The Europeans*, *Great Peace*).

The 1990s is best characterized as the triumph of the late capitalist effect, an effect that in fact has its roots in the deterritorializing industrialization that under-girded the 1960s promise itself. The curious effects of postmodernity upon sub-jectivity are at the heart of playwriting in the 1990s, and key here is the repression of the other, the disavowal of the unconscious itself, with the effect of engendering a toxic social environment (*Lives of the Great Poisoners*, *The Skriker*, *Thyestes*, *Far Away*) characterized by the failure of human emotion and the pressing need to re-engage the crucial tragic activity of human mourning (*Skylight*, *Amy's View*, *The Permanent Way*), specifically through the tragic avowal of loss, mortality, and the unconscious (*Gertrude – The Cry*, *Dead Hands*, *My Zinc Bed*). Into this post-modern situation have come the new generation of dramatists who are the subject of the previous chapter, who respond to the death of the tragic within postmoder-nity through an assertion of tragedy's absolute necessity.

This brings us to the new millennium and to plays that are more difficult to historicize because they are so proximate to our understanding. Yet by situating them in relation to this ongoing discourse regarding the tragic, we can see a continued investment in the avowal of the other, in a sense of acknowledging absence as such, in whatever guise it appears. This might be the children in *Seven Jewish Children* or it might be the absent central character at the heart of *pool (no water)*. It might be a simultaneous acknowledgment of both profound loss and affirmative difference (*A Number*), or an insistence on ecstatic experience of an absent and perhaps non-existent god (*The Seduction of Almighty God*). It might be the representation of quietly contrarian characters who have absented themselves from their societies and who can only be described as possessing grace (*Gethsemane*), or it might be an assertion of the fatal necessity of tiny, humanizing gestures of the 'freedom-tragic,' the Promethean assertions of humanization within situations that render it deadly (*Olly's Prison, At the Inland Sea, Coffee, The Crime of the Twenty-First Century, Chair*).

Quietly permeating this analysis has been the insistence by these playwrights upon the metaphysical, if we take the avowal of the Other, in its most elementary sense, to mean the openness to what is outside of the mundane material boundaries of the human. Hare explores spiritual experience through curiously self-possessed social saints and martyrs, Barker seeks to create an ecstatic experience of the unconscious, Bond seeks to stage the radical innocent and confront the audience with this core self, a self that resembles the integrity of the human soul,[1] Churchill explores the human relationship to Dionysian desire and Otherness, while Ravenhill and Kane stage tragedies of evil and love. Significantly, these artistic visions all function as tragic interventions into the discourse of Englishness. As I discussed earlier, Antony Easthope proposes a theory of Englishness as an empiricist discourse, one characterized by a professed transparency of thinking, of common sense built upon a rigid binary logic of clear oppositions. To engage with such discourse by demystifying it as 'ideological' is to engage in its own binary logic of false and true. (The flat positivism of postmodernity is a similar kind of rationalist discourse of transparency, one having dispelled the other altogether from its plane through its dialectic of Enlightenment.) The tragic insistence upon the metaphysical can be understood as a disruption of the discourse of Englishness, if we understand that the purpose of this insistence is not merely to *negate* the rational, material plane with the intrusion of the metaphysical but rather to provoke a properly dialectical, tragic action, asserting an identity of opposites between the material and the metaphysical, to infuse the profane with the sacred. This promise, impossible to the categories of the rational mind, is the key claim to the absolute made by the tragic.

While insisting upon the importance of metaphysical experience as an aspect of social life, virtually all of the playwrights whose oeuvres are on display here have demonstrated a movement away from social realism and towards increasing stylization, as I have noted over the course of this study, and have shown a growing emphasis upon the formal qualities of theatre art itself. Politicized materialism, again and again, drifts into the materialism of the aesthetic. The autonomy of art, or the sense that art's content is itself, seems to lurk at the margins of this political theatre. On the one hand, this is a familiar issue that we could argue Brecht's work grappled with and solved by demonstrating that form is political. Yet the plays I have studied here are, in my analysis, not instances of *Verfremdungseffekt*. Neither, for that matter, are they instances of the clichés of 'postmodern' art. They do not operate through pastiche; they do not internalize the logic of late capitalism within their forms, mimicking reification as style. While they often demonstrate traits associated with metatheatre (as does the Epic theatre), like Brecht's plays they are not simply metatheatrical, in the sense of being obsessed primarily and hermetically with their own status as theatre. They do not parody their own forms or undermine their own status as aesthetic objects. They are not engaged in complicitous critique. Neither are they 'post-dramatic' theatre: they pursue plot, character, and theme.

The plays' formalism and their interest in metaphysical experience may both be understood to be manifestations of the same impulse, manifestations united in the assertion of the tragic. Their formalism, even in the sense of writing 'tragedies' rather than 'realistic' plays, is parallel to the turn away from material experience (realism) and towards metaphysical experience (formalism). While they share with Brecht's work a modernist sense of the autonomy of the aesthetic, an underlying premise here has been that in pursuing a dialectic of the tragic, these plays may be understood to be emulating another aspect of the ideology of modernism: not simply the autonomy of art, but the modernist assertion that what makes art 'political' is in the final instance its disengagement from quotidian social life. This is the paradox of a politicized formalism, since formalism always implies a seemingly neo-modernist abandonment of the social in favour of artistic autonomy. Howard Barker, whose adoption of the ideology of modernism is evident in his epigraphs from Adorno, is only the most ostentatious example of this formalism.[2] Tragedy resembles high modernism in its refusal of everyday life, its formal self-possession, and most importantly, in its appeal to a dialectical unity of opposites. As I mentioned at the outset, the concept of the tragic that I articulate here is for all appearances a Romantic vision of the sublime that transcends the everyday. The tragic is a window into the transcendent, yes, but crucial for our consideration here is that the tragic is, paradoxically, also the necessary failure of transcendence.

Fredric Jameson borrows the term 'the Absolute' from André Malraux to characterize an essential feature of high modernism. The Absolute represents that to which modernist art refers by being absolutely non-referential. The Absolute prevents the aesthetic from 'passing over into autism and schizophrenia' and 'in an extraordinary dialectical reversal, endows it with its revolutionary power' (*A Singular Modernity* 160). This autonomous imperative is not a creed of art for art's sake, or of art itself as religion: 'the very term Absolute, if it means anything, designates a transcendental motivation, an appeal to something outside the practice in question, and enveloping it' (163). It represents a utopian vision of 'total social transformation which includes a return of art to some putative earlier wholeness' (164). As Jameson notes, 'art, even in its modernist form as the Absolute – especially in its modernist form as the Absolute – has a genuine function to redeem and transfigure a fallen society' (178). High modernism is a paradigm for sublime, tragic art.

However, I evoke this theory of modernism only to demonstrate how insufficient it finally is as a description of the plays under consideration. They do, I think, bear within themselves the impulse towards autonomy, and this impulse is mired in the possibility of tragic experience as a transcendence of the quotidian: 'The sublimity of tragedy transports its readers into a disinterested contemplation of the universal, the necessary, and the purposive without purpose,' writes Simon Goldhill (50). Yet I have observed a productive paradox in contemporary English tragedy that distinguishes it from modernism proper: the autonomous, formal impulse here is at all times placed in a sharp and conscious tension with the political energies circulating throughout these plays, energies that are most in evidence at the level of content. When form is politicized in these plays, such as in Bond's and Churchill's stylistic innovations, this formalism is not harmonized with politicized content but stands in distinction from it. Yet formalism never escapes the social. Even Barker and Kane, who turn their gazes so resolutely away from everyday life, perform this gesture so ostentatiously that they seem to constantly keep the world just at the edge of their visions, a barely discernible glimpse that is all the more significant for being so fleeting. Bond, who casts his gaze far forward into future dystopias and wastelands, seems to do so only to drag those vistas directly into the present. Churchill's strange, formal gems are baroque, stylized objects that nevertheless refract through themselves a social content so seemingly didactic and stark that the plays appear to be torn from newspaper headlines, and have the inflammatory effect of agitational propaganda. Form and content are neither completely separate, nor completely harmonious.

With this deliberate tension between social content and aesthetic formalism in mind, the presence of the third term, the tragic, offers a particular, teasing suggestion. The plays in this study do not undo themselves with an anachronistic modernism. They are not some naive appeal to the sublime or to the authenticity of the Absolute. This becomes apparent if we consider them in contrast to Eugene O'Neill's more earnest modernist spirit, particularly in his masterwork of tragedy, *Long Day's Journey into Night*, with its aching, agonizing appeal to the fleeting yet desperately necessary spiritual transcendence of material existence.[3] The forebears of contemporary English tragedians are not the Romantics, as they were for the modernists, but the modernists. English tragedians now have no interest in a banal assertion of the autonomy of the aesthetic, knowing as they do that this is merely an accommodation to the postmodern condition. It is postmodernity, the end result of the modernization process itself, that has created impossible conditions for art. When industrial modernization was transitional, modernism was able to take an artistic position in relation to it. After the Second World War, conditions changed. The plays I have studied here chart a knowing passage through the Cold War, the end of Empire, the failure of consensus, the end of History, the demise of politics in England, and the emergence of an all-encompassing culture of consumerism. Jameson suggests the term 'late modernism' to describe some art that emerges out of this increasingly postmodern landscape. He calls it 'late modernism' because it looks a lot like modernism and is specifically made possible by the critical theorization of modernism in the post-war period (thus through the development of an ideology out of experience), but it is late because it is lacking the key authentic aspect essential to modernism's elevation of itself into the realm of high art: the utopian, Romantic commitment to the Absolute, the authentic promise of transcendence. In abandoning the authenticity of this ideal, late modernism deliberately (and for Jameson fortunately) ruins itself. The tragic in postmodernity is that deliberate ruin, the lingering, hollow promise of transcendence that simultaneously bars access to the Absolute.

Jameson argues that the late plays of Samuel Beckett, instances of this late modernism, demonstrate a war between form and content without recourse to the sublimity of the Absolute. Formally, they enact aesthetic autonomy and withdrawal from daily life, constructing 'eternally recurring spectacles' that are, however, marred by the 'empirical content' lurking at their cores: 'unhappy marriage, intolerable youthful memories, a banal family structure' – queasy, drab lumps of realism that Beckett's formalism can never digest. 'The form itself – autonomy – and the anecdotal content on which it depends yet which it cannot manage to appropriate into its own substance – these stand in a necessary dialectical relation with each other and indeed produce each other reciprocally' (*A Singular Modernity* 209). This contradiction of late modernism is, Jameson suggests, particularly productive, for the tension between form and content also breaks down the high modernist distinction between art and culture, allowing for the emergence of a post-war literature within the developing consumer culture that Jameson optimistically calls 'middlebrow late modernist' (210). It is, he suggests, what the student and academic classes study in universities today as 'the canon.'

Taking my cue from Jameson, I want to assert the general appropriateness of this category – the late modern – for the work studied here. From the two essential theatrical (late) modernists, Brecht and Beckett – key influences at the Royal Court Theatre from its inception – the playwrights who have moved through these pages have inherited the tension between form and content that leans more towards social content on the one hand (Brecht) and more towards abstract form on the other (Beckett), without in either case being able to resolve the tension. Yet what makes the contemporary political playwrights studied here *late* late modernists is that not only have they inherited the theory and ideology of modernism that made late modernism possible, they have also inherited the theory and ideology of late modernism, namely postmodernism. Jameson tells us cryptically, '[I]t is with this late modernism that postmodernism attempts radically to break, imagining that it is thereby breaking with classical modernism, or even modernity, in general and as such' (210).

The arrival of the tragic is the sign of late late modernism's particular intervention into postmodernity. This intervention is not simply the aesthetic tension between form and content or between aesthetic autonomy and social engagement, but also the dialectical mediation between these oppositions, mediation that tragic experience enables and that postmodernism has abandoned. Tragic mediation is ambivalent here: this mediation is a promise of a unity of form and content that is implied by the tension between them, but this promise also ruins itself and maintains the unresolved, tragic mediation. What the tragic offers to us is a dialectic between political content and aesthetic form, between autonomy from and engagement with the world, and thus tragic theatre occupies this space between literature (the aesthetic) and the popular (the social), between art (form) and daily life (content). But the dialectic is not resolved, because it is an historical, ongoing progression. If Romanticism called the promise of the aesthetic the sublime, and modernism envisioned it as the Absolute, then contemporary English tragedy is the transcendence of postmodernity through access not to the Absolute but to the human-as-historical. Yet paradoxically, this historicized subjectivity demands the avowal of the metaphysical, the outside of the human that appears under the guise of the Absolute. This human, importantly, includes the Other, whose voice is the unconscious. Even in Barker's quasi-modernist, seemingly metaphysical theatre, it is after all the unconscious that is the transcendent. This human also includes features of humanity, which Ravenhill and Kane point out for us still bear the conceptual residue of metaphysical absolutes: evil and love. Postmodernity, Jameson reminds us, includes not just the modernization of industry and the industrialization of agriculture, but also 'the colonization and commercialization of the Unconscious or, in other words, mass culture and the culture industry' (*A Singular Modernity* 12). The tragic now has as its ideal the articulation of the image of the human within a horizon of complete reification, and the principal action of this tragic is the avowal of the Other. The ends of such a tragic action are the historicization of Englishness through the inhabitation of this discourse by that which it represses, as a means of promising the dialectical identity of the material and the metaphysical. A very high-profile example of contemporary English tragedy speaks directly to this question of the infusion of the sacred into contemporary English life.

Jerusalem

Jez Butterworth's 2009 Royal Court sensation and 2010 West End transfer *Jerusalem* (dir. Ian Rickson) makes a startlingly forceful assertion of the political value of tragic social loss for a contemporary sense of national identity. From its evocative title to its singular locale – a clearing in a wood at the edge of a local township – *Jerusalem* conjures a highly self-aware sense of the role of location and place within the ongoing creation and maintenance of a community. 'What the fuck do you think an English forest is for?' growls the play's protagonist in the faces of the local town officials who have served him and his old trailer eviction papers (98). It is a question that announces to us just what is at stake here in the play's forest locale: the desperate matter of what it means to be English. 'Rooster' Johnny Byron has been living in this glade for twenty-seven years, and in that time this social dropout with Romany blood in his veins has both lived at the outskirts of local civilization and embodied its heart. Byron is both the unacceptable liminal excess that will not be domesticated by modern life and the essential outsider whose life force fuels the vitality and energy of his community. It is no wonder, then, that he serves as a convenient scapegoat for the township on its St George's Day festivities, as he is both the king and the fool, the insider who is the outsider, the most valued member of his society and simultaneously the most reviled. He is the man everyone seems to love and hate at the same time. He is taboo, both sacred and profane. *Jerusalem* is at once a modern May Day ritual with Byron as the fool-king who will be offered up in bloody sacrifice at the end, and equally a modern Oedipus plot in which the heroic saviour of the community is revealed to be the loathed abject scum living at the edge of town.

What is startlingly apposite to the present study is not just the thematic and political concerns of *Jerusalem*, and not just that they should be articulated by a younger member of the contemporary English theatre scene, one who was deemed a member of the mid-nineties 'in-yer-face' generation early in his career. What will ultimately be most important for us here is that formally, *Jerusalem* knows it is expected to be an instance of scandalous, contemporary shock theatre and references this awareness in its raucous, ear-splitting opening moments, but does so only to finally offer the audience an experience that, while containing within itself this contemporary discourse about new English theatre also frames this issue within a larger and more evocative message. Plays like *Jerusalem* make apparent for us that for this younger generation of writers, shock is a profound and crucial form of communication.

The humour of *Jerusalem* is expressed through an ongoing dramatic tension between tradition and modernity, between values and the death of values, between meaning and meaninglessness. A new housing estate has been built at the edge of the fictional village of Flintock,[4] a small town in Wiltshire along the Kennet and Avon Canal. 'Rooster' Byron and his decrepit old trailer are now considered to be unwanted intruders, unwelcome squatters within view of the new estate and are served an eviction notice within the first few minutes of the action. In response, Byron shakes off his hangover with a flamboyantly prepared concoction of milk, vodka, speed, and a raw egg, and pisses against a tree in an act of ostentatious territoriality: 'I dreamt last night of waterfalls. (*Beat.*) Riches. Fame. A glimpse of God's tail … Comes a time you'd swap it all for a solid golden piss on English soil,' he opines (10). Established here are the stakes at play in *Jerusalem*: the forces of change that provoke the compressed action of the play are expressed in modernization, gentrification, and an abandonment of a sense of community and tradition in favour of the commercialized heritage industry represented by the Flintock Fair. In contrast, Byron is a living embodiment of tradition and a sense of belonging. He is, essentially, the perennial town drunk, a fifty-year-old who knows everyone and whom everyone knows, a living legend and constant nuisance who has finally been banned from every pub in Flintock. Most importantly, the positive values that Byron expresses through the rhetoric of Englishness and location cannot be separated from the fact that he articulates these values by pissing on them, and that this piss constitutes a sacrament. The effect of his twenty-seven-year squat in this wood is that he embodies and protects a space, a space that seemingly is highly endangered within contemporary England, because it is nothing less than a public space rather than a privatized space. 'Rooster's Wood,' as it is colloquially called (15), is not simply the convenient dramatic location for the play's action, it is a refuge for the town's misfits, young and old. One of the more quietly moving aspects of the play is the tangible fabric of social connection that emerges as it becomes clear that Byron's camper is a public locus, a hangout, a place where the cast of youthful characters know they can come day and night and find welcome, community, and even protection from the dangers of their homes.

Rooster's Wood is not so much a sanctified haven of English greenery as it is a rubbish tip where teenagers go to buy drugs, drink, and party, but it is precisely this that makes it sacred.

And this is why it is both a threat and something vital to the town, serving as a raw, profane, and pagan contrast to the Flintock Fair happening nearby over the course of the play: Rooster's Wood is the obscene excess without which the community cannot function. In contrast, the Flintock Fair is represented humorously throughout *Jerusalem* as a hollow, commercialized mockery of May fertility and hunt rituals, plastic and vapid and meaningless for its pointless repetition of activities that were once lively collective expressions of human experience and community. Twenty years ago, we are told, 'Johnny Byron *was* the Flintock Fair' (30). In former days Byron wasn't simply the town drunk, he was a motorcycle daredevil whose stunts drew crowds from neighbouring communities and who was apparently pronounced dead for a few minutes at the Flintock Fair in 1981 after botching a jump, only to later be found in the beer tent downing a pint. Throughout the play, Byron amazes his youthful entourage with narratives of his mythological exploits: two of his most memorable stories are that his mother was a virgin when she bore him, and that he once met a giant on the A14 who claimed to have built Stonehenge. The point of such narratives is not whether or not they are true, but that they accord to Byron the status of myth and legend, a person composed of the tall tales he tells and others tell about him: 'What did King Arthur ever do to top that?' a credulous youth remarks of Byron's reported resurrection (32).

The risk of such a portrayal is the possibility of a shallow and insubstantial heroization of the play's protagonist, and to offset this aspect of the story, Byron himself is portrayed not simply as a living legend but also as a self-destructive drunk and a painfully embarrassing failure as a husband and father, as we learn in the second act when his ex-wife and six-year-old son pay him a visit. At the same time, Butterworth also balances the valorization of locality with the narrow-minded chauvinism that comes hand in hand with it. While lamenting the decline in local news coverage on the BBC, the gang of teens point out that they can only care about terrible events that happen nearby: they couldn't care less about victims of violence in Wales. 'Show me a good house fire in Salisbury. Now *that's* tragic,' one remarks (60). Yet while most of the group are determined never to travel beyond their narrow confines, one amongst them, Lee Piper, is about to escape to Australia, and his departure constitutes a significant subplot as his friends quiz him about his incomprehensible motivations for leaving Flintock. Their befuddlement demonstrates their ultimate spiritual impoverishment, and reveals their non-stop ingestion of speed, ecstasy, and cocaine as, finally, symptoms of an emptiness of working-class experience rather than an embracing of vitality and the expression of a life force. The depressed economic class of the characters that embody the play's heart are key to its political timeliness, essential to the material groundedness of a drama that might otherwise risk a flight into escapist celebrations of antique images of Englishness. Byron and his entourage are society's abject, the first to be scapegoated during the bad economic times emerging in the wake of the global financial crisis that began in 2007 and as of 2012 shows no sign of ending,[5] and the image of a man living in a local forest brings to mind contemporary images of unemployed immigrant workers living in tents in England's woods.

And so the play moves back and forth between enchantment and demystification, between mythological heroism and banal reality, particularly with reference to Byron himself, who impresses his gang of admirers by memorizing the answers to an entire set of *Trivial Pursuit* questions, trying to convince them that he is 'Fuckin' magic Johnny Byron. I got X-ray vision. I'm Spiderman, me' (78), when meanwhile the truth is less enchanting: 'How sad would I have to be to sit and learn every question of every card of the fucking Genus 2000 Edition of Trivial Pursuit?' he asks rhetorically, indirectly revealing that it is very sad indeed (76). This tenuous vacillation between marvel and mundanity is preface to the final lowering of Byron into the status of abject outsider. The arrival of a local man, Tony, searching for his missing stepdaughter, Phaedra, ushers in the murderous social ostracism that is the violent and bloody underside of the official town eviction notice. Tony signals a change in tone and focusses a new lens upon Byron:

> You deaf as well as daft? We'll bury the hatchet all right. Right in your fuckin' skull, pikey. You *did*. You *diddicoy* maggot. Living on a rubbish tip. Worzel Maggot. Stig of the Dump. Thinks he's the Pied Piper. You're the lowest piece of shit in this forest, mate. It's you and me now, you fucking snake. I will beat you into your grave. Into your grave, Gypsy. Now, one more time, cunt. Where's my daughter? (80)

For Tony, Byron's status as an outsider living in a caravan in a forest finds expression in terms like 'pikey,' a word used to describe pseudo-transient Anglo-Irish caravan-dwellers in England, or 'diddicoy,' a word used to describe British Romany of mixed blood. While it is Tony and his associates who eventually behave in the violent and anti-social manner associated with derogatory stereotypes like 'pikey,' *Jerusalem* does not so much reject the designation of Johnny Byron as 'the lowest piece of shit in the forest' as embrace it dramatically, rendering Byron a figure of debased satire as a passage to his elevation into a tragic figure. Tony tells a story of his two brothers finding Byron passed out in the woods, having urinated all over himself in his inebriated state. In turn, the brothers too urinated on Byron, on his clothes, his face, and in his mouth, while Davey, one of Byron's friends, filmed the degradation with a camera-phone and distributed the video to Byron's youthful entourage. Learning of this past betrayal, Byron, humiliated, goes into his caravan, and the teens are left to admit the shame of their treatment of him: they all laughed at him, 'but it's not funny, is it' (83). The laughter at the scapegoat, while it is laughter, is not the laughter of comedy.

From out of this isolation of Byron from his former friends and surroundings, the play generates a powerfully self-aware fantasy of tragic experience. Byron is described at various times in the play as a troll, an ogre, Stig of the Dump; the Pied Piper, a magician, Spiderman, Supertramp, and, indirectly, as a knight who saved the children of a town from the menace of a dragon (83–4). The original promotional imagery for the Royal Court portrays a stylized image of a Green Man, mythological figure of fertility and rebirth. Twice in the play Byron levels his gaze at others and asks them to look deeply into his eyes and tell him what they see: the implication is that '[w]ritten there is old words that will shake you. Shake you down' (49). While constantly portraying Byron as a tale-teller, the play also seduces the audience with the potential that he is nevertheless a shaman who guards something precious in this wood. At the end of the second act, it is revealed that Phaedra, the missing girl, is being harboured in his caravan by Byron, who is protecting her specifically from her stepfather, whom Byron suggests has malign sexual designs upon the fifteen-year-old.

Phaedra has spent the entire play dressed in her homemade fairy outfit, lurking at the edges of the action. Her scene with Byron near the play's conclusion constitutes a solid, burning emotional core against which the cynicism, satire, and humour of the play dissolves. Despite the fact that she is in hiding, Phaedra is about to conclude her year as the Flintock Fair May Queen, and this maturing awareness on her part is conflated with a fall from innocence into experience that collides meaningfully with Byron's looming eviction from the wood, and the associated implication that all that is connoted by this green space will too be destroyed. The scene between Byron and Phaedra, masterfully directed by Ian Rickson, figures Byron as a weary and beleaguered knight and Phaedra as his fearsome Queen in the midst of an enchanted forest that is now passing from the mortal world. The desperate, heartfelt, and prolonged embrace between Byron and Phaedra, performed on stage but not described in the script, communicated the subtext of the moment clearly: Byron's desire to protect her from her brute reality, to stop time and maintain her youth, and the futility of these desires were all evoked by the embrace. This embrace was broken by the arrival of Tony and his brothers, armed with a blowtorch and a branding iron, serving as the figurative dragon from which Byron would protect Phaedra.

The lyricism of the scene between Byron and Phaedra is inverted into the violent purging of the liminal excess. Byron is brutally assaulted by Tony and his brothers, who leave Byron a bloody mass of gore, broken teeth, and brand-marks; a pariah. The shock value of this moment, when Byron emerges from his trailer following the assault, practically unrecognizable under a vivid coating of blood and in a state denoting permanent physical damage if not impending death, is certainly as much an in-yer-face moment as anything produced by the young generation of playwrights in the 1990s. But it is precisely here that the play rejects the idea that this is a shock effect, a symptom of modern theatre or of postmodern cynicism. In the image of the bloody, broken man, rendered most visibly untouchable and tangibly taboo, the play finds not only its most meaningful image but also its most forceful assertion of the idea of meaningful-ness itself. In his moment of his most abject debasement, Byron is suddenly confronted by his six-year-old son, Marky, and he tells the boy a secret that is in fact a birthright: the blood Marky sees on his father is rare and valuable blood. After his legendary motorcycle crash, Byron explains, the doctors at the hospi-tal discovered that Byron has a rare blood type due to the Romany blood in his heritage, and when Byron goes to donate blood they pay him very well for it and treat him 'like a king' (107). He can smoke and drink in the waiting room and they cannot touch him because, quite simply, they need him (107).

A king with holy blood in his veins, Byron becomes, in these final moments of the play, a purely taboo figure, sacred and profane at the same time. He is also an embodiment of the ideal of the Englishman on the first of May, whose tradi-tional duty, we learn earlier, is 'to be free from constraint. [It is a] time to com-mune with flora and the fauna of this enchanted isle. To abandon oneself to the rhythms of the earth' (52). It is such a wisdom that Byron offers to Marky: 'Don't listen to no one and nothing but what your own heart bids. Lie. Cheat. Steal. Fight to the death' (107). What Byron offers to his son and what he him-self embodies is the fleeting phantasy of unalienated existence, true to itself and not blemished by bad faith, at one with its surroundings and at home in the universe. Yet importantly, this image must be embodied by a man rendered purely untouchable and taboo: ironically, there is no place in this universe for the man fully at home in the world.

The final moment of the play brings home the potency of this phantasy, as Byron's tall tales bear fruit. As the police bear down upon his camper, he calls down a curse upon the Kennet and Avon Council who have evicted him from the wood, and then this seemingly performative rhetorical bombast changes in tone as he begins to beat a large drum and starts to methodically calls out the names of his ancestors. The drum, we learned earlier, was given to him by the giant he met on the A14, who explained that if Byron ever needed help, he was to bang the drum and the giants would come. Accordingly, the long list Byron names gives way to 'Cormoran. Woden. Jack-of-Green. Jack-in-Irons,' and the names of other giants and Norse gods (109). In performance (though not in the published script), this incantation concluded with a moment of silence, and then the deafening pounding of enormous thudding footsteps and the final rustling of trees and leaves as a rising wind began to shake Rooster's Wood. This marvellously potent theatrical moment willfully denies the parameters of realistic consideration: the play ends there, and we will not know if giants will in fact come to fight the police for Byron. Our imaginations have been seduced into accepting the conceit that he is indeed a shaman, a knight, and a dragon-slayer: the moment when the ground thuds and the branches of trees begin to weave silently and then the leaves rustle on the branches is the moment of enchantment, of meaningfulness that the play has promised all along, but it is only accessible to us once the dramatic passage through debasement and shock has been travelled imaginatively.

Which returns us to a significant stylistic flourish with which the play opens, and which, retroactively, stands as *Jerusalem*'s metatheatrical comment upon the state of English theatre itself. The play opens with the fire curtain lowered, and painted with images of dragons, maidens, and a cross of St George. On the beam above the stage reads 'the English Stage Company,' gesturing consciously towards the Royal Court and its resident company. In front of this appears Phaedra in her fairy outfit, and she begins to sing Blake's hymn 'Jerusalem,' only to find herself disrupted by thumping modern trance music, growing louder and louder, until she flees in terror and the curtain rises to reveal a remarkably contemporary scene: Byron's camper at night, the scene of a raucous, deafeningly loud party. The opening montage of the play seems to gesture towards the passing away of traditional Englishness and its replacement by 'in-yer-face' theatre, a loud, sensory experience replicating on stage the cacophony and meaninglessness of modern life. The old gives way to the new. Yet by the play's conclusion this simple opposition has been overcome: the violence of 'in-yer-face' theatre, figured in Byron's bloody last stand, is the place that the traditional English values are actually being protected from the postmodern assault.

Thus *Jerusalem* describes the possibility of building a holy land within present-day England rather than in an antique past, just as Blake's hymn begins with the question of whether Christ walked in England in ancient time but concludes with the promise to build the Holy City in the present. Alternately, a less evident and more subtextual reading of the play's title is possible if we relate it not to the popular, though technically untitled, hymn but instead to the actual epic poem Blake titled *Jerusalem the Emanation of the Giant Albion*, in which the Giant Albion stands for Britain and Humanity. The poem describes, among other things, the fall of Albion, and this grants another resonance to the fact that it is 'Brutus of Albion' who is the final giant Byron names in his incantation (109). The rustling of the leaves and the thumping of giant footsteps then herald the return of Britain and Humanity to the world. The sacred in *Jerusalem* lies not in the past, the future, or the outside of material existence, but at the very heart of it, in the moment of historicized humanity.

Byron's quiet act of heroism, his doomed attempt to protect a girl from her abusive stepfather, places *Jerusalem* within a dramatic discourse concerning the fate of English youth within an emotionally detached and uncaring society. The tragedies I have studied here seek to historicize the present as a means of rendering the present historical, which means viewing it as open-ended and incomplete. It is a small but crucial shift in understanding within tragic thought: from a flawed, fallen, decayed world, imperfect, despairing, and resentful, to an affirmative, future-oriented vision that celebrates this unfinished state of affairs. Tragedy is a representation of an alienated, fallen world that through this representation reveals alienation to be not a loss but rather the signs of difference, of the unfinished future. Perhaps it is Jez Butterworth's titular reminder to us of Blake's progressive hymn that captures this sentiment best: beginning with the question of Christ's fabled presence in England, and thus a lamentable absence lost to the past, the poem concludes instead with the promise to build Jerusalem within the present, not return to an antique fiction.

Notes

Introduction

1 Dominic Shellard's *British Theatre since the War* is an important recent corrective to this inadvertent historical myth. Another work of note includes Dan Rebellato's *1956 and All That*, which proposes a counter-narrative regarding the effect of *Look Back in Anger* on the London theatre scene. Similarly, Susan Bennett's 'A Commercial Success' investigates the historical occlusion of women's theatre by the success of *Look Back in Anger*. Alternately, Luc Gilleman, in 'From Coward and Rattigan to Osborne,' demonstrates the stylistic inheritance that Osborne's play owes to Noël Coward and Terrence Rattigan, playwrights who were overshadowed by Osborne's success.

2 See Philip Roberts, *The Royal Court Theatre and the Modern Stage* 56–7.

3 In *John Osborne, Vituperative Artist*, Luc Gilleman argues that Osborne is best understood as a tragedian with a philosophical investment in the beauty and value of the experience of loss. Osborne's early success was contingent upon a coincidence with his historical moment: 'The late fifties and early sixties were so congenial to Osborne because it was a period of transition when old structures were fast becoming useless while new ideas were not yet solidified into stifling conventions.' This moment was suitable to Osborne's tragic universe, where '[t]he sun is always setting or rising' (195). In an analysis of Osborne's 1972 *A Sense of Detachment*, Gilleman argues persuasively that this strange, self-destructive piece of metatheatre embodies Osborne's 'tragic conception of theatre' (178) as a representation whose purpose 'is to demonstrate its own necessary failure' and allow an audience to 'experience loss' (183). It is not as content that theatre is most effectively tragic but as form, and Gilleman extends this consideration to the tragic aesthetics of Osborne's own life (197).

4 Orr, writing at the end of the 1970s, engages in a largely frustrated, and to my mind myopic, search for post-war English tragedy. His approach is a useful contrast to my own. Like George Steiner, Orr begins with an ideal concept of tragedy and then

finds that all actual instances of tragedy fall short. Arnold Wesker's trilogy of working-class social realist plays are explored for their dramatization of 'a painful kind of loss over the space of two generations' (251), yet are finally deemed to be social realist rejections of the tragic (253), while David Rudkin's *Afore Night Come* (1962) and Harold Pinter's *The Caretaker* (1960) display 'a minimal sense of the tragic' (253). Pinter, in particular, serves Orr as an elegiac symbol of the death of tragedy: 'The effect is to see tragedy through a glass darkly aided by many of the familiar props of the traditional English drama, and to feel once one has seen it, that the real experience of tragedy is no longer accessible' (254). He concludes his study with a suggestion that Christopher Hampton's *Savages* (1973) hints at new directions: a link between tragic drama and Brechtian Epic techniques (262). Here, I am interested in a more capacious sense of the tragic, one that allows plays themselves, rather than abstract theory, to articulate the nature of tragic experience.

5 See Luc Gilleman (2007) for a recent analysis of the play that highlights how *Saved* challenged its audience by refusing to provide traditional explanations for character behaviour, and in a manner akin to Pinter and Strindberg uses 'linguistic opacity' to undercut traditional conventions of realism ('"Juss Round an' Round"' 55).

6 See Roberts, *About Churchill* for Churchill's account of how the piece was solicited and her underlying motivations (xxv–xxvii).

7 See, for instance, Howard Barker's recent comment that '[i]f I hadn't entered the Royal Court in the 1970s and encountered so much middle-class Marxist theatre, I probably would never have moved so violently towards tragedy and tragedy's ambiguity' ('Art Is About Going into the Dark' 197).

8 See chapters 2 and 3 of Stanton B. Garner Jr's study of Griffiths for a resonant and evocative discussion of the failure of the 1960s, in particular Griffiths's sense by 1970 that the revolutionary moment was a failure (49). See also Howard Brenton's more optimistic assessment: 'May '68 disinherited my generation in two ways. First, it destroyed any remaining affection for the official culture. [...] But it also, secondly, destroyed the notions of personal freedom, freak out and drug culture, anarchist notions of spontaneous freedom, anarchist political action. And it failed. It was defeated. A generation dreaming of a beautiful utopia was kicked – kicked awake and not dead. I've got to believe not kicked dead' ('Petrol Bombs' 20).

9 For an erudite and lucid study of the influence of Brecht and the Berliner Ensemble on British theatre (and particularly the Royal Court) in the 1950s and 1960s, see Janelle Reinelt's *After Brecht* (5–16). While scholars have frequently been comfortable associating political playwrights with Brecht, the writers themselves, particularly in the 1970s, have commonly distanced themselves from Brechtian theatre. See, for instance, Brenton's 1975 comments in interview: 'I'm anti-Brechtian, a Left anti-Brechtian. I think his plays are museum pieces now and are messing up a lot of young theatre workers' ('Petrol Bombs' 14). Brenton would shortly go on to

adapt Brecht's *Life of Galileo* for the National Theatre. Bond's self-distancing from Brecht, while more measured and thought out, remains a constant refrain for him. For Bond's attitude in the late 1970s, see 'On Brecht: A Letter to Peter Holland.' For a recent analysis of Bond's critical distance from Brecht, see Kate Katafiasz, 'Alienation Is the "Theatre of Auschwitz."'

10 For an analysis of the relationship between the tragic ideology and the tragic within Brecht's theatre, see my *Brecht and Critical Theory: Dialectics and Contemporary Aesthetics* (152–84).

11 For an excellent overview, see Hugh Grady, 'Tragedy and Marxist Thought.'

12 See also Charles Segal's lucid discussion of this dialectical aspect of Greek tragedy and the Oedipus narrative in *Oedipus Tyrannus: Tragic Heroism and the Limits of Knowledge*, particularly ch. 6 (53–70).

13 It is much like Northrop Frye's 'order of words,' a zone that dramas like Shakespeare's *The Tempest* seem to approach, in Frye's estimation. Frye borrows the phrase 'the order of words' from T.S. Eliot (*Anatomy of Criticism* 117).

14 In contrast, Orr argues forcefully that Eugene O'Neill's *Long Day's Journey into Night* occupies a zone 'of darkness more intense and resounding than anything Beckett subsequently created […]. The night of O'Neill's play is the darkness of the twentieth century fully brought to light' (205).

1. David Hare: The Work of Mourning, or, The Agony and the Ecstasy of the Bourgeoisie

1 The irony of Hare's usage of the term should be noted. Bertolt Brecht coined the concept of the 'Learning Play' to describe his didactic Marxist-Leninist plays for revolutionary workers in the early 1930s (see *Brecht on Theatre* 79–80). Hare's point is that *The Year of Magical Thinking* is confrontational and didactic in its assertion of the tragic aspects of the human, as formed around loss, grief, and the contradictions of the self.

2 Director Richard Eyre praises Hare's 'attempt to speak to the much-derided middle-class audience' (qtd in Boon, *About Hare* 226). Carol Homden's study of Hare asserts that 'David Hare understands to this day that the English middle classes do not speak their feelings' (200). She argues that the development of his work moves away from class-conscious political theatre and towards the articulation of 'middle-class liberal values born of man's humanity' (179). Homden's study also appears to endorse these values. More anecdotally, I recall a public Q and A about Gregory Burke's *Black Watch* at the New Zealand International Arts Festival in Wellington in March 2008, in which the director, John Tiffany, explained that *Black Watch*'s writer character was modelled on David Hare, a 'very middle-class playwright.' This derisive comment provoked knowing laughter from the very middle-class New Zealand audience.

3 See Tony Bicât's short memoir, 'Portable Theatre,' for a lucid description of Hare's early development. Richard Boon's 'Keeping Turning Up' provides a complementary critical analysis of the Portable Theatre's unique contribution to political theatre in England, as well as Hare's gradual move to the mainstream London theatre institutions.

4 Carol Homden's study of Hare serves as a productive contrast to my own approach. Like me, Homden tracks a tragic genealogy from *Teeth 'n' Smiles* through *Plenty* and finds its full culmination in *The Secret Rapture*. However, we differ significantly in our approaches to the tragic. Homden's is firmly Aristotelian in its terminology, for instance referencing a character's 'fatal flaw' (175) and asserting that Hare's tragic characters are 'heroic' in their individualistic stances (18). While Homden's study pays significant attention to issues of class in Hare's work, it also endorses an uninterrogated valorization of his protagonists as moral models of 'meaningful action' (18).

5 The lecture was Hare's first and was published as the introduction to *The Early Plays*. It has been reprinted as 'The Play is in the Air' in Hare's collected lectures, *Obedience, Struggle and Revolt*.

6 Hare discusses the poor reception of this talk in interview with Hersh Zeifman (Hare, 'An Interview with David Hare' 19–20).

7 In his review of the initial production, Michael Billington found strong parallels between *Teeth 'n' Smiles* and John Osborne's *The Entertainer* (1957) (see Page, *File on Hare* 35). While *The Entertainer* uses the backdrop of the Suez Crisis as an elegy for Empire, Hare uses the end of the 1960s as an elegy for the post-war dream. It is worth noting that the anger of Hare's protagonists against the complacency of English middle-class life recalls John Osborne's work in general, and particularly the railing frustration of Jimmy Porter in *Look Back in Anger* (1956). John Deeney notes Hare's admiration of and desire to emulate Osborne's impact (430). Hare himself observes his increasing identification with Osborne (Boon, *About Hare* 164–5). Finlay Donesky situates Hare in the tradition of Osborne's drama of angry protest. However, Donesky also argues that this emphasis on emotions rather than social analysis is a flaw in Hare's work, resulting in 'an absence of alternative principles and values undergirding the emotion' (13).

8 Hersh Zeifman discusses how 'Hare's deliberate evenhandedness [...] has infuriated ideologues from both the Left and the Right' and notes in particular how *Plenty* 'managed to outrage a large portion of its audiences' (Zeifman, Introduction xiii).

9 'I stopped admiring the woman. I really wanted to pummel her. I would come to the middle of the second act, and I would just withdraw my consent from that woman. I don't think the audience ever knew, but I was very worried about it' (Kate Nelligan, qtd in Page, *File on Hare* 44). In an assessment of Hare's 'Virtuous

Women,' Anne Nothof notes some of the vitriolic criticism leveled against Hare's women protagonists as so-called 'plaster saints' (186).

10 'Selfishness is not living as one wishes to live, it is asking others to live as one wishes to live. And unselfishness is letting other people's lives alone, not interfering with them. Selfishness always aims at creating around it an absolute uniformity of type. Unselfishness recognises infinite variety of type as a delightful thing, accepts it, acquiesces in it, enjoys it' ('The Soul of Man under Socialism' 1194–5). Hare's familiarity with this material can be surmised from the fact that he named his play *A Map of the World* after a quotation from Wilde's essay.

11 See, for instance, Lacan's *The Seminar Book VII*: 'My egoism is quite content with a certain altruism, altruism of the kind that is situated on the level of the useful. […] It is a fact of experience that what I want is the good of others in the image of my own. That doesn't cost so much. What I want is the good of others provided it remain in the image of my own' (187).

12 This aspect of *Plenty* becomes a point of criticism for Donesky later in his study: 'In these last scenes the most naked individuality is yoked to a public morality at its most abstract and general. No intermediate levels of solidarity exist between Susan and her soaring national ideals' (149). Individualistic morality is, for Donesky, a holdover of the post-war consensus itself, which he assesses as an individualistic 'moral idealism' based solely on nationalistic forms of solidarity, to the exclusion of other forms of collective activism (148–9). He also suggests that Hare is nostalgic for this consensus because of 'the undemocratic, hierarchical, nonparticipatory way the postwar consensus was sustained almost from its inception. The consensus as administered encouraged individualistic support of collective ideals and thus sowed the seeds for Hare's inwards-turning solution' (147).

13 Lib Taylor explores Hare's response to Thatcherism and discusses how in the 1980s, '[t]he tradition of epic dramas which dissected the condition of Britain, so prevalent in the 1970s, was subdued in a theatre either too timid or too financially insecure to challenge the prevailing climate' (49). Taylor argues that *The Secret Rapture* is 'Hare's most direct theatrical response to Thatcherism to date' and that the play 'does mourn the passing of a gentler, more caring society,' thus suggesting that Isobel does represent traditional English values (57). In contrast, Finlay Donesky is critical of this criticism of Thatcherism. He argues that Isobel represents Hare's 'retreat to the soul' (150) and is Hare's nostalgic attempt to revitalize the moral values associated with the post-war consensus as a means of countering Thatcherism. Donesky criticizes such liberal posturing: 'Like Hare, these people, who tend to gravitate to the center of British political and cultural life, invested heavily in the egalitarian reformist ideals of the consensus while remaining largely oblivious to the elitist, undemocratic, paternalistic manner in which such ideals were administered' (150). While Donesky finds Isobel to be a nostalgic figure for

liberal, middle-class English values, my argument suggests that she is an affront to Englishness itself.

14 'It is an unfashionable play in that it is a tragedy. We don't have many plays with heroines or many tragedies in England at the moment. It is commonly said that it's not possible to write a tragedy nowadays and I was interested to see whether it was' (Hare, qtd in Page, *File on Hare* 75; see also Boon, *About Hare* 121).

15 See Carol Homden (173–4) for Isobel's fatal flaw. Homden, in an Aristotelian mode, suggests that Hare seeks to offer his audience an emotional experience through Isobel's tragedy: 'The true source of salvation is tragedy – not so much the pure form and order of art itself, but the emotion which it generates. In *The Secret Rapture* that emotion is one of pity and fear' (180). It is ultimately a diagnosis of Hare's late-1980s playwriting as post-political and concerned with 'the eternal situation' (180). John S. Su sees Isobel as a moral role model: 'Isobel's actions have good ramifications because she herself becomes a nostalgic figure, her sacrifice a guiding principle for others' (34).

16 See *The Seminar Book VII*, in particular pp. 247–83.

17 In performance, director Howard Davies decided to have Isobel appear in a ghost-like manner at her sister's side. Su is certainly correct is pointing out that this eliminates the play's ambiguities (35). I would add that it crassly literalizes and undercuts what Marion's dialogue achieves with understated finesse: the tragic opening of the Tory self to the experience of mortality.

18 Finlay Donesky's assessment of Kyra is an illustrative example of frustration with the character: 'Although she earns very little money and lives in a shabby apart-ment, Kyra brims over with confidence, happiness, vocational purpose, and a sense of personal worth' (193). In contrast, Tom, financially successful, 'is a hollow man plagued with guilt and low self-esteem' (193). Donesky finds this situation implausible and accordingly interprets Kyra's spiritual serenity and self-possession as symbolic of cultural privilege and elitism, '[l]ike the undemocratic viruses that infect the intestinal workings of the British state and society' (193). Meanwhile her antagonist, Tom, represents commerce, long tolerated as a necessary evil by the English ruling classes. Donesky's analysis is an intriguing coding of the play as a conflict between the traditional values of the upper class and the upward-mobility of the working and lower middle classes in England. It ultimately holds the play accountable for a disingenuous, nostalgic investment in the ruling caste. In other words, Kyra is a spiritual aristocrat with 'the right breeding' (191). This interpretation is based on a reading of their class backgrounds rather than their current class situations (Kyra is from the middle class, Tom from the working class), a rejection of the terms in which Kyra describes her commitment as a teacher (which Donesky criticizes for having 'no institutional or structural dimension' [192]) and a lack of engagement with Tom's subtextual action of mourning in the drama.

19 *Ressentiment* is the concept developed by Nietzsche to describe inauthentic consciousness and actions, grounded on hypocritical envy and loathing of others rather than
upon affirmation of the self. It is reactive rather than active existence, a form of
consciousness based upon negativity. *Ressentiment's* key assumption is to first figure
the other as 'evil' so that one can then describe oneself as 'good.' In other words, by first
finding an other to vilify, *ressentiment* can then allow one to valorize one's own being
in contrast to this other (see *On the Genealogy of Morals*, 39).

20 Lacan makes a similar comment with reference to Antigone's insistence on burying
Polynices: 'One cannot finish off someone who is a man as if he were a dog. [...]
[I]t can be seen that Antigone's position represents the radical limit that affirms the
unique value of his being without reference to any content, to whatever good or
evil Polynices may have done' (*The Seminar Book VII* 279).

21 See Judith Butler's *The Psychic Life of Power* for a discussion of how the heterosexual ego is predicated upon the disavowal of homosexual attachment: '[T]he
man who insists upon the coherence of his heterosexuality will claim that he never
loved another man, and hence never lost another man' (139). Butler calls this
disavowal of loss 'ungrieved homosexual cathexis' (139) and politicizes this psychic
action by relating it to the cultural refusal to grieve those lost to the ravages of
AIDS in America (138).

22 The published script refers to a haemorrhage, but this detail was cut from the
original production (121).

23 See Liorah Anne Golomb for a reading of the play as Christian allegory. In
contrast, see John S. Su, who rejects readings of *The Secret Rapture* that argue it is
a Christian allegory (37), and insists that it is an open-ended questioning of ethics
and whether or not personal morality can offer political solutions (35). Carol
Homden also argues that 'Isobel is neither a Christian nor a Christ figure and in
her death she does not so much absolve the family and the audience of sin or guilt
but charge [*sic*] them with it' (178).

2. Howard Barker: Will and Desire – From the Tragedy of Socialism to the Ecstasy of the Unconscious

1 See Rabey, *Howard Barker: Politics and Desire* (254–86) and *Howard Barker:
Ecstasy and Death* (254–60) for appraisals by actors who have performed Barker's
plays and worked with him as director. See *Howard Barker: Ecstasy and Death*
(33–5) for a discussion of Barker's gradual ostracism from the English theatre
establishment in the 1980s and the creation of The Wrestling School, a theatre
company dedicated to performing Barker's texts alone. See Barker's *Arguments*
(32–7) for his own description of this systematic ostracism.

2 'They have this act, this thing called the Defence of the Realm Act and it means
they can shut papers down and stick the editors in gaol, all right? It's very like what

Hitler's got. Only they had it long before Hitler. And it means we can end up in a concentration camp. And they had that long before Hitler, too' (Barker, *No End of Blame* 35).

3   Rabey observes that Barker, in his recent manifesto *Death, the One and the Art of Theatre*, seems to prefer the term 'tragic' over the 'catastrophic' (*Howard Barker: Ecstasy and Death* 27).

4   In an insightful study of the concept of tragedy in Adorno's work, Karoline Gritzner similarly situates Barker in relation to Adorno's 'late capitalist' thought: 'The argument shared by both Adorno and Barker is that individual experience in late capitalist culture has become dangerously diminished – this constitutes tragic experience today. [...] [Barker's] work is therefore a contemporary example of Adorno's call for a changed, post-metaphysical form of tragedy that neither lays an affirmative claim on the construction of positive meaning through art (by suggesting the possibility of reconciliation or redemption), nor abnegates the possibility of the impossible' ('Adorno on Tragedy' 47).

5   See Karoline Gritzner's excellent 2006 essay on Barker's theatre ('Towards an Aesthetic of the Sublime'), which, while arguing for the relevance of the theory of the sublime in relation to Barker's aesthetic, in fact also draws upon modernist theory (Adorno, Lacan) in grounding her argument. Similarly, Liz Tomlin's thoughtful 2006 essay on Romantic tragedy in Barker draws upon Nietzschean theories of the *Übermensch* to describe characters whose acts of will 'reclaim and reconstitute the divine' ('A New Tremendous Aristocracy' 114). Both essays operate upon premises fundamentally akin to mine, though I am resistant to heroic Romanticism or to sublime transcendence, which I see as finally foreign to Barker's aesthetic, and I thus suggest the idea of the unconscious as a translation of the idea of the Absolute or transcendent.

6   David Ian Rabey suggests that it was with *Victory* (1983) that Barker made a substantial break from his 1970s aesthetic, and with *The Bite of the Night* (1988) that Barker manifested a full example of the Theatre of Catastrophe. Rabey, 'Raising Hell' 15.

7   Heiner Müller's *Mauser* is the most articulate exploration of this gap between immediate dehumanizing killing and the long-term goals of revolutionary activity.

8   Barker comments on this final moment: 'The will to be whole, and perhaps more than whole, is discovered in opposition to collective sentiment. Dramatically, the technique for summoning the will for this act of persistent rupture consists in constant self-description, the exhortation which found its first expression in a rudimentary form in Billy McPhee's last words in *That Good Between Us*' (*Arguments* 194).

9   I capitalize the word 'History' to reflect how Barker himself capitalizes it in his plays (albeit inconsistently) as a means of highlighting the philosophical concept

of History as a grand narrative of progress. See also the discussion of *The Europeans* below.

10 See *The Love of a Good Man* for the articulation of the idea that 'God likes pain' (54).

11 Barker describes her as 'an atrocity addict, [...] not easily prised open by psychological or political interpretation. She is a self-invention of the historical moment, absurd and yet powerfully evocative of wrong-rightness' (*Arguments* 200).

12 'The Play for an age of fracture is itself fractured, and hard to hold, as a broken bottle is hard to hold. It is without a message. (Who trusts the message-giver any more?) But not without meaning. It is the audience who constructs the meaning. The audience experiences the play individually and not collectively. It is not led, but makes its own way through a play whose effects are cumulative. The restoration of dignity to the audience begins when the text and production accept ambiguity. If it is prepared, the audience will not struggle for permanent coherence, which is associated with the narrative of naturalism, but experience the play moment by moment, truth by truth, contradiction by contradiction' (*Arguments* 38).

13 'As Adorno wrote of the great nineteenth-century novels, whose ambition the theatre must imitate if it is not to be made yet more tolerable and yet more brief, it derives its meaning precisely from the dissolution of coherent meaning' (*Arguments* 53).

14 It is only when he restaged and revised *Man Equals Man* that Brecht began to criticize Galy Gay and reconsider him as the dehumanized weapon of fascism and the ideal soldier. See *Brecht on Theatre* (18–19) for Brecht's praise of Galy Gay as a new human type whose strength comes from surrendering his ego.

15 See Nietzsche, *On the Genealogy of Morals* (94).

16 See Irigaray, 'The Eternal Irony of the Community' and Butler, *Antigone's Claim*, particularly the essay 'Promiscuous Obedience' (57–82).

17 Nietzsche's full exploration of the concept of cruelty is found in *On the Genealogy of Morals*, while Artaud's is in the essays collected in *The Theatre and Its Double*.

18 The women's movement-driven, anti-nuclear Greenham Common protests of the 1980s are the historical event with which *The Castle*'s feminist utopia echoes most forcibly. Barker acknowledges this influence and explains that his wife was involved in these events ('Articulate Explorers' 39).

19 On the subject of nuclear disarmament in the 1980s, Barker's most forceful, direct, and unambiguous statement is found in *A Passion in Six Days: The Curse of Debate* (1983), in which an octogenarian Labour peer, Lord Isted, who was imprisoned as a pacifist in 1916, gives a merciless and impassioned speech to his juniors explaining that disarmament is not an optional party policy but an inarguable aspect of the Labour party's identity. Nuclear capabilities have made human freedom obsolete, he explains: none of them have the right to be alive. They are

enslaved, freedom meaningless, when nuclear extinction mocks the idea of the future. Once, an individual might die but his neighbour would survive. A slave might have a chance. This nuclear slavery 'mocks this democracy! It laughs in the face of your so-called choice!' The possibility of total extinction robs humanity of the 'endless chain which is the greatest comfort of mortality' (49). This speech is an indication that Barker is perfectly capable of making a direct political statement when such didacticism is imperative.

20 My sense that there is a fundamental affinity between *Übermensch* and Antichrist in Nietzsche's thought arises from the Second Essay in *On the Genealogy of Morals*: 'This man of the future, who will redeem us […] from […] the great nausea, the will to nothingness, nihilism; […] this Antichrist and antinihilist; this victor over God and nothingness' (96). Nietzsche then defers this prophecy to Zarathustra, his fictional prophet of the *Übermensch*, in the following, final paragraph of the essay.

21 David Barnett ('Howard Barker: Polemical Theory and Dramatic Practice') gives a very detailed and insightful analysis of Barker's Nietzschean rhetoric and analyses *The Europeans* in these terms, but, as I mentioned earlier, also suggests that Barker's emphasis on these philosophical ideas is uninterrogated and reminiscent of 'bourgeois individualism of the nineteenth century' (463). Barnett is ultimately critical of Barker's polemical assertion of the need for, as Barnett sees it, 'authentic' individuality and suggests that Barker 'fails to problematize the sovereign indi-vidual subject' (462). However, he then argues that *The Europeans* is somewhat less polemical and more open to interpretation than Barker's essays are (465). Barnett also proposes that the play's ambiguity is specifically due to the element of self-performance that the characters engage in, which leaves the question of authenticity of character open to debate. As is evident from my analysis I am in accord with this reading; however, my interpretation of *The Europeans* is otherwise at odds with Barnett's. For instance, his emphasis on Starhemberg's 'tragic seriousness' (467) overlooks the comical situations into which his self-performance brings him, and I disagree with Barnett's estimation that Leopold's laughter in the play is a 'protection from the pain and cruelty of existence' (466). In Barnett's reading, the psychological motivations of Barker's characters are withheld but hint at the possibility of authentic selfhood. In my analysis, Barker's characters are beyond authenticity altogether.

22 'I believe like Barker that Tragedy is the dramatic form for our times and subscribe to Nietzsche's aphorism: "the tragic artist is not a pessimist. He says Yes to every thing questionable and terrible"' (qtd in Rabey, *Howard Barker: Politics and Desire* 286).

23 Rabey compares *The Possibilities* to Brecht's *Lehrstücke* briefly, and suggests they may be called 'discord pieces' rather than Learning Plays (*Howard Barker: Politics*

and Desire 246). I suggest that *The Possibilities* is very much in keeping with the contradictory spirit of the Learning Plays, rather than the letter of Brecht's texts.

24 Rabey describes Barker's state of ecstasy as 'the most intensively convulsive drama of the body and the self experienced between life and death, where rapture mingles with ordeal, involving the possible sense of disintegration from a former bodily centre and sensory relocation in other constituent parts, perhaps involving the sense of being outside oneself, looking in' (*Howard Barker: Ecstasy and Death* 15).

25 The stylistic effect of these breathless, run-on sentences as embodiments of unconscious desire resembles Lacan's theory of the invocatory drive (the partial drive that Lacan suggests in Seminar XI is closest to the symbolic register of consciousness): 'At the scopic level, we are no longer at the level of demand, but of desire, of the desire of the Other. It is the same at the level of the invocatory drive, which is the closest to the experience of the unconscious.' Lacan, *The Seminar Book XI* 104.

26 See *The Seminar Book VII*, where Lacan describes extimacy as 'intimate exteriority' (139).

27 Bruce Fink suggests a connection between the word 'ecstasy' and the word 'extimate' to describe how unconscious desire, or as he puts it, 'Other jouissance,' is unrepresentable and 'outside' the symbolic order (*The Lacanian Subject* 122).

28 '[T]he true formula of atheism is *God is unconscious*' (Lacan, *The Seminar Book XI* 59).

29 David Ian Rabey writes that 'Loftus's fall can appear conventionally tragic, like that of an over-reaching protagonist in a Marlowe play which (at least nominally) restores order by punishing the would-be superhuman' (*Howard Barker: Ecstasy and Death* 185).

30 'I think of anxiety in my theatre as a state quite different to fear … rather it is a troubling of the fixed strata of moral conventions … a sort of low quaking that threatens the foundations of the stable personality … the public doesn't quite know where to place its feet, there is an insecurity, but one which is simultaneously exhilarating' (Rabey and Gritzner, 'Howard Barker in Conversation' 34).

3. Edward Bond: Tragedy and Postmodernity, or, The Promethean Impulse

1 Nothing more is known of this text, written around 1957, but it is mentioned by both Mangan (4) and Hay and Roberts (301).

2 One of Barker's earliest staged plays is called *No One Was Saved* (1970), written as a satiric, critical response to Bond's representation of working-class life in *Saved* (1965). See Rabey, *Howard Barker: Politics and Desire* (20–2).

3 This image of broader and broader horizons of interpretation is borrowed from Fredric Jameson's *The Political Unconscious*. Jameson, in turn, has adapted the idea from Northrop Frye's *Anatomy of Criticism*.

4 At the same time, we can observe that there is a simulacrum of an historical movement in the logic of this book: from realism, to expressionism, to orthodox political formalism, to identity politics (chapter 4), and finally fin-de-siècle malaise (chapter 5).

5 Michael Mangan describes Bond's estrangement from the Royal Court (30–2), gives a good account of Peter Hall's uneasiness with Bond's politics during the rehearsal of the 1980 Royal National Theatre production of *The Woman*, and describes Bond's alienation from this theatrical institution (61–4).

6 The recent essay collection *Edward Bond and the Dramatic Child* (ed. David Davis) is focused specifically upon Bond's work with Theatre in Education since he turned his back on the professional English theatre at the end of the 1980s, and contains a wealth of insight into the unique challenges of Bond's highly unorthodox dramaturgy. The book is particularly valuable for the insights provided by theatre practitioners such as Chris Cooper, who has staged Bond's plays with young actors and who demonstrates that Bond's theoretical ideas are in fact highly practical tools for realizing his plays onstage. In particular, the ideas of 'radical innocence' and the 'object-moment of the freedom-tragic,' two of Bond's concepts that are also of sustained interest in this chapter, are discussed at many points in *Edward Bond and the Dramatic Child*.

7 Spencer's approach, for instance, is most persuasive when she analyses more 'optimistic' plays, such as *The Woman*, which she studies as a response to and in some ways a corrective to *Lear*. Whereas *Lear* presents problems, *The Woman* presents solutions to problems, the result of a 'socialist vision of history' (96).

8 Georg Lukács gives an eloquent description of this concept of nature in Rousseau's bourgeois thought: 'nature becomes the repository of all these inner tendencies opposing the growth of mechanisation, dehumanisation and reification. Nature thereby acquires the meaning of what has grown organically, what was not created by man, in contrast to the artificial structures of human civilisation. But, at the same time, it can be understood as that aspect of human inwardness which has remained natural, or at least tends or longs to become natural once more. […] 'Nature' here refers to authentic humanity, the true essence of man liberated from the false, mechanising forms of society: man as a perfected whole who has inwardly overcome, or is in the process of overcoming, the dichotomies of theory and practice, reason and the senses, form and content; […] man for whom freedom and necessity are identical' (*History and Class Consciousness* 137).

9 In fact it is exactly as such a character that Spencer reads Shakespeare in *Bingo*. Spencer's interpretation is based on the estimation that his insights are disappointing and 'seem limited for a man of vision and cannot account for nor explain the social contradictions set up in the play. […] If it is Shakespeare's ego-centred and metaphoric reading of events which leads to suicide in lieu of progressive political

action, then we are confronted with the particular limits of Shakespeare's imagination' (50). Spencer, reading the play as social realism rather than tragedy, turns to the gardener's son as a possible model for political engagement, while acknowledging that his pointless murder of his own father and his subsequent compromises make him a deeply ambiguous character. My suggestion is that this is an interpretive pitfall resulting from the attempt to read the play as a political polemic on socialist activism. See also Bond's assessment: 'Shakespeare acts fraudulently but he doesn't deceive himself mentally, he judges himself. The Son does not. He, I think, accepts a series of false values, false beliefs, false attitudes. I think he lies' (qtd in Roberts, *Bond on File* 33).

10 A possible rebuttal of this interpretation comes from one of Bond's companion poems to the play, in which he suggests that Clare's historical obsession with a young woman he had loved early in his life was elemental in his destruction. 'Mary' is Clare's fantasized other wife and the subject of some of his later poetry. Bond writes in the poem 'Mary,' 'They took your wife / Now they will take your woman / You are a poet and should have known / You must imagine the real and not the illusion […] Clare, you created illusions / And they destroy poets' (*The Fool* 77–8). Yet to think this is some kind of accusation on Bond's part would be a misleadingly simplistic reading of the drama, one in which Clare's madness is demonstrated to be as much a question of social prejudice as it is to be found in the poverty that results in his physical and mental degeneration. Moreover, Bond's Clare indicates clearly that he knows the Mary he writes poetry to is a figure from his past, long gone (56). Nevertheless, this poetic fantasy is taken as an excuse to have him confined to an asylum.

11 See Hegel, *Aesthetics: Lectures on Fine Art*, 2:1158–1237. See particularly 1162–3, and 1195–6 and 1217–18 for Hegel's reading of *Antigone*.

12 Spencer notes the echoes of *Saved* in *The War Plays* and also records that this was a parallel observed by several theatre critics (226).

13 Ian Stuart gives an excellent account of the production history of *The War Plays*, in particular the fraught rehearsal process in the original Royal Shakespeare Company production and his estimation that the RSC had undermined the production through its decisions (139). He also compares the original production to a subsequent production in France in 1994 and praises the success of this latter production (142).

14 Yet Steiner cautions us against the imposition of this precept onto tragic drama in general: 'The tragic postulate, in this pure and defining expression, cannot, in any strict sense, be "lived,"' and moreover, 'the translation of the pure tragic axiom into a performative act is infrequent' ('Tragedy, Pure and Simple' 536–7). Singling out *The Bacchae* as a rare instance of 'absolute tragedy,' Steiner also observes that 'absolute "pure" tragedies, enactments or articulations of the death of hope, do,

in a sense, contradict or deconstruct themselves, just because they exist, because they are there for us to ponder or stage. [...] By virtue of its bare existentiality, the absolute tragic statement implies positive values of survivance, of formal beauty or innovation, of repeatability. In some ways, it cheats' (544).

15 See Adorno, 'Trying to Understand *Endgame*,' in *The Adorno Reader*.

16 *At the Inland Sea*, *Eleven Vests*, and *Have I None* are grouped together since they were written for Big Brum Theatre-in-Education, while *Coffee*, *The Crime of the Twenty-First Century*, *Born*, and *People* are grouped together and called the Colline tetralogy after the Théâtre Nationale de la Colline in Paris. Of note here is Bond's acknowledgment of these theatre companies as essential venues that give dramatically correct performances of his work.

17 For an in-depth interpretation of *Blasted* please see my article 'The Tragedy of History in Sarah Kane's *Blasted*' and the reading of *Blasted* in chapter 5 of this book.

18 Once more, it is hard to imagine that Bond has not been inspired by similar imagery of mutilation in Sarah Kane's *Blasted* (Ian's blinding by soldiers) and *Cleansed* (Carl, who loses first his hands and then his feet to Tinker).

4. Caryl Churchill: The Dionysian Möbius Strip

1 It has by now become *de rigueur* to quote a 1982 interview where Churchill describes the society she would like: 'decentralized, nonauthoritarian, communist, nonsexist.' See Reinelt, 'Caryl Churchill and the Politics of Style' (190) and Adiseshiah, *Churchill's Socialism* (1). This statement is frequently used as a means of explaining her plays.

2 A recent exception to this reticence on her part is her comments on *Drunk Enough to Say I Love You?*, which indicate clear frustration over the reading of the play as an allegory about Tony Blair and George W. Bush. However, the frustration seems to be directed at herself for not having anticipated this reading (see Introduction, *Plays: Four* ix).

3 This lack of a positive historical vision has resulted in one trend in Churchill scholarship, which argues against reading her as a socialist due to her avowed appropriation of some ideas from Michel Foucault's *Discipline and Punish* for her play *Softcops*. A Foucauldian reading is then imposed on other Churchill plays, despite the fact that Foucault has little general relevance to her oeuvre. See Jane Thomas ('The Plays of Caryl Churchill'), Dimple Godiwala (*Breaking the Bounds*) and Daniel Jernigan ('*Traps*, *Softcops*, *Blue Heart*, and *This Is a Chair*').

4 Churchill's use of the Möbius strip as an image of selfhood without alienation, outside of time and space, appears in *Traps*, to be discussed below. The Möbius strip is an impossible object, having only one surface but two sides when represented. The commonplace representation of a Möbius strip with a strip of paper is a

three-dimensional rendition of the mathematical abstraction. A Möbius strip proper is a single continuous plane with zero thickness, something that is impossible to achieve in a three-dimensional object. While a Möbius strip is impossible, its representation demonstrates an identity between time and space, and thus promises an escape from time, distance, difference, history, and alienation for the subject. It has been noted by a number of recent critics as a Churchillian intervention into subjectivity (Jernigan 27; Gobert 112; Diamond, 'Beckett and Caryl Churchill' 288). My interest in the Möbius strip is found in its Lacanian resonance. For Lacan, the Möbius strip was a useful image of the obverse side of the subject (thus unconscious desire) as merely the same side of the subject at a different point in space and time. See Lacan, *The Seminar Book XI* for Lacan's playful discussion of desire as illustrated by a Möbius strip: 'not to want to desire and to desire are the same thing' (235).

5 This image of Dionysus as an 'absent presence' is drawn from J.P. Vernant's reading of Euripides's *The Bacchae*, in which Vernant suggests that it is the player's smiling mask itself that is the image of the god in the play, and that the mask is thus the sign of 'the presence of a being that is not where it seems to be, a being that is also elsewhere, perhaps inside one, perhaps nowhere. It is the presence of one who is absent' ('The Masked Dionysus of Euripides' *Bacchae*' 383).

6 'Tell Her the Truth.' *The Nation*, 13 April 2009. 6 June 2012. http://www.thenation .com/article/tell-her-truth?page=0,1.

7 The word 'frightening' is discussed in Aston and Diamond, *The Cambridge Companion to Caryl Churchill* (2, 114, 127, 168), and recent scholars have noted that this is a recurrent refrain throughout Churchill's work. See, in particular, Rebellato 'On Churchill's Influences' (168).

8 In *The Dialogic Imagination*, Bakhtin theorizes that '[e]very concrete utterance of a speaking subject serves as a point where centrifugal as well as centripetal forces are brought to bear' (272). Centripetal force is the force of ideology, which seeks to unify sense in a monologic shape, while centrifugal force is the aspect of language that spins outwards from this ideological centre of gravity, seeking to disperse sense in multiplicity and openness of dialogue. This multiplicity is what Bakhtin calls 'dialogized heteroglossia, in which is embodied the centrifugal forces in the life of language' (273). Bakhtin sees these aspects of language at work in fiction with many diverse voices presented, much as is presented in *Seven Jewish Children*, where the play's only ideological monologue is surrounded by a multiplicity of dissenting voices.

9 'The notion of a "message" in art, even when politically radical, already contains an accommodation to the world: the stance of the lecturer conceals a clandestine entente with the listeners' (Adorno, 'Commitment' 193).

10 This openness and multiplicity of meaning may be extended further: I was struck by the strange resonances created by the premiere of *Seven Jewish Children* at the

Royal Court in February 2009. The play was performed each night after Marius von Mayenburg's *The Stone* (2009) and on the same stark white set. A staging decision presumably borne from necessity created inevitable and provocative resonances, since Mayenburg's play concerns three generations of a German family. The first generation displaces a Jewish family from its home before the Second World War and then concocts a lie claiming to have helped this family escape, a lie mythologized through transmission to successive generations into a narrative about the heroic patriarch's anti-Nazi resistance activities. Over the course of the drama we are shown the historical events that have been displaced by the family's fictions. It is this juxtaposition of Mayenburg's play with Churchill's that creates, more than anything in *Seven Jewish Children* itself, a provocative if unintentional echo between the treatment of Jews during World War Two and the treatment of Palestinians in the Occupied Territories.

11 The challenges of understanding *Traps* extend to interpretations of the conclusion of the play, but Kritzer (*The Plays of Caryl Churchill*) suggests that this final commune is affirmative and socially progressive (81). Jernigan also raises this interpretation as a possibility (33).

12 Gobert appears to be dialoguing with Elin Diamond's reading of this moment as a phenomenological sleight of hand. Diamond writes, 'The one-by-one bathing ritual injects, for the first time, an impression of temporality and focused space. [...] At this point the spectator might also insist that the illusionistic surface has cracked [...]. But of course this is just another sleight of hand. Our belief in an orificial non-illusionistic body is *produced* by a representational system' ('(In)visible Bodies in Churchill's Theatre' 192).

13 Such an insistence on the social context of *Englishness* in a reading of *Cloud Nine* helps us to avoid turning the play into a straw man to knock down. See, for example, Harding's critical assessment of *Cloud Nine*'s 'safe' representation of sexuality, a reading that must abstract the play from its ideological context and read it as primarily about gender and sexuality, rather than about gender and sexuality as couched within the framework of a nationalist consciousness, in order to make its point.

14 See Apollo Amoko's critical assessment of *Cloud Nine* for using the colonization of Africa as a metaphor and for excluding the literal representation of Africans in the play.

15 Kim Solga's critical review of a Canadian production of *Top Girls* in 2007 assumes that *Top Girls* is a Brechtian play, and in response to this production suggests that the play may be most productively performed as a hybrid of Brechtian *Verfremdungseffekte* and Stanislavskian realism within the actor's performances. It is an important indicator that character in *Top Girls* operates, in the final instance, within the parameters of realism.

16 The historical anachronism of the first scene is the play's most deliberate break from realism, but the scene itself is otherwise resolutely couched within the codes of realism: the characters have lunch and engage in a long series of self-revealing monologues. The focus is upon character revelation. Even the overlapping dialogue of the first act may ultimately be an assay at hyper-verisimilitude, the ultimate point of which was to offer the audience a novel theatrical 'special effect' within a cultural moment when the market was dictating the survival of theatres and companies. Finally, the multiple role playing in the play does not function as it does in *Cloud Nine* or *Light Shining in Buckinghamshire*; it is done for the sake of economy.

17 Alicia Tycer's study *Caryl Churchill's Top Girls* is a detailed, book-length study of the play, its performances, and its reception both with the public and with critics. See Tycer (64–5) for an overview of such readings of the play as anti-feminist.

18 Tycer surveys the academic scholarship on the dinner party scene and highlights the broad disagreement over the politics of the scene amongst, for instance, feminist critics (*Caryl Churchill's* Top Girls 63–5).

19 When I have studied this play with students they have speculated, with a fresh, clear-eyed perspective, whether Marlene is an alcoholic or not.

20 See the discussion of *Abortive* in this chapter for a discussion of the *tuché*.

21 Here I am distancing my understanding of Dionysos from Kritzer's reading of the character as 'a model of nature' as 'organic disunity' (*The Plays of Caryl Churchill* 178, 179).

22 It also draws our attention towards the set (which Churchill does not describe in her published script): in the original production, it was a dilapidated, multi-storied house, with walls removed to expose the interior to the audience and with a tree growing up through the centre of the building. One reading of this image is as the uncanny itself: the rendering of the home strange through the intrusion of the unfamiliar, the decentring of the stable origin.

23 I am alluding here to Harold Bloom's theory of misprision in *The Anxiety of Influence: A Theory of Poetry*.

24 Gilles Deleuze suggests the 'spirit of revenge' as an umbrella phrase covering several Nietzschean concepts: 'Nietzsche calls the enterprise of denying life and depreciating existence nihilism. He analyses the principal forms of nihilism, *ressentiment*, bad conscience, ascetic ideal; the whole of nihilism and its forms he calls the spirit of revenge' (*Nietzsche and Philosophy* 34). Fredric Jameson suggests that Nietzsche's theory of *ressentiment* 'is ostensibly proposed as a kind of psychological mechanism in the service of a critique of Victorian moralism and hypocrisy,' but that in fact 'Nietzsche's whole vision of history, his historical master narrative, is organized around this proposition' (*The Political Unconscious* 201).

25 Elaine Aston describes the Skriker as a figure for the damaged maternal semiotic (in a Kristevan sense) and the Skriker's language as hysterical (*Feminist Views on*

the English Stage 29–30). The Skriker is thus a disavowed goddess figure. Inasmuch as Kristeva's concept of the semiotic is a description of the pre-symbolic maternal as it irrupts into the symbolic order of language, Aston's sense of the Skriker is proximate to the understanding I present here. Other readings of the Skriker include Elin Diamond's analysis of the death of the natural world in this play as an image of the postmodern condition of late capitalism. This leads Diamond to read the Skriker's 'schizoid' language as the pathological, deterritorializing underside of capitalism itself ('Caryl Churchill: Feeling Global' 483). Building on Diamond's reading, Candice Amich gives a detailed close reading of the play as a demystification of the machinations of late capitalist globalization and the Skriker as the postmodern 'agent of space-time compression' (400).

26 The Skriker's convoluted poetry has been the subject of much critical speculation. Ann Wilson argues that its purpose is to actually be, to some degree, incomprehensible, and thus refuse the audience's mastery in a form of pseudo-Brechtian alienation (187). Candice Amich surveys the readings of the language as 'Joycean' or 'schizophrenic' and reads the language as a mirror of postmodern capitalist time-space compression (396–7). All responses to this language will be subjective. The Skriker's run-on sentences are challenging poetry but not incomprehensible, and are certainly more accessible to an audience than Vincentio's opening speeches in *Measure for Measure*.

5. New English Tragedians: The Tragedy of the Tragic

1 Moreover, recent scholarship has turned its attention to playwrights of the 1990s who do not fit comfortably into the 'in-yer-face' thesis. See particularly the collection of essays *Cool Britannia? British Political Drama in the 1990s*, edited by Rebecca D'Monté and Graham Saunders.

2 For instance, in an essay comparing the violent imagery in Kane's *Blasted* to similar imagery in *King Lear*, Graham Saunders notes how Samuel Johnson had the same reaction to *King Lear* as contemporary critics had to Kane: 'namely that the acts of sexual and physical violence in Kane's play lacked a dramatic context' ('"Out Vile Jelly"' 70). Saunders maps out the influence of Shakespeare on Kane and concludes that far from an 'in-yer-face' dramatist 'questioning postmodern dilemmas,' Kane addresses issues that are 'essentially existential, concerning man's place in the universe and relationship with God, love as an obsession, and sexual fulfilment as both ecstatic and destructive' (77). Saunders has elsewhere argued against the idea that Kane was solely interested in 'experiential' theatre, although she was inspired by it early on in her career. See '"Just a Word on a Page"' 100.

3 Consider, for example, Kritzer's *Political Theatre in Post-Thatcher Britain: New Writing 1995–2005*, which begins in the mid-nineties, thus implying a remarkable

moment of break or *newness*, the emergence of an historical period (despite the fact that Thatcher resigned in 1990): 'Despite their stylistic debts to earlier eras of theatre, the in-yer-face plays do not express a sense of continuity; rather, they signify a break with the immediate past' (30).

4 The rape of Ian in the 2001 Royal Court remounting of *Blasted* 'was unlike any other experience that I've had in the theatre. […] It makes an argument about our notions of sexuality and violence, an argument that is *felt*, not heard: no dialectical conversations, instead, the power of the image, of Dudgeon's exposed buttocks and Jordan Murphy's incessant sobs' (370). Urban does not explain what this felt argument was, preferring to let the 'experiential' speak for itself.

5 David Edgar suggests a similar way of understanding the 1990s generation: 'Far from celebrating the death of the class struggle, it seems to me that one of the great subjects of in-yer-face theatre is mourning its loss' (301).

6 Consider also Ravenhill's recent criticism of the popularity of Richard Dawkins in the UK. While not a spiritual person, Ravenhill cherishes his Methodist education and attributes a similar sentiment to Kane: 'The late Sarah Kane acknowledged that her youthful Christianity was the single most formative influence on her playwriting. It's strange to think that her Blasted [*sic*] and my Shopping and Fucking [*sic*] wouldn't have been written without the Christian church. But that's the truth. There's something about their sharp iconography and intense language that suggests a youthful experience of Christianity on the part of the writer. And I resent the possibility that aggressive secularism would deny future generations this inspiration.' 7 June 2012. http://www.guardian.co.uk/stage/theatreblog/2008/apr/14/godisbehindsomeofourgrea.

7 A company that, incidentally, while claiming that this was the first Disney movie derived from an original story, in fact committed international intellectual property theft by appropriating a beloved contemporary Japanese cultural icon. This moving emotional content is in fact stolen property.

8 Ravenhill's familiarity with this character is indicated in an article where he compares notorious advertising guru Charles Saatchi to Mauler. See 'Me, My iBook, and Writing in America' (132).

9 Ravenhill discusses how the first German production redressed this by staging a seven-minute- long scene of anal stabbing, a sharp departure from the script (see Sierz, *In-Yer-Face Theatre* 133).

10 Rabey observes that 'the surprising persistence of blood is a running motif in the play' (*English Drama* 201).

11 Alderson analyses the influence of Baudrillard's book *America* on Ravenhill's satiric characterization of Alain (869).

12 And in this the representation of Alain is a strong echo of Bond's Lear, who is humanized first by the apprehension of his dead daughter's humanity as he beholds

her physical corpse and then further humanized by his interactions with the swineherd's ghost. As in *Lear*, Ravenhill is attempting to negotiate a passage through traditional paradigms of tragic selfhood without abandoning them altogether.

13 I am deriving this idea from Scottish science fiction writer Ken MacLeod's introduction to the American edition of his novel *The Star Fraction*. The book explores the same problem for socialism, but within a near-future setting.

14 Ravenhill based the character of Jonathan on Charles Saatchi, advertising guru and campaign designer for Thatcher. Saatchi's agency coined the phrase 'Labour Isn't Working' for Thatcher's first campaign. Ravenhill describes Jonathan as 'charismatic but rather evil' ('Better to risk,' *The Guardian* 6 Feb. 2006: 21).

15 Elsewhere, he writes of the effect of globalization and financial success upon theatre artists such as Robert Lepage, Robert Wilson, and Peter Brook: after the relative vitality of his early play *The Dragons' Trilogy*, Lepage's 'subsequent work has relied on some hazy thinking, generalized cultural references and a great deal of spectacle. Not a million miles away from Cats.' Robert Wilson initially developed a highly original theatre language and then spent 'the rest of his time selling that language as an international brand' ('Better to risk,' *The Guardian* 6 Feb. 2006: 21).

16 Michael Billington praised *Some Explicit Polaroids* for its content but criticized its style, suggesting that it 'falls prey to the soundbite values it condemns' ('A return to old fights,' *The Guardian* 16 Oct. 1999: 19).

17 Horkheimer and Adorno discuss how metaphysics is the dialectical element of Enlightenment that would save it from its own totalitarianism, but is also that which Enlightenment eventually eliminates: 'The denial of God contains an irresolvable contradiction; it negates knowledge itself' (*Dialectic of Enlightenment* 90). This is where Enlightenment turns against itself, because in the absence of divinity, the concept of truth loses its grounding in the absolute.

18 See Max Stafford-Clark's discussion of working-class playwright and single mother Andrea Dunbar's work at the Royal Court, in Roberts and Stafford-Clark, *Taking Stock* 113. See also chapter 5 of Gregory Motton's *Helping Themselves: The Left-Wing Middle Classes in Theatre and the Arts* for an acerbic, critical discussion of the Royal Court's relationship to working-class playwrights. Motton also cites the search for authenticity as the reason for the Royal Court's championing of Sarah Kane: 'It was the search for authenticity that resulted in a girl suffering from a serious psychotic condition being made into a playwright [...]. Only such a hunger could cause a whole culture to mistake the symptomatic writing of a psychotic for something which ought to be played and watched' (164). While I take serious issue with Motton's callous and ignorant assessment of Kane's artistry (an assessment concealed behind a mask of humane concern), his contrarian assessment of British theatre is, potentially, an important corrective to a self-congratulatory and uncritical theatre environment.

19 See Carney, 'The Tragedy of History in Sarah Kane's *Blasted*.' Other essays of mine also explore some preliminary groundwork for this book. See 'The Art of Living: History as Use-Value in *The Romans in Britain*'; 'Edward Bond: Tragedy, Postmodernity, *The Woman*'; and 'Capitalism's *Pharmakos*: David Edgar's *Destiny* and *Pentecost*.'

20 Aleks Sierz describes *Blasted*'s evasion of the political in a recent essay: '[I]t feels experientially like a profound political statement, and emotionally makes links between private abuse and public war crimes, but its moral absolutism and ferocity of feeling are also a way of avoiding political discussion' ("'Looks like there's a war on,"' 54). Sierz's essay is an admirable example of resistance to what he calls the 'cult of Kane' (52), a posthumous canonization of the writer that makes it difficult to engage critically with her brief and fraught body of work.

21 Graham Saunders suggests recently that Kane's 'concerns predominantly occupy a metaphysical terrain' ('The Beckettian World of Sarah Kane' 78).

22 Kane herself objected to a European production that placed Cate on stage nude and covered in blood in the second scene on the grounds that it was psychologically indefensible, considering she had been raped. See Sierz, *In-Yer-Face Theatre* 105.

23 For an alternate reading that interprets *Blasted*'s rejection of realism from a feminist perspective, see Solga, '*Blasted*'s Hysteria.'

24 Peter A. Campbell ('Sarah Kane's *Phaedra's Love*') gives a lively description of his and other directors' unsuccessful attempts to stage this scene without descending into risible comedy. Dogs that won't follow stage directions, animal puppets that provoke bathetic laughter, and audiences rendered nauseous by the smell of burning meat are a few of the risks that the high tragic approach founders against. The possibility that Kane is parodying her own reputation as an 'in-yer-face' playwright seems to be overlooked by such literal staging.

25 See Sierz, *In-Yer-Face Theatre* 116–17.

26 Originally played by Sharon Duncan-Brewster, a British actress of black African heritage.

27 See Alicia Tycer, '"Victim. Perpetrator. Bystander": Melancholic Witnessing of Sarah Kane's *4.48 Psychosis*,' particularly pages 33–4.

28 See Graham Saunders, '*Love Me or Kill Me*' 116–17 for a description of this moment. Elsewhere Saunders describes a personal correspondence with Edward Bond in which Bond suggests that the line functions in two ways: as a description of living as a fully conscious and aware person, and as an exposure of the undead hollowness of late capitalist society in the emptiness behind the curtains. See Saunders, '"Just a Word on a Page"' 104.

29 Theatre In Actu's production, performed in the Lab Space of the Segal Centre for the Performing Arts, Montreal, 26 September 2009; dir. Liz Truchanowicz, perf. by Stéphanie Breton and Shaune Houlston.

Conclusion: Late Modernism in *Jerusalem*

1   I am not arguing that Bond believes in the soul or that he is a metaphysician. I am arguing that he, like the other playwrights studied here, are materialist tragedians whose art forces a confrontation with the aspects of the human that are invisible to vulgar materialism, and these aspects can only be described with metaphysical contours precisely because they are those blind spots in material existence. While Bond insists that 'There is no homunculus in the brain, no "ghost in the machine," no soul in the imagination, no centre in the psyche' ('Notes on Imagination' 97), the figure of the radical innocent nevertheless serves the functional role of such a metaphysical core. Bond indicates his awareness that his idea might be understood as metaphysical: 'There is the danger that this might be understood transcendentally, as Geist or elan vital or some other abstraction' (Letter to Graham Saunders 7.11.04 in *Edward Bond and the Dramatic Child* [184]).

2   Hunka suggests that Barker, while not necessarily considering himself a modernist, seems to endorse Adorno's modernist sentiments as an anachronistic rebuttal to the condition of postmodernity (107–8).

3   See for instance John Orr's reading of the play in *Tragic Drama and Modern Society* 196–205.

4   It has been observed that the referent for Flintock is Pewsey. See http://www.marlboroughpeople.co.uk/news/Pewsey-set-play-good-critics-say/article-1814069-detail/article.html (accessed 11 May 2010).

5   See for example journalist Paul Mason's sensitive estimation of the political timeliness of *Jerusalem*, one notable because written not by a theatre critic but an economics commentator: http://www.bbc.co.uk/blogs/newsnight/paulmason/2009/12/butterworths_jerusalem_the_ful.html (accessed 11 May 2010).

Works Cited

Note: in the case of a play, the date of first performance or broadcast follows directly after the title.

Adiseshiah, Siân. *Churchill's Socialism: Political Resistance in the Plays of Caryl Churchill*. Newcastle upon Tyne: Cambridge Scholar's Publishing, 2009.

Adorno, Theodor W. 'Commitment.' *Aesthetics and Politics*. Ed. Ronald Taylor. Trans. Francis McDonagh. London: Verso, 1977. 177–95.

– *Negative Dialectics*. 1966. Trans. E.B. Ashton. New York: Seabury, 1973.

– 'Trying to Understand *Endgame*.' Trans. Michael Jones. *The Adorno Reader*. Ed. Brian O'Connor. Oxford: Blackwell, 2000. 319–52.

Alderson, David. 'Postgay Drama: Sexuality, Narration and History in the Plays of Mark Ravenhill.' *Textual Practice* 24.5 (2010): 863–82.

Amich, Candice. 'Bringing the Global Home: The Commitment of Caryl Churchill's *The Skriker*.' *Modern Drama* 50.3 (2007): 394–413.

Amoko, Apollo. 'Casting Aside Colonial Occupation: Intersections of Race, Sex, and Gender in *Cloud Nine* and *Cloud Nine* Criticism.' *Modern Drama* 42.1 (1999): 45–58.

Artaud, Antonin. *The Theatre and Its Double*. Trans. Mary Caroline Richards. New York: Grove, 1958.

Aston, Elaine. *Feminist Views on the English Stage: Women Playwrights, 1990–2000*. Cambridge: Cambridge UP, 2003.

– 'Reviewing the Fabric of *Blasted*.' *Sarah Kane in Context*. Ed. Laurens de Vos and Graham Saunders. Manchester: Manchester UP, 2010. 13–27.

– and Elin Diamond, eds. *The Cambridge Companion to Caryl Churchill*. Cambridge: Cambridge UP, 2009.

– and Elin Diamond. 'Introduction: On Caryl Churchill.' *The Cambridge Companion to Caryl Churchill*. Ed. Elaine Aston and Elin Diamond. Cambridge: Cambridge UP, 2009. 1–17.

Bakhtin, Mikhail Mikhailovich. *The Dialogic Imagination*. Ed. Michael Holquist. Trans. Caryl Emerson and Michael Holquist. Austin: U of Texas P, 1994.

Barker, Howard. *Arguments for a Theatre*. 3rd edition. Manchester: Manchester UP, 1997.

– 'Art is About Going into the Dark.'' Interview. With Mark Brown. *Howard Barker Interviews 1980–2010: Conversations in Catastrophe*. Ed Mark Brown. Chicago: Intellect, 2011. 187–202.

– 'Articulate Explorers in an Age of Populism.' Interview. With Charles Lamb. *Howard Barker Interviews 1980–2010: Conversations in Catastrophe*. Ed Mark Brown. Chicago: Intellect, 2011. 39–53.

– *The Castle*. 1985. *Plays Two*. London: Oberon, 2006. 7–77.

– *Claw*. 1975. *Stripwell; with Claw*. London: John Calder, 1977. 123–230.

– *Dead Hands*. 2004. London: Oberon, 2004.

– *Death, the One and the Art of Theatre*. London: Routledge, 2005.

– *The Europeans: Struggles to Love*. 1991. *Plays One*. London: Oberon, 2006. 87–156.

– *Fair Slaughter*. 1977. *Crimes in Hot Countries; with Fair Slaughter*. London: John Calder, 1984. 59–105.

– *Gertrude–The Cry*. 2002. *Plays Two*. London: Oberon, 2006. 79–175.

– *The Love of a Good Man*. 1978. *The Love of a Good Man; with All Bleeding*. London: John Calder, 1980. 1–70.

– *No End of Blame: Scenes of Overcoming*. 1981. London: John Calder, 1981.

– *A Passion in Six Days*. 1983. *A Passion in Six Days; with Downchild*. London: John Calder, 1985. 1–53.

– *The Possibilities*. 1988. *Plays One*. London: Oberon, 2006. 157–216.

– *The Power of the Dog*. 1984. London: John Calder, 1985.

– Preface. *The Ecstatic Bible*. London: Oberon, 2004. 7–8.

– *The Seduction of Almighty God by the Boy Priest Loftus in the Abbey of Calcetto, 1539*. 2006. London: Oberon, 2006.

– *That Good Between Us*. 1977. *That Good Between Us; with Credentials of a Sympathizer*. London: John Calder, 1980. 1–59.

– *Victory: Choices in Reaction*. 1983. *Plays One*. London: Oberon, 2006. 7–85.

Barnett, David. 'Howard Barker: Polemic Theory and Dramatic Practice. Nietzsche, Metatheatre, and the Play *The Europeans*.' *Modern Drama* 44.4 (2001): 458–75.

Benjamin, Walter. *The Origin of German Tragic Drama*. 1928. Trans. John Osborne. London: Verso, 1994.

Bennett, Susan. 'A Commercial Success: Women Playwrights in the 1950s.' *A Companion to Modern British and Irish Drama: 1880–2005*. Ed. Mary Luckhurst. Oxford: Blackwell, 2006. 175–87.

Bicât, Tony. 'Portable Theatre: "fine detail, rough theatre." A Personal Memoir.' *The Cambridge Companion to David Hare*. Ed. Richard Boon. Cambridge: Cambridge UP, 2007. 15–30.

Bloom, Harold. *The Anxiety of Influence: A Theory of Poetry*. Oxford: Oxford UP, 1973.

Bond, Edward. *The Activists Papers. The Worlds, with The Activists Papers*. London: Methuen, 1980. 85–174.

– Appendix. *Plays: One*. London: Methuen, 1977. 309–12.

– *At the Inland Sea*. 1995. London: Methuen, 1997.

– Author's Note. *Olly's Prison. Plays: 7*. London: Methuen, 2003. 75.

– Author's Preface. *Lear. Plays: Two*. London: Methuen, 1978. 3–12.

– *Bingo: Scenes of Money and Death*. 1973. *Plays: Three*. London: Methuen, 1978. 1–66.

– *The Bundle*. 1978. London: Methuen, 1978.

– *Chair*. 2001. *Plays: 8*. London: Methuen, 2006. 109–44.

– *Coffee: A Tragedy*. 1996. *Plays: 7*. London: Methuen, 2003. 123–216.

– Commentary on *The War Plays. The War Plays: A Trilogy*. London: Methuen, 1991. 245–363.

– *The Crime of the Twenty-First Century*. 2001. *Plays: 7*. London: Methuen, 2003. 217–74.

– *Existence*. 2002. *Plays: 8*. London: Methuen, 2006. 145–67.

– *The Fool: Scenes of Bread and Love*. 1975. *The Fool and We Come to the River*. London: Methuen, 1976. 1–79.

– 'Freedom and Drama.' *Plays: 8*. London: Methuen, 2006. 205–22.

– *Great Peace*. 1985. *The War Plays: A Trilogy*. London: Methuen, 1991. 99–244.

– Introduction. *Bingo. Plays: Three*. London: Methuen, 1978. 3–12.

– 'Introduction: The Cap.' *Plays: 7*. London: Methuen, 2003. ix–xliii.

– Introduction. *The Fool. The Fool and We Come to the River*. London: Methuen, 1976. vi–xvi.

– 'Introduction: The Rational Theatre.' *Plays: Two*. London: Methuen, 1978. ix–xviii.

– *Lear*. 1971. *Plays: Two*. London: Methuen, 1978. 1–102.

– Letter to Graham Saunders 7.11.04. *Edward Bond and the Dramatic Child*. Ed. David Davis. Stoke-on-Trent: Trentham Books, 2005. 184–5.

– 'Modern Drama.' *The Hidden Plot: Notes on Theatre and the State*. London: Methuen, 2000. 10–19.

– 'Notes on Acting *The Woman*.' 1979. *Plays: Three*. London: Methuen, 1987. 285–9.

– 'Notes on *Coffee* for Le Théâtre Nationale de la Colline.' *The Hidden Plot: Notes on Theatre and the State*. London: Methuen, 2000. 165–70.

– 'Notes on Imagination.' *Plays: 7*. London: Methuen, 2003. 95–122.

– 'Notes on Post-Modernism.' 1990. *Two Post-Modern Plays: Jackets and In the Company of Men*. London: Methuen, 1990. 211–44.

– *Olly's Prison*. 1993. *Plays: 7*. London: Methuen, 2003. 1–91.

– 'On Brecht: A Letter to Peter Holland.' *Theatre Quarterly* 30 (1978): 34–5.

– 'On Violence.' *Plays: One*. London: Methuen, 1977. 9–17.

– 'The Reason for Theatre.' *The Hidden Plot: Notes on Theatre and the State*. London: Methuen, 2000. 113–61.

- *Red Black and Ignorant*. 1985. *The War Plays: A Trilogy*. London: Methuen, 1991. 1–48.
- *Restoration: A Pastoral*. 1981. *Restoration and The Cat*. London: Methuen, 1982. 1–101.
- *Saved*. 1965. *Plays: One*. London: Methuen, 1977. 19–133.
- *The Tin Can People*. 1985. *The War Plays: A Trilogy*. London: Methuen, 1991. 49–97.

Boon, Richard. *About Hare: The Playwright and the Work*. London: Faber and Faber, 2003.
- 'Keeping Turning Up: Hare's Early Career.' *The Cambridge Companion to David Hare*. Ed. Richard Boon. Cambridge: Cambridge UP, 2007. 31–48.

Brecht, Bertolt. *Brecht on Theatre*. Ed. and trans. John Willett. London: Methuen, 1964.
- *Collected Plays*. Ed. John Willett and Ralph Manheim. 8 vols. London: Eyre Methuen, 1979–85.

Brenton, Howard. 'Petrol Bombs through the Proscenium Arch.' Interview with Catherine Itzin and Simon Trussler. *Theatre Quarterly* 17 (1975): 4–20.

Brown, Sarah Annes. 'Introduction: Tragedy in Transition.' *Tragedy in Transition*. Ed. Sarah Annes Brown and Catherine Silverstone. Oxford: Blackwell, 2007. 1–15.

Butler, Judith. *Antigone's Claim: Kinship Between Life and Death*. New York: Columbia UP, 2000.
- *The Psychic Life of Power: Theories in Subjection*. Stanford: Stanford UP, 1997.

Butterworth, Jez. *Jerusalem*. 2009. London: Nick Hern, 2010.

Campbell, Peter A. 'Sarah Kane's *Phaedra's Love*: Staging the Implacable.' *Sarah Kane in Context*. Ed. Laurens de Vos and Graham Saunders. Manchester: Manchester UP, 2010. 173–83.

Carney, Sean. 'The Art of Living: History as Use-Value in *The Romans in Britain*.' *Modern Drama* 47.3 (2004): 423–45.
- *Brecht and Critical Theory: Dialectics and Contemporary Aesthetics*. London: Routledge, 2005.
- 'Capitalism's *Pharmakos*: David Edgar's *Destiny* and *Pentecost*.' *Essays in Theatre / Études Théâtrales* 18.2 (2000): 131–48.
- 'Edward Bond: Tragedy, Postmodernity, *The Woman*.' *Journal of Dramatic Theory and Criticism* 19.1 (2004): 5–33.
- 'The Tragedy of History in Sarah Kane's *Blasted*.' *Theater Survey* 46.2 (2005): 275–96.

Chaudhuri, Una. 'Different Hats.' *Theater* 33.3 (2003): 132–4.

Churchill, Caryl. *Abortive*. 1971. *Churchill: Shorts*. London: Nick Hern, 1990. 21–36.
- *Cloud Nine*. 1979. *Plays: One*. London: Methuen, 1985. 248–320.
- *Far Away*. 2000. London: Nick Hern, 2000.
- *Fen*. 1983. *Plays: Two*. London: Methuen, 1990. 143–92.
- *Light Shining in Buckinghamshire*. 1976. *Plays: One*. London: Methuen, 1985. 181–241.
- *Lives of the Great Poisoners*. 1991. *Plays: 3*. London: Nick Hern, 1998. 183–237.

- *Lovesick*. 1966. *Churchill: Shorts*. London: Nick Hern, 1990. 1–19.
- 'Not Ordinary, Not Safe.' *The Twentieth Century* 168 (Nov 1960): 443–51.
- *A Number*. 2002. London: Nick Hern, 2002.
- *Owners*. 1972. *Plays: One*. London: Methuen, 1985. 1–67.
- Interview. With Kathleen Betsko and Rachel Koenig. *Interviews with Contemporary Women Playwrights*. New York: Beech Tree Books, 1987. 75–84.
- Introduction. *Plays: Four*. London: Nick Hern, 2008. vii–x.
- Introduction. *Thyestes*. *Plays: 3*. London: Nick Hern, 1998. 295–301.
- Preface. *Cloud Nine*. *Plays: One*. London: Methuen, 1985. 245–7.
- *Seven Jewish Children: A Play for Gaza*. 2009. London: Nick Hern, 2009.
- *The Skriker*. 1994. *Plays: 3*. London: Nick Hern, 1998. 239–91.
- *Thyestes*. 1994. *Plays: 3*. London: Nick Hern, 1998. 295–344.
- *Top Girls*. 1982. *Plays: Two*. London: Methuen, 1990. 51–141.
- *Traps*. 1977. *Plays: One*. London: Methuen, 1985. 69–125.
- and David Lan. *A Mouthful of Birds*. 1986. *Plays: 3*. London: Nick Hern, 1998. 1–53.
Clute, John. 'Thinning.' *The Encyclopedia of Fantasy*. Ed. John Clute and John Grant. London: Orbit, 1997. 942–3.
Critchley, Simon. 'I Want to Die, I Hate My Life – Phaedra's Malaise.' *Rethinking Tragedy*. Ed. Rita Felski. Baltimore: Johns Hopkins UP, 2008. 170–95.
Davis, David, ed. *Edward Bond and the Dramatic Child: Edward Bond's Plays for Young People*. Stoke-on-Trent: Trentham Books, 2005.
Deeney, John. 'David Hare and Political Playwriting: Between the Third Way and the Permanent Way.' *A Companion to Modern British and Irish Drama: 1880–2005*. Ed. Mary Luckhurst. Oxford: Blackwell, 2006. 429–40.
Deleuze, Gilles. *Nietzsche and Philosophy*. Trans. Hugh Tomlinson. New York: Columbia UP, 1983.
Diamond, Elin. 'Beckett and Caryl Churchill along the Möbius Strip.' *Beckett at 100: Revolving It All*. Ed. Linda Ben-Zvi and Angela Moorjani. Oxford: Oxford UP, 2008. 285–98.
- 'Caryl Churchill: Feeling Global.' *A Companion to Modern British and Irish Drama: 1880–2005*. Ed. Mary Luckhurst. Oxford: Blackwell, 2006. 476–87.
- '(In)visible Bodies in Churchill's Theatre.' *Theatre Journal* 40.2 (1988): 188–204.
- 'On Churchill and Terror.' *The Cambridge Companion to Caryl Churchill*. Ed. Elaine Aston and Elin Diamond. Cambridge: Cambridge UP, 2009. 125–43.
Didion, Joan. *The Year of Magical Thinking: The Play*. 2007. London: Fourth Estate, 2008.
D'Monté, Rebecca, and Graham Saunders, eds. *Cool Britannia? British Political Drama in the 1990s*. London: Palgrave Macmillan, 2008.
Donesky, Finlay. *David Hare: Moral and Historical Perspectives*. Westport: Greenwood, 1996.

Eagleton, Terry. *After Theory*. New York: Basic Books, 2003.

– *Sweet Violence: The Idea of the Tragic*. Oxford: Blackwell, 2003.

Easthope, Antony. *Englishness and National Culture*. London: Routledge, 1999.

Edgar, David. 'Unsteady States: Theories of Contemporary New Writing.' *Contemporary Theatre Review* 15.3 (2005): 297–308.

Evans, Dylan. *An Introductory Dictionary of Lacanian Psychoanalysis*. New York: Routledge, 1996.

Fink, Bruce. *The Lacanian Subject: Between Language and Jouissance*. Princeton: Princton UP, 1995.

Frye, Northrop. *Anatomy of Criticism: Four Essays*. 1957. Princeton: Princeton UP, 1971.

Garner, Stanton B., Jr. *Trevor Griffiths: Politics, Drama, History*. Ann Arbor: U of Michigan P, 1999.

Gilleman, Luc. 'From Coward and Rattigan to Osborne: Or the Enduring Importance of *Look Back in Anger*.' *Modern Drama* 51.1 (2008): 104–25.

– *John Osborne, Vituperative Artist: A Reading of His Life and Work*. London: Routledge, 2002.

– '"Juss Round an' Round": Edward Bond's *Saved* and the Family Machine.' *New England Theatre Journal* 18 (2007): 49–76.

Gobert, R. Darren. 'On Performance and Selfhood in Caryl Churchill.' *The Cambridge Companion to Caryl Churchill*. Ed. Elaine Aston and Elin Diamond. Cambridge: Cambridge UP, 2009. 105–24.

Godiwala, Dimple. *Breaking the Bounds: British Feminist Dramatists Writing in the Mainstream since c. 1980*. New York: Peter Lang, 2003.

Goldhill, Simon. 'Generalizing about Tragedy.' *Rethinking Tragedy*. Ed. Rita Felski. Baltimore: Johns Hopkins UP, 2008. 45–65.

Golomb, Liorah Anne. 'Saint Isobel: David Hare's *The Secret Rapture* as Christian Allegory.' *Modern Drama* 33.4 (1990): 563–74.

Goodman, Lizbeth. 'Overlapping Dialogue in Overlapping Media: Behind the Scenes of *Top Girls*.' *Essays on Caryl Churchill: Contemporary Representations*. Ed. Sheila Rabillard. Winnipeg: Blizzard, 1998. 69–102.

Grady, Hugh. 'Tragedy and Marxist Thought.' *A Companion to Tragedy*. Ed. Rebecca Bushnell. Oxford: Blackwell, 2005. 128–44.

Griffiths, Trevor. *The Party*. 1973. *Plays One*. London: Faber and Faber, 1996. 91–185.

Gritzner, Karoline. 'Adorno on Tragedy: Reading Catastrophe in Late Capitalist Culture.' *Critical Engagements* 1.2 (2007): 25–52.

– '(Post)modern Subjectivity and the New Expressionism: Howard Barker, Sarah Kane, and Forced Entertainment.' *Contemporary Theatre Review* 18.3 (2008): 328–40.

– 'Towards an Aesthetic of the Sublime in Howard Barker's Theatre.' *Theatre of Catastrophe: New Essays on Howard Barker*. Ed. Karoline Gritzner and David Ian Rabey. London: Oberon, 2006. 83–94.

Hall, Edith. 'Trojan Suffering, Tragic Gods, and Transhistorical Metaphysics.' *Tragedy in Transition*. Ed. Sarah Annes Brown and Catherine Silverstone. Oxford: Blackwell, 2007. 16–33.

Harding, James M. 'Cloud Cover: (Re)Dressing Desire and Comfortable Subversions in Caryl Churchill's *Cloud Nine*.' *PMLA* 113.2 (1998): 258–72.

Hare, David. *Amy's View*. 1997. London: Faber and Faber, 1997.

– Author's Preface. *Fanshen*. London: Faber and Faber, 1976. 7–10.

– *The Blue Room*. 1998. New York: Grove, 1998.

– *Gethsemane*. 2008. London: Faber and Faber, 2008.

– Interview. With Harriet Devine. *Looking Back: Playwrights at the Royal Court 1956–2000*. Interviews by Harriet Devine. London: Faber and Faber, 2006. 149–60.

– 'An Interview with David Hare.' With Hersh Zeifman. *David Hare: A Casebook*. Ed. Hersh Zeifman. New York: Garland, 1994. 3–21.

– Introduction. *The Asian Plays*. London: Faber and Faber, 1986. vii–xiv.

– Introduction. *The Early Plays*. London: Faber and Faber, 1992. 1–11.

– Introduction. *The History Plays*. London: Faber and Faber, 1984. 9–16.

– Introduction. *The Year of Magical Thinking: The Play*. By Joan Didion. London: Fourth Estate, 2008. vii–xvii.

– *The Judas Kiss*. 1998. London: Faber and Faber, 1998.

– *My Zinc Bed*. 2000. London: Faber and Faber, 2000.

– *The Permanent Way, or La Voie Anglaise*. 2003. London: Faber and Faber, 2003.

– 'The Play is in the Air.' *Obedience, Struggle and Revolt: Lectures on Theatre*. London, Faber and Faber, 2005. 111–26.

– *Plenty*. 1978. *The History Plays*. London: Faber and Faber, 1984. 129–207.

– *Racing Demon*. 1990. London: Faber and Faber, 1990.

– *The Secret Rapture*. 1988. London: Faber and Faber, 1988.

– *Skylight*. 1995. London: Faber and Faber, 1995.

– *Teeth 'n' Smiles*. 1975. *The Early Plays*. London: Faber and Faber, 1992. 163–249.

– *The Vertical Hour*. 2006. London: Faber and Faber, 2008.

– 'When Shall We Live?' *Via Dolorosa and When Shall We Live?* London: Faber and Faber, 1998. 45–72.

Hay, Malcolm, and Philip Roberts. *Bond: A Study of His Plays*. London: Eyre Methuen, 1980.

Hegel, G.W.F. *Aesthetics: Lectures on Fine Art*. Trans. T.M. Knox. 2 vols. Oxford: Clarendon, 1975.

Homden, Carol. *The Plays of David Hare*. Cambridge: Cambridge UP, 1995.

Horkheimer, Max, and Theodor W. Adorno. *Dialectic of Enlightenment: Philosophical Fragments*. Ed. Gunzelin Schmid Noerr. Trans. Edmund Jephcott. Stanford: Stanford UP, 2002.

Howard, Jean E. 'On Owning and Owing: Caryl Churchill and the Nightmare of Capital.' *The Cambridge Companion to Caryl Churchill*. Ed. Elaine Aston and Elin Diamond. Cambridge: Cambridge UP, 2009. 36–51.

Hunka, George. *Word Made Flesh: Philosophy, Eros, and Contemporary Tragic Drama*. Gainesville, GA: Eyecorner Press, 2011.

Huyssen, Andreas. 'Producing Revolution: Heiner Müller's *Mauser* as Learning Play.' *After the Great Divide: Modernism, Mass Culture, Postmodernism*. Bloomington: Indiana UP, 1986. 82–93.

Irigaray, Luce. 'The Eternal Irony of the Community.' *Speculum of the Other Woman*. Trans. Gillian C. Gill. Ithaca, NY: Cornell UP, 1985. 214–26.

Jameson, Fredric. *A Singular Modernity: Essay on the Ontology of the Present*. London: Verso, 2002.

– 'Periodizing the 60s.' *Social Text* 9/10 (1984): 178–209.

– *The Political Unconscious: Narrative as a Socially Symbolic Act*. Ithaca, NY: Cornell UP, 1981.

Jernigan, Daniel. '*Traps, Softcops, Blue Heart*, and *This Is a Chair*: Tracking Epistemological Upheaval in Caryl Churchill's Shorter Plays.' *Modern Drama* 47.1 (2004): 21–43.

Kane, Sarah. *4.48 Psychosis*. 2000. *Complete Plays*. London: Methuen, 2001. 203–45.

– *Blasted*. 1995. *Complete Plays*. London: Methuen, 2001. 1–61.

– *Cleansed*. 1998. *Complete Plays*. London: Methuen, 2001. 105–51.

– *Crave*. 1998. *Complete Plays*. London: Methuen, 2001. 153–201.

– *Phaedra's Love*. 1996. *Complete Plays*. London: Methuen, 2001. 63–103.

Katafiasz, Kate. 'Alienation Is the "Theatre of Auschwitz": An Exploration of Form in Edward Bond's Theatre.' *Edward Bond and the Dramatic Child: Edward Bond's Plays for Young People*. Ed. David Davis. Stoke-on-Trent: Trentham Books, 2005. 25–48.

Kritzer, Amelia Howe. *The Plays of Caryl Churchill: Theatre of Empowerment*. New York: St Martin's, 1991.

– *Political Theatre in Post-Thatcher Britain: New Writing 1995–2005*. Houndmills: Palgrave Macmillan, 2008.

Kuti, Elizabeth. 'Tragic Plots from Bootle to Baghdad.' *Contemporary Theatre Review* 18.4 (2008): 457–69.

Lacan, Jacques. *The Seminar of Jacques Lacan. Book VII: The Ethics of Psychoanalysis, 1959–1960*. 1986. Trans. Dennis Porter. Ed. Jacques-Alain Miller. London: Routledge, 1992.

– *The Seminar of Jacques Lacan. Book XI: The Four Fundamental Concepts of Psychoanalysis*. 1973. Trans. Alan Sheridan. Ed. Jacques-Alain Miller. New York: Norton, 1981.

Lacey, Stephen. *British Realist Theatre: The New Wave in Its Context 1956–1965*. London: Routledge, 1995.

Lamb, Charles. *Howard Barker's Theatre of Seduction*. Amsterdam: Harwood, 1997.

Lukács, Georg. *History and Class Consciousness: Studies in Marxist Dialectics*. 1922. New edition. 1968. Trans. Rodney Livingstone. Cambridge, MA: MIT, 1997.

MacLeod, Ken. Introduction to the American Edition. *The Star Fraction*. 1995. New York: Tor Books, 2001. 11–12.

Mangan, Michael. *Edward Bond*. Plymouth: Northcote House, 1998.

Megson, Chris. '"England brings you down at last." Politics and Passion in Barker's "State of England" Drama.' *Theatre of Catastrophe: New Essays on Howard Barker*. Ed. Karoline Gritzner and David Ian Rabey. London: Oberon, 2006. 124–35.

Motton, Gregory. *Helping Themselves: The Left-Wing Middle Classes in Theatre and the Arts*. Deal, Kent: Levellers Press, 2009.

Müller, Heiner. *Mauser*. 1970. Trans. Helen Fehervary and Marc D. Silberman. *New German Critique* 8 (1976): 122–49.

Nietzsche, Friedrich. *The Birth of Tragedy*. *The Basic Writings of Nietzsche*. Trans. Walter Kaufmann. New York: Modern Library, 1968. 1–144.

– *On the Genealogy of Morals*. *On the Genealogy of Morals and Ecce Homo*. Ed. and trans. Walter Kaufmann. New York: Vintage, 1969. 15–198.

Nothof, Anne. 'Virtuous Women: Portraits of Goodness in *The Secret Rapture*, *Racing Demon*, and *Strapless*.' *David Hare: A Casebook*. Ed. Hersh Zeifman. New York: Garland, 1994. 185–200.

Orr, John. *Tragic Drama and Modern Society*. London: Macmillan, 1981.

Page, Malcolm, ed. *File on Hare*. London: Methuen, 1990.

Patterson, Michael. *Strategies of Political Theatre: Post-War British Playwrights*. Cambridge: Cambridge UP, 2003.

Pavis, Patrice. 'Ravenhill and Durringer, or the *Entente Cordiale* Misunderstood.' *Contemporary Theatre Review* 14.2 (2004): 4–16.

Porter, James I. 'Nietzsche and Tragedy.' *A Companion to Tragedy*. Ed. Rebecca Bushnell. Oxford: Blackwell, 2005. 68–87.

Rabey, David Ian. *English Drama since 1940*. London: Longman, 2003.

– *Howard Barker: Ecstasy and Death. An Expository Study of His Drama, Theory and Production Work, 1988–2008*. New York: Palgrave Macmillan, 2009.

– *Howard Barker: Politics and Desire. An Expository Study of His Drama and Poetry, 1969–87*. London: Macmillan, 1989.

– 'Raising Hell: An Introduction to Howard Barker's Theatre of Catastrophe.' *Theatre of Catastrophe: New Essays on Howard Barker*. Ed. Karoline Gritzner and David Ian Rabey. London: Oberon, 2006. 13–29.

– and Karoline Gritzner. 'Howard Barker in Conversation.' *Theatre of Catastrophe: New Essays on Howard Barker*. Ed. Karoline Gritzner and David Ian Rabey. London: Oberon, 2006. 30–7.

Rabillard, Sheila. 'On Caryl Churchill's Ecological Drama: Right to Poison the Wasps?' *The Cambridge Companion to Caryl Churchill*. Ed. Elaine Aston and Elin Diamond. Cambridge: Cambridge UP, 2009. 88–104.

Ravenhill, Mark. *The Cut*. 2006. *Plays: 2*. London: Methuen, 2008. 179–231.

– *Faust Is Dead*. 1997. *Plays: 1*. London: Methuen, 2001. 93–140.
– *Handbag*. 1998. *Plays: 1*. London: Methuen, 2001. 141–226.
– Introduction. *Shoot / Get Treasure / Repeat*. London: Methuen, 2008. 5.
– 'Me, My iBook, and Writing in America.' *Contemporary Theatre Review* 16.1 (2006): 131–8.
– *pool (no water)*. 2006. *Plays: 2*. London: Methuen, 2008. 293–323.
– *Product*. 2005. *Plays: 2*. London: Methuen, 2008. 153–78.
– *Shopping and Fucking*. 1996. *Plays: 1*. London: Methuen, 2001. 1–91.
– *Some Explicit Polaroids*. 1999. *Plays: 1*. London: Methuen, 2001. 227–314.
– 'A Tear in the Fabric: The James Bulger Murder and New Theatre Writing in the 'Nineties.' *New Theatre Quarterly* 20.4 (2004): 305–14.
Rebellato, Dan. *1956 and All That: The Making of Modern British Drama*. London: Routledge, 1999.
– 'On Churchill's Influences.' *The Cambridge Companion to Caryl Churchill*. Ed. Elaine Aston and Elin Diamond. Cambridge: Cambridge UP, 2009. 163–79.
Reinelt, Janelle. *After Brecht: British Epic Theater*. Ann Arbor: U of Michigan P, 1994.
– 'Caryl Churchill and the Politics of Style.' *The Cambridge Companion to Modern British Women Playwrights*. Ed. Elaine Aston and Janelle Reinelt. Cambridge: Cambridge UP, 2000. 174–93.
Roberts, Philip. *About Churchill: The Playwright and the Work*. London: Faber and Faber, 2008.
– ed. *Bond on File*. London: Methuen, 1985.
– *The Royal Court Theatre and the Modern Stage*. Cambridge: Cambridge UP, 1999.
– and Max Stafford-Clark. *Taking Stock: The Theatre of Max Stafford-Clark*. London: Nick Hern, 2007.
Saunders, Graham. 'The Beckettian World of Sarah Kane.' *Sarah Kane in Context*. Ed. Laurens de Vos and Graham Saunders. Manchester: Manchester UP, 2010. 68–79.
– '"Just a Word on a Page and There Is the Drama." Sarah Kane's Theatrical Legacy.' *Contemporary Theatre Review* 13.1 (2003): 97–110.
– *'Love Me or Kill Me': Sarah Kane and the Theatre of Extremes*. Manchester: Manchester UP, 2002.
– '"Out Vile Jelly": Sarah Kane's "Blasted" and Shakespeare's "King Lear."' *New Theatre Quarterly* 20.1 (2004): 69–78.
Segal, Charles. *Oedipus Tyrannus: Tragic Heroism and the Limits of Knowledge*. 2nd ed. Oxford: Oxford UP, 2001.
Shellard, Dominic. *British Theatre since the War*. New Haven, CT: Yale UP, 1999.
Sierz, Aleks. *In-Yer-Face Theatre: British Drama Today*. London: Faber and Faber, 2001.
– '"Looks like there's a war on": Sarah Kane's *Blasted*, Political Theatre and the Muslim Other.' *Sarah Kane in Context*. Ed. Laurens de Vos and Graham Saunders. Manchester: Manchester UP, 2010. 45–56.

Solga, Kim. '*Blasted*'s Hysteria: Rape, Realism, and the Thresholds of the Visible.' *Modern Drama* 50.3 (Fall 2007): 346–74.

– Review of *Top Girls*, by Caryl Churchill. *Theatre Journal* 60.2 (2008): 300–1.

Spencer, Jenny S. *Dramatic Strategies in the Plays of Edward Bond*. Cambridge: Cambridge UP, 1992.

States, Bert. O. *Great Reckonings in Little Rooms: On the Phenomenology of Theater*. Berkeley: U of California P, 1985.

Steiner, George. *The Death of Tragedy*. 1961. Rev. ed. New Haven, CT: Yale UP, 1996.

– 'Tragedy, Pure and Simple.' *Tragedy and the Tragic: Greek Theatre and Beyond*. Ed. M.S. Silk. Oxford, Clarendon, 1996. 534–46.

– '"Tragedy," Reconsidered.' *Rethinking Tragedy*. Ed. Rita Felski. Baltimore: Johns Hopkins UP, 2008. 29–44.

Storm, William. *After Dionysus: A Theory of the Tragic*. Ithaca, NY: Cornell UP, 1998.

Stuart, Ian. *Politics in Performance: The Production Work of Edward Bond, 1978–1990*. New York: Peter Lang, 1996.

Su, John S. 'Nostalgic Rapture: Interpreting Moral Commitments in David Hare's Drama.' *Modern Drama* 40.1 (1997): 23–37.

Svich, Caridad. 'Commerce and Morality in the Theatre of Mark Ravenhill.' *Contemporary Theatre Review* 13.1 (2003): 81–95.

Szondi, Peter. *An Essay on the Tragic*. Trans. Paul Fleming. Stanford: Stanford UP, 2002.

Taylor, Lib. 'In Opposition: Hare's Response to Thatcherism.' *The Cambridge Companion to David Hare*. Ed. Richard Boon. Cambridge: Cambridge UP, 2007. 49–63.

Thomas, Jane. 'The Plays of Caryl Churchill: Essays in Refusal.' *The Death of the Playwright? Modern British Drama and Literary Theory*. Ed. Adrian Page. London: Macmillan, 1992. 160–85.

Tomlin, Liz. 'A New Tremendous Aristocracy: Tragedy and the Meta-Tragic in Barker's Theatre of Catastrophe.' *Theatre of Catastrophe: New Essays on Howard Barker*. Ed. Karoline Gritzner and David Ian Rabey. London: Oberon, 2006. 109–23.

Tycer, Alicia. *Caryl Churchill's Top Girls*. London: Continuum, 2008.

– '"Victim. Perpetrator. Bystander": Melancholic Witnessing of Sarah Kane's *4.48 Psychosis*.' *Theatre Journal* 60 (2008): 23–36.

Urban, Ken. 'Towards a Theory of Cruel Britannia: Coolness, Cruelty, and the 'Nineties.' *New Theatre Quarterly* 20.4 (2004): 354–72.

Vernant, Jean-Pierre. 'The Masked Dionysus of Euripides' *Bacchae*.' *Myth and Tragedy in Ancient Greece*. By Jean-Pierre Vernant and Pierre Vidal-Naquet. Trans. Janet Lloyd. New York: Zone, 1990. 381–412.

Wilde, Oscar. 'The Soul of Man under Socialism.' *Complete Works of Oscar Wilde*. 3rd ed. Ed. Owen Dudley Edwards, Terence Brown, Declan Kibred, and Merlin Holland. Glasgow: HarperCollins, 1994. 1174–97.

Williams, Raymond. *Drama from Ibsen to Brecht*. 2nd ed. London: Chatto and Windus, 1968.

– *Modern Tragedy*. London: Chatto and Windus, 1966.

Wilson, Ann. 'Failure and the Limits of Representation in *The Skriker*.' *Essays on Caryl Churchill: Contemporary Representations*. Ed. Sheila Rabillard. Winnipeg: Blizzard, 1998. 174–88.

Zeifman, Hersh. Introduction. *David Hare: A Casebook*. Ed. Hersh Zeifman. New York: Garland, 1994. xi–xvii.

Žižek, Slavoj. *The Sublime Object of Ideology*. London: Verso, 1989.

Index

absolute, the, 11, 12, 13, 14, 19, 22, 24, 192, 229, 235–7, 253, 260, 272, 276, 284, 285, 287, 288–9, 290, 291, 308n5, 320n17 .

Adiseshiah, Siân, 314n1

Adorno, Theodor W., 68, 84, 109, 180, 253, 266, 288, 308nn4–5, 309n13, 314n15, 315n9, 320n17; on committed art, 180, 315n9; on *Endgame*, 151, 314n15

affirmation, 16, 20, 23, 80, 89, 102, 122, 128, 138, 170, 174, 181, 185, 193, 211–12, 216, 229, 233, 307n19

Alderson, David, 241, 254, 319n11

alienation, 6, 11, 13, 15, 23, 25, 34, 35, 37, 38, 50, 55, 60, 65, 69, 75, 77, 94, 96, 107, 128, 131, 132, 133, 134, 135, 144, 146, 149, 157, 159, 167, 176, 177, 180, 181, 184, 196, 209, 214, 226, 228, 229, 258, 283, 284, 299, 312n5, 314–15n4, 318n26

Althusser, Louis, 17

altruism, 305n11

Amich, Candice, 318nn25–6

Amoko, Apollo, 316n14

anagnorisis, 107, 133, 154

Antichrist, 101, 118, 195, 310n20

Antigone, 18–19, 20, 21, 28, 29, 34, 43, 46, 87–8, 121, 144, 162, 163, 267, 313n11

anxiety, 22, 73, 74, 87, 92, 108, 114, 121, 122, 183, 185, 192, 206, 210, 214, 221, 228, 229, 230, 239, 253, 254, 311n30. *See also* fear, being frightened

Aristotle, 15, 107, 127, 169

Artaud, Antonin, 22, 89; *The Theatre and Its Double*, 89, 309n17

Aston, Elaine, 175, 268, 315n7, 317n25

atè, 267–8, 271–2, 275, 280, 282, 283

Bakhtin, Mikhail Mikhailovich, 178, 315n8

Barker, Howard: on ambiguity, 309n12; on anxiety, 73, 121, 311n30; on audiences, 309n12; on beauty, 73, 76, 121; on being European, 76; on being human, 69, 107; on catastrophe, 69, 84, 87, 102–3, 121; on *catharsis*, 84; on *The Castle*, 93, 95, 309n18; on *Claw*, 72, 73; on ecstasy, 107, 108, 121; on Epic Theatre, 84; on *Fair Slaughter*, 76; on pain, 75, 76, 80, 121; on performances of Bradshaw in *Victory*, 91; on *The Possibilities*, 107; on *The Power of the Dog*, 309n11; on prayer, 70; on Royal Court Marxist theatre, 302n7; on socialism as tragedy, 76; on tragedy, 70, 76, 102, 108; on the unconscious, 102–3

Barker, Howard, works of: *The Bite of the Night*, 308n6; *The Castle*, 92–6, 122, 286, 309n18; *Claw*, 71–7, 122, 286; *Dead Hands*, 112–16, 122, 286; *Death, the One and the Art of Theatre*, 70, 308n3; *The Europeans: Struggles to Love*, 96–102, 122, 286, 308–9n9, 310n21; *Fair Slaughter*, 74–7, 122, 286; *Gertrude–The Cry*, 108–12, 113, 286; *The Love of a Good Man,* 309n10; *No End of Blame: Scenes of Overcoming*, 307–8n2; *No One Was Saved*, 311n2; *A Passion in Six Days*, 309n19; *The Possibilities*, 102–8, 122, 310–11n23; *The Power of the Dog*, 80–6, 87, 122, 286; Preface, *The Ecstatic Bible*, 108; *The Seduction of Almighty God by the Boy Priest Loftus in the Abbey of Calcetto, 1539*, 116–20, 287; *That Good Between Us*, 77–80, 122, 286, 308n8; *Victory: Choices in Reaction*, 86–96, 122, 286, 308n6

Barnett, David, 70, 310n21

Baudrillard, Jean, 245, 319n11

beauty, the beautiful, 19, 22, 57, 69, 73, 76, 82, 96, 107, 108, 119, 121–2, 133, 138, 139, 142, 165, 183, 210, 226, 239, 260, 266, 301n3, 302n8, 313–14n14

Beckett, Samuel, 5, 14, 131, 176, 285, 290–1, 303n14; *Endgame*, 150, 151, 272, 314n15; *Waiting for Godot*, 8, 268

being, 43, 46, 60, 63, 88, 107, 249, 276, 307n20; non-being, 60

Benjamin, Walter, *The Origin of German Tragic Drama*, 108

Bennett, Susan, 301n1

Berliner Ensemble, the, 159, 302–3n9

Bicât, Tony, 304n3

Big Brum Theatre Company, 124, 164, 314n16

Billington, Michael, 304n7, 320n16

Blair, Tony, 251, 252, 314n2

Blake, William, 298–9

Blanchett, Cate, 34

Bloom, Harold, *The Anxiety of Influence: A Theory of Poetry*, 317n23

Bond, Edward: on aggression, 133; on Aristotle, 169; on art, 142, 149; on art as tragic, 142; on being human, 148; on *Bingo*, 312–13n9; on the boundary, 156; on the child, 158, 162; on *Coffee*, 166–7; on contradictions, 149, 172; on the core self, 171–2; on the definition of culture, 142–3; on drama, 157–8, 172; on evil, 167; on fate, 152; on *The Fool*, 313n10; on the freedom-tragic, 126, 161, 162; on free will, 148–9; on Freud, 171; on *Great Peace*, 151, 153, 156; on Greek drama, 149, 152, 157, 162; on Greeks and the gods, 152; on guilt, 171; on history, 144; on history as tragic, 168; on *hubris*, 169; on ideology, 172; on imagination, 157–8, 162; on Kane's *4.48 Psychosis*, 321n28; on *Lear*, 134; on V.I. Lenin, 130; on machines, 148, 149; on Marx, 130; on metatexts, 146; on mortality, 162; on the neonate, 162; on objects as tragic, 126, 161, 172; on *Olly's Prison*, 159, 160–1; on the Palermo paradox, 147, 149, 156, 172; on post-modernity, 156–7; on the Promethean, 171; on the Promethean imperative, 169; on psychoanalysis, 171; on radical innocence, 147, 148, 152, 158, 171–2; on recognition, 154–5;

on *Restoration*, 145–6; on *Saved*, 127, 128; on the self, 157; on self-consciousness, 162; on Shakespeare, 130, 135; on socialism, 144; on socialist theatre, 143–4; on technology, 148; on Theatre Events, 146; on time, 162; on tragedy, 158; on the tragic, 162, 172; on the unconscious, 148

Bond, Edward, works of: *The Activists Papers*, 143; *At the Inland Sea*, 163–6, 167, 287, 314n16; *Bingo: Scenes of Money and Death*, 123, 124, 130, 135–9, 140, 286, 312–13n9; *The Bundle*, 142–3; *Chair*, 172–4, 297; *Coffee: A Tragedy*, 164, 166–8, 174, 287, 314n16; Commentary on *The War Plays*, 146, 147, 148, 151, 152, 153, 155, 156, 158; *The Crime of the Twenty-First Century*, 169–72, 287, 314n16; *Existence*, 172; *The Fool: Scenes of Bread and Love*, 123, 138, 139–42, 286, 313n10; 'Freedom and Drama,' 168, 169, 171, 172; *Great Peace*, 149, 150–6, 158, 162, 174, 286; *Have I None*, 172, 314n16; *Lear*, 123, 128–34, 140, 157, 169, 174, 286, 312n7, 319–20n12; 'Modern Drama,' 126, 159, 161, 162; 'Notes on *Coffee* for Le Théâtre Nationale de la Colline,' 167; 'Notes on Imagination,' 157, 158, 322n1; 'Notes on Post-Modernism,' 156–7; *Olly's Prison*, 159–63, 174, 287; 'On Brecht: A Letter to Peter Holland,' 302–3n9; 'On Violence,' 133; 'The Reason for Theatre,' 162; *Red Black and Ignorant*, 149, 286; *Restoration: A Pastoral*, 123, 145–7; *Saved*, 7, 123, 125–8, 129, 147, 169, 174, 286, 302n5, 311n2, 313n12; *The Tin Can People*, 149–50, 286; *The Under Room*, 172

Boon, Richard, 47, 48, 55, 303n2, 304nn3, 7, 306n14
Bradley, A.C., 131
Brecht, Bertolt, 3, 4, 5, 6, 7, 10–11, 24, 41, 54, 55, 62, 71, 79, 82, 83–4, 85, 92, 99, 103, 104, 108–9, 133, 142, 146, 149, 151, 168, 174, 187, 193, 197, 239, 263, 272, 285, 288, 291, 302–3n9, 303nn10, 1, 309n14, 310–11n23, 316n15, 318n26
Brecht, Bertolt, works of: *Baal*, 72, 272; *Brecht on Theatre*, 63, 108, 303n1, 309n14; *The Caucasian Chalk Circle*, 99; *The Good Person of Setzuan*, 41, 153; *Life of Galileo*, 302–3n9; *Man Equals Man*, 72, 84, 309n14; *Mother Courage and her Children*, 10, 83, 99, 103, 151, 168; *Saint Joan of the Stockyards*, 239
Brenton, Howard, 29, 302nn8–9
Brook, Peter, 131, 225, 320n15
Brown, Sarah Annes, 15
Büchner, Georg, 206; *Woyzeck*, 14, 207
Bulger, James, 234–5, 272
Burke, Gregory, *Black Watch*, 303n2
Butler, Judith, 87, 307n21, 309n16
Butterworth, Jez, 3, 24, 231; *Jerusalem*, 24, 285, 292–9, 322n5

Campaign for Nuclear Disarmament, 6
Campbell, Peter A., 321n24
capitalism, late capitalism, 9, 10, 11, 23, 35, 48, 55, 56, 62, 77, 123, 131, 133, 136, 137, 147, 156, 174, 195, 209–10, 235, 237, 238, 251, 252, 253, 255, 257, 266, 286, 288, 317–18n25
Carney, Sean, 303n10, 314n17, 321n19
catharsis, 84, 87, 96, 157, 232, 240, 265
Chaudhuri, Una, 224
Chekhov, Anton, *Three Sisters*, 238

Christ. *See* Jesus Christ

Christian, Christianity, 41, 67, 71, 92, 101, 103, 104, 108, 116–21, 131, 193, 194–6, 198, 307n23, 319n6. *See also* Jesus Christ

Churchill, Caryl: on *The Caretaker*, 8; on *Cloud Nine*, 197; on *Drunk Enough to Say I Love You?*, 314n2; on kitchen sink realism, 7–8; on *Look Back in Anger*, 7; on Seneca's *Thyestes*, 221; on *Top Girls*, 200, 205; on tragedy, 8; on *Waiting for Godot*, 8

Churchill, Caryl, works of: *Abortive*, 178, 183–5, 229, 317n20; *Cloud Nine*, 178, 197–9, 200, 229, 286, 316nn13–14, 317n16; *Far Away*, 223–6, 229, 286; *Fen*, 23, 175, 206–10, 229, 286; *Light Shining in Buckinghamshire*, 193–7, 229, 286, 317n16; *Lives of the Great Poisoners*, 214–16, 229, 286; *Lovesick*, 181–3, 229; 'Not Ordinary, Not Safe,' 7; *A Number*, 226–9, 287; *Owners*, 186–9, 229, 286; *Seven Jewish Children: A Play for Gaza*, 177–81, 183, 230, 287, 315n8, 315–16n10; *The Skriker*, 216–21, 229, 286, 317–18n25; 318n16; *Thyestes*, 175, 221–3, 229, 286; *Top Girls*, 178, 183, 199–206, 210, 229, 286, 316n15, 317nn17–18; *Traps*, 189–93, 229, 286, 314–15n4, 316n11; and David Lan, *A Mouthful of Birds*, 175, 176, 211–14, 229, 286

class, class consciousness, class struggle, class war, 6, 8, 9–10, 17, 29, 33, 40, 44, 48, 49–50, 52, 62, 67, 72, 73, 74, 123, 125, 129, 130, 132, 139, 143, 148, 159, 169, 184, 186, 203–4, 206, 240, 247, 252, 253, 256, 259, 260–2, 295, 303n2, 304n4, 306n18, 319n5. *See also* middle class, working class

Clute, John, 216

Cock Tavern Theatre, 124

commodity fetishism, 150

communism, 6, 56, 57, 72, 78, 81, 105, 198, 254, 314n1

concrete, the, 15, 126, 144, 147, 168, 172, 247, 249

'Cool Britannia,' 251, 252

Covington, Julie, 91

Coward, Nöel, 48, 72, 301n1; *Hay Fever*, 49

Craig, Daniel, 227

Critchley, Simon, 274, 275

cruelty, 22, 72, 85, 89, 94, 95, 97, 99, 100, 101, 102, 110, 115, 119, 120, 121, 138, 155, 184, 211–13, 243, 245–7, 260, 268, 309n17, 310n21

Davies, Howard, 306n17

Davis, David, 312n6

Dawkins, Richard, 319n6

death of tragedy, 13, 24, 157, 222, 223, 236, 301–2n4

dehumanization, 22–3, 73, 75, 77, 81, 82, 83, 90, 93, 100, 107, 120, 130, 136, 138, 141, 147–8, 150, 156, 166–8, 261, 262, 276, 308n7. *See also* humanization

Deeney, John, 304n7

Deleuze, Gilles, 317n24

Dench, Judi, 48, 49, 51

desire, 19, 20, 23, 24, 38, 39, 43, 57, 59, 69, 70, 71, 80, 85, 86, 90, 93–6, 98, 102, 105, 106, 107, 109–22, 125, 162, 171, 176, 181–3, 185, 186, 197–9, 202, 206–14, 218, 229, 233, 243, 287, 311nn25, 27, 314–15n4

Devine, George, 5

dialectics, dialectical, dialectical contradictions, dialectical materialism, 10,

11, 12–13, 15–16, 18, 21, 22, 24, 29,
    33, 36, 38, 48, 64, 68, 69, 72, 74, 81,
    83, 84, 85, 93, 99, 103, 104, 105, 106,
    126, 130, 140, 144, 147, 158, 174,
    180, 196, 208, 210, 212, 214, 215,
    229, 245, 248, 249, 253, 262, 265,
    284, 285–92, 303nn10, 12, 319n4,
    320n17
dialogism, 178, 315n8
Diamond, Elin, 175, 176, 314–15n4,
    315n7, 316n12, 317–18n25
Didion, Joan, 25–9
différance, 15, 60, 130
difference, 23, 43, 93, 94, 112, 120, 176,
    180, 181, 192, 201, 211, 213, 214, 226,
    228–9, 243, 259, 283–4, 287, 299
Dionysus, Dionysian, 12–13, 18–20, 23,
    24, 30, 57, 101–3, 120, 169, 175–7,
    180–3, 184, 192–9, 202, 211–14, 220,
    229–30, 233, 264, 287, 315n5; as char-
    acter in *A Mouthful of Birds*, 211–14,
    229, 317n21
D'Monté, Rebecca, 318n1
Donesky, Finlay, 37–8, 60, 304n7,
    305n12, 305–6n13, 306n18
Dunbar, Andrea, 320n18
Duncan-Brewster, Sharon, 321n26

Eagleton, Terry, 11, 13, 60, 209, 210
Easthope, Antony, 16–18, 287
ecstasy, ecstatic experience, 21–2, 24, 25,
    68–70, 80, 103, 106, 107–12, 115–16,
    117, 119–21, 122, 170, 198, 287,
    311n27, 318n2
Edgar, David, 319n5, 321n19
ego, 17, 19, 36–7, 41, 42–3, 46, 48, 55, 59,
    99, 111, 114, 116, 121–2, 149, 157,
    176, 183, 188, 204, 210, 219, 307n21,
    309n14, 312–13n9
Eliot, T.S., 303n13

emotions, feelings, authentic emotions,
    emotions as commodities, 31–4, 36, 37,
    38, 42, 53, 61, 63, 65, 102, 112, 118, 134,
    138, 151, 177, 182, 204, 227, 228, 237–
    9, 241, 242, 243, 248, 253–5, 257, 259,
    266, 273, 274, 276, 282, 303n2, 304n7
empiricism, 17–18, 287
English Civil War (English Revolution),
    87, 193, 194, 195
Englishness, being English, 16–18, 21,
    22, 23, 24, 28, 35, 40, 41, 52, 54, 63,
    67, 77, 80, 123, 174, 198, 276, 287,
    292, 293, 295, 298, 305–6n13. *See also*
    repression, emotional
English Stage Company, 3, 5, 9, 298
Enlightenment, counter-Enlightenment,
    81, 84, 93, 108–9, 116, 133, 234, 253,
    260–2, 287, 320n17
Epic theatre, 10, 61, 83–4, 144, 193, 199,
    288, 301–2n4
Erinyes, 216
Euripides, *The Bacchae*, 14, 103, 199,
    211, 213, 264, 313–14n14, 315n5
Evans, Dylan, 121
evil, 24, 101, 163, 167, 202, 225, 235–7,
    251, 256, 260–2, 268, 272, 280, 284,
    287, 291, 307nn19–20, 320n14
existential, existentialism, 54, 71, 82,
    126, 171, 174, 279, 313–14n14, 318n2
expressionism, 22, 68, 69, 91, 92, 94, 96,
    97, 102, 106, 111, 116, 120, 133, 134,
    151, 183, 186, 198, 199, 206–7, 208,
    229, 234, 275, 280, 283, 312n4
extimacy, 111, 122, 311n26
Eyre, Richard, 48, 303n2

Faust, Faustian Man, 239, 240, 244, 245,
    247, 249
fear, being frightened, 8, 27, 42, 44, 56,
    57, 90, 100, 106, 114, 115, 162, 171,

177–81, 183, 185, 190, 192, 194, 196,
205–6, 210, 214, 219–20, 222–3, 228–
30, 253–4, 256, 257, 270, 276, 279,
284, 306n15, 311n30, 315n7. *See also*
anxiety
feminism, 23, 175, 176, 190, 197, 200–1,
204, 268, 309n18, 317nn17–18, 317–
18n25, 321n23
Findlay, Deborah, 203
Fink, Bruce, 311n27
formalism, dramatic, 5, 7, 21, 24, 27, 68,
102, 125, 132, 145, 174, 184, 259,
262–3, 266, 288–9, 290, 312n4
Foucault, Michel, 245, 314n3
Frantic Assembly Theatre Company, 263
freedom-tragic, the, 126–7, 152, 161,
162, 165, 174, 287, 312n6
Freud, Sigmund, 17, 18, 23, 31, 111, 121,
125, 171, 176, 177, 181, 182–3, 201,
203, 216, 218, 229
Frye, Northrop, 303n13, 311n3

Gambon, Michael, 47
Garner, Stanton B., Jr, 302n8
Gaskill, William, 7
Genet, Jean, 88
gestus, 7, 146, 151
Gilleman, Luc, 125, 301nn1, 3, 302n5
Gobert, R. Darren, 192, 314–15n4, 316n12
Godiwala, Dimple, 314n3
Goldhill, Simon, 20, 289
Golomb, Liorah Anne, 307n23
Goodman, Lizbeth, 203, 205
Grady, Hugh, 12, 303n11
Greenham Common protests, 309n18
Griffiths, Trevor: on May 1968, 302n8;
The Party, 10
Gritzner, Karoline, 70, 76, 232, 308nn4–
5, 311n30

Hall, Peter, 312n5
hamartia, 107
Hampton, Christopher, *Savages*,
301–2n4
Harding, James M., 198, 316n13
Hare, David: as actor, 51; on addiction,
55; on communicating with the audience, 33; on Didion's *The Year of
Magical Thinking*, 25, 26, 27; as director, 25–7; compared to John Osborne,
304n7; on consumer capitalist culture,
55; on England, 30; on free will, 55;
on *Plenty*, 35; on the reception of his
plays, 29, 35; on the Second World
War, 34; on *The Secret Rapture* as
tragedy, 42, 306n14; on *Teeth 'n'
Smiles*, 29; on tragedy, 42, 306n14
Hare, David, works of: *Amy's View*, 28,
48–54, 286; *The Blue Room*, 53;
Fanshen, 61; *Gethsemane*, 65–7, 120,
287; *The Judas Kiss*, 28, 36, 48, 51–4;
A Map of the World, 305n10; *My Zinc
Bed*, 32, 54–60, 286; *The Permanent
Way, or La Voie Anglaise*, 60–4, 66,
286; 'The Play is in the Air,' 33, 68,
304n5; *Plenty*, 28, 30, 34–40, 240, 286,
304nn4, 8, 305n12; *Racing Demon*, 25;
The Secret Rapture, 30, 40–3, 67, 286,
304n4, 305–6n13, 306n15, 307n23;
Skylight, 40, 43–8, 66, 286; *Stuff
Happens*, 66, 233; *Teeth 'n' Smiles*, 28,
29–34, 39, 40, 51, 59, 286, 304nn4, 7;
The Vertical Hour, 64–5; 'When Shall
We Live?' 34
Hašek, Jaroslav, 79
Hay, Malcolm, and Philip Roberts,
311n1
Hegel, G.W.F., 15, 144, 163; *Aesthetics:
Lectures on Fine Art*, 152, 313n11

heteroglossia, 178, 315n8
history, anti-history, end of history, 57,
   72, 80–6, 96, 100, 103–5, 122, 123,
   131, 138, 142, 143–5, 147, 156, 164–5,
   167, 168, 177, 186, 234, 236, 245–6,
   248, 251, 253, 260, 262, 290, 308–9n9,
   312n7, 317n24
Homden, Carol, 30, 303n2, 304n4,
   306n15, 307n23
Horkheimer, Max, 68, 109, 253, 266,
   320n17
Howard, Jean E., 187, 197
hubris, 23, 27, 47, 56, 59, 169, 219, 264, 265
humanism, 88, 136, 173, 244, 246, 286
humanization, 126, 129, 133, 134, 138,
   148, 150, 152, 153, 155–6, 165, 258,
   287. See also dehumanization
Hunka, George, 12, 322n2
Huyssen, Andreas, 103

Ibsen, Henrik, 28–9, 38, 47, 207; Hedda
   Gabler, 39
ideal, idealism, 13, 17, 20, 21, 28, 34, 36,
   38, 40, 41, 45, 46, 50, 52–3, 56, 60, 63,
   65, 66, 67, 70, 74, 75, 77, 78, 90, 91,
   92, 105, 121, 124, 129, 139, 196, 197,
   198, 224, 235, 253, 254, 262, 266, 290,
   292, 297, 301–2n4, 305n12, 305–6n13,
   317n24
ideology, ideological, 6, 10–11, 16–17,
   21, 22–3, 28, 35, 37, 40, 42, 48, 49, 53,
   54, 58–9, 61, 67, 69, 71, 74, 78, 80,
   113, 117, 121, 123, 132, 135, 141, 145,
   146, 148, 157, 159, 160, 161, 162, 165,
   170, 171, 172, 174, 179, 194, 197–8,
   199, 207, 208, 210, 233, 236, 237, 239,
   244, 248, 252, 257, 258, 259, 263, 264,
   265, 266, 267, 287, 288, 290, 291,
   303n10, 304n8, 315n8, 316n13

imaginary register of consciousness, 19,
   122, 188
In-Yer-Face Theatre, 24, 231, 233, 235,
   251, 265, 266, 292, 297, 298, 318nn1–
   2, 318–19n3, 319n5, 321n24
Ionesco, Eugene, 5
Irigaray, Luce, 87, 309n16

Jameson, Fredric, 9–10, 24, 288–92,
   311n3, 317n24
Jernigan, Daniel, 314n3, 314–15n4,
   316n11
Jesus Christ, 41, 66, 95, 97, 100, 101, 102,
   117, 119, 120, 122, 195–6, 245, 247,
   298, 299, 307n23
Joint Stock Theatre Company, 61, 81, 193,
   206
Joplin, Janis, 29
jouissance, 41, 111, 311n27

Kane, Sarah, on Blasted, 321n22
Kane, Sarah, works of: 4.48 Psychosis,
   280–4; Blasted, 163–4, 232, 233, 266–
   72, 275, 314nn17–18, 318n2, 319nn4,
   6, 321nn19–20, 23; Cleansed, 275–8,
   314n18; Crave, 279–80; Phaedra's
   Love, 272–5, 321n24
Katafiasz, Kate, 302–3n9
Kelly, Tricia, 91
Kendal, Felicity, 49
Kott, Jan, 131
Kritzer, Amelia Howe, 176, 232–3, 236,
   254, 266–7, 316n11, 317n21, 318–19n3
Kushner, Tony, 177
Kuti, Elizabeth, 233, 240

Labour Party, Labour Government, the,
   78, 234, 251, 261–2, 309–10n19,
   320n14

Lacan, Jacques, 15, 17, 18–19, 22, 36, 42, 43, 70, 111, 114, 121–2, 148, 185, 206, 210, 267, 283, 305n11, 307n20, 308n5, 311nn25–8, 314–15n4
Lacey, Stephen, 4–7, 10
Lan, David, 176, 211
Lehrstück, 26, 103, 180, 263, 310–11n23
Lenin, V.I., Leninism, 75, 77, 83, 103, 130, 303n1
love, 24, 28, 40, 44, 45, 50, 52–3, 56–7, 59, 67, 100, 105, 176, 181, 185, 187, 188, 192–3, 232, 236–7, 241, 254, 266–9, 271–2, 274, 276–8, 280, 282, 283, 284, 287, 291, 318n2
Lukács, Georg, 312n8
Luther, Martin, Lutheranism, 117

Macdonald, James, 283
MacLeod, Ken, 320n13
Macmillan, Harold, 6
Malraux, André, 288
Mangan, Michael, 124, 125–6, 145, 152, 160, 311n1, 312n5
Marber, Patrick, 231
Marx, Karl, Marxist, 9, 10, 17, 23, 56, 57, 70, 71, 72, 81, 83, 99, 103, 130, 147, 176, 302n7, 303nn11, 1
May 1968, 9, 10, 302n8
Mayenburg, Marius von, The Stone, 315–16n10
McCarthy, Eoin, 49
McDiarmid, Ian, 101
McDonagh, Martin, 231
McKellen, Ian, 259
Megson, Chris, 77
metanarratives, 236, 238, 244, 251, 267
metaphysics, metaphysical, metaphysical experience, 11, 12, 14, 16, 19, 20, 24, 32, 40, 43, 46, 58, 60, 69, 70, 75, 84, 89, 94, 95, 110, 116, 117, 118, 157,

196, 202, 235–7, 249, 256, 267, 268, 271–2, 276, 277, 279, 280, 284, 285, 287–8, 291–2, 308n4, 320n17, 321n21, 322n1
middle class, 5, 6, 21–2, 25, 28–9, 33, 37, 44–5, 46, 47–8, 50, 51, 54, 67, 68, 123, 124–5, 137, 181, 183–5, 187, 204, 207, 239, 249, 259, 262, 302n7, 303n2, 304n7, 305–6n13, 306n18, 320n18
Mirren, Helen, 29, 33
misprision, 213, 317n23
Möbius strip, 103, 175, 176–7, 189, 191–2, 214, 229, 283, 314–15n4
modernism, high modernism, late modernism, late late modernism, 14, 20, 22, 24, 70, 285, 288–92
modernity, 11, 179, 215, 291, 293
Monstrous Regiment, 193
Motton, Gregory, 320n18
mourning, 3, 10, 16, 19, 23, 24, 25, 27, 34, 40–1, 43, 46–8, 58, 60–4, 67, 87, 111, 112, 134, 142, 156, 163, 173, 200, 201, 204–5, 214, 222, 229, 235, 236, 255, 265–6, 275–8, 279, 280, 286, 305–6n13, 306n18, 319n5
Müller, Heiner, Mauser, 168, 308n7
multiplicity, 178, 180–1, 193, 194, 199, 212, 213, 229, 315n8, 315–16n10

necessity, 11–12, 15, 24, 32–3, 69, 74, 76, 80–1, 103, 119, 122, 126, 152, 156, 162, 165, 202, 204, 207, 208, 246, 262, 312n8
Neeson, Liam, 51, 53
negative dialectic, 84, 180
Neilson, Anthony, 231
Nelligan, Kate, 36, 304–5n9
New Left, 6, 8, 9–10, 17
New Zealand International Arts Festival, 303n2

Nietzsche, Friedrich, 19–20, 22, 30, 70, 79, 84–5, 89, 99, 101–2, 150, 169, 195, 224–5, 233, 236, 243, 246, 286, 307n19, 308n5, 309n15, 310nn20–2, 317n24; on Dionysus, 169; on Oedipus, 169; on Prometheus, 169

Nighy, Bill, 47

nostalgia, 10, 30, 37–40, 55, 58–9, 60, 147, 218, 254, 256, 262, 305n12, 305–6n13, 306nn15, 18

Nothof, Anne, 304–5n9

object-moment, 126, 152, 161–2, 165, 166, 172, 174, 312n6. *See also* freedom-tragic

Oedipus, Oedipal, 12, 18–19, 20, 29, 31, 69, 87, 95, 112, 127, 150, 169–70, 180, 181, 182, 202–3, 227, 250, 292, 303n12

O'Neill, Eugene, *Long Day's Journey into Night*, 290, 303n14

Oresteia, the, 216, 221, 236

Orr, John, 6, 13, 301–2n4, 303n14, 322n3

Orwell, George, *1984*, 18

Osborne, John, 301nn1, 3; *The Entertainer*, 304n7; *Look Back in Anger*, 5–6, 304n7; *A Sense of Detachment*, 301n3

Other, Otherness, 17, 18–19, 22, 23, 24, 185, 193, 198–9, 206, 219, 222, 229, 282, 283, 286, 287, 291–2, 311nn25, 27

Out of Joint Theatre Company, 61

overcoming, 79, 94, 99, 100, 101, 191, 193, 195, 214, 286

Page, Malcolm, 304n7, 304–5n9, 306n14

pathos, 127, 137, 240, 257, 259, 273

Patterson, Michael, 9

Pavis, Patrice, 254

Penhall, Joe, 231

pharmakos, 95, 156, 197, 209, 215, 216

Pinter, Harold, 302n5; *The Caretaker*, 8, 301–2n4

poison, poisoning, 109, 111, 214–16, 217, 219, 224, 229, 286

Portable Theatre, 28, 30, 304n3

Porter, James I., 19

positivism, 14, 16, 253, 256, 284, 287

post-Freudian, 23

postmodern, postmodernity, 10, 12, 14, 16, 23, 24, 51, 54, 59, 69, 70–1, 123, 147, 148, 149, 150, 157, 174, 215, 216, 217, 220, 222, 223, 224, 229, 230, 231–3, 236–8, 241, 242, 244–5, 246, 247, 248, 249, 266, 267, 268, 284, 285, 286, 287, 288, 290, 291, 297, 298, 317–18n25, 318nn26, 2, 321n19, 322n2

post-structuralism, post-structuralist, 23, 71, 176, 245

post-war consensus, 6, 60, 305n12, 305–6n13

Prometheus, Promethean, 18–20, 23, 24, 69, 123, 157, 169–72, 174, 236, 287

Queen's Theatre, 239

Rabey, David Ian, 70, 71, 76, 79, 101, 307n1, 308n6, 310n22, 311nn29–30, 2

Rabillard, Sheila, 216

Racine, Jean, *Phèdre*, 274–5

radical innocent, 24, 158, 287, 322n1

rape, 78, 80, 82, 90, 98, 100, 106, 118, 132, 181, 184, 240, 243, 249, 268–74, 277, 279–80, 319n4, 321n22

Rational Theatre Company, 168

Rattigan, Terrence, 301n1

Ravenhill, Mark: on aggressive secularism, 319n6; on the James Bulger murder, 233–5; on contemporary audiences, 236; on evil, 235; on grand narrative, 236; on his plays, 235; on the In-Yer-Face generation, 233–5; on Robert Lepage, 320n15; on his Methodist education, 319n6; on Robert Wilson, 320n15

Ravenhill, Mark, works of: *The Cut*, 231, 259–62; *Faust Is Dead*, 244–9, 255; *Handbag*, 249–51; 'Me, My iBook, and Writing in America,' 319n8; *pool (no water)*, 262–6, 287; *Product*, 242, 256–9; *Shoot / Get Treasure / Repeat*, 236; *Shopping and Fucking*, 233, 237–44, 253, 319n6; *Some Explicit Polaroids*, 251–6, 258, 320n16; 'A Tear in the Fabric: The James Bulger Murder and New Theatre Writing in the 'Nineties,' 234–5

real, the, 16, 185, 206, 209, 256–7, 259, 263, 265

realism, dramatic, kitchen sink realism, social realism, 5, 7–9, 21–2, 27–8, 29–30, 46, 54–5, 59, 68, 82, 86, 106, 112, 121, 123, 125, 127, 131, 132, 145, 147, 159, 163, 174, 186, 190, 199–200, 205, 206, 223, 240, 255, 262, 263, 266, 267, 269, 270, 281, 284, 285, 288, 290, 302n5, 312n4, 312–13n9, 316n15, 317n16, 321n23

realpolitik, 56, 77, 103

Rebellato, Dan, 176, 301n1, 315n7

Redgrave, Vanessa, 25–6, 27

reification, 32, 55, 116, 136, 147, 151, 174, 188, 266, 288, 292, 312n8

Reinelt, Janelle, 302n9, 314n1

repression, emotional, 16, 18–19, 22–4, 36, 37, 40–8, 64–5, 67, 89, 91, 94, 97, 109, 111, 116, 119, 176–7, 180–3, 197–9, 201–4, 229, 254, 256, 276, 286,

292. *See also* Englishness, being English

ressentiment, 23, 45, 87, 89, 115, 134, 140, 206, 214, 216, 224–5, 229, 253, 265, 269, 307n19, 317n24

return of the repressed, the, 94, 177, 178, 184, 198–9, 217, 227, 229, 253, 262

revenge, 53, 62, 91, 93, 118, 214–23, 227, 229, 317n24

Rickson, Ian, 292, 296

Roberts, Philip, 301n2, 302n6, 311n1, 312–13n9, 320n18

Romantic, Romanticism, German Romantics, 20, 22, 52, 53, 57, 70–1, 108, 288–9, 290, 291, 308n5

Rose, Jacqueline, 179

Rousseau, Jean-Jacques, 312n8

Royal Court Theatre, 3, 5–7, 9, 21–2, 24, 29, 68, 123, 145, 163, 178, 186, 231, 291, 292, 296, 298, 301n2, 302n7, 302–3n9, 312n5, 315–16n10, 319n4, 320n18; Jerwood Upstairs, 283

Royal National Theatre, 10, 25, 65, 302–3n9, 312n5

Royal Shakespeare Company, 123–4, 131, 313n13

Rudkin, David, *Afore Night Come*, 301–2n4

Saunders, Graham, 232, 268, 318nn1–2, 321nn21, 28, 322n1

Saussure, Ferdinand de, 148

Schelling, Friedrich Wilhelm Joseph, 15

Schnitzler, Arthur, *Reigen*, 53

Second World War, 33, 34, 72, 77, 87, 177, 290, 315–16n10

Segal, Charles, 303n12

Seneca, 221, 222, 272; *Thyestes*, 221

Shakespeare, William, 8, 15, 60, 109, 130, 131, 135, 139, 143, 236, 303n13,

318n2; as character in *Bingo*, 124,
135–9, 140, 174, 312–13n9; *Hamlet*,
108–9, 112; *King Lear*, 75, 81, 129,
131, 132, 134, 135, 232, 318n2;
Measure for Measure, 318n26; *Romeo
and Juliet*, 244; *The Tempest*, 303n13
Shellard, Dominic, 301n1
Sierz, Aleks, 231, 268, 319n9, 321nn20,
22, 25
Silenus, wisdom of, 150–1
socialism, 6, 9, 21–2, 24, 56, 68, 69, 74,
75, 76–7, 84, 122, 124, 125, 130, 144,
232, 251, 252, 253, 286, 320n13
Solga, Kim, 316n15, 321n23
Solomon, Alisa, 177
Sophocles, 18, 28, 87, 96, 107, 138, 150,
267
soul, the, 16, 24, 36, 43, 52, 53, 67, 76,
107, 157, 223, 236–7, 238, 239, 245–6,
249, 250, 258–9, 260, 267, 283, 287,
305n10, 305–6n13, 322n1
sparagmos, 12, 18, 111, 196, 211, 213, 264
Spencer, Jenny S., 131–2, 312–13n9
Spink, Ian, 211
spirituality, spiritual experience, 24, 31,
40, 46, 58, 70, 88, 93, 98, 107, 109,
116, 195, 236, 254–5, 260, 261, 287,
290, 294, 306n18, 319n6
Stafford-Clark, Max, 61, 203, 205, 320n18
States, Bert O., 128
Steiner, George, 13–14, 19, 24, 150, 157,
301–2n4, 313–14n14
Stewart, Patrick, 124
Storm, William, 12–13, 18
Strindberg, August, 206–7, 302n5; *Miss
Julie*, 83, 269–70
structure of feeling, 3–4, 5, 10, 210, 234,
235
Stuart, Ian, 145, 153, 313n13
Su, John S., 30, 306nn15, 17, 307n23

subject, subjectivity, tragic subjectivity,
15, 17, 19, 23–4, 51, 54, 55, 57, 58, 69,
79, 80, 84, 86, 87, 88, 108, 111, 114,
116–17, 121, 122, 132, 134, 144, 171,
176, 177, 178, 183, 185, 188–9, 192,
199, 202, 209, 212, 214, 232, 237, 240,
243, 250–1, 258, 260, 279, 286, 291,
310n21, 314–15n4, 315n8
sublime, sublimity, 19, 20, 22, 70, 107,
120, 162, 188, 236, 289–91, 308n5
subtext, 88, 129, 132, 139, 197, 200, 202,
203, 227, 228, 268, 270, 296, 306n18
Suez Canal Crisis, 6, 36, 37, 304n7
superego, 243
Svich, Caridad, 241
symbolic, the, 19, 148, 149, 156, 311nn25,
27, 317–18n25
Szondi, Peter, 15

Taylor, Lib, 305–6n13
techne, 149
Thatcher, Margaret, 9, 40, 42, 49, 117,
123, 145, 199, 203, 204, 205, 214, 235,
251, 252, 253, 261, 286, 305–6n13,
318–19n3, 320n14
Theatre of Catastrophe, 21–2, 69, 70–1,
73, 76, 77, 79, 81, 84, 87, 88, 91, 96,
102, 103, 109, 121, 122, 232, 308n6
Theatre of Cruelty, 89
Théâtre Nationale de la Colline, 314n16
Theognis, elegies of, 150
Thomas, Jane, 314n3
Tiffany, John, 303n2
Tomlin, Liz, 308n5
totalitarianism, 18, 69, 78, 104, 109, 130,
223, 224, 262, 320n17
tragedy, 6–24, 27, 29, 37, 38, 40, 42, 60,
61, 68, 69, 70, 74, 76, 84, 88, 96, 102,
107, 108–9, 112, 114, 115, 116, 117,
118, 120, 121, 123, 128, 129, 130, 131–2,

138, 142, 144, 145, 149, 150, 151, 154, 157, 160, 162, 163, 165, 166, 167, 169, 174, 175, 176, 177, 179, 180, 185, 206, 209, 210, 221, 222, 223, 227–9, 232, 233, 236, 237, 238, 243, 244, 247, 249, 250, 251, 254, 262, 267, 272–3, 275, 278, 279, 280, 284, 285–92, 299, 301n3, 301–2n4, 302n7, 303n12, 306nn14–15, 308nn4–5, 310n22, 312–13n9, 313–14n14, 321n19, 322n1
tragedy, absolute, 13–14, 313–14n14
tragedy, liberal, 29, 38–9, 240
tragic authenticity, 33
tragic experience, 3, 9, 12–13, 15–16, 19, 20, 21, 23, 24, 31, 32, 67, 71, 108, 122, 123, 145, 174, 200, 202, 214, 216, 229, 231–2, 233, 234, 236, 239, 251, 254, 255, 257, 258, 259, 266, 289, 291, 301–2n4, 308n4
tragic heroism, 23, 303n12
tragic ideologeme, 11, 264, 265
tragic joy, Dionysian joy, 18, 19, 20, 101–2, 180–1, 193, 202, 213, 228–9
tragic protagonist, 22, 29, 48, 51, 53–4, 59, 67, 87, 96, 107, 114, 132, 134, 152, 241, 267, 273
tragic stalemate, 229
tuché, 185, 206, 209, 317n20
Tycer, Alicia, 205, 317n17, 321n27

Übermensch, 71, 79, 100, 233, 308n5, 310n20
unconscious, the, 15, 18, 19, 22, 23, 24, 43, 47, 58, 59, 64, 68, 69, 70–1, 102, 103, 104, 106, 111, 114, 116, 121, 122, 123, 124–5, 148–9, 176, 182, 185, 197, 209, 210, 214, 217, 219, 220, 229, 236, 276, 283, 286, 287, 291–2, 308n5, 311nn25, 28

Unheimlichkeit, 13, 122, 202, 228
Urban, Ken, 233, 319n4
utopia, the utopian, 10, 23, 34, 45, 75, 91, 92–5, 127, 144, 156, 171, 176, 188, 190–3, 196–7, 199, 211, 212, 214, 226, 229, 245, 276, 284, 289, 290, 302n8, 309n18; anti-utopia, 91, 122; false utopia, 144

Verfremdungseffekt, 7, 61, 83, 197, 199, 288, 316n15
Vernant, Jean-Pierre, 199, 315n5

Walker, Nicola, 66
Waters, Les, 211
Wesker, Arnold, 5, 301–2n4
Wilde, Oscar, 36, 51, 249–50, 305n10; as character in The Judas Kiss, 28, 51–4, 59; The Importance of Being Earnest, 249–51; 'The Soul of Man under Socialism,' 36, 305n10
Williams, Raymond, 4–6, 11–15, 29, 38–9, 61, 221, 233, 240
Wilson, Ann, 217, 318n26
working class, 5–6, 7, 17, 33, 44, 68, 123, 125, 129, 141, 145, 146, 165, 185, 200, 203, 204, 205, 227, 240, 247, 249, 250, 257, 274, 294, 301–2n4, 306n18, 311n2, 320n18
Wrestling School, the, 307n1

Yeats, William Butler, Purgatory, 14
Young Vic Theatre, 124

Zeifman, Hersh, 304nn6, 8
Žižek, Slavoj, 206
Zola, Emile, 206